Dictionary of Symbols

The Third Branch may be called *semeiotike,* or *the Doctrine of Signs,*
the most usual whereof being Words, . . .
the business whereof, is to consider the Nature of Signs,
the Mind makes use of for the understanding of Things,
or conveying its Knowledge to others.

John Locke
Essay on Human Understanding

Dictionary
of
Symbols

Carl G. Liungman

W. W. Norton & Company
New York • London

English translation of *Symboler—västerländska ideogram* © 1974 by Carl G. Liungman

Originally published by Merkur International KB, Malmö, Sweden.
First published as a Norton paperback 1994
Published by arrangement with ABC-CLIO

Library of Congress Cataloging-in-Publication Data

Liungman, Carl G., 1938–
        [Symboler. English]
        Dictionary of Symbols / Carl G. Liungman.
            p.   cm.
        Translation of: Symboler
        Includes bibliographical references and indexes.
        1. Signs and symbols. 2. Picture-writing. I. Title
    BL603.L5413   1991   302.2′22—dc20   91-36657

ISBN 0-393-31236-4

W. W. Norton & Company, Inc., 500 Fifth Avenue, New York, N.Y. 10110
W. W. Norton & Company Ltd., 10 Coptic Street, London WC1A 1PU

Contents

Preface, vii

Part I: Introduction, 3

Part II: Ideographic Dictionary, 83

Part III: Word Index, 537

Part IV: Graphic Index, 555

Part V: Graphic Search Index, 593

Preface

The intention of this work is that it should function both as a reference work in Western cultural history and as a tool for those working with ideograms, e.g., logotype and trademark designers, those engaged in advertising, interior designers, researchers in communication, art historians, art and history teachers, etc.

Dictionary of Symbols is also a voyage of discovery into the realm of Western thought. Ideograms such as ♀, ♡, ⊗, and ♙ illustrate the ways in which we perceive relationships, functions, and continuity in the world. The historical development of these different forms reflects the ways in which our understanding and perception of the world have changed.

Basic graphic gestalts such as ⊙, +, ෨, and ☆ were created thousands of years ago (or discovered, see ⊛) in specific historical situations. They later became integrated parts of Western culture. For example, there is a distinct relationship between the way that the sign ★ is used on military uniforms, tanks, and airplanes and the discovery made in the Euphrates-Tigris area, approximately

4000 B.C., of the way in which the planet Venus moves around the earth.

A strong parallel can be found between the ancient, ideographic basic forms and the collective archetypes that exist in our subconscious. One cannot discount their influence and correlation with basic psychological functions. The Nazi movement in Germany between 1930 and 1945 would not have had the same success over such a short period of time if its rallying sign had been ◉ instead of 卐.

Apart from its function as a cultural historical reference book, *Dictionary of Symbols* is also intended to provide guidance in the design of new ideograms on signposts and instrument panels. For this reason the graphic index lists both modern ideograms, such as ⚡, ◰, and •ⷦ, and older ideograms that are no longer in use, such as ⚱ and ≞. Those who advocate ideals of standardization and uniformity will perhaps be annoyed when they discover ideograms like ◁, ⟲, and ♭ on the same page, but this is unavoidable. Versatility and usefulness have been the predominant guidelines.

The section "An ideographic system of writing ready for use" in Part I, the introduction, discusses ideograms that are easily understood by most adult Europeans and Americans. These ideograms could be used much more in everyday life than is the case today. Ideographic writing has the advantages of being understood much faster than the written word, taking up less space, and being easier to write. Compare the sign 📦, which consists of three signs, with *This parcel should be protected from cold*, which has 35 separate signs.

Such differences emphasize the time factor involved between perception and comprehension. The time it takes to comprehend a message concerning a specific situation, especially in traffic, emergency situations, and military contexts, can often be the decisive factor between life and death.

Part II is the ideographic dictionary. The entries in this dictionary number approximately 1,500. This part of the book makes available to the reader practically all the ideograms used in the history of the Western world and also covers the ideograms that are in use today. It does not, however, account for those signs that denote sounds — letters and spelling signs — nor many of the signs that are used in technical engineering. The graphical dictionary gives the history of each symbol, lists the systems in which it is used, and gives cross-references to other ideograms with the same meaning or with a similar graphic structure.

Part III is *Dictionary of Symbols'* first large index: the word index. Here the reader can look up the name of the sign (e.g., fylfoot) or the system that it belongs to (e.g., genealogy) or terms from the ideographic terminology. This index also lists the meanings, e.g., *dangerous power*, and gives all pages where signs with these meanings are shown.

Part IV is the graphic index. Here all the images in the dictionary (Part II) are listed in 54 groups with references to the numbers of the pages where the signs are discussed. A new system has been devised to subdivide the graphic signs. This system allows for easy access to the graphic symbols and has made them as easy to find as Linn's sexual system made the different species of the vegetable world. If one knows the exact form of the ideogram one is looking for, then looking up this sign in the graphic index will be as easy as looking up a word in an ordinary dictionary.

The facts and ideograms presented in *Dictionary of Symbols* were originally collected on punched cards, coded with a ticket collector's clipper, and computed with the help of two knitting needles. Each card had a picture of one sign or symbol. All around the cards were 80 holes. The holes were about the size of a medium-thick knitting needle. Through a system of clipping open specific holes, thousands of different characteristics could be coded. If, for example, a group of cards were penetrated with a needle, then all those cards that had been clipped at this particular hole would fall out. Using this system it was possible to find, for instance, all the signs from the period between 1000 B.C. and 500 B.C. or all the signs made up of curved lines only. With two needles it was therefore possible to extract the signs that came from this period and were made of curved lines only.

The new graphical system was tested in a pilot edition. Over a period of several years, the material was revised, fed into an electronic computer, and rearranged until its present form was reached. In the first edition the author invited readers to write letters with comments and to call attention to any relevant fact that had been overlooked, so that the following edition might be improved and made accessible to a wider audience. The responses were very valuable. For this reason the invitation remains open, with the conviction that a two-way communication with the readers of *Dictionary of Symbols* is as important today as it was then.

Malmö, Sweden
Carl G. Liungman

Dictionary of Symbols

Part I: Introduction

Signs, symbols, and ideograms

Any object can be called a symbol as long as a group of people agrees that it means more than just itself. A rose can be a symbol for love; two crossed swords, a symbol for war. Graphic symbols are signs or pictures that have been drawn, written, painted, or engraved. They can also be called graphs. Drawings found on toilet stall doors or along the walls in the underground are called *graffiti*.

In this book I have chosen to refer to graphs like ⺐ as signs rather than symbols. This is because the word *symbol* is sometimes used in a special way. For example, the sign ⚖ depicts or represents a pair of scales, which is a symbol for the part of the zodiac called *Libra*.

The word *symbol* is derived from the Greek word *symbolon*. In ancient Greece it was a custom to break a slate of burned clay into several pieces and give each individual in a group one piece as a mark of identification. When, at a later date, they met and fitted the pieces together (Greek *symbollein*) it confirmed that the persons were the same ones, or representa-tives of those, who had received the pieces of clay in the first place.

The use of the word *symbol* was widened to include the engraved shells that were employed by those initiated in the mysteries, both as marks of identification and as essential components in ritual gatherings. It was only a short step away to the word's eventual meaning, in which an object, either through a visual similarity or a common agreement between those using it, represented something other than itself.

An ideogram is a special type of symbol, a graphic sign that illustrates an idea or a concept. The graph 𝄞 represents the *G-clef* in musical notation, the *treble range* on sound reproducing appliances, and is, in a variety of ways, always related to music. 𝄞 is an ideogram.

The concept or idea of *rain* and the physical phenomenon of raindrops falling from clouds is symbolized by the graph ▽̇. This graph is therefore an ideogram. There also exists a large group of non-iconic graphs that represent different sounds rather than things or relationships – i.e., letters and syllabic signs. K, G, and Q are not considered as ideograms in this book and therefore are not listed in the dictionary section or the graphic index.

The letter A, however, not only is a sign for a specific sound but is also a true ideogram. A is the first letter of the alphabet and because of this has been used to denote the idea of something that comes *first*, which indirectly suggests the idea of something *good, the best, of the highest quality*, etc. Consider expressions like "A-child," the "A-team," or the "A grade."

Iconic and non-iconic signs

To say that a graphic sign, a graph, is iconic means that it is an icon (Greek *eikon* = image) of something or someone. ☽ is an iconic graph representing the crescent of the moon. Twice a month, for a few days only, the moon is visible as a crescent against the evening or morning sky.

I have decided to refer to all graphic symbols and signs that are not pictures of easily recognized objects as non-iconic. These non-iconic symbols and signs are the subject matter of this book.

Iconic signs such as pictures, photographs, and stylized reproductions of the type used for certain road signs only mean something if the observer is able to associate them with what they portray or with something closely related to it. The signs dealt with in this book, however, are given their meaning in another way. They might be said to be similar to the idea represented, not in the same way as a picture of a cow is similar to a living cow, but more like ∿ is "similar" to two witnesses, one who speaks the truth and one who lies. ∿ is an ideogram in which the idea of truth is represented by the straight line and the idea of dishonesty is represented by the wavy line, the two lines woven together symbolizing two statements about the same reality.

Although non-iconic signs can be considered as pictures resembling something, they reflect the way in which we think, our knowledge of the world, and the way we create visual interpretations of the world's relations rather than the things and relationships themselves.

Signs and meanings

The meaning of a sign is something collective. Each person, during his or her childhood, acquires a whole series of conventions (implicit and often subconscious, tacit agreements). Graphic structures rely upon these conventions for their various meanings.

There are, for example, analogical conventions – something that is placed above something, as ✕ in ⬚, is also evident in the relationship between heaven and earth, father and son, cause and effect, etc.; conventions that decide the way in which time is to be represented graphically – the future to the right or under, the past to the left or above (in the Western world); and conventions that determine the way in which we experience what is outside and what is inside – on the one hand · ○ , and ⊙ on the other, etc.

The meaning of a sign can, in this way, be either related to a specific cultural sphere or accepted universally. The former can be exemplified by comparing the meaning of a vertical line, |, in the West with the meaning of a horizontal line, —, in the East.

Both have approximately the same spectrum of meaning.

The central nervous systems of human bodies are organized in a similar way. Most people live the greater part of their lives in a vertical position and all people experience the horizon as something horizontal, etc. Moreover, there undoubtedly exist certain genetically inherited mechanisms in the human nervous system that are similar to those found, for example, in an octopus. An animal of this type can perceive certain visual structures but not others. It is probably this last element that accounts for the fact that ⊙ implies the same thing today as it did in Babylon, China, pre-Columbian America, and many other areas over thousands of years.

The meaning of a sign (as *meaning* is used in this book) can be interpreted as consisting of the ideas shared by the majority of the people familiar with the sign – that which remains when the associations unique to each individual's experiences are neglected.

At any given moment, the meaning of a sign will depend upon its historical background. For example, 卐 and what it stood for changed dramatically after 1935. Its historical background and, as a result, its meaning as a sign were altered.

A sign and the way it is experienced are affected by the sign's immediate surroundings. Take, for example, $ on a banknote and the same sign in the eyes of a Donald Duck on a political poster, or otherwise compare + in the expression 1+1 with the + on one end of a torch battery.

Nor can the observer of the sign be ignored, the individual whose experiences, education, and general frame of mind will affect the way in which a given sign is understood.

To summarize the main elements that constitute and affect the meaning of a sign, the meaning is a function of:

1. the structure of a sign,

2. the immediate background of the sign and whether there are other signs in the vicinity,

3. the individual observer's background,

4. the social and historical background of the sign.

It is easy to see that the meaning of a sign is constantly changing. Only such signs as those for the sun, moon, and planets can be said to be relatively stable. Their immediate backgrounds are similar – natal charts, astrological tables – and they are often observed by individuals with a similar background – astronomers, astrologers, and psychologists.

In the case of this type of signs, it is their social and historical background, the fourth factor, that, over a span of thousands of years, has undergone the greatest change. Such changes, often slow and hardly discernible, are reflected in the way a sign changes in meaning.

The sign ♂, 2000 years ago, represented Mars, the god of war and aggression. Today it stands for the planet Mars. The earlier associations with war and aggression have weakened considerably. In some cases they have disappeared altogether or been replaced with other meanings such as *self-assertion, the planetary system, iron, cars,* etc.

The polarity of meanings of elementary graphs

Dr. Liz Greene, a psychoanalyst who has done considerable research on the subject of symbols, writes in her book *Relating*:

A symbol is not the same thing as a sign – something which merely represents something else. Road signs, for example, are signs with a specific meaning: *one-way traffic, road works, waiting is prohibited*. A symbol, on the other hand, suggests or generates an aspect of life where the number of possible interpretations is infinite and eludes all attempts on the part of the intellect to fix or establish a single meaning.

One can never fully account for the manifold meanings that any given symbol has, nor is it possible to categorize them in intellectual terms because there is often an antithesis – an opposite – which the conscious mind is unable to grasp simultaneously.

Liz Greene writes about something that I will call *the polarity of meanings of elementary graphs*. The simplest or most elementary signs have diametrically opposed meanings.

The initial or primary meaning of a vertical straight line, |, in the West, is *one thing, something unique*, and its opposite, *something that is continuous, endless*. The line in a vertical position will more often, although not always, bear the former meaning, while in a horizontal position it will have the latter meaning.

The cross, †, stands for *death* and *sorrow* and their opposites: *eternal life* and *salvation*.

The circle, ○, means primarily *all that exists, all time, all possibilities*. But it also means *nothingness, zero, no entry, no possibilities, disconnect*.

The triangle, △, means not only *the supreme power, prosperity, fire* but also *danger, evil power, water*.

The square, □, is synonymous with *the ground, the earth* and also with *a house, a building* — i.e., something that removes a person from the ground.

Finally, the five-pointed star, ☆, is the sign for both *war* and *pain* and their opposites: *festivities, favorable opportunities, enjoyment*.

From this we can infer the following rule: *the most elementary signs always signify at least two opposite or almost opposite meanings.*

This rule, however, seems only to apply to the most elementary structures. As soon as a sign structure becomes slightly more complex its meanings no longer present themselves as opposites. ⊙ stands for *the sun* and *gold* but nothing else. ⚠ only means *danger*.

There are also other elementary signs that do not carry opposite meanings. ♡ does not mean *love* and *hate*. ♄ does not mean both *heat* and *power* and *weakness* and *cold*. The six-pointed star, ✡, is the sign for Judaism, but not its opposite, heathenism. Nor does it stand for other beliefs or religion in general.

The basic ideographic structures

There are four or five *basic elements* in Western ideography, depending on how one chooses to count. They include the *straight line,* —; the *circle segment,* ⌒; the *spiral* or *exponential curve,* ⊚ and ⊚ (or in one form ⊚⊚); and · , the *dot* or *small, filled circle.* With these basic components it is possible to draw all the ideograms in Western ideography.

Gestalts in Western ideography are those basic signs that have been created as complete entities, i.e., those that have not been built up by more elementary components or are not the result of a dividing of a larger structure. It is, however, difficult to draw a clear dividing line between basic elements and gestalts. Is it possible for the human mind to combine V with a straight line and produce ↓, or is ↓ a holistic psychological gestalt? Is ⌒ a gestalt or does the human mind create a uniformly curved line ⌒ by dividing ○, which would mean that ⌒ is not a gestalt?

Here are some structures that could be considered gestalts: +, △, ⅄, □, ⌁, ⋎, ⊚, ☆, and ⍜⍜. One only has to look at some of the signs from prehistoric ideography to see that all basic elements were being used between 10,000 and 20,000 years ago, during the Neolithic Age: +, ⚲, ⋎, ♡, and ⊞. Primary gestalts such as △, ⊚⊚, ⅄, and ☆ came into use thousands of years later.

The development of sign structures through the ages

It would be logical to assume that signs like +, ☐, △, and ☽ were among the first to be used by the human race – if we disregard the iconic signs that represented animals in paintings and engravings, etc. – but in reality this is not the case.

The oldest signs consisted of strange combinations of the five basic elements: —, ⌒, ☺, ☻ , and •. Examples include signs such as ⛩ and :::: from the caves in Niaux, ⚘ and ⋔ from the El Castillo cave, and the remarkable graphic structure ⫴⫲⫴ from the La Pasiega cave. Signs such as ⚱, crosses combined with arches, seem to have appeared at a later stage.

The oldest engravings and paintings found in the caves of Europe are said to be between 10,000 and 20,000 years old. Whether this estimation is correct or not, it is possible to date the signs in relation to each other by studying the style of the paintings and engravings and the number of layers on cave walls.

More advanced sign structures have also been found in caves and on rock faces, such as ⚲, ⛩, ⋁, ◎, 人, and ⊕. Other common signs at this time were those that depicted *hands*, ✋ and 🖐, and *footprints*, ⫯⫯ and ⫮⫮. Even today footprints are used in Buddhist symbolism, often drawn and combined with other symbols, as in ⫯⫯. During the Algerian war of independence, at the end of the 1950s, the French made use of the sign ⫯ on the sides of buildings and on walls. These black feet, *pieds noirs*, signified the secret army organized by the French inhabitants of Algeria. The sign for the soles of feet is also common in Nordic rock engravings from about 1500 B.C.

Curiously enough, one of the oldest structures is ♥, the heart. Furthermore, þ and �, the Nordic runes representing *troll* or *giant*, have also been found in South European caves and even on rock faces in the interior of the Sahara.

The next development of sign structures can be exemplified by Egyptian hieroglyphs from around 4000 B.C. Among these there are advanced forms such as ⌀, ⌀, ⌀, and ⌀. It was at about this time that the pentagram, ⛤, appeared for the first time in the area that is now the state of Israel. Also the sign ⌀, and ⊕, the *sun wheel*, materialized, the latter in the form of the hieroglyph ⊗, which was possibly an ideogram for a *town* or *city*.

In approximately the year 3000 B.C. the sign 卐 emerged in the Indus and Harappa cultures. Such signs as ⌀, ⌀, ⊗, ⌀, and ⌀ began to be used by the other societies around the Persian Gulf.

At about the same time, the Assyro-Babylonian culture introduced ⁂ and ►, the basic cuneiform sign. It was the Cretian culture, however, that around the year 2000 B.C. introduced what might be considered the first modern alphabet with signs like ⌀, ⌀, ‡, ⌀, and φ.

It was not until approximately 1000 B.C. that ✿ appeared, coinciding with the emergence of the first Greek cultures. Several centuries later other structures like ⌀, φ, ⌀, Σ, ⌀, ⌀, ⌀, and ⌀ began to be used.

Later, the Celts introduced variations like ⌀ and ⌀, as well as many other beautiful patterns based on the exponential curve, which the Egyptians had mastered so well (e.g., φ and ⊙).

It was not until the sixteenth and seventeenth centuries that radically new structures began to emerge. In the interval between, old and new patterns were combined in more complex and sophisticated ways, as in ‡, ⊙, ⌀, and ⁂.

In about A.D. 1500 groups became common ideographic structures. They had existed at an earlier stage – the Egyptian hieroglyph ⌀, the Roman numeral Ⅲ, and many of the Mayan hieroglyphs – but these were more often exceptions to the rule. There also appeared new forms such as ⌀, ⌀, ?, and ⊕.

The next significant change in graphic form occurred during the nineteenth century. Rather than the sign itself being colored, it was the background that was filled in: ⬛. Although this technique had already been practiced during the Neolithic period (e.g., ⌀), it was hardly to be seen in antiquity. With this new development signs were framed or inscribed so that the graphs did not touch one another, as in ⌀; sometimes signs were placed one on top of another, as in $. Also, a cog-like form came into use, as in ⌀.

The groupings became gradually more advanced, for example, ⌀ and ⌀. Old, well-known structures were combined in new and innovative ways. A circle with "moveable segments," ◖, and systems of co-ordinates with different types of curves appeared in different contexts. See, for example, ⊰ and ∟ .

During the twentieth century the synthesis of old patterns became more advanced, as exemplified by ⊗, ⊙, and the larger illustration below. New structures emerged that looked like ◁| and ⨌. The technical perfection of this age has been responsible for the creation of new variations based on the old structures, such as ⌁ and ✦.

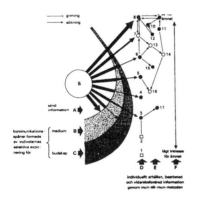

It was in the twentieth century that the network first came into use as an ideographic structure. An example of this is ⨇, which represents part of a net of benzene rings in chemistry. It should not be forgotten, however, that interlacing patterns were in use at a much earlier stage. The Celts, the Nordic peoples, and others, at the time of Christ's birth, were already in the habit of using complicated, woven patterns in their work. The woven structure can only be expanded within limits set by its structure, but the network has the advantage of not being closed – it can be added to indefinitely. The same possibility also characterizes co-ordinate structures.

Around the middle of the twentieth century there appeared numerous new ideograms. They first appeared in the world of comic strips and advertising. Examples are ꙮ, ✑, ⸙, and ⸙.

If one could discern the rules that have governed the development of ideographic structures one would be able to predict the forms of future structures. No one has yet been able to isolate these rules, although the network coincided with the discovery of electricity and its wider use in society. Co-ordinate structures and exponentially ordered groups (e.g., ▮▮▮▮▮) became more common around the middle of the twentieth century.

Strangely enough, the period between 10,000 B.C. and 4000 B.C. seems to be totally devoid of signs. It is as if a symbolic void had occurred in the period between the birth of the first known civilizations – in Egypt, around Euphrates and Tigris, in the Indus Valley, and in China – and the

Neolithic and prehistoric rock paintings and engravings.

It might be that the science of history has made an error in its calculations and that the Neolithic Age occurred, not as is supposed, 10,000 years before Christ's birth, but immediately before the appearance of the first known civilizations.

Another possibility is the occurrence of a natural catastrophe such as the shifting of the earth's polar axis, resulting in large-scale floods and ice ages sometime between 15,000 B.C. and 10,000 B.C. The known expansion of the ice-cap of the North Pole, which principally affected the Northern European regions, can hardly account for this void in ideographic development.

The relationship between visual perception, thought, and graphic form

The Chinese ideogram 古 represents the idea *prehistoric, long since past, ancient*. This sign is derived from ⼝, which means *mouth, opening*, and ⼗, which means *10*. The lines of association behind the concept *ancient* in Chinese ideography can be expressed by the following: "that which takes *ten mouths*" (ten generations) "to convey to posterity."

Although a system such as the Egyptian hieroglyphs is considered to be a pictorial writing system, this does not imply that it is possible to derive all hieroglyphs from visual impressions found in peoples' everyday lives. Signs such as ⼘ and ⼤ resemble the staffs carried by the gods and goddesses drawn in or around the hieroglyphs found on wall paintings in burial chambers and temples. It is not known, however, whether the staffs existed first and later were depicted on wall paintings or whether they first existed as signs, which then were used to create the staffs. Whatever the truth, ⼘ means *gold, kingdom*, and *happiness*, while ⼤, called *ankh*, is a common symbol for *life, rebirth*, and *sexual union*.

Certain ideograms are easy to understand once the primary meaning of a basic ideogram has been learned. ⼀, for example, means *the sky, the heavens* and is placed high up. Compare this with 雷, which means *lightning, something that shines*; 雨, which means *rain, to rain*; and 夜, which means *night*.

Other ideograms, however, would be totally incomprehensible without additional information. Take 凵, which stands for *Egypt*. Among the more interesting hieroglyphs are those that, once their meaning is revealed, seem to induce a recognition of the relationship between the graphic form and what it implies: ideograms such as ⼯, *unite, union*; ⼬, *imprison, close in*; ⼫, *sweet*; and ⼭, *meat*. Most hieroglyphs, however, are reproductions of visual impressions, which with time became associated with relationships that were often quite remote from their sources. ⼝ exemplifies this.

The meanings and grammatical construction of the old systems of writing were undoubtedly influenced by the uses they were put to. If, for instance, one wanted to write a letter to a servant, specifying what one wanted done, it would have been necessary to know the meanings and signs for many trivial and earthly relationships and objects. If, on the other hand, one wrote to pacify the gods or to pay tribute to a ruler, the signs used would in some way reflect religious, metaphysical, and moralistic meanings. Such things as voyages, victories, prisoners, victims, titles, and superior qualities would be signified.

The same principle applies to modern-day sign systems, such as the hobo signs. These signs have in common the fact that they represent things relevant to the beggars and the hobos. ⊙ means *food and money is given*; ✕ means *nothing given*; and ⊘ means *snappy people, likely to run you in*.

The sign ⊙ is found in the most ancient of Chinese writings, among the Egyptian hieroglyphs, and in modern astronomy. In each case it has been used to represent the *sun*. For the botanist, the same sign stands for *plants with a one-year life cycle*; on maps, ⊙, which is similar to the above, is used to denote *towns, centers of communica-*

tion, and other centers of human conglomeration; in alchemy the sign means *gold*. There is a logical connection between the graphic form and what it means. The sign ⊙ means *sun* in a system of planets moving in circles around a center. Likewise, a system not necessitating a sign for the sun but containing the concept of a yearly cycle (the sun's cycle) will use the sign ⊙ to represent *yearly*. This sign's meaning of life-giving force has been given a more concrete and practical significance — *food* and *money* — by hobos and beggars.

In all probability there exist certain sign structures that, owing to certain peculiarities in the human nerve system and sensory organs, are more easily associated to outer phenomena. We can take as an example the sign for *danger*, ⚡. Among tramps in Sweden the sign ⁓ means *look out, danger*. For a train engineer ⁓ marks the beginning of a risk zone for *landslides* or *avalanches*. The well-known sign ⚡ means *Danger! High Voltage!* In runic characters ⚡ was sometimes used instead of ⟨, *sun, s-sound,* or ⟨, *yew tree,* and was thereby associated to the most dangerous of weapons, the bow. Furthermore, the pine needles of the yew tree were especially poisonous for horses.

The structure doubled becomes ⫪, which in the Hittite hieroglyphic system meant *state of siege*. In Linear B, from about 1000 B.C., ⸗ represented the syllable *ra*, which had the same intonation and sound as the name given to the all-powerful Egyptian sun-god. The more modern ⚡ was used to warn those resisting the Nazi ideas.

Doubling is one of the simplest and most fundamental relationships that make meanings. In the world of languages, primitive types are often recognized by this process of doubling. Examples from the germanic languages are "ma-ma," "pa-pa," and "to-to." Similar rules are at work in the world of ideograms, but here doubling is not associated with primitiveness.

The sign -, a relatively short horizontal line, is used both to separate and to join as a hyphen, a minus sign, a dash, etc. Doubled, it becomes the familiar =, *equals*, and tripled, it forms ≡, which represents in the field of mathematics and logic *absolute likeness*, *identity*.

When the single warning sign ϟ is doubled, we have the symbol for Hitler's frightening *Schutz-Staffeln* and their abominable activities. In the game of chess † means *check, your king is being attacked by an enemy piece*, †† means *checkmate, your king is being attacked and cannot move*. If used in connection with the picking of mushrooms, † stands for *poisonous* and †† stands for *extremely poisonous*.

On nautical charts the sign ₊₊₊ is used to denote *shipwreck at a depth that is of no danger to passing sea traffic*. An anchor might become entangled in the wreck but the likelihood of collision is limited. This sign is not found doubled on nautical charts, but instead ‡‡ is found in the Swedish system of hobo signs and means *police, danger*.

There are also situations where doubling does not necessarily imply an amplification of the single sign's meaning. On the contrary, the sign doubled may imply the opposite meaning, as in – and = and in • and : . The full stop marks the *end* of a line of thought – a sentence. Doubled, the full-stop becomes : – a colon – which signals the *beginning* of an enumeration, rather than the termination of a line of thought. These exceptions, however, are few. The symbolism of military rank illustrates the principle of augmentation. Every person who has been in the military knows that an increase in the number of ★ is synonymous with a higher rank, more power, a higher wage, etc.

As I have indicated, all ideograms are analogies, i.e., they resemble, in one way or another, the thing or idea they represent or mean. With the sign =, for example, there exists an analogy between the visual appearance and the meaning. Two exactly similar lines form a parallel and horizontal relationship between two other signs or groups of signs.

The sign system is also constructed on similarities, where the relative height of the note in relation to the horizontal lines corresponds to the pitch of the frequency of sound waves.

Tones can be heard but other analogies can only be understood by thought. ☯, for example, is the sign from Chinese philosophy and cosmology in which the world's most basic relationships are perceived as a balancing act between two opposing life forces, *yin* (the white) and *yang* (the black). Everything in the universe (symbolized by the outer circle) embodies both *yin* (the untouched matter, the receptive, the cold) and *yang* (light, life force, the masculine, activity, warmth). Nothing exists in the universe that is all yin or all yang (this fact is symbolized by the two smaller circles within the sign).

where the analogy is not so self-evident, as with the sign 〾. This structure has become common in psychology textbooks and other literature written during the twentieth century. It represents the *normal distribution curve*, the distribution curve of measured values that are grouped as the natural variations in height of a group of people whose age and sex are the same.

The vertical dimension, symbolized by the vertical line to the left, is used to indicate the number of people. Body height is measured along the horizontal line. By splitting a large number of people into groups of similar height and by then counting the number in each group and, for each interval of height, marking the corresponding point on the diagram, the figure ∧ is achieved. The points joined together create a curve that is recognized in science as the *curve of normal distribution*.

The analogy between the yin-yang philosophy and the structure of the sign ☯ is quite clear. There are cases

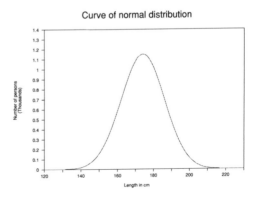

Curve of normal distribution

The uses of this curve have, in recent times, become more numerous in Western culture as a model for the ideal distribution of measured values. For example, in an intelligence test, the degree of difficulty of the questions has been adjusted so that the results form a normal distribution curve when a large group of people of the same race, social status, and age is tested.

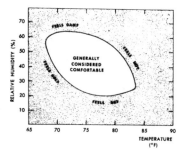

The illustration above provides another example of modern Western graphical analogies. In the diagram, the area within the curve shows the varying temperatures and intervals of atmospheric humidity that are experienced as pleasant by a specific number of individuals. The vertical line represents atmospheric humidity, and the horizontal line represents the temperature.

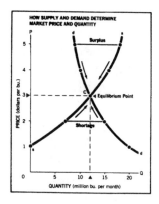

The ideogram above illustrates the way in which supply and demand (the two curves) decide the price and the quantity of a chosen product. The values that appear at the intersection of the two curves, marked by the broken lines, indicate those prices and quantities where there exists a balance between supply and demand.

Ideographic systems of writing

The human systems of writing in Europe, the Near East, and North Africa have developed along similar lines. Iconic signs were the primary source. Over a period of time these iconic signs were simplified and made more uniform. This period is referred to as the period of pictography. Below are examples discovered on a clay tablet from the period 3500–3000 B.C.

The simplification proceeds at the same time as the sign's meanings (which were originally related to its prototype) are expanded to include a number of objects and relations associated with the original prototype. ⊙ means *one year* in a specific context, a *great power* in another, *gold* in a third, and *life* in still other contexts, although the original meaning is the *sun*. When an iconic sign is simplified so that it no longer resembles what is visually perceived and when its meaning is at the same time ex-

panded, then it is appropriate to use the term *ideogram*.

In an earlier section I mentioned that ideograms have been found sporadically in cave paintings and rock engravings from the period 20,000 B.C. to 10,000 B.C. On the other hand, genuine picture or ideographic writing, i.e., longer strings or groups of signs, did not appear until 4000 B.C. This seems to have occurred simultaneously in the Indus Valley (India), the Nile Valley (Egypt) and the Euphrates-Tigris basin (Babylon). About 2,000 years later (the exact time is not known) the oldest Chinese picture writing began to be used.

The term *hieroglyph* was originally used to mean the ancient Egyptian signs, but today its meaning has been expanded to include all more or less stylized depictions carved into stone or other materials. The term is derived from the Greek words *hieros* = holy and *glyfein* = to carve in.

Egyptian hieroglyphs are often simplified pictures of animals, ⤚, parts of the body, ⋀ (two legs), tools, and so on, but there also exist more abstract signs such as ⊗, ◊, and Γ.

The Egyptian hieroglyphic writing abandoned early on, perhaps as early as 3000 B.C., the ideographic level and moved on to the next stage of development. The pattern of sounds — words — associated with a specific sign became more important than the thing or idea it represented.

Let me explain this with an imaginary example. If ▽ was originally the iconic sign used in ancient Egypt to represent an everyday basket, and if it had eventually been given the meanings *basket*, *basket shaped*, the *amount contained in a basket*, and if the equivalent word in ancient Egypt was pronounced *nöbböt*, the sign would in time incorporate all meanings of these and related sound patterns. ▽ would, therefore, eventually not only mean *basket* but also *master* (ancient Egypt: *nöbb*) and *all* (ancient Egypt: *nebbet*).

The result of this development was that certain signs could not be used without indicating which of all the possible homonyms — similar sounding words — was referred to. New signs had to be invented to mark which of the original sign's meanings was intended.

This stage of linguistic development is therefore recognized by the presence of two types of written characters: those signs representing the sound pattern (which could have several different meanings) and those signs specifying the intended meaning of the signs of the first type.

Eventually, most of the original hieroglyphs ceased being ideograms in the proper sense and instead adopted a function similar to that of letters: they came to represent single sounds, syllables, and short words instead of things, living organisms, ideas, and relationships. At about this time, with the hieroglyphs used primarily for worldly purposes and to facilitate communication — letters, accounts, written contracts — the hieroglyphs were simplified so that they came to resemble the written characters used by the Arabs.

All the ideographic systems of writing in the Near East seem to have undergone a similar metamorphosis. The ancient Sumerian ideography in Mesopotamia (see the picture writing at the beginning of this chapter) was simplified into what is known as cuneiform writing. The signs were produced by pressing wedge-shaped writing tools into slates of soft clay, which were then dried in the sun or in ovens. There existed about 700 such signs during the Babylonian period. Half of these were sound signs, the other half, ideograms.

Most old systems of writing consisted eventually of between 100 and 300 signs for syllables and short words and several hundred signs that were still proper ideograms. Usually the central concept of a sentence was an ideogram, while sound signs were used to indicate grammatical inflections and other less essential meanings.

The development toward a phonetically based written language seems to have been concluded in about 2000 B.C. During the next thousand years a completely new system was to develop: writing with signs for single sounds – the alphabetical characters. Somewhere in between these two fundamentally different systems for the conveyance of information lie what are known as Linear A and Linear B, from Crete and the time around the year 500 B.C. Linear A had approximately 80 sound signs and about 35 ideograms. Linear B, which early on was transferred to the mainland of Greece, had about 90 signs, most of which were syllable signs. The following are examples of syllable signs from Linear B: ǂ, ┝, ╤, Υ, ʃ, ν, ʃʃ, ⊕, ⊘.

During the millennium before the birth of Christ, phonetic writing systems replaced the ideographic and mixed systems in the Mediterranean region. Fifteen hundred years later the new phonetic writing system reached Scandinavia, and the first runic carvings were made around A.D. 500.

A discussion of the ideographic writing systems would not be complete without mention of the system used by the Hittites. They lived in what are now Turkey and Syria and have left behind them a great number of stone slabs engraved with hieroglyphs. They used, among others, the sign ⊕, God, and ⊡, house. Their graphic logic was simple: ⊕⊡, for instance, meant God's house, i.e., temple.

The East Asian systems of writing have to some extent progressed along other lines than the Western. Unlike the hieroglyphs used in ancient Egypt, which underwent a radical metamorphosis to sound signs, the Chinese system of writing retained its ideogrammatical character. This may have been because of the great number of nationalities, with more or less different languages, living within the borders of the Chinese Empire. Thanks to what one might call a lack of modernism, Chinese literature and therefore a greater part of China's cultural heritage have remained accessible to all Chinese who can read, despite the fact that people from different regions often cannot understand each other when they talk.

As a matter of course, the Chinese have made use of phonetical signs to help clarify their language. The

Chinese word that stands for the abstract idea *to come* was formally pronounced in the same way as the word for *wheat* (in the predominant language minority). The sentence, "The king is coming to the city" was written by painting with a brush the signs for *king*, *wheat*, and *city*.

The Chinese often made use of interesting analogies to create an ideogram with an abstract meaning. The sign for *human speech*, for example, is a combination of the signs for *mouth* and *trumpet*: in other words "sound from the mouth." The idea of *clear* or *shining* was represented by combining the signs for *sun* and *moon*. "Three women in company," i.e., the sign for *a woman* repeated three times, served to illustrate the idea of *falsehood, dishonesty*, and *thoughtlessness*.

The ideograms used in the modern Chinese system of writing are abstract. The original imagery has been simplified and conventionalized so that it is now impossible to perceive the structural relationship between the sign and the object it initially represented. Take, for example, ☉, which in the oldest Chinese writing means *sun*, and compare it with its modern equivalent: 日.

Today's most voluminous Chinese dictionaries contain approximately 40,000 signs and essential combinations, but according to authorities on the subject one can manage with between 3,000 and 4,000 signs. Even well-educated Chinese seldom have at their disposal more than 6,000 signs.

Ideographic writing systems were also used on the American continents. Several pre-Columbian cultures in what today is known as Mexico developed such systems between the years A.D. 200 and 1500. The oldest and most advanced system is that of the Mayan people. A jade plate engraved with hieroglyphs, dating from about 300 B.C., has been found.

Only three books written in the Mayan language exist today, but the Mayans left a treasury of hieroglyphs on the walls and pillars of their temples. Only a small part of these signs has been deciphered. They represent the more important gods, weekdays, months, and years.

The fragment below gives an idea of what Mayan writing looks like:

Altogether some 400 to 500 signs have been catalogued, of which approximately 150 are deciphered.

The Mayan counting system, like their calendar, was based on the number 20. The Mayans also recognized the idea of zero. Mayan numbers were often written from the bottom upward. Whereas in our system a figure to the left of another in the same group means that its value is incremented by a factor of 10, in the Mayan system the number sign above another meant that its value should be incremented by a factor of 20. The sum 37 was therefore written with three bars (3×5), two points (+2), and one point above the others (+20): ⋮⋮ .

Like the Aztecs and many other Central American cultures, the Mayan people had developed a very exact chronology. As a result it has been calculated that the Mayan people's chronology began with an event that took place in the year 3113 B.C. A peculiarity – which, by the way, characterized most of the Central American chronological systems – was the Mayan use of two parallel chronologies: the first was the sun year, consisting of 365 days, and the second, a religious year made up of 20 groups of 13 days. The latter cycle of 260 days is undoubtedly of an earlier origin than the 365-day year.

The number 52 was important as a common denominator in their chronology (260/52=5, 364/52=7). The two chronologies made it possible to name each day in a 52-year cycle, a name that was given to all the children born on that day. The Mayan people were deeply religious, indulged in human sacrifice, and believed that suicide was the most direct way to heaven.

The most surprising aspect, however, of the Mayan culture was the accuracy of their astronomical measurements, something that was directly related to their having two parallel chronologies. In one of the books written by the Mayans, which has been preserved, is a calendar charting the movements of the planet Venus over a period of 384 years. The Mayan astronomers had calculated the time of Venus's rotation to be 584 days; their exactitude is reflected by today's astronomers, who have calculated the planet's rotation to be 583.92 days.

In all probability the Mayan culture did not undergo any appreciable changes. The shape of the written characters and their buildings (they did not know the technique for building arches), dress, and customs seem to have remained the same throughout the ages. The only exception is the introduction of a few new ideograms during the tenth century: 🔲 often occurred in combination with 🔺 on temple facades. Both of these signs are very "un-Mayan." The curving form is typical for Mayan writing, but their palaces and buildings always had a very straight linearity. Both 🔲 and 🔺, and combinations of the two, 🔲🔺, became frequent in the whole of

Central America from about the year A.D. 1000.

It has, however, been impossible to find any connection between the Mayan and other cultures, with the exception of those of the nearest Indian peoples. It might be that the Mayans' religious attitude was one in which anything new or foreign was prohibited and where the existing cultural heritage was fanatically preserved. This is the impression that one is left with when studying their writings, architecture, and relics.

Several other cultures in Central America developed writing systems, but none as advanced as the Mayans'. The Incas in Peru did not have a written language, but the Aztecs in Mexico had a very primitive pictographic system.

On Easter Island in the Pacific wooden tablets filled with rows of ideograms have been found. Nothing is known about them. The natives say that their ancestors already had the tablets when they came to the island in the twelfth century.

Ancient American ideograms

The sign ∂, which stands for the *j-sound*, *a good year's crop*, and *year*, is one of the oldest signs in the runic alphabet. The mirror image of this sign was used by the Hopi Indians in Arizona and represents the word *nakwach*, meaning *universal brotherhood*.

Perhaps the oldest cult object of the Hopis is a square stone or clay tablet that is roughly 10 centimeters in diameter. Part of it has been broken off and has disappeared. On the tablet are several signs, three of them being ⌁, ⟡, and ☺.

On similar tablets, although probably not as old as the above, the following series has been found:

O + ◎ ☽ +
ʕ ʕ ʕ ʕ ʕ

The sign + is recognized in other contexts as meaning the *star of haste*. When the nomadic Hopi people saw this star they knew that it was time to complete their regular migrations. If this is the case, then + may represent the planet Venus. The other signs in the series signify *full moon*, *half moon*, and *sun*. Each sign is accompanied by the symbol for *universal brotherhood* placed below. Another common sign among the Hopis is ⊕, the *wheel cross*. It represents the four parts of the earth and signifies the *earth*, the *ground*.

Rock engravings have been found in Colorado that in all likelihood are very old. Among them is the sign ⚞. This is also an old Celtic sign that is still in use today as a symbol for the Bretonic separatist movement. The somewhat similar ideogram ϒ, the **triskele** or **three-leg**, is common in Greece after A.D. 400.

Among the signs engraved on the rocks at Pictograph Point in Colorado, the symbol for brotherhood, ʕ, has been found in the form ⌐⌐. Furthermore, there is the sign ⌂, which probably means *village*, *cave*, or *cave village*. The *black hand*, ✋, is also depicted. This iconic sign has been found in many prehistoric sites in Europe, on cliff faces in the Sahara, and elsewhere. What it represented is still unknown, but it is used even today in Europe.

On other engravings in Colorado one finds the structure ⬚. It belongs to a group of signs that are often found in Central America. Variations of this sign are engraved on cliff faces, on Mayan temples, painted on clay jugs, etc. Its original meaning is not known. It is interesting, therefore, to compare similar structures from different times found in many places on the planet.

The sign ⬚ is often joined to the **staircase**, ⌐. ⌐⬚ is the most usual combination of these two. The sign ⌐ is difficult to grasp. It is similar to the Egyptian hieroglyph representing *water*, ∿. The structure ⬚ is found among the Egyptian hieroglyphs in the form ⊓. In the oldest Chinese alphabet ⓐ means a *completed circle*, a *return*. The Hopi Indians seem to have used ⬚ to mean, or be connected to, *migratory paths* and *migration*. The combination of signs to form ⌐⬚ might therefore represent a migration across the seas.

⬚⬚⬚ is the Hopi sign for the *water clan* or *tribe*. The same sign can be found on Greek amphoras decorated with mythological motifs from 500 B.C. The water tribe or clan used ◎ to represent a *movement outward* and ⊚ for a *return*. The sign ⊚ is also found on ceramics from Troy about 1300 B.C. A slightly different version of the sign appears among the Mayan hieroglyphs, where it is related to *water*. In Tibet the sign ꝯ is the symbol for *potential power*. On modern washing machines it is used as the sign for *spin drying*. The Egyptians used its mirror image, ⊘, to mean *thread* and *measurement*.

To the right is the old Hopi symbol **mother and child** or **mother earth**. Exactly the same sign is found on certain coins from Crete about 300 B.C. There it probably represented the famous

labyrinth in Knossos. It is also possible that both the sign and the labyrinth symbolized something else. In Scandinavia the structure appears from the Middle Ages onward.

It becomes clear that there is still a lot of research to be done here. Many of these ideograms were used by the Hopi Indians alone, and they were just one of hundreds of Indian civilizations existing on the American continents. Take, for example, the structure to the right. It is a rock relief from Uxmal in Yucatan in Central America, a region once ruled by the Mayans. It is not

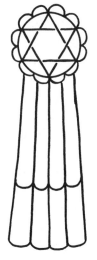

known what this sign represented, but the addition of a pendant or hanging element was often used in China around 500 B.C. and in the Phoenician Empire around 1000 B.C.

The **six-pointed star** is believed to have already been used in the time of Solomon and is sometimes called **David's shield**. Nowadays it is almost exclusively associated with the Israeli people and Judaism.

The Mayan and Egyptian hieroglyph systems had roughly the same scope and usages. The Mayan hieroglyphs are always in the shape of a TV screen: ⬛, ⬛, ⬛, and ⬛. Note that the sign ⊗ in the last hieroglyph is identical to the Egyptian hieroglyph denoting *city*.

The cross is common everywhere in pre-Columbian America, and even the swastika was used, for example, ⊹ in Peru, home of the imperialistic, state communistic, Inca culture. Also from Peru, but before the time of the Inca culture, is this combination of a sun sign and a cross: ⊞.

The Aztec Empire is considered to be the next greatest pre-Columbian empire. It existed in what is now Mexico. The Aztecs' pictography was different from the Mayans'. All their signs were iconic – i.e., pictures of people and gods in human and animal forms engaged in different activities. The Aztecs had a peculiar sign, ⌇, that was often drawn in front of the mouths of depicted people. It is quite likely that it had the same function as speech balloons in comic strips.

In 1960 a very conventionalized statuette of a human being was found in a sealed room in an old Indian temple, a *kiva*, in the United States. Next to the statue lay this small button (seen from above): ⬣.

Compare this with the two buttons, ⬣ and ⬣, found at excavations of Troy in Crete. They are dated to about 3000 B.C. An analogous structure, ⬣, is found on a dress ornament in Scania, Sweden, from 800 B.C.

The arm of the small statue had been broken off and could not be found. It might not mean anything, but one remembers the ancient Greek tradition of breaking an object into pieces and giving the bits to other persons to be used, at a later stage, as proof of one's identity.

A few thousand years ago sea voyages over the oceans and back often took many years. Therefore, it was often representatives for or descendants of the original voyagers who returned to renew the communication in foreign lands. To obtain the goodwill from an earlier meeting it was necessary to bring a token or sign. Showing a part of a broken object was therefore a very practical way of ensuring that one represented the original party.

Finally, a parenthetical remark concerning ⟅, the Hopi Indians' symbol for *universal brotherhood*. This sign is similar in structure to)(from the oldest Chinese system, meaning *to split or cleave*. A sign such as () ought, therefore, to denote *unite* or *join*. This sign has been found in prehistoric European caves. The symbol (), however, is difficult to draw and can easily end up as ◯, a circle, with the result that the meaning is difficult to decipher. By displacing the parts of the sign in relation to each other, as in ⟋, this risk disappears. It is impossible to say for certain whether ⟅ used as a Hopi ideogram and in the Scandinavian runic alphabet has a direct semiotical or cultural connection with the Chinese sign)(, but it is a fascinating possibility. One can hardly refrain from believing that there has existed some sort of contact between the American civilizations and those on other continents, long before Columbus and even before Leif Eriksson's voyage to Vinland. If this, however, is not true, then one has to conclude that C.G. Jung was correct when he assumed that certain signs are psychological archetypes, the same for the whole of humankind.

I would suggest as highly probable that the Greek, Phoenician, Egyptian, and Chinese cultures were in contact with cultures in pre-Columbian America. The contentions that signs such as ⌁, ⊕, ▣, ⅋, ⊗, ✡, and ⊚ appeared "out of the blue" or were Jungian archetypes are unsatisfactory to say the least.

The astrological system of symbols

Astrology is the theory of relationships said to exist between the changing positions of the planets in the sun's system and those characteristics, occurrences, and lines of developments that exist in the life of a person.

Until the seventeenth century astronomy and astrology were the same science. This changed during the following centuries. Then the whole conception of the existing world changed and science as we know it started. The older science, astrology, continued to exist, but as a sort of psychology, whereas astronomy was the new science, quantitative by its nature, studying the positioning of celestial bodies, their composition, temperatures and radiations, chemical compositions, and gravitational fields.

Between the seventeenth century and the twentieth century astrology became almost religious in its emphasis. It lost much of its credibility, especially in the eyes of the new scientific establishment, which treated it as pure superstition. During the twentieth century astrology has developed into a ramification or branch of psychology, with connections to psychoanalysis. The astrological symbols have been used to identify and bring light to more or less unconscious psychological factors. This development has been especially prominent in the United States.

There is a general agreement that the first astrological work to be undertaken occurred in the Euphrates-Tigris region about 6000 years ago. See ✪ in Group 29 for more facts in this respect.

Astrology makes use of between 40 and 50 signs. The principal sign (above) is the pattern of the natal chart, or horoscope. The 12 sectors along the periphery correspond to the zodiac's 12 signs. The zodiac begins in the spring, when day and night have the same length. This is the spring equinox, when the sun enters the sign of Aries, ♈. Astrologers perceive the system of planets from a geocentric point of view, i.e., they view the earth as its center, this being the reason that the celestial bodies in the sun's system are seen as moving counterclockwise in the zodiac.

The signs of the zodiac are: ♈, *Aries – the ram;* ♉, *Taurus – the ox;* ♊, *Gemini – the twins;* ♋, *Cancer – the crayfish;* ♌, *Leo – the lion;* ♍, *Virgo – the virgin;* ♎, *Libra – the scales;* ♏, *Scorpio – the scorpion;* ♐, *Sagittarius – the archer, half human, half horse;* ♑, *Capricorn – the ibex;* ♒, *Aquarius – the water bearer;* ♓, *Pisces – the fishes.*

The signs of the zodiac are partly symbols for the month-long periods when the sun moves through the respective signs and partly symbols for that part of space against which the sun, moon, and planets move, as seen from the earth, during this time.

The signs of the zodiac are said to "color," each in its own specific way, the planets that happen to be passing against or "through" them at the time of birth of an individual. This "coloring" is symbolized by three types of sign groupings:

1. A sign is either positive–active–male or negative–passive–female.

2. Furthermore, a sign belongs to a specific **triplicity**. In other words, it is related to one of the four elements: ⊕, *earth,* which means that the individual experiences and understands the external world primarily through his or her sensory organs; △, *fire,* which means that the individual initially perceives the ingredients of the surrounding world via the possibilities that these wake in him or her; ▽, *water,* where the individual depends upon the feelings experienced on contact with the external world for his or her understanding; and ══, *air,* in which the individual's personal system of ideas reflects the way in which he or she relates to what is experienced.

3. Last, a sign belongs to one of three **quadruplicities**: ∧, the *cardinal* signs, which commence with the sun's position at midwinter, midsummer, spring equinox, or autumn equinox and are considered to stamp the individual with the qualities of self-assertion and initiative; ◼, the *fixed* signs, said to make the individual consistent and trustworthy; or ◠, the *variable* signs, which are said to make the individual adaptable and flexible.

The astronomical background to triplicities and quadruplicities is based on the fact that the earth, during the solar year, is influenced by different gravitational fields that reach their maximum strength in different periods of the solar year.

During the first half of the solar year the gravities of both the sun and the center of the galaxy (GC) are united, while during the second half they counteract one another.

The earth's orbital speed and acceleration are, in relation to GC, greater during that half of the year in which both the earth and the sun move in the same direction and slower during the other half.

We have, therefore, three factors to contend with: the speed of the earth's orbit as seen from the GC; the earth's acceleration and retardation in relation to GC; and the cooperation or counteraction of the sun's and GC's gravitational fields. These are shown in the diagram to the right.

Notice that this zodiac has, at its center, the sun, not the earth. For example, when the sun moves against ♋, the earth is moving through ♑. The earth's phase of acceleration is therefore finishing and it has a maximum speed relative to GC.

In astrology the planets are "the wandering stars" and thus different from the fixed stars. They represent the psychological aspects of an individual in his or her natal chart, the map in which each planet's position at the individual's birth is given.

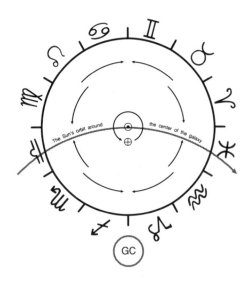

Following are concise descriptions of each planet's meaning in the natal chart. For a more detailed description, refer to the respective planets in the dictionary section.

☉, the *sun*, symbolizes the individual's conscious self and character.

☽, the *moon*, is the symbol denoting one's personality, which from the astrological point of view is the unconscious self – that which the individual subconsciously has incorporated from parents, siblings, and other people during his or her lifetime.

☿, *Mercury*, symbolizes the intellect.

♀, *Venus*, symbolizes the need to belong, to join together.

♂, *Mars*, symbolizes the drive to self-assertion.

♃, *Jupiter*, symbolizes the desire and ability to incorporate those values that exist in society and the desire to expand both materially and spiritually through increased knowledge.

♄, *Saturn*, symbolizes the instinct to build permanent structures in life, restrictions, discipline, and rigidity.

♅, *Uranus*, symbolizes the instinct to break free from routine and inhibiting situations to give free rein to one's individuality.

♆, *Neptune*, symbolizes fantasy, intuition, spiritual seeking, idealism, and the capacity to go beyond existing boundaries on the psychological plane.

♇ , *Pluto*, symbolizes deep transformations, willpower, recklessness, and the individual's capacity to change totally and start anew.

Another important aspect of astrological symbolism, apart from the zodiac signs in which the planets are (the signs that "color" the planets), is the angles between the planets. The planets represent psychological factors, and the angles, known as *aspects*, symbolize the way in which these qualities harmonize or conflict with one another.

The most important aspects in astrological symbolism are based on the division of the zodiac circle into two, three, four, five, and six. Here are their names and qualities:

☌, *conjunction*, means that two planets lie close to one another. This is either positive or negative depending on which signs and planets are involved.

☍, *opposition*, where two planets lie 180 degrees from each other, i.e., oppose one another. This is considered a "difficult" aspect and suggests conflict or a state of opposition.

△, *trine*, means that the angle between two planets is 120 degrees. This is the most positive aspect of all.

□, *square*, where the angle between two planets is 90 degrees. This is considered one of the most "difficult" of aspects and suggests a crisis situation between the psychological elements symbolized by the two planets.

⚹, *sextile*, where the angle between two planets is 60 degrees. This aspect is almost as positive as the trine.

The following aspects are considered less important. They are also called weak aspects. They are less positive or negative than the main aspects:

⚼, *sesqui-square*, denotes an angle of 135 degrees between two planets. It is slightly discordant.

⌐, *semi-square*, where the angle between two planets is 45 degrees. It is slightly discordant.

⊻, *half-sextile*, where the angle between two planets is 30 degrees. This aspect is considered slightly harmonious.

⊼, *inconjunct* or *quincunx*, means that the angle between two planets is 150 degrees. It is considered to be slightly discordant.

Q, *quintile*, where the angle between two planets is 72 degrees. This aspect is slightly harmonious.

⊥, *half quintile*, in which the angle between two planets is 144 degrees. It is very slightly harmonious.

⊥, *semi-quintile*, where the angle between two planets is 36 degrees. This aspect is very slightly harmonious.

☊ and ☋, the two signs representing the nodes of the moon, also play a significant role in the astrological system of symbols. These nodes move through the zodiac and return to the same position every 18 years.

The moon does not move in exactly the same orbital plane as that of the earth around the sun. These two orbiting planes cross one another so that the moon intersects the plane of the earth's orbit twice a month. When the moon crosses the earth's orbital plane from the "under" side on the way "up," the intersection is called the moon's north node. These two points,

seen from the earth, are symbolized by ☊, denoting the *moon's north node, caput draconis,* or *the dragon's head,* and ☋, denoting the *moon's south node, cauda draconis,* or *the dragon's tail.*

From the earth it appears as if all the planets, apart from the sun and the moon, follow a pattern of movement that first seems to go backward, to stop, and then to move forward. The sign ⊠, *station*, signifies the point in the zodiac where a planet is said to be "standing still" before it changes direction; and ℞, *retrograde,* denotes that the planet is moving backward, i.e., clockwise in the horoscope circle.

The signs ⊕ and ⊕ are less often seen. ⊕ represents (besides the *earth* in the zodiac) the *Part of Fortune,* that point in the zodiac that lies as far before or after the ascendant (the ascendant being the point in the zodiac that rises at the horizon at the moment of birth) as the moon is ahead of or behind the sun. It is considered to be related to an individual's material fortune. The sign ⊕, the *Part of Spirit,* lies equally far from the ascendant, but on the other side. It is believed to have been introduced by the Arabs during the Middle Ages. In today's astrology, however, it is rarely used.

A complete description covering the basic structure of astrology's symbolism necessitates the explanation of the concept of "the 12 houses." They are not symbolized by ideograms but by Latin or Arabic numerals. The 12 houses represent 12 different areas of life. Houses affect the planets passing through them in much the same way as the signs of the zodiac do.

The first house begins at the ascendant. There exist several methods of charting the houses. The simplest method considers each house to be as big as a sign, i.e., 30 degrees. But according to other, more complicated methods, the house sizes vary corresponding to the distance of the place of birth from the earth's Equator.

The *first house* indicates the self and those interests that are self-centered and is linked to ♈ and ♂. The ascendant, as the **cusp** or **first point** of the house, represents a person's way of appearing to others: the way he or she looks, dresses, behaves, and so on.

The *second house* indicates moveable property, material security, and values, and it is related to ♉ and ♀.

The *third house* is representative of relationships between the self and its surroundings, communication with relatives and neighbors, and the school years, and it is related to ♊ and ☿.

The *fourth house* represents the base for different types of growth, and home and family. It is related to ♋ and ☽.

The *fifth house* denotes the active participation of the self in the environment, children, own productivity, leisure, and enjoyment. It is related to ♌ and ☉.

The *sixth house* denotes the adaptation to the surrounding world and service to others or society, and it is related to ♍ and ☿.

The *seventh house* indicates relationships to partners, husband or wife, enemies, and the public, and it is related to ♎ and ♀.

The *eighth house* represents sexuality, death and rebirth, ownership shared with others, and inheritance, and it is related to ♏ and ☿.

The *ninth house* represents the self's ability to approach new horizons, also, literally, long voyages, and immersion in the studies of new areas, and it is related to ♐ and ♃.

The *tenth house* denotes social status, career, professional activities, and parents, and it is related to ♑ and ♄.

The *eleventh house* represents ideals, friends, group goals and activities, and hopes and fears. It is related to ♒ and ♅.

The *twelfth house* denotes the karma, hidden abilities and motives, enemies and dangers, secrets, self-denial, escapism, and isolation, and it is related to ♓ and ♆.

And so we come to the semiotics of the zodiac signs. The signs used for the aspects, at least those that are considered stronger, ☌, □, and △, are based on simple and easily understood analogies. The same applies to the signs of the zodiac, although the analogies are somewhat more complicated.

♈, *Aries*, resembles the head of a ram, but also brings to mind the fountain of life or a growing shoot that comes up at the spring equinox.

♉, *Taurus*, resembles the head of an ox. The empty circle is a sign for unlimited potential, the half circle a symbol denoting receptivity. These two signs combined, the half moon above the full circle, symbolize an exceptionally good receptivity.

♊, *Gemini*, symbolizes dualism.

♋, *Cancer*, is more difficult to analyze. The British astrologer R.C. Davison suggested that the two horizontal lines in the sign represented the same dualism as in the vertical ♊, but in the passive form. The smaller circles at one end of each line signify a potential whereby the passive dualism can give birth to something new.

♌, *Leo*, suggests Davison, is a symbol signifying creative energy that can be compared to the snake energy, kundalini, in Indian mythology.

♍, *Virgo*, is based on the Hebraic letter *mem* and the Phoenician symbol ♌, meaning fish. It became, early on, a sign representing Jesus and the mystery of his virginal birth.

♎, *Libra*, depicts a pair of scales, but perhaps more accurately resembles a stylized sunset. ♎ corresponds with the beginning of the autumn equinox, when the sun, figuratively speaking, sinks, so that the night becomes longer than the day. It also symbolizes the two opposites that are weighed and balanced in the search for harmony. This balancing process is a typical characteristic of those born in this sign.

♏, *Scorpio*, is based on the Hebraic letter *mem* and the stinging arrow in the sign ♂, or the scorpion's tail. ♂, Mars, was, according to the old astrological traditions, the planet that ruled ♏.

♐, *Sagittarius*, is a symbol signifying the projection of the self toward new horizons.

♑, *Capricorn*, is a stylized symbol for a being that is half billy goat and half fish. The sign is a combination of the horns of the billy goat and the tail of a fish. ♑ is also similar to ⩘, the sign representing the Greek god Chronos, later written ♄, Saturn, Capricorn's ruling planet.

♒, *Aquarius*, conveys the same idea of passive dualism as ♎ and ♋.

♓, *Pisces*, is a stylized representation of two fish swimming in opposite directions but bound to each other. This glyph can be compared to the ancient Chinese)(, *to split*, and also to)(, the Pisces' glyph in ancient Greece.

In conclusion it can be said that the graphs of the zodiac used in ancient Egypt at about the time of Christ's birth look much the same as those used today. Those symbols that the graphs represented – ✗ was, for example, a graph for the symbol *centaur with bow aiming his arrow* – were already known and used among the Egyptians in 600 B.C.

Many of the old signs for the then-known planets were being used in ancient Greece, but today's planetary signs most probably had their origins in Assyria and Babylon.

The structure shown on this page, found in the Euphrates-Tigris area, is believed to be a map of the world. It was drawn in Babylon either around 2300 B.C. or around 700 B.C.

Whatever difficulties might be involved in dating such a structure, it contains all those elements that are now in use and that were apparently used to designate the planets known at that time: the cross, the crescent moon, the circle, the sign of the sun, and the arrow.

The presence of the signs for the sun and moon suggests that this stone tablet was more likely a map of the planetary system than of the earth. A comparison with a symbol for our solar system from the fifteenth century, illustrated in the chapter entitled "The signs of the alchemists," supports this statement.

The symbolism of the astrological ages

In approximately the year 200 B.C. (findings are not concordant) the zodiac star signs were located in the constellations of fixed stars bearing their respective names. Since then the signs of the zodiac have drifted farther and farther away from their corresponding constellations.

The longer an astronomical time cycle is, the more difficult its existence becomes to discover. The earth's polar axis moves as if the earth had been hung from a string attached to the South Pole and swung slowly round, i.e., the earth's polar axis describes a circular movement through space. One full circle takes approximately 26,000 years.

The zodiac symbolizes the 12 periods of the solar year — the first beginning at the vernal equinox, when day and night are of the same length — and the different sections of the ecliptic (that "band" of fixed star constellations around the earth against which sun, moon, and other planets seem to move). During the first 4000 years of astrological development the fact that the equinox was not fixed in relation to the constellations of stars was prob-

ably not known. But when this was discovered it necessitated the making of two zodiacs: one for the 12 periods of the solar year — the one commonly used for astrology, called the **tropical zodiac** — and the zodiac of fixed stars, the so-called **sidereal zodiac**.

Over a period of 26,000 years the vernal equinox moves through each of the sidereal zodiac's 12 signs. This means that the solar year always begins in (and is in this way influenced by) a specific sign of the fixed star or sidereal zodiac. According to astrological symbolism, the movement of the vernal equinox (marking the beginning of a new solar year) over the boundary between two signs in the fixed star zodiac heralds the beginning of a new era.

If astrologers take as their starting point the idea that the tropical and sidereal zodiacs were identical around 200 B.C., they can divide human history in the following way:

With the dawn of historical time after the last Ice Age, between 8800 and 6650 B.C., the vernal equinox moved through the sign of Cancer. According to historical research this epoch was dominated by tribal societies that tended toward worship of the mother figure and moon cults. This period marked the end of the so-called Stone Age, or Neolithic time.

In the epoch between 6650 and 4500 B.C. the vernal equinox moved through Gemini. Little is known about this Age of Gemini although it was then that the so-called Bronze Age began. This epoch, in accordance with astrological symbolism, would have been characterized by a great amount of trade and voyages of discovery: in short, by more and farther communications and by intellectual speculations.

The next era, 4500 to 2350 B.C., was the Age of Taurus. It was believed by astrologers to have been influenced by Venus, ♀, the ruling planet of Taurus. Venus also represents the metal copper. It brought the Bronze Age to its ripeness and end. In this period the majority of mankind ceased being hunters and shepherds and turned their attention to agriculture. This encouraged the development of towns and a more complex social structure, which in turn favored more centralized rulership and greater geographical and demo-graphical units. Important, long-lasting civilizations appeared along many of the earth's major river valleys. A common symbol at this time was ⊕ , the **sun cross** or **four-spoked wheel,** symbolizing the revolutionary effect that agriculture, and those discoveries that followed as a result, had on the existing societies.

The time between 2350 and 200 B.C. was the Age of Aries, influenced by ♂, the planet Mars, which represents the metal iron. The great pyramids of Gizeh were built around 2400 B.C. and mark the transition to the Age of Aries. The path to the enormous temple of the sun god, Aman-Res, at Karnak near Thebe in Egypt, leads through an alley surrounded by giant sculptures bearing Aries heads. The temple was built around 2400 B.C. Aries was the symbol for the god Amon. In the Karnak temple, the seat of Amon was a sphinx bearing an Aries head. In Greek mythology, Jason set out on a dangerous voyage to retrieve the golden (Aries) fleece, which was believed to have the power to speak, think, and fly.

For many, the Iron Age was a time marked by endless wars, a time when new trade routes were discovered, and long voyages into uncharted regions of the world were embarked upon; a time of struggle and daring escapades; an age dominated by man, not woman. The goddess Venus, who had had a predominant position during the Age of Taurus, was now superseded by the male Mars and the sun. They now became the dominant gods in the mythologies of different cultures.

In this period ♈ and ♋ became common symbols in temples, on the sides of buildings, and on clay tablets. In 900 B.C., on a relief from Babylon, ⊕, the sun, appears rising from the sign ♋. It was at the end of this age that the following epoch's most important signs, ✚ and ✝ , became common.

According to astrological symbolism, the **Age of Pisces** began around the year 200 B.C. It is represented by two fish trying to swim in opposite directions while bound together, depicted in the sign ♓. The symbol illustrates the conflict between spiritual and material values. The epoch was characterized by continuous conflicts, brother against brother.

Christ, one of the central characters of this particular epoch, is symbolized by a fish drawn as ⌒ and by an instrument of torture, ✝. The cross has become the symbol *par preferénce* for the Western world. Faith in God and compassion have been widely propagated under this sign. At the same time, it has served as an excuse for some of the most ruthless wars and atrocities encountered throughout the history of humankind. These wars have been fought for the accumulation of material wealth and power and for the suppression of peoples.

The next age is that of Aquarius. It is said to have begun in the middle of the twentieth century. Some astrologers pinpoint its birth to 1962. The sign ♒ represents water: not the water we drink, but the river of consciousness that flows over the earth from the source of intuition and the water of knowledge that all men and women are brothers and sisters. The ruling planet of Aquarius is ♅, Uranus, which stands for modern science, humanism, and the desire to overcome all obstacles that hinder human growth, the development of societies, and human fellowship.

The transition into this epoch was marked by the creation of humanity's hitherto most destructive weapon, the atom bomb. According to astrological symbolism this age, which will last until 4100, will be an epoch of humanism, expansion of consciousness, and social and scientific progress.

The mystical pentagram

The **five-pointed star** is one of the most common ideograms in both the West and the East and is almost as frequently used as the cross. The sign ☆ is used on uniforms by most of the world's armies and on tanks and fighter jets in the U.S.S.R., the United States, and other countries. It also appears on many national flags.

We also know that ☆ is derived from ✩, which in turn is not an invented structure but one that has been discovered. The earliest evidence for the existence of ✩ is from about 4000 B.C., whereas ✡ which is similar, did not appear until around 800 B.C. If ✩ had been invented, i.e., created by random drawing, it is unlikely that it would have appeared long before ✡, as the combination of two equilateral triangles to form ✡ is an easier pattern to achieve than ✩ when drawing at random.

The pentagram, ✩, was probably discovered as a result of astronomical research. The sign is the structure that results if one plots the movement of the planet Venus as seen from the earth in the zodiac. A more thorough description of the origin of this structure is given under ⊕ in Group 29.

The knowledge that linked ☆ with the planet ♀ was somehow lost or repressed from the earliest Sumerian times until the present day.

The first mystery concerning ☆ is that it does not appear in astrology. It could well have stood for the planet Venus instead of ♀ or for the quintile aspect (which divides the circle into five parts, 72 degrees each, and was first used around 1600, probably by Johannes Kepler).

The goddess of Venus, Ischtar, from the ancient Euphrates-Tigris culture, appeared both as the Morning and the Evening star. As the Morning star it was the deity of battle, hunting, and physical activity. As the Evening star it was the goddess of beauty, sexuality, and fertility. This is illustrated in the way ☆ and ✩ are used in modern Western societies. When ☆ is used, it is often related to war and military power and signifies the ruling power's sovereignty (as in flags). Most of the time its use is of a serious nature. ✩, however, appears in the West as a sign to denote feasting, happiness, festivities, and favorable opportunities (e.g., price reduction sales). During the Middle Ages ☆ was associated with *Antichrist* – the *Devil*.

The second mystery is why the West has associated the pentagram primarily with military concerns and the assertion of nationalism, and then never in its crossed version, ☆. Sometimes it is used with lines that emanate from a central point in these connections, ☆, but never in other ways.

The third mystery is why ☆ appears as a sign for the planet Venus only in the Arabic cultural sphere. In many of the Arabic nations' flags, the sign ☆, representing the planet Venus as the Morning star, appears. In the sign ☾ the moon is represented as being on the wane, i.e., the way it looks from the Northern Hemisphere at dawn a few days each month. In this sign, therefore, ☆ is the Morning star, the deity of war and action. On the other hand, one seldom, if ever, finds the variation ☽ in the Arabic symbolism, which would have shown Venus as the Evening star together with the crescent of the new moon, ☽ .

It is quite possible that the European crusaders first came across ☆ when they went to war with the Muslims to win back Jerusalem. The sign ☆ had been used to symbolize the city of Jerusalem a few hundred years before the birth of Christ. The war over Jerusalem ended with the defeat of the crusaders, who were forced to leave the city. It was then that the defeated Western powers adopted the sign ☆ from their victorious enemies. Maybe they began to make use of it in the hope that it would ensure them victories. This development was further strengthened when the Turks during the seventeenth century moved through Southeast Europe, defeating all nations in their path. It is natural for the symbol used by a victorious enemy to become a sign denoting military power, and the negative pole (the Devil) in a dualistic dichotomy between Good and Evil, God and the Devil. As a symbol for the Evil One the sign is taken over unchanged, i.e., both ☆ and ☾ are attributed to the Devil, while ☾, as a sign for military power and success, is modified. ☆ as a military symbol avoids being associated with ☾.

Those graphs that can be called true symbols in the sense that they actualize subconscious archetypes in all people follow the law of polarity of meaning. ☆ is such a symbol, its dualistic meaning being both war and the principle of dominance and beauty, pleasure, and unity. For this reason the Arabs joined ☆ with ☾, the sign for the waning moon, the morning crescent, and in this way ensured that only one of the meanings was represented: war, dominance, and action.

☆ is not found in astrological symbolism, which is a mystery. But a symbol adopted by a military establishment and used as its leading symbol would become "locked" to this use and therefore be unsuitable for use in any other serious context. Compare this with the disparity of ⚡ as a sign denoting power stations on maps and large-scale electric power industries when ⚡ became the main ideological and military symbol in Germany during the 1930s.

Yet another mystery concerning the use of ★ is why it never appears in the Arab world *behind* ☾ (as in ★ ☾), but always on the crescent moon's concave side. One of the reasons may be that an ideographic symbol, once it is established as an ideological and religious structure, is unlikely to change as long as the ideology continues to predominate. It becomes, so to speak,

holy, and as such unchangeable, one of the qualities of holiness.

In conclusion I draw your attention to the fact that the planet Venus is bound to a *four-year period*. This is the time it takes for ♀ to return to the same point in the zodiac (if one realizes that ♀ is both the Morning and Evening star). The zodiacal cycle of the Morning star (Evening star) is thus eight years.

The planet Venus is related to the number 4 through its cycle in the geocentric zodiac and to the number 5 through its appearance as graph.

When the Olympic Games took place in Los Angeles in 1984, this relationship was visualized in the Olympic logotype above, consisting primarily of the five-pointed star of Venus.

The sign of the cross in Western ideography

The cross is one of the most common structures in Western cultures. In the same way that ☾ often represents the *Muslim-Oriental culture*, † is the most universal symbol for the *Christian-Western world*.

Many an ideogram is referred to as a cross even when it does not look like a cross. Take ⳹ as an example. It is often called the cross of Christ. ⳹ is made up by the Greek letters X and P, which correspond to the letters K (or C) and R in the Latin alphabet (Greek ΧΡΙΣΤΟΣ = Christ). If one discounts letter monograms in cross forms there exist over 50 different and easily distinguished variations, all of which are called crosses and are used in Christian symbolism. The most common of these is the **Latin cross**, †, which appears daily in newspapers' obituary notices. Another variation is the **cross of Peter**, an upside down Latin cross used in memory of the apostle Peter, who was supposedly crucified upside down. There is ✳ , the **Maltese cross**, whose eight points symbolize the eight virtues of the knights: loyalty, piety, generosity, courage, modesty, contempt of death, helpfulness to-

ward the poor and helpless, and respect for the church. There is ☨, the **cross of the pope**, which is slightly more adorned than ☨ , the **cross of the patriarch** (*patriarch* is the term for the highest dignitaries in the Greek Orthodox Church). This, in turn, is related to ☦, the **cross of the Russian Orthodox Church**.

The Christian Church has often adopted cross-like ideograms from earlier ideologies that have had a positive meaning. The **Egyptian cross**, ⚲, is an adaption of ☥, the ancient Egyptian hieroglyph **ankh**, a symbol for *life* and *rebirth*. ⊕, the **inaugural cross**, is identical to the ancient ideogram found in the Bronze Age. ⊕ is used by most races. It has been found, for example, on rock carvings in the Nordic countries, and the form ⊕ has been discovered on pre-Christian altars of bronze in Scania, Sweden, and other regions.

Even the sign +, the cross with arms of equal length, has been found in the Nordic countries dating long before the time of Christ, as in rock engravings in Dalsland, Sweden, from about 800 B.C. Otherwise it seems that the earliest crosses appeared in Sweden during the eighth and ninth centuries after the birth of Christ. They were often complicated structures like ⚛.

From the beginning of modern times ⇨, the **cross of Philip,** has become the sign representing the Nordic countries because of its use in their flags (no other country's flag bears this sign).

In this context I would like to discuss an interesting semiotic problem. To what extent must a structure such as ✝ be changed for it no longer to be considered a Christian symbol partaking of the cross structure's spectrum of meaning? (By "spectrum of meaning" I refer to those associations and emotional responses that the sign awakens in all those belonging to a culture where the sign is in use – apart from those meanings that are private, i.e., that belong to the experiences that are unique for each individual. In this case the spectrum of meaning is associated to burials, sorrow, death, God, salvation, priesthood, the Church, heaven, hell, sin, etc.

The answer to this question can supply us with a key to the interpretation of systems of signs. We find that the form of cross where the arms are diagonal instead of horizontal and vertical still partakes of the spectrum of meaning of the Christian cross. An example is **✕** , **St. Andrew's cross,** after the apostle Andrew, who, not feeling himself worthy of being executed on a cross of the same form as Christ's, is said to have asked to be crucified on a diagonal cross.

If a sign structure has a central point, its movement around that point hardly seems to affect the sign's meaning. Other changes, however, minor as they may seem, do affect the meaning. Take ⊢ as an example. This is a metallographic sign that denotes a specific type of amalgamation characteristic in metals. In this case the slight lengthening of the horizontal arms affects the meaning of the sign so that it is no longer associated to the Christian faith.

Neither ⊢ nor ⊢ are considered Christian crosses. ⊢ was used in Nordic calendars of the Middle Ages and in older moon calendars on what were called calendar sticks, a sort of almanac of the times, and signified the *number 10* (one of the "golden numbers" that described the phases of the moon in relation to the days of the week).

Apart from all the different Christian variations of the cross there exist some 20 or 30 older cross forms in the Greek cultural sphere from about 1000 B.C. There is, for example, ⊹, which is often found on antique vases decorated with mythological motifs and which is used today on nautical charts to signify *breakers* or *stone bottom at water's edge*. Others are ⚹, 卐, etc.

The sign 卐 is of special interest because it has also been used in the Buddhist cultural sphere to signify *rebirth* and *prosperity*. 卐 is called **swastika** in Sanskrit, which means *well-being* or *positive being*. It is often found on the statues of Buddha and is a common sign in the symbol 🦶, the **footprints of Buddha**. The mirror image of this sign, 卍, is called **sauvastika** in Sanskrit, and is associated with *darkness, misfortune,* and *suffering*. Both these signs are also found in pre-Columbian America.

The earliest occurrences of the swastika in Europe are in ancient Greece. There are many variations, such as ✕, used to decorate vases. In Christian symbolism 卐 is called **Crux Gammata**. The name, as does the Greek *gammadion*, comes from the Greek letter Γ, *gamma*. It is as if four gamma signs have been put together to make 卐. Another Greek name for it is **tetraskele**, the four-legged one. In England it is called **fylfot**. In ancient China the symbol 卐 stood for *wan*, *10,000* (compare this with the single cross +, 10, which was not only a large number, but also a general superlative).

It was not until the 1920s that Hitler adopted the swastika, and 卐 (for the first time?) was used drawn within the circle, the symbol for eternity. In Finland the swastika was used from 1918, in connection with the war of liberation from the Russian Empire. Even today the swastika is a common Finnish symbol. More will be said about this particular sign's history in Finland and Germany under the heading "The ideographic struggle in Europe during the 1930's."

It is clear that 卐 is strongly associated with *power* and *energy*. In Scandinavia it was once known as **Tor's hammer**. Today it is used on some maps to signify *electric power stations*. ASEA, now ABB, a Swedish manufacturer of electrical machines, used 卐 in its logotype until the Second World War.

The more common cross with arms of equal length is found used prolifically in Europe, but also in all-important Oriental cultural spheres and pre-Columbian American cultures. In America + was used to symbolize *Thaloc*, the god of weather. The four arms of the cross probably symbolized the four corners of the world from which the wind blew. The structure ⊕ is also quite common. Among the hieroglyphs used by the Mayans there is 🔘, the **Kan cross**, a common sign denoting something *expensive* or *valuable*. It is often related to water. Another of their hieroglyphs is ⊕ , and although its meaning is not yet known it seems to have something to do with the planet Venus.

The cross, by the way, is one of the oldest human ideograms. It has been found in prehistoric caves in Western Europe. The symbol ♀, painted on small round stones in red, has been found in the Mas d'Azil cave in France. The signs, carvings, and paintings in these caves are between 10,000 and 20,000 years old. Crosses have also been discovered on rock faces in the inner Sahara. These rock paintings are said to have been made 10,000 years ago.

The Hittites used variations of the common cross in their hieroglyphs. Babylon was also acquainted with several types of crosses. The god Anu was sometimes symbolized with ✕. Anu was the highest of the gods — the highest among the 2,000 or so mythological characters that existed — the god of the heavens. Different variations of the **sun cross**, ⊕, appeared in the Assyrian-Babylonian culture. Other signs used in this culture to represent the highest god were ✳ and ⊕ . These last two signs combine the cross structure with star-like shapes.

To sum up, the cross long ago was common in the Americas, China, the Near East, and Europe. Obviously a structure that is simple and widely used will find a place in many ideographic systems and be given a wide variety of meanings. Nevertheless, the form of the cross, like that of the rectangle and square, has a strong connection to the earth, the ground. In flags it represents nations, countries — claims to a right of possession of different parts of the earth's surface. In obituary notices the association to the ground is obvious. The sign ⊥ in ancient China meant *earth*, *land*, *ground*. Likewise, ⊞ on nautical maps has a similar relationship by the fact that it marks those places where land meets water. In an astrological context, the sun cross, ⊕, means the planet earth, sometimes the element earth, and sometimes the Part of Fortune (see "The astrological system of symbols"), which represents matter, worldly things, and success in earthly matters. ⊕ is also used on the American continent to denote *land* or *ground*.

Different types of crosses are common in the fields of astrology and alchemy. From the Middle Ages up until the nineteenth century, the signs used to represent chemical substances consisted of a cross in combination with other structures, as in ⦵, which stood for *olive oil*. Most of the astrological signs for the planets depict a cross.

As for the diagonal cross it seems that in the West it has partaken of the same meanings as the horizontal-vertical cross. Between the sixteenth and seventeenth centuries $+$, and 150 years later $\times$ began to be used as mathematical symbols for the mathematical operations *addition* and *multiplication*.

The diagonal cross has, since then, more and more come to mean *prohibition, invalid, the opposite is true,* whereas the "normal" cross has been given positive meanings. The diagonal cross has had its spectrum of meaning centered on the idea of something that crosses, or a crossing, more so than the cross, an idea aptly illustrated by the use of the diagonal cross as one of the signs for multiplication.

The signs of the alchemists

The science that studies the chemical elements and compounds was known during the period from the Middle Ages until approximately 1700 as alchemy. After this time it became known as chemistry, and the term *alchemy* was used primarily to indicate the art of making gold, which was only one of the many activities and areas that interested the alchemists.

It was the Swedish chemist Jöns Jacob Berzelius, working during the first part of the nineteenth century, who introduced the method of representing the elements with the letters of the alphabet. He chose the initials of the elements' Latin names. Before Berzelius' time many different sign systems were used to identify the elements. As there did not exist any universally accepted scientific terminology, it was not uncommon for one element to be symbolized by several different signs.

There exist, therefore, innumerable signs for the elements, chemical compounds, different ways of treating them, and so on. In Part II, the dictionary, there are hundreds of such signs: those in use after approximately 1700 are called chemical signs; the earlier signs are called alchemic. There is no reason, however, to take strict measures to separate the early chemical signs from the alchemical signs.

It is not clear when the science of alchemy began. There exist writings suggesting that attempts were made to produce gold from less precious substances in China hundreds of years before the birth of Christ. And knowledge of chemistry began to accumulate in Alexandria, in Hellenic Egypt, at the time of the birth of Christ. After the fall of Alexandria, this knowledge, reproduced in Arabic, spread throughout the Arab world. Traces of this are the Arabic chemical terms that are used or have been used: *al-chimaya* (alchemy), *al-kuhl* (alcohol), *al-kali, al-iksir* (elixir), *natron*, etc.

Alchemy had its heyday from the ninth century until the time it was transformed into modern chemistry at about the beginning of the eighteenth century. But the term *alchemy* is still used in places to denote the practice of making gold. August

Strindberg, among others, was periodically interested in this art.

Alchemy was a practical science concerned with the art of transforming elements and compounds, and a religious-philosophical system, esoteric alchemy, was connected to older traditions. Esoteric alchemy — *esoteric* (Greek) = *for the initiated only* — rested on the idea of the existence of a substance called *lapis philosophorum, the philosopher's stone* (*philosopher* used in the sense of wise man), which could change base elements into more precious substances without itself being changed — i.e., the Middle Ages' equivalent to what is today called a *catalyst*. Sometimes the term *elixir* was used for similar, sought-after substances.

The ideogram above is a symbol for the *moon elixir* and is said to have been drawn around the middle of the fifteenth century. The most interesting aspect of this combination of signs is that it is a graphic model of our planetary system. The sun is at the center and the moon lies within the sun, while the five known planets have been placed outside. The ideogram

has empty places for the remaining three planets in our solar system – unknown in the fifteenth century, but discovered within 200 years: Uranus, Neptune, and Pluto.

Strong links exist between the signs and theories of astrology and alchemy. Each of the five planets was associated with a primary element: ☿, mercury, signified by *Mercury*; ♂, iron, signified by *Mars*; ♀, copper, signified by *Venus*; ♃, tin and zinc, signified by *Jupiter*; and ♄, lead, signified by *Saturn*.

Furthermore, each sign of the zodiac was associated with an alchemical process: ♈, Aries, meant *calcination*, reduction through the application of intense heat; ♉, Taurus, meant *coagulation*, the process whereby a liquid substance changed into a jelly-like form. Gemini, ♊, and sometimes the sign ♇, denoted *fixation*, the process whereby a volatile substance became less volatile. Cancer, ♋, denoted the *dissolution* of a substance in a solvent. Leo, ♌, denoted the absorption or assimilation of one substance by another. Virgo, ♍, or the sign ◯, denoting the distillation flask, or the sign ♐ stood for *distillation*, the process where a substance is heated until it vaporizes, and the steam then is cooled so that the substance passes back into a liquid form. Libra's sign, ♎, or the sign ♒ , denoted *sublimation,* whereby a substance is heated until it is transformed into a gas and then cooled to such an extent and with such rapidity that it becomes a solid without having passed through the liquid stage. The upside down Libra sign, ⊽, denoted *precipitation,* a process where an element or a compound is dissolved in a solvent and then the solvent is allowed to evaporate, leaving a deposit. Scorpio, ♏, signifies *separation,* a process by which two joined substances are separated. Sagittarius, ♐, stands for *ceration,* whereby an element is transformed into a partly solid, wax-like consistency. Capricorn, ♑, denoted *putreficatio,* the process of decomposition or rotting. Aquarius, ♒, signified the key concept of alchemy, *transmutation,* a process whereby one element is transformed into another (more precious) element. Finally, Pisces, ♓, represented the *process where lapis philosophorum or some similar elixir was transmitted to that material one intended to transform, i.e., had prepared for transmutation.*

The various signs used by alchemists to denote the different primary materials could be combined and, as such, denoted chemical compounds. One obtained, for example, the sign ⚴, *brass,* by combining the sign for *copper,* ♀, and the sign for *zinc,* Z♃. The sign for *arsenic sulphate,* 🜍, is a combination of the sign 🜍, *sulphur,* and 🜺, *arsenic.*

The alchemists' primary elements were not only those substances that we today term chemical. There were others such as ⚴, *wood;* ⛬, *gravel;* ✢, *soot;* 🝎, *stone;* and ⊡, *urine.*

The number of signs that existed for one and the same element were many. Mercury or quicksilver, for example, whose name translated literally means silver that is alive (*argent vif* in French), fascinated the alchemists. It was, without doubt, a metal and classified as such, but at the same time it was fluid and formed drops like water. For this reason it was given over ten different signs. Among them were ☿, ☿, ⊖, ∞, and ∝.

Sulphur was another element that attracted the alchemists' interest. It was usually represented by the sign 🜍, but at different times and in different countries it was also represented by 🜍, ⊕, 🜎, and 🜍.

As a matter of course the alchemists were very interested in gold and silver. The most common sign for *gold* was the sun sign, ☉, but others were ☉, ℘, and ϭ. The new moon, ☽, was the sign used to denote *silver.* Others were ⌒, ◡, and ⟁, to mention but a few. The precious metal *platinum,* which was first recognized in the middle of the eighteenth century, was sometimes drawn as ☽☉, a combination of the signs for silver and gold.

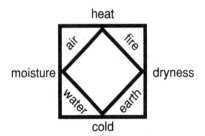

The signs representing the four elements were used frequently in alchemy. They were usually represented in the form of triangles: △ denoted *fire*, ▽ denoted *water*, *air* was represented by the sign △̶, and *earth*, as ▽̶. The relationship between these four elements, and also their respective qualities or characteristics, is expressed in the diagram above.

It is interesting to note that the ancient Tibetan sign for the element of  fire was a triangle with its point upward. This particular sign is also an intercultural sign for *God, king, spirituality,* and *power*.

Because of the close relationship that *sulphur* and *phosphorus* have to the fire element, they are often represented with the signs ♀ and ⅄, respectively. A liquid such as *aqua fortis*, strong water (*nitric acid*), was denoted by the sign ▽̶, composed of ▽, water, and an *F*, the initial of *fortis*.

Clay, closely related to water and earth, was drawn ▽̸. Another enlightening example of the graphic logic of the alchemists was the way the signs for fire and water were combined in ✡ to mean *alcohol*, i.e., fire water. It was more usual, however, to denote *alcohol* with the signs V̇ and ⅋.

Salt is a vital substance for humankind. *Salt from salt mines* was represented with the signs □ , ⊖, or ⊖. *Sea salt*, however, was drawn as ⊙ or ⊕. Acids were also of import, especially *aqua regia*, the *king's water* (a mixture of three parts concentrated hydrochloric acid and one part concentrated nitric acid), which was the only liquid that could dissolve the king of metals, gold. *Hydrochloric acid* was represented by ⊢⊖ and other signs; *nitric acid* as ε─⊕ (composed of ①, *nitrogen*). It follows that one of the signs used to denote *aqua regia* was ε⊕.

Acetum, ⅄, *wine spirit*, ◺ (which in all probability was the same as acetum), *olive oil*, ⟡, and *etheric oil* (i.e., volatile oil), ⅄, were among the other liquids that both alchemists and chemists worked with. Signs for *water* existed, of course, e.g., ⊞ and later ∞. *Lye* could be represented with the sign ◺.

Soap was usually represented by a diamond-shaped sign, ◊. The *saltpeter flower* was given the artistic sign ☡, although the substance is not a flower but a chemical precipitate. The sign ⏃ was supposed to stand for *phosphorus*, but it was also represented by ⊗, which the reader may associate with the South American girl Mercedes, whose name later became the trademark of a car. Finally we have the substance *glass*. It, too, was given many different signs, such as XX, ⚲, and o-o.

In Part II, the dictionary, are listed several hundred different signs used to represent primary elements, compounds, and combinations. The more important of them are also described briefly, with explanations of why they were of special interest to the chemists of former times.

Esoteric alchemy

One of the reasons that there were so many varying alchemical names for the primary elements and chemical compounds was that the science of alchemy was only partly a natural science concerned with the chemical substances and their reactions. Alchemy was also a secret and coveted science. It embraced humankind's search for the highest knowledge and an eventual unity with God. Naturally, many charlatans, impressed by the mystery-making, saw an opportunity to hide their ignorance behind a babble of words and signs, thinking it an easy way to recognition and money.

The first stage of esoteric alchemy was known as *nigredo*, a state or condition of gloom and decay that necessitated a change. The symbol used to represent this condition was ☻, *caput mortuum*, or the *skull*.

Then came the stage for the preparation of the raw material: *preparatio*. The three most important elements were ♠, *sulphur*; ⊖, *salt*, to protect against decay; and ☿, *mercury*, which represented the embryo of wisdom. Earthbound mercury contained some-

thing heavenly, but it was impure and had to be *sublimated,* ⚺, and *precipitated,* ⚏, until all the impurities had been removed.

Once the raw material, *materia tertia*, had been produced, the alchemical process could begin. The first step was known as *purificatio*, ♒, cleansing or purification. The result of this process was known as *materia secunda*. This material could be dissolved in the water of truth. Any impurities left could then be removed by the process of decomposition, *putreficatio;* and with the help of *sapiens sapientia*, the wisest of wisdoms, *materia secunda* could be cleansed further via *calcination*, ♈, i.e., reduction by roasting or burning the substance to ashes.

The next stage was that of *sublimation*, ♐. It demanded a greater degree of both inspiration and concentration. The element, having been sublimated, was once again a solid substance. It was now a question of detaching *half parallels*, compounds that were unwanted. The process of *distillation*, ♍, was used to achieve this. If the substance — after having undergone the secret method of *coagulation* ⊏⊐ — coagulated (i.e., became solid), the process had been successful and all that was left to do was to control the result. This test was known as the *peacock test* and consisted of a carefully controlled warming up. When the substance cooled it was expected to radiate all the colors of the spectrum, from infrared to ultraviolet. If this happened then all was as it should be, and one had in one's hand what was known as ♁ or , *lapis philosophorum*, the *stone of wisdom.*

This stone was a deep red crystal that when placed with the common earthly elements would turn them into gold. The aim of esoteric

Catena Aurea Homeri

1. ♁ is the symbol for the earth and matter. On top of the sun sign, ☉, it represents *chaos*: matter over ☉, *God*.

2. The divine spirit pushes up into matter.

3. In ⊕ the spirit has pierced matter. This is the alchemistic sign for *nitrum*, the gas *nitrogen.*

4. Here matter has become ethereal. ⊖ is the alchemical symbol for *salt,* which permeates, cleanses, and conserves matter.

5. The *sun cross* denotes that the ethereal process is complete and that matter is now permeated with the spirit.

6. The consciously created life begins to leave matter – man has separated himself from the animal.

7. This symbol represents the way in which the soul of man rises to a higher plane of awareness.

8. The soul of man has become eternal. It can no longer sink into the unconsciousness of matter.

9. The symbol denotes how matter becomes less and less important and returns to its original state before the creation of man.

10. When *matter* is finally placed under *God*, the *spirit*, and the *divine consciousness,* perfection has been reached – Man has returned to God. This is humankind's divine condition, closely related to *quinta essentia*, or the *fifth element, coniunctio,* — the *merging with God.*

alchemy, however, was primarily to improve the state of man, not to turn base elements into gold.

The stone of wisdom was considered to be extremely powerful and dangerous if used for any purpose not truly altruistic. For this reason the method for producing it was a well-kept secret.

During the eighteenth century the esoteric work of alchemy to achieve a refined human being was symbolized by *Catena aurea Homeri*, the *golden chain of Homer*, shown here with explanations for each of the stages involved.

Coniunctio, the ultimate aim of esoteric alchemy, is symbolized in different ways. We have just seen it represented as ☿. It is also quite commonly symbolized by ☿ and ⚹.

In the same way as do some Eastern philosophies, the esoteric alchemists regarded existence as a game between opposites, first and foremost between matter and spirit, or the four elements and God. *Coniunctio* is synonymous with the Indian *yoga* (union), the Chinese ☯ , and the Christian mystical ascendance into God. On the way to *coniunctio* man must pass through different stages, shown by the golden chain of Homer.

Other descriptions of the way to *coniunctio* are, for example, the *red and white rose*, the *snake* or *dragon that bites its own tail*, and the *sun and moon that are united*.

Behind esoteric alchemy lies an old tradition of sign and speech symbolism, with its roots in ancient Egypt and the Jewish *kabbala*. In the ideograms below the association is apparent.

Systems of hobo signs

Hobo signs, sometimes called gypsy signs in Sweden, is a comprehensive name for a group of similar ideographic systems used for drawing or carving into trees, walls, doors, or other surfaces. Each ideogram gives specific information concerning the place where it is found. The type of signs and their meanings are influenced by the situations the vagabonds, tramps, homeless, and destitute found themselves in up to the time of the Second World War.

Different parts of the world produce their own, individualized systems of hobo signs. I have chosen to describe three specific types: a Swedish, an English, and an American system. They consist of approximately 30, 40, and 60 ideograms, respectively.

What these systems have in common is their mutual concern with basic tramp problems, such as the availability of food, money, a night's lodging, or temporary work. They also serve as warning systems that inform whether the inhabitants of approached houses are unpleasant, or whether there are police or dogs to deal with. All three systems also contain ideograms for a kindhearted woman.

Yet there are clearly defined differences. The American system has signs that cover more modern phenomena like bus-stop shelters and places that are suitable for boarding freight trains free of charge. In the other two systems there are no such signs.

In England there is the sign ⊟, which means *here live working people – talk a lot*.

The sign V exists only in Sweden and means *they give only if you are ill*.

Interesting analogies appear such as ⛄, *a good woman lives here*, found in the American system. A woman who has a cat is apparently more kindhearted than one without.

It is also noticeable that the Swedish system is characterized by a certain straightforward, unimaginative beggar spirit, whereas in England the signs often supply information about the possibility of temporary work.

The American system is often concerned with the dangers involved in being a tramp. For example, the sign ⟡ stands for *prepare to defend yourself,* and 🖳 stands for *this water is danger-ous to drink*. There are no scruples when it comes to deceiving gullible people. This is even encouraged with signs such as ₿o, *sucker* = easy catch or easily deceived person. There is also a clear distinction between thieves and criminals on the one hand and tramps and hobos on the other, as signs such as ⌇, meaning *here lives a dishonest person*, and $\frac{2}{10}$, *there are thieves in the neighborhood*, show. $\frac{2}{10}$ was probably a warning to fellow tramps that there was a risk they would be accused by the local population for any crimes that were committed while they were in the vicinity.

The American designer Dreyfuss writes that the American system of hobo signs is international. According to him the same signs could be found in several different countries. It is, however, the meanings that are often similar in Sweden, England, and the United States. The actual graphs vary from country to country, although there do exist certain signs that are the same and have the same meaning in all three countries. They are:

〰, or 〰, which mean *unpleasant people* and *angry dogs*;

△▴▴▴, *the wife is alone with daughters or maid*;

###, #, or ###, which mean *bypass this place – risk of being arrested*;

‡ or ‡‡, *danger, police*; and

†, *speak religiously and they'll give*.

There exist several ideograms that look the same in two of the systems but have different meanings:

⌐+, *stay here* (U.S.); *knock – they buy if you have what they want* (England).

ooo, *here they give you money* (England and Sweden).

⊙, *be careful – hot-tempered people* (England). Compare this with ⊚, which means *food and money are given* (Sweden).

⊙⊙, *danger – they'll try to run you in* (England); and ⊙⊡, *man with a bad temper living here* (U.S.).

▽, *ruined – too many have been here* (England); *bad road – too many hobos* (U.S.).

⊞, *frightened of tramps* (England); *here live frightened people* (Sweden). Compare this with ⊞, *here live frightened people – they give to get rid of you* (U.S.).

⌐⌐, *invalids live here – show compassion* (England); *accommodation for the night* (Sweden); *you can camp here* (U.S.).

⟨⟨, *tell a moving story* (England); *keep on begging* (Sweden); *the police here are not friendly to hobos* (U.S.).

⊖, *unfriendly people* (Sweden); *leave quickly* (U.S.).

⊕, *a day's work can be found* (England). Compare this with ⊗, *good place for food and money* (U.S.); ⊗, *very hospitable people* (England); and ⊕, *food given here* (Sweden).

⊘, *irritable people* (England); *look out – the police will be called* (Sweden). Compare with ⊙, *people here may try to get you arrested* (England).

=, *here they give you a place to sleep* (England). Compare with ‖, *here you'll get whatever you want* (U.S.).

Naturally there does not exist a dictionary that covers hobo signs. A long period of time would be needed in their company to learn the signs and their meanings and uses.

The systems of hobo signs show, however, that even the poorest and least educated create their own communicative medium to help them survive. The most interesting aspect of this is that it shows the latent goodwill of people, a sort of subconscious tendency to help each other survive. No superior authority has forced this troublesome tribe of vagabonds to create their own system of writing. Nor does there exist any clear reason that a miserably poor tramp should inform others of his or her kind as to whether a place will offer them food and money or not. On the contrary, it may spoil his or her chances to use the place a second time.

One can of course be the hardboiled cynic and refuse to believe in a natural, subconscious, and inherent tendency toward social behavior and altruism among the poorest and most rejected stratum of society. But in that case one would have to admit the existence of a more or less conscious intention behind the development of these signs. The lesson learned then would seem to be that it is more valuable for everyone's survival to share whatever is found out and that this is of greater value than the damage done by not keeping it to oneself.

Below are three lists, one for each group, of those signs not yet shown.

First the Swedish:

⊙ *here food and money are given*

⊙ *here money is given*

ooo *here money is given*

▱ *this house's owner is brutal and ruthless*

◇ *a certain resistance to be expected. Compare with* ♡, *prepare to defend yourself* (U.S.).

○ *here food is given*

⊕ *no money but food*

∪ *here you'll be given a place to sleep*

∨ᴀᴀ *here lives a kindhearted or sympathetic woman*

⅄ *leave quickly*

ȼ *keep walking in this direction*

⤳ *warning – guard dog or other danger*

ᴡᴡᴡ *beware of the dog*

Next come the English hobo signs:

Ψ *if you work you'll be given food*

✕ *don't knock here*

◇ *generous people – but don't expect too much*

⣿ or ▱ *danger – they'll try and put you away*

▨ *a brutal man lives here*

ⅠⅠ *there are several tramps on this road*

Ƶ *strangers live here – tell them you've been in the army*

⋀ *here they sometimes give food*

⸸ *they'll usually give money*

⊃ *keep away – there's no use knocking*

∩ *a good haystack or barn for a night's rest*

◎ *a good place for a job*

⊙ *here lives a kind woman*

⋇ *there is fruit in the garden*

⏣ *a policeman lives here*

⊃− *take this direction preferably*

Ⲙ *the work is hard here*

Finally, the American:

↞ *no point in going in this direction*

↦ *go this way*

↤ or *disappear quickly*

Ⓠ *a good road to follow*

— *doubtful*

this is the place

a dangerous neighborhood

(•) *this neighborhood leaves hobos alone*

fresh water and a safe place to camp

or *the house is well guarded*

þ *the owner is at home*

ç *the owner is not at home*

Π *here lives a gentleman*

ΠΔ *here live rich people*

a kindhearted woman – give her a moving story

or *you'll be given food if you work*

Γ *if you are sick they will help*

here lives a doctor who gives free care

you can use their phone free of charge

□/ *in this town there is alcohol* (from the time of Prohibition in the United States during the 1920s and 1930s)

or *you can sleep in the barn*

∞ *keep quiet*

◊ *say nothing*

ᗯᗯ *guard dog*

look out for four dogs

trolley bus stop

a good place for jumping onto a train

/// *this is not a safe place*

man with firearms lives here

crime has been committed here – dangerous for strangers

here people tell you to go to hell

here you'll be manhandled

the authorities here are on the alert

a judge lives here

tribunal or police station

The ideographic struggle in Europe during the 1930s

The most successful and in many ways most conscious attempt to manipulate the masses with the help of ideograms was undertaken in Germany. It might even be true that Nazi Germany never would have come into existence without the use of ideograms.

In *Mein Kampf* Adolf Hitler wrote: "The question of the new banner, i.e., how it should look, occupied our minds considerably. . . . The reason being that not only was it to be a symbol for our struggle, but also had to be very effective on posters and placards. Those who have had experience with the masses realize just how important such a seemingly trivial thing is. A working and effective sign can be the deciding factor in hundreds of separate instances as to whether an interest is awoken for a movement."

The swastika was already being used in both Germany and Austria at the turn of the century. 卐 had an anti-Semitic undertone. The advocates of racial purity had used 卐 in anti-Semitic journals, in leaflets and on posters. This movement was most likely an expression of aggression against the socioeconomic repression practiced by the capital-owning class, where the number of Jews was disproportionately high considering the relative size of the group.

The sign had also been used by a number of the so-called free corps, independent paramilitary units in Germany, such as the Ehrhardt Brigade and the Rossback Free Corps, who used the swastika in their standards.

Hitler's main supporter at this time was the air force officer and former commander of the Richthofen Squadron during the First World War, Hermann Göring. After World War I, Göring worked as a taxi pilot in Stockholm. One day he was given the job of flying the Swedish explorer Count Erik von Rosen to his castle, Rockelstad. Once they had reached their destination Göring was invited to warm himself against the winter cold in front of the fireplace. In the wrought iron that decorated the fireplace Göring noticed the symbol 卐, a symbol that Erik von Rosen had already made use of as a type of owner's mark when travelling in South America and Africa among primitive peoples.

Having eventually warmed up and enjoying a toddy, Göring turned his attention to the rest of the interior. It was then that a beautiful woman made her way down the stairs that led into the hall of the castle, where Göring was sitting in the company of his host. The woman was Carin von Kantzow, a relative of the family through her marriage to a Swedish officer. Göring was struck by amour's arrow where he sat in front of the fire. On this particular night Göring had been struck twice: first by a symbol and second by the love of his life. Both were to follow him and his future commander, Hitler, in the coming years.

A few years earlier Erik von Rosen's favorite symbol had spread eastward. Finland had been, since the fifteenth century, a part of Svea Rike, i.e., Sweden. But Russia expanded and challenged the power of Svea Rike and in the seventeenth century conquered the eastern part of the Swedish Empire, which became the Grand Princedom of Finland in the tsar's empire.

After the October Revolution many peoples took the opportunity to free themselves from their Russian shackles. Among these were the inhabitants of Finland. This resulted in civil war between the Reds – the Communist workers and crafters – and the Whites – the aristocracy, the landowners, and the farmers who owned their fields, the freeholders.

It was during this struggle for independence that the embryo for the independent Finnish Air Force was conceived. Its first fighter plane was a gift from Count Erik von Rosen. It was, as a matter of course, decorated with his favorite sign, 卐, painted on the wings of the single-engine skiplane. From this year, 1918, until shortly after World War II, the swastika, blue on a white background, was the symbol used by the Finnish Air Force.

During the years that preceded Hitler's eventual seizure of power in Germany in 1933, he spent much time in the company of Göring and Göring's wife, Carin. There is hardly any doubt that the Nazi swastika that led the wave of blood and fire over the greater part of Europe between 1930 and 1940 had roots that stretched from South American voyages of discovery to a castle in the Valley of Mälaren and then on into the Bavarian Alps, cared for by an addicted German pilot ace and a Swedish woman from an aristocratic family.

Hitler made use of this ancient Greek and Indian sign: "The swastika is the symbol of national socialism. . . . Already in the year before the war (World War I), German groups had taken the swastika as their sign. It stood for their struggle against all that was harmful to a pure race, all that was un-German, and the destructive influence of the Jews. In this way the swastika became a particularly powerful anti-Semitic sign" (*Taschenbuch des Nationalsozialismus*).

Hitler turned 卐 into an effective tool of propaganda. He succeeded in this by simplifying the structure and creating a uniformity, 卐; by perpetual repetition through all possible media; and last, but most important of all, by an almost religious worship of the symbol. We can exemplify this with one cult object, *die Blutfahne*, the *blood banner*. This was a swastika banner that had been used in the failed attempted coup in Munich on 9 November 1923. In the ensuing battle, the banner was sprayed with the blood of one of the coup perpetrators. Hitler made a solemn point of touching every new Nazi, SA, and SS banner with this blood-stained cloth.

On other occasions a large wagon decorated with flowers and bearing a giant swastika banner was pulled by Aryan people dressed in white cloaks through the centers of the towns un-changed since the Middle Ages. The political sessions in Nuremberg likewise had the Nazi symbol as the cult object. Hitler cried, "Hail, my men!" and a hundred thousand Nazis replied, "Hail, my leader!" It was then, to the accompaniment of low drum rolls, that thousands of banners and standards were unfurled. Military music, resounding commands, and straight lines of uniformed soldiers all added to the intensity of the moment.

The swastika banner was red (representing socialism) with a white circular area (for eternity, virginity, and the Aryan ideal) and within this circle 卐 (for the people, power, the movement, and anti-Semitism).

The swastika was officially recognized as the Nazi party's sign on 7 August 1920. Hitler wrote: "During the Summer of 1920, the new banner was publicly revealed for the first time. It suited our movement perfectly. It was as young and new as our movement. No one had ever seen it before. The effect was the same as if we had dropped a bomb" (from *Mein Kampf*).

Doctor Joseph Goebbels, head of Nazi propaganda, believed that banners were more valuable and effective than Nazi party newspapers.

"Mit einer Fahne führt man Millionen in den Kampf," wrote another prominent Nazi personality, Alfred Rosenberg.

There were, at that time, several other political symbols in current use. One of them was 𝄃𝄃𝄃, the sign used by *Eiserne Front*, the *Iron Front*. This was a union of social democrats during the first half of the 1930s who were working against their main enemy, national socialism. When the Nazi party came into power a law was passed on 28 February 1933 forbidding all other political symbols used on banners. The reason given was that the Nazis wanted to "protect the people and state." This was less than a month after Hitler had taken office as chancellor of the reich.

The swastika was then adopted by several other countries. In 1933, the English fascist party, the Imperial Fascists, swapped another well-known fascist symbol, **fasces** – with the broad axe – for the swastika. The swastika even appeared in Sweden, Holland, and the United States. The symbol for the American Nazi party is still today ⊕, a swastika with a small circle at its middle, suggesting a claim to world domination.

The Hungarian fascist movement used their own cross: ✛, the **arrow cross**. This symbol was used by the Magyarian people when they conquered Hungary around A.D. 1000. It is recognized as the next most anti-Semitic sign after the swastika.

Two other symbols also are related to the swastika. In the 1920s the Nazi party had already begun to organize what was called *Sturmabteilungen*, the SA, groups dressed in brown uniforms who fought against the Communists for supremacy in the streets and squares. To protect the Nazi speakers attacked by Communists and other hecklers, a group called *Schutzstaffeln*, the SS, was formed. The SS were protection units in black uniforms bearing the symbol ⚡⚡. By the middle of the 1930s the SA and SS together numbered approximately half a million men.

The prototype for the symbol ⚡⚡ was the rune known in Germany as **Sigrune**, the **victory rune**, ⚡. Among the Nordic runes it appears as the sign for both an s-sound and an e-sound. It was known as the sun-rune or the yew-rune. The yew tree was formerly used for making battle bows.

The SS troops managed the concentration camps, and for this reason their sign, ⚡⚡, is associated with the camps. A total of about 53,000 men were involved in the starvation and extermination of several million people. (Of those involved in West Germany, approximately 600 have been tried and convicted.)

The sign ⬤, black against a white background, for instance, on black uniforms, was also used by the Nazis. ↑ is the old Nordic rune **Tyr**. It is associated with *law and order, sword and fighting, and victory and death.*

Another sign that was used to win the favor of the masses in this ideographic struggle during the 1930s was the **crutch cross**, ✛, which was related to the cross on the standards used by the Order of the Knights of the Teutonic Crusade during the fourteenth century, **T**. This sign was used by Dolfuss's anti-Nazi party in Austria. To fight against Nazism it was considered necessary to find a graphic symbol that was at least as powerful as ⚡, and for this reason the crutch cross was chosen. If this was the intention, however, another sign ought to have been used. If one compares the two signs ✛ and ⚡ there is no doubt that ⚡ is more eye-catching. Because of its asymmetry and diagonal structure, ⚡ "rotates" while ✛ is static.

If we look back at the sign ⚡, it is self-evident that it was well chosen. It was associated with ancient concepts of power, energy, and prosperity. It was easily distinguished from other signs. It was easy to copy. In Germany it was associated to old and respected ideograms such as the Christian cross and the Iron cross. It was also related to migration, returns, and rebirth. In addition, it was a new and exotic sign, and consequently it appealed to the masses from the very beginning.

It is also worth noting that 卐 and 卍 have never had much to do with the Germanic and Nordic races. The few swastikas that have been found in the Nordic countries are engraved on a few runic stones, pictorial slabs, and gravestones. None of these are older than A.D. 500. These few examples appear almost 1500 years after their initial occurrences in ancient Greece.

There are several other ideograms associated with fascist movements. For example, ⚡ stands for the new fascist movement, *Mouvement populaire français*. The **sun cross** or **Celtic cross**, ⊕, is used in Sweden to represent the small Nazi party with the name *Nordiska Rikspartiet*. In France, the same sign has been adopted by the new fascist party, *Jeune Nation*.

The **yoke and arrows** is an old fascist symbol that was used by right-wing extremists in several countries, e.g., in Spain by the Falanga.

Fasces was the name for the bundle of rods carried as a symbol by the highest public officials in Rome. It symbolized the right to order bodily punishment or death sentences, which was a prerogative only for high officials. The fasces was carried by civil servants, known as *lictors*, in the retinue of the highest governing officials, and for this reason it is also called a **lictor bundle**.

At a later stage in history fasces (from the Latin word for rods) became an emblem for the *republican form of state* as opposed to the monarchy. As a symbol for republicanism, the sign depicts the executioner's axe in the middle of the bundle of rods.

A survey of the ideographic struggle during the 1930s would not be complete without mentioning a couple of other relevant ideograms. The Polish resistance movement in Warsaw used the sign ⚓, which stood for *Polska Walczy*, the struggling Poland.

In occupied areas during the Second World War the Germans used ideograms in the form of bits of cloth attached to the clothes to distinguish specific ethnic or sexual groups. Every Jew over six years old was ordered to wear a yellow, six-pointed star, sewn or pinned on the outer garment over his or her chest. Homosexuals were forced to carry pink triangles in the same way.

This order, however, was never enforced in the Nordic occupied countries, thanks to King Christian of Denmark. He informed the German authorities that if it was enforced he himself would wear this sign when taking his daily ride through Copenhagen. This was a sufficient deterrent and the Germans never enforced the order.

(During the Middle Ages this habit of forcing Jews to wear some sign that separated them from other people was practiced in many cities and towns in Europe. At that time the sign was a special type of hat, and later it became a yellow circle of cloth.)

Forced laborers of different nationalities were also made to wear ideograms for their identification. The Poles, for example, wore a P made of cloth.

The world of business and ideograms

The immense Krupp Werke was one of the most important weapons producers for Hitler's senseless attempt to dominate the world. Its logo was the ancient symbol for spirituality from the Christian symbology, meaning the *Holy Trinity*, ⊛.

The number 3, the holy number, is very popular with big corporations. The large Japanese company Mitsubishi, uses ⚛ as its logotype, Mercedes-Benz uses Ⓐ, and Sweden's Skandinaviska Enskilda Banken uses ◉.

McDonald's, the worldwide hamburger chain, has taken as their logotype the ancient alchemical sign for fire, ⋔, and developed it so that it has become **M**, similar to the M in the Western alphabet.

One of the oldest symbols on earth, ⊙, representing the sun and the metal gold, has been adopted by a worldwide advertising agency, Ted Bates, but in the "negative" form ●.

It might seem a little odd for an ironworks to use ♀, as this is the symbol for copper. But this can be explained by the fact that the company, Stora, during its first few centuries, dealt only with the extraction of copper. The primary symbol for the planet Venus, womanhood, and fertility, ♀, has become a symbol for the emancipation of women, with the addition of a closed fist, ✊, to emphasize the movement's aggressiveness and self-assertiveness.

Ancient ideograms have otherwise been used by car manufacturers as weapons against other car manufacturers. The sign often appears on the radiator as a sort of standard that accentuates the superiority of this type of car in comparison to others.

Volvo earlier used the old sign for the planet Mars, iron, and self-assertion, ♂. Italian Fiat uses the sun cross, ⊕. Volkswagen has successfully used the sign for *viva!, hail!*, Ⓦ, written within a circle. Opel used the old rune ϟ, which represents victory and power, and has placed it, like Volkswagen, within a circle, ⊖. The ancient structure for the sun's energy, the sun cross, has been adopted by BMW, but with a slight alteration, as ◑. Many car manufacturers use the symbol $\bigvee$, which represents victory and military superiority. Among those manufacturers that use this sign are Buick, Cadillac, Daimler, and DeSoto. The French car manufacturer Citroën also uses this symbol, but doubled, ⋀. Chrysler has taken the pentagon and filled it with a stylized version of the pentagram, ✪. Audi has chosen the linked circles, ⃝⃝⃝⃝, a symbol denoting *unity* and *togetherness*.

The modern-day selling enterprises use many of the same structures the old military establishments used. Consequently one often sees flags outlined against the blue sky outside shopping centers. This type of symbolism is similar to that in the Middle Ages, when banners, flags, and graphic symbols were used in battle as means of ensuring attention and loyalty.

An ideographic system of writing ready for use

The most important prerequisites for an ideographic system of writing are that the signs should be easy to draw and that their meaning should be understood by the greater part of a society. The rules that govern the syntax (rules that decide in what way the signs can be combined) must also be relatively simple.

In the Orient there exist ideographic systems of writing that are still in use even though they have become almost incomprehensible due to their formalized and stylized nature. The West stopped using ideographic systems of writing about two thousand years ago with the advent of the phonetic system of writing, which reproduced the sounds of a particular language and due to its versatility could express most meanings using some 20 signs (the alphabet), whereas the ideographic systems needed several thousand signs to reach the same capacity.

However, in situations where the message is short and simple and there is a need for speed, the ideographic system is far better. For this reason it is still used in traffic, war, and emergency situations. Many people in the West know, without being aware of it, several hundred ideographic signs. If one puts these ideograms together with a few simple rules about how to combine them (which are also well known), one can create a modern Western ideographic system of writing that can be used at an advantage in advertising, communications, and other areas where speed of comprehension is essential.

In Part II, the dictionary, one can find hundreds of signs that nearly all Westerners comprehend directly.

Syntactic rules, also immediately understood, include inscription and doubling.

The sign ⌐, which stands for *(material) protection* or *shelter*, can be combined with ⓒ, *radiation*, to form ⌐ⓒ, *shelter from radiation*. But ⓒ can also be combined with ☐ or ☐, both of which mean a *closed room*. Thus, ☐ⓒ denotes a *microwave oven*. The sign for *radiation* combined with the sign for *house*, *room*, or *building* becomes the sign for *solarium*. The sign denoting *thought*, or *thinking*, ℘°°°, becomes, when combined with ☐ , a *room for meditation*, ☐ .

If we take ☐ , which stands for an *enclosed space*, and write in it ☒, denoting *mixing* or *mixture*, we end up with a *mixing machine*. And with #, denoting *order* or *ordering*, written in ☐ , we arrive at ☐# , a *sorting machine*. Put in ♩ instead and we have a *music machine*, such as a *synthesizer*, denoted by ☐ .

The syntactic doubling is as simple. A double arrow, ⇥, suggests an *extra fast movement*. The sign ↯ , *heat*, can be doubled to mean *extreme heat*, ↯ ↯ . The sign ⌇, for *water*, doubled to ⌇, means even more water, such as a *lake* or *swimming pool*.

Other syntactic combination rules are as self-evident.

When →, which stands for *directed movement or force*, is combined with ↯ , representing *heat*, we end up with the ideogram ↯ , *lightning*. When ♡, which denotes *togetherness* or *feelings*, is combined with →, we are given ♡⃗, which means *love, jealousy*, and *infatuation*. When ♡ is combined with †, *death* and *burial*, it produces ♡, denoting *deep sorrow*.

There does exist a basic syntax, but it is continuously changing. New combinations occur, for example, on computer screens and TV and in comic strips, which create new syntactic patterns. The sign ⟨●⟩, denot-ing *see, search, eye*, or *sight*, can be combined with ! , for *success*, to make ⟨●⟩, which means *found*.

Up to now, the most intelligent attempt to exploit all Western men's and women's common ideographic heritage has been made by the Australian Charles Bliss, who was born in Austria during the time of the Hapsburg empire and was named Karl Blitz.

In the Double Monarchy about ten different nationalities lived under the same reign. They "hated each other because they thought in, and talked with, different languages." Karl's interests as a young student were music, mathematics, and chemistry – three subjects with symbols that were universal, something that young Karl noticed with great satisfaction. He got his degree at the polytechnic institute in Vienna and then took a job as director of the patent division of a manufacturer of electrical machinery. There he often had to struggle with complicated specifications written in some ten languages.

Then Hitler came to power. A Jew, Karl Blitz was sent to Dachau concentration camp and then to Buchenwald. Unbelievable as it may sound, he managed to escape with the help of some of the wardens and arrived in England. He changed his name to Charles Bliss and got a job as a production manager in London. Later he was sent to Shanghai. Shortly afterward his wife Claire travelled eastward from Germany through Russia and China, and joined her husband on Christmas Eve, 1940.

It was in Shanghai that Charles found the key to what would be his life's work. He began to study the Chinese ideographic writing system, in which each sign stood for an idea, a concept. When he discovered how many different nationalities were united through this writing system in spite of the fact that they spoke different languages, he started to dream about a universal language of graphical symbols.

He and Claire were put in a prisoners' camp by the Japanese invaders. When they were liberated at the end of the war they emigrated to Australia, where Charles got a job on the assembly line of a car factory in Sydney. In his free time he immersed himself in the work on his symbol system. In 1949 he at last finished his manuscript. It was published in three volumes with the title *Semantography* (from the Greek words *semantikos*, meaning, and *grafein*, to write).

The Bliss system had a hundred basic symbols and a handful of syntactic rules.

Today his system does not seem very self-evident or clear and requires conscious learning for its use. But his basic idea was both correct and innovative, and surely someone soon will create a useable ideographic system that every Westerner can understand without other learning than that which all Westerners subconsciously receive during childhood and youth.

Modern ideographic systems

There are roughly 40 ideographic systems in use in Western countries. The boundary between what can be called an ideographic system and what perhaps should be called something else is difficult to define. First, there is the difference between iconic and non-iconic ideograms. To call a photograph an ideographic system does not make sense, and therefore we prefer to use the terms *picture* or *copy*.

In plumbing, iconic signs are used for things like *washbasin*, ▭, *WC*, ▢, etc. There are also non-iconic signs such as ∅, *automatic closing valve*. As only a few of the plumbing signs are non-iconic it is sometimes not considered to be an ideographic system. The same applies to the system of welding signs, with graphs like ∨, *on the rootside crowned welding*, or ⌴, *three plate welding*.

Metallography uses a whole series of signs to denote different chemical characteristics, such as *binary eutectoid* and *monotectic joining*. Here, the sign structures are not easily related to what they mean by the way they look. The signs used in metallography can,

therefore, be regarded as an ideographic system.

Then there is the question of what ought to be meant by *system*. There is the class of signs used for sailboats, such as ⌒, ≡, and ≈, which appear at the top of the sails. The chemical sign system and the systems of music, mathematics, and logic all have their own signs. The differences between the systems are great. Compare, for example, the relationship between those signs used on the sails of sailboats and the logic signs combining the numbers in mathematical expressions.

A system of signs can be split up in different ways. There are those systems that are self-sufficient in that the signs of the systems can be understood by themselves without any explicative additions. To this group belong mathematics, logic, music, timetable systems, and chemical and electrical systems. Maps and meteorological systems, however, become understandable only when placed on a background of iconic signs: maps of parts of the earth's surface.

Then there are all those systems of signs that refer to words or other entities in printed or otherwise written text: metric, genealogical, and typographic systems, the proofreading system, dictionary signs, the metallographic and botanical signs, etc.

Last, there are those systems of signs that only occur with a specific type of background. Examples include military group–affiliation signs, which are only found on heavy-duty war material such as trucks, fighter planes, and tanks; sailboat signs that are found only on sails; flag and weapon signs; and symbols worn on uniforms denoting rank.

There are also a few common ideographic sign groups that hardly can be regarded as systems. There are the washing signs, which have meanings such as *do not tumble dry*, etc., and ten or so other signs that are common in pharmaceutical contexts, such as ❖, *narcotics – danger of habituation*, and ☿, *poison*. There are perhaps a handful of signs that appear in commercial contexts: &, %, etc.; signs to denote the various currencies: $, £, ¥, etc.; the signs denoting the different suits in a standard deck of cards: ♣, ♦, ♥, and ♠; non- iconic signs from the world of comics; and scattered, non-iconic astronomical signs.

Below is a listing (by no means complete) of modern Western subjects and areas in which non-iconic ideograms play an important part.

almanacs and calendars

pharmaceuticals

architecture

astrology

botany

fire prevention

building construction

choreography

data processing and programming

electronics

business symbolism

trademarks

genealogy

geology

geometry

trading (the system of measurements on packages)

ground-to-air emergency code

agriculture and horticulture

rail traffic

cartography

chemistry

card games

proofreading

Christian symbolism

logic

hobo signs (tramps' and thieves' systems of signs)

mathematics

medical techniques

metallography

metric signs

military techniques

music

coins and currencies

systems of measurement

pronunciation instructions in dictionaries

political symbolism

plumbing

radio techniques

chess

sailing

comic strips

nautical charts

mushroom picking

welding techniques

telephone techniques

timetables

traffic signs

traffic accident descriptions

typography

household appliances and machines

An annotated bibliography

Those works mentioned below are especially informative and worth knowing about.

SIGN DICTIONARIES

Cooper, J.C. *Symboler – en uppslagsbok* (Symbols – a reference book), Forum, Helsingborg, Sweden, 1963.

Warning! This book contains too many faults. When collecting many facts, as, for example, in the compilation of a reference book, mistakes are almost inevitable. However, the number in this book is far too great.

Dreyfuss, Henry. *Symbol Sourcebook*, McGraw-Hill Book Co., New York, 1972.

Compiled by one of America's leading graphic designers, this work contains many ideograms used in industry, agriculture, medicine, architecture, meteorology, etc. It is based almost entirely on the graphic form and has very little accompanying text. An extensive and useful list of further reading is included.

Estrin, Michael. *2000 Designs, Forms and Ornaments*, W.M. Penn Publ. Co., New York, 1947.

A "picture book" useful to the advertiser and designer.

Holmquist, Herman. *En liten samling tecken samt deras betydelse* (A small collection of signs and their meanings), Lund, Sweden, 1964.

This is an interesting and original book. Holmquist worked as a foreman with a large printing house that specialized in scientific publications and succeeded, over the years, in accumulating a large number of ideograms in the form of types and plates.

Koch, Rudolf. *The Book of Signs*, Dover Publ. Inc., New York, 1955.

A small book without text that contains approximately 500 non-iconic ideograms. Among these are runes and a large number of cross forms from Christian symbolism. It was originally published in German at the beginning of the twentieth century.

Lehner, Ernst. *Picture Book of Symbols*, W.M. Penn Publ. Co., New York, 1956.

Similar to the book above but more interesting. It contains some 800 ideograms that are mainly iconic and used in the United States.

Shepherd, Walter. *Glossary of Graphic Signs and Symbols*, J.M. Dent & Sons Ltd., London, 1971. 600 p.

This book is the first of its kind. It is an ideographic dictionary with some 6,000 (Western) ideograms arranged in groups according to form. For each sign there is a short description of its system and its meaning. This book is dominated by technical and scientific ideograms.

GENERAL WORKS ON SYMBOLS

Chetwynd, Tom. *A Dictionary of Symbols*, Granada, Reading, England, 1982.

This book's 450 pages deal with the symbols in dreams.

Chevalier, Jean, and Alain Gheerbrant. *Dictionnaire des symboles*, 6th edition, Seghers, Paris, 1973.

This is a big dictionary in four volumes, put together by 16 French and non-French professors. Its subtitle is *Myths, dreams, customs, gestures, forms, colors, numbers*. It gives much information about historical backgrounds and meanings of Western symbols, though mostly of other types than graphical and non-iconic. Few illustrations, but the text is loaded with facts and not at all superficial.

Cirlot, Juan-Eduardo. *Diccionario de simbolos* (Dictionary of symbols), 2nd edition, Editorial Labor S.A., Barcelona, 1969.

A 500-page dictionary of symbols. It has the most exhaustive bibliography of literature related to symbols that I have ever seen. It has been translated into English.

Cista, Joan. *La imagen y el impacto psicovisual* (The image and its psychovisual impact), Ediciones Zeus, Barcelona, 1971.

With 250 pages, this work covers roughly the same subject area as the above book. The pages are larger and most of the collected material consists of pictures. These are varied and interesting.

d'Alviella, Goblet. *The Migration of Symbols*, London, 1894. A facsimile edition published by Aquarian Press, Wellingborough, England, 1979.

A famous work that discusses the spread of symbols like the sun cross, the swastika, the trident, etc., in different cultures.

Whittick, Arnold. *Symbols, Signs and Their Meaning*, London, 1960.

A general book on symbolism that shows the more important of the earlier symbols, both iconic and non-iconic.

Zehren, Erich. *Das Testament der Sterne*, Berlin, 1957.

A thorough and exhaustive exposition of those deities that are represented by or related to the sun, the moon, and Venus. The survey stretches from prehistoric times to the beginning of the Christian era. Special attention is given to the Euphrates-Tigris, the Nile Delta, and the Palestine regions.

ALPHABETICAL WRITING AND CHARACTERS

Cohen, Marcel. *La grande invention de l'écriture et son évolution* (The great invention of writing and its evolution), 3 volumes, Paris, 1958.

A large work, richly illustrated, that outlines the development of writing from simple pictography to the modern alphabetical systems.

Diringer, David. *The Alphabet*, London, 1962.

Deals with the same subject as the above but is compiled in one volume instead of three. Some questions as to its factual correctness.

POLITICAL SYMBOLISM

Rabbow, Arnold. *Dtv-Lexikon politischer Symbole* (Dictionary of political symbols), Deutsche Taschenbuch Verlag, Munich, 1970.

A summary of those modern political symbols that appear on flags, posters, etc. In this 250-page book Rabbow successfully presents to the reader a well-defined picture of modern political symbolism.

ALCHEMICAL SYMBOLISM

Jung, Carl Gustav. *Psychology and Alchemy*, Collected Works, Vol. 12, New York, 1952.

A richly illustrated and comprehensive work that concentrates on the esoteric aspect of the alchemy tradition. Included is a bibliographic reference guide for the reader who wants to pursue other aspects of the subject.

Junius, Manfred M. *Praktisches Handbuch der Pflanzen-Alchemie*, Interlaken, Switzerland, 1982.

This book has at the end a short dictionary with approximately 700 alchemical signs, ordered after approximately 250 words for their meanings. This German revised book was originally published in Italian.

Scheffer, H.T. *Chemiske föreläsninger* (chemical lectures), Uppsala, Sweden, 1775.

This work contains some pages filled with old chemistry signs and their meanings, as well as some pages with (for the uninitiated) unintelligible combinations of the same signs in a lot of tables. Table I, "Characteres Chemici praecipii," is the dictionary part.

ROCK ENGRAVINGS AND PAINTINGS

Brate, Erik. *Sveriges runinskrifter* (The rune inscriptions of Sweden), 2nd edition, Stockholm, 1928.

Fredsjö - Jansson - Moberg. *Hällristningar i Sverige* (Rock carvings in Sweden), Stockholm, 1929.

Jansson, Sven B. *Runinskrifter i Sverige* (Rune inscriptions in Sweden), Uppsala, Sweden, 1965.

Moberg, Carl-Axel. *Kiviksgraven* (The tomb of Kivik), Stockholm, 1963.

These four books are short works. Fredsjö et al. is easy to read and gives a good outline of both rock carvings and paintings. Together with these books one should also read:

Lhote, Henri. *Klippmålningarna i Sahara* (Rock paintings in the Sahara), Tidens Book Club, Stockholm, 1959.

Well illustrated and presents interesting facts about some of the oldest ideograms of the human race.

MEDICAL SYMBOLISM

Bergman, Emmanuel. *Medicinska emblem och symboler* (Medical emblems and symbols), Sweden's Union of Doctors' Publishing Company, Karlshamn, Sweden, 1941.

A small, concise book with many illustrations showing mostly iconic symbols.

CHRISTIAN SYMBOLISM

Dahlby, Frithiof. *De heliga tecknens hemlighet* (The secret of the holy signs), Stockholm, 1963.

A relatively comprehensive survey of both iconic and non-iconic Christian graphic symbols.

ASTROLOGICAL SYMBOLISM

Greene, Liz. *Relating — An Astrological Guide to Living with Others on a Small Planet*, Samuel Weiser, Binghamton, New York, 1983.

Dr. Greene explains the psychoanalytical theory of C.G. Jung in relation to astrological symbolism. It is a very enjoyable and well-written book. The author has a thorough knowledge of the subconscious archetypes.

Hand, Robert. *Horoscope Symbols*, Para Research, Rockport, Massachusetts, 1981.
Horoscope Symbols consists almost entirely of text. Its 350 pages give a thorough and exhaustive account of the meanings of all astrological symbols. Hand is one of the foremost humanistic astrologers in the United States today.

de Vore, Nicholas. *Encyclopedia of Astrology*, Littlefields, Adams & Co., Totowa, New Jersey, 1976.

With its 450 pages, this is the most comprehensive dictionary of astrological terms that exists today.

CARTOGRAPHIC SIGNS

Jonsson, Åke. *Allt möjligt om alla möjliga karttecken* (Everything possible on all possible map signs), Generalstabens Litografiska Anstalt, Kartförlaget, Stockholm, 1959.
An enjoyable little book (99 pages) full of information on cartography and its signs. It deals mostly with older signs.

Part II: Ideographic Dictionary

Group 1

Single-axis symmetric, soft, open signs with crossing lines

This group is rather slight as far as Western signs are concerned. The reason is not that Western ideography avoids this type of sign, but that there are very few signs possible to draw according to the definition of the graphical characteristics.

The clothes sign from Ghana shown here belongs to this group. It means *come back and fetch it*. The graphs ♡ and ⚇ in Group 2 have the same meaning.

The sign ⚘ can be seen as a combination of the elements ☺, representing a *return*, and ☻, for *to catch or keep*.

Group 2

Single-axis symmetric, soft, open signs without crossing lines

The curved line or segment of a circle that is less than a half-circle is one of a group of basic elements of Western ideography.

The structure ∩ appears in a dozen or so different ideographic systems ranging from modern logic to astrology. In the astrological system of symbols ∪ stands for the *assimilating, receptive aspect of man* that the *spirit, life*, ○, creates in its interplay with *matter*, +. Example: ☿.

In those instances where ∩ and ∪ appear between other signs, the idea represented (or the signs themselves) should be *merged or brought close together*. In logic (a∩b) means the *sum* of everything that is contained in a and b. In proofreading, the sign ∪ denotes that the *space between should be lessened*. Used in musical notation, ∪ means that the *tones covered should be brought together to form a whole*.

In certain systems ∩ stands for the *faculty of reason*, and its double, ∧, stands for the *conscience*, the *higher reason*.

When this sign is curved downward, ∪, it often represents a *boat*. In the Swedish system of hobo signs it denotes a *sleeping place*.

∩ is occasionally used to mean *sky*, and in some meteorological contexts it can mean *rainbow*. In early chemistry ∩ could mean *phosphorus*, as could ⊕.

Compare with)(in Group 8 and ♭ in Group 14.

A segment of a circle that is greater than half a circle, or as big, represents *elements or substances fundamental to a specific society's or individual's livelihood*.

In the English system of hobo signs ⊃ means *keep away – no use knocking*, and ⌒ in the same system means a *good haystack for the night*.

Compare with the following signs from Group 24: ◗, *spring or well*; the modern ◪, *water for firefighting* or *firefighting equipment*; and ◯.

This ideogram is a modern sign used in comic strips to denote *movement* and *direction of movement* when drawn next to a picture of a figure or an object that is represented as moving. The sign �=☽ has a similar meaning.

This is a modern ideogram for *undulations* or *radiation* moving from an oscillating body. It appears in comic strips and physics textbooks. Compare with ☌ in Group 44, which has a similar meaning.

The appearance of **parentheses** in modern typography indicates that what is contained within the parentheses is *relevant, but somewhat specialized material*. The uniting quality of ∪ becomes an isolating quality when the sign is turned 90 degrees.

This is one of the most common structures in Western ideography. The signs ε, Ɜ, ω, and ᴍ are used with different meanings in some 30 well-known ideographic systems from the Bronze Age to the present day. The structure is especially common in modern-day technical and scientific systems (because of its function as a letter of the Greek alphabet).

The sign ᴍ has been used to represent *fire* in alchemy, but in military contexts it indicates *transport by plane*.

Turned upside down, ω, it becomes a meteorological sign for *certain types of high, thin clouds*.

This sign for *water* appears both as a modern ideogram and as an alchemical sign. Other ways of representing water are ⌇⌇ and ∿.

In eighteenth-century chemistry, ᙊᙊ could mean *coquere* or *ebullire*, i.e., *boil*.

For the other water signs, see the word index (Part III).

The symbol for an *active intellect*, often also drawn |||. It is of unknown origin. Compare with ≡, the *passive intellect*. ᙊ also appears as a sign for *water*, *bathing*, and *swimming pool*. See ⊕→ in Group 54.

This is a common ideogram for *vessel* or *bowl*. See also ᙳ in this group. According to Koch (see the bibliography), ᴜ is an ancient Germanic **time sign** for *summer*. The other seasons in this particular system are drawn as follows: ᙘ, *spring*; ♏, *autumn*; and ᙏ, *winter*.

Purificatio. The *process of purification* in alchemy is explained in the section "Esoteric alchemy." This sign is based on the signs ᙊ, *water*, and ᴜ, *vessel*.

This is a variation of the entry sign above for *purificatio*. The point often is used to represent water in Western ideography.

ᙳ is a synonymous graph.

This ideogram is a combination of ᙊᙊ, *water*, and ᙏ, for *flight*.

⌇ is used in some genealogical systems with the meaning *baptized*. It depicts graphically the pouring of water and the acceptance of the recently baptized soul as a candidate for the heavenly paradise, shown by the similarity to ᙏ.

This structure has been used by many cultures and through many ages. During the Middle Ages ☽ was used in Europe to denote the *moon*. In musical terminology ⌒ is called a **fermata** and signifies *hold that tone longer than usual*.

In astrology ⌒ represents the qu*adruplicity* or *mutable quality* of zodiacal signs. The mutable signs of the zodiac are ♓, Pisces; ♊, Gemini; ♍, Virgo; and ♐, Sagittarius. ⌒ here stands for *orbital movement*, as ◙, the *fixed quality*, stands for *gravitation*, and ⋀, the *cardinal quality* stands for *radiation*.

Persons with many planets in mutable signs are considered to be *easily adaptable and flexible*, and to be *flexible of intellect*.

In the U.S. system of hobo signs ⌒ means *look out – the authorities here are on the watch*. The sign inverted, ⌣, means *no trouble in this community*.

In some meteorological sign systems ⌒ is used to represent *rain that does not reach the ground*. The uniting quality of ⌒ has here adopted, in accordance with the **law of the polarity of meanings of elementary graphs,** an isolating signification.

Compare with)·(, *precipitation far from the observation station*.

See ⸎ in Group 20 and)(in Group 8.

The wavy line is the sign used for *water, watercourse, water surface*, and the *sea*. In music it is used as an "iconic sound" to denote *trills*.

Placed vertically, ⟨, it stands for *arpeggio,* in which the tones are played in quick succession, usually toward a higher register: a *rising trill*.

In nautical charts ⌇ can represent *underwater cables*.

In some U.S. meteorological systems ⟨ can mean *unstable barometric readings*.

The wavy line was already in use 4000 years ago as a sign for *radiation*. It can be seen in the Babylonian sun sign, ✳, which is similar to the modern ☀, signifying radiation.

A doubling of this sign, ∿, is often used to denote *water*. In astrology it represents the zodiacal sign of *Aquarius*. For more information about the sign of Aquarius, turn to ∿ in Group 14.

This is the well-known modern ideogram, **braces**, for *bringing together several elements* and for *grouping elements*.

This structure is one of the oldest ideograms. It has been found on the walls of prehistoric caves, on rocks and pottery from pre-Columbian America, and in Bronze Age Europe. The sign is associated with *growing*, *(re)birth*, and *genesis*.

In the system of Egyptian hieroglyphs it was used to signify *woman* and the *female* sex. As a sign for growing it implied that woman, the female, was the originator of life. Parallels can be found between similar structures that appear both in different contexts and different ages, such as ↤, found among Egyptian hieroglyphs and meaning *lock up* or *contain*, and in geometrical contexts, where B⟶A means that *A is a part of B*.

The ideogram ⋎ illustrates the idea *one becomes two* in the same way as its "graphical opposite," ♡, illustrates the idea *two becomes one*. This is what is behind the meaning *woman* in the hieroglyphic system and the *sexual love* meaning of ♡.

⋏ is sometimes used in astronomy for *mean distance*.

The ideogram ♈ is most commonly associated with *Aries*, the zodiacal sign represented by the *ram*. The sign ♈ denotes both the part of the zodiac through which the sun moves during the period from around 21 March to around 19 April each year and this particular period of time. It is related to the **element of fire** in the astrological symbolism of the elements: temperamental personality types. This implies that a person born during this period in all probability has a temperament characterized by dynamic creativity and a tendency to perceive the environment in terms of intuitively perceived possibilities for the individual.

See △ in Group 28 for a further description of the astrological elements.

♈ belongs to ⋀, the **cardinal signs**. To this **quadruplicity** belong the sun signs ♋, ♑, and ♎. If one happens to be born in one of the cardinal signs, i.e., has one's sun in such a sign, astrologers believe that one is more aggressive and pioneering than others. Look up **quadruplicities** in the word index to get information about this concept of astrology.

The planet Mars (see ♂ in Group 42) is the so-called ruler of Aries. The planets ☉, the sun, and ♃, Jupiter, are considered well placed in ♈, whereas ♀, Venus, and ♄, Saturn, as psychological complexes, do not function smoothly in Aries.

♈, the ram with its horns, is very prominent and important in the mythology of antiquity and in the architecture of that epoch. The Greek hero Jason tried to bring home the **golden fleece of the ram** and some very old temples in Egypt are approached by walks surrounded by statues of rams.

See the section "The symbolism of the astrological ages," in Part I, for more data in this respect.

The **lyre** was the attribute of the Greek god *Apollo*. ☿, **Hermes**, who later became the messenger of the Greek gods and, as Mercury, became the god of merchants and thieves in Rome, stole some oxen from Apollo. The dispute was settled when Mercury gave Apollo the lyre.

Between 600 and 400 B.C. the **lyre and the flower** were the attributes of **Eros**, the god of sexual love. The Greek Eros and his Roman counterpart, **Amor**, and also **Cupid** (derived from the Latin word for *desire* or *lust*) later got the **bow and arrow** as their attributes.

See ♂ in Group 53 for the modern ideogram that incorporates this myth inherited from antiquity.

The sign ☽, a main element of this entry's sign structure, is a **basic element** in Western ideography.

Turn back and fetch it is the significance of this clothes sign from Ghana. It is synonymous with 卍 in Group 1. It can be analyzed as a combination of ↓, representing the direction *back*, and ☽ for a *return*, with the sign ☾ for *capture*.

See also ♡ in Group 20.

This is another Ghana sign decorating garments. It has the meaning *return and fetch it!* It is synonymous with ♡ above and 卍 in Group 1.

This is an alchemical **time sign** for *winter*. See the word index for synonymous signs and for other time signs.

Group 3

Single-axis symmetric, straight-lined, open signs with crossing
lines

The **Latin cross**. This cross has been the Western world's symbol par excellence. It is chiefly associated with the cross on which Jesus Christ was crucified.

Before the time of Jesus, † represented, among other things, the **staff of Apollo**, the sun god, and appeared on ancient coins. A cross with arms of equal length was used in pre-Columbian America, the Euphrates-Tigris region, and other parts of the world long before and was associated to the sun and other powers that controlled the weather. It was only when + was used to represent the staff of Apollo that one of its arms was lengthened to form †.

Earlier still, in Babylon, the cross was considered as one of the attributes of **Anu**, god of the heavens.

Sometime during the first centuries of the Western calendar the Latin cross was adopted by the Christian ideology. Instead of being associated with the sun, the heavens, and the weather, both + and even more so †, God's staff, became the symbols for *death*, *sin*, *guilt*, and *burial* and — according to the **law of the polarity of meanings of elementary graphs** — referred to the *resurrection, rebirth,* and *eternal life after bodily death.*

On gravestones and in genealogy † means *dead, has died,* or *a death.*

Compare with and ☆, which stand for *born.*

The Latin cross turned upside down is known as **St. Peter's cross** after Peter, the disciple of Jesus who is believed to have been executed by crucifixion on an upside down cross.

The cross placed over the globe is a symbol for the *evangelization of the world*. The ideograms ⬧ and ⬧, and others, have the same meaning.

This cross represents *the four evangelists, Matthew, Mark, Luke, and John,* and is the **cross of the Evangelists**. The graph ⊚ in Group 26 is a synonym.

The **cross of the archangels**. It is also known as the **Golgata cross**. The Greek word *archangel* meant chief angel, from *archos*, chief or first, and *angelos*, messenger. **Archangels** were angels protecting the religion, while ordinary angels protected individual human beings.

A variation of the **cross of the archangels**.

A Latin cross with two beams instead of one is known as the **croix de Lorraine** or the **patriarchal cross**. Lothringen, or Lorraine, is a province on the border between France and Germany. During the Middle Ages this province was a principality. In the crusade that culminated with the siege and eventual fall of Jerusalem in 1099, the victory was dedicated to the duke of Lorraine.

This cross is also used by the **Greek Orthodox Church**. In 1940, it was taken as the symbol representing the *French resistance movement* against Germany.

After 1963 this entry sign was used as a symbol representing the *exiled Cubans* and their (unsuccessful) attempt to invade Cuba and conquer Fidel Castro's forces.

✝ has been used in alchemy to denote *white lead*. Today, it has become the international symbol for the *battle against tuberculosis*.

This sign often appears in heraldic contexts, sometimes in the form ✝, but more often as ⛊.

Compare with the Egyptian hieroglyph ⚱.

The Latin cross that has three horizontal beams is the **cross of the pope**. The beams represent the pope's threefold rule: as *highest priest*, *highest teacher*, and *chief shepherd*. They also symbolize the idea that the pope, as Christ's representative on earth, is the *co-ruler of the three kingdoms: heaven, earth, and hell*. The number 3 has long been recognized as divine in most early cultures.

This entry sign is also known as the **Western triple cross**.

This is the **ladder of transmigration**, the *soul's pilgrimage from the earthly existence to paradise*. ⛊ was used during the sixteenth century to signify an increase of awareness and is therefore also a synonym to the alchemical symbol, the **golden chain of Homer**.

Refer to the section "Esoteric alchemy" in Part I.

This cross is used in Christian symbolism. It is associated with X as a symbol for ΧΡΙΣΤΟΣ, *Christ*, and is called the **cross of Christ**.

In botany, ideograms are needed to denote where on earth different plants grow. The sign taken for this purpose is that meaning *fixed star*, ✳, the **symbol of orientation**. By adding a straight line above, below, or on one of its sides, the different parts of the earth can be represented. The graph here shown denotes the *old world*, the *Eastern Hemisphere*, i.e., *Eurasia*.

The cross form where one of the vertical arms is longer than the other, as in the Latin cross, is closely associated to *death*. Two such signs crossing one another logically ought to be even more closely associated to *death*. However, the ideogram here is used in dictionaries to denote *military expression* and in genealogy to denote that someone has *died in battle*.

One can also perceive ✕ as an iconic sign representing two crossing swords or sabres, a symbol for *battle* or *military power*.

This is of the many signs of alchemy and early chemistry for *iron*. ♂ was the most common sign for iron.

The similar ↦ is a **scout sign** meaning *a hindrance to be overcome*.

Potash is sometimes written in this way in alchemy. The ash left after the burning of plants contains this substance (*potassium carbonate*). It is used in baking to help the dough rise, and in the production of soft soap, glass, and potassium cyanide. The last is a highly poisonous substance used in the extraction of gold from minerals containing gold. *Potash* was written ⦿ in Dalton's nineteenth-century system.

Potassium carbonate was also drawn ♀, ⯜, and otherwise.

This sign for *cinis*, *ash*, was used in alchemy during the seventeenth century. Note its relation to ♉, the *lightning* sign, in this group, and to the above sign for *potash*.

In eighteenth-century chemistry this sign could mean *combustion* and *incinerare*, or *burn*.

This sign means *etheric oil*, i.e., oil that evaporates easily. The graph was used in alchemy and early chemistry.

See the word index for more signs for different types of oil.

The **staff of Poseidon** (in Greece; the **staff of Neptune** in the Roman Empire). Poseidon was the younger brother of **Zeus** (see ♃ in Group 17), and **master of the seas, rivers, and earthquakes** in Greek mythology. The **trident** has since the beginning of time, in the Euphrates-Tigris region and along the eastern Mediterranean coast, been a symbol of *thunder and lightning*. It is also the **staff of the Devil**.

It can be drawn ψ.

See also ♅ in Group 11 and ♉ in Group 39.

This sign stands for *viva!*, *live!*, *hail!* (e.g., on walls and build-ings combined with political slogans – W *MAO*). Turned up-side down it means *down with!* (e.g., /M FASCISMO). It is common in Italy. Compare with ⚡ in Group 4.

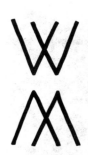

This sign is from the U.S. system of hobo signs. It means *danger, barking dogs!*

For synonyms in similar systems, refer to the section "Systems of hobo signs" in Part I.

A sign for the *asteroid Juno*. See ⚲ in Group 17 for further details concerning the asteroids.

Juno could also be represented by ♀.

This is a sign for *metal* used by the alchemists.

For synonyms, refer to the word index.

An alchemical or early chemical sign for *sal ammoniacus*, or *ammonium salt*.

See)(in Group 11 for a synonymous sign.

The sign ↦ is common in geological, logical, and mathematical systems. It is made up of → as its basic structure and a crossing line whose meaning is *cancelled*. The sign becomes a **fascist symbol** when the arrow points upward.

See ↥ in Group 22. Compare with ♐, the Sagittarius zodiacal sign.

Group 4

Single-axis symmetric, straight-lined, open signs without crossing lines

This structure is common in military and heraldic contexts and is often called a **chevron**. It denotes rank when used on military uniforms; when doubled, the rank increases. The car manufacturer Citroën has taken ⊠ as the emblem of its cars.

The rune named **kaun** or **kaen** is associated with *openings* and *opening up*, according to the Anglo-Saxon tradition.

The sign ⟨ is a rune from the earliest rune alphabet. Its name meant *boil* or *pustule*. Apart from plague, boils occurred only as a result of infections in wounds. Here we have an association between → and ⟨ as a military sign.

In the ground-to-air emergency code used by pilots who have managed an emergency landing, or crashed but survived, ⋀ signifies that *ammunition and firearms are needed*, i.e., there exists a relationship to the military use of ∧ and ⋀.

It is also found on tape recorders and video appliances, but turned on its side as ≫ and ≪. The meanings are *fast forward* and *reverse*. In this use ≫, for instance, is synonymous with ▷▷.

This is a **scout sign** indicating that the *group has or desires a peaceful relation*.

Here we have a **scout sign** indicating that the *group is in conflict*.

This is the same structure as the chevron, but with a much sharper angle. It is used in logic to signify *all that lacks existence*, *nothing*, or the *zero class*. An ideographic opposite is O.

/\ is also used to denote the concept *and* in logic.

Between other signs, /\ denotes a direction upward in the same way as ↑ does.

The above sign, when turned upside down, is used in logic to signify the *whole universe*, *all that in one way or another exists*. V can also denote the logical concept *or* when used between expressions of the notation of formal logic.

Alone, V can mean *victory*. It was used extensively during the Second World War.

In some U.S. meteorological contexts it has the meaning *white frost* or *frost*.

When the pointed angle is turned to one side and the sign is placed between other signs, it means that the relationship between their denotations is *less than*, *greater than*, *derived from*, *changes to*, etc. It has the same function as → , i.e., it denotes a *relation of direction and ordering*.

By doubling a sign the original meaning usually becomes stronger, as when > for *greater than* becomes >> for *much greater than*.

The variation ⇀ and other forms that are similar are found in musical notation and signify a *decrease in volume*, or *diminuendo*. When placed the other way, ↽, it denotes the opposite – *crescendo*.

Compare with ⌐ in Group 34 and ↷ in Group 36, which have similar functions.

When the combination of two straight lines is drawn ∟ and appears in an astrological context, it strangely enough signifies half a right angle, i.e., 45 degrees. (□ is used to denote an angle of 90 degrees.)

The astrological sign ∟ has its origins in Greece and is more than 2000 years old. In ancient Greece this sign was used to denote half of something. It is also used in the ground-to-air emergency code and means *need fuel and oil*.

Two of the above sign placed side by side are used in the ground-to-air emergency code to denote *have not understood*.

The two halves of the square need to be combined to a square.

This is a modern ideogram used on radios and TV sets. It means *inlet for antenna*. Signs such as ◠◦ in Group 42 and ◁ in Group 22 are used for a similar type of in- or outlets.

This sign is a rune with a name that associates with *horse*, *movement*, and the *orbit of the sun*.

The angle is like the arrow sign associated with energy. The spectrum of meaning of this entry sign is centered around the concepts of *work, energy*, and *effect*. We meet the structure as ⧢ , the **sun rune**, in the earliest runic alphabet, and as W today in technical and electrical contexts.

In the ground-to-air emergency code, W means *mechanic is needed*, i.e., something is wrong with the source of energy, the engine. In the English system of hobo signs, ⧢ drawn on a wall denotes *they demand hard work here*.

This is one of the alchemists' signs for *transform into liquid form*.

It is also one of the graphs for the zodiac sign *Aquarius*.

This sign means *water* in all times and all cultures. It is among the earliest Egyptian hieroglyphs. Today it is still used to signify water. It has also been adopted as a general sign for *resistance* of some kind, especially in electrical contexts, where it can stand for *resistor* or *rheostat*. The structure warns that something is *dangerous* or *resistant*.

It is also a Swedish hobo sign meaning *danger – angry dog*.

After electricity had become a common feature in our daily lives, ᴍᴍ was seldom used for water. But when doubled ᴍᴍ still has its close relation to water by being one of the graphs for the zodiac sign *Aquarius*, the *water-bearer*.

See ≈ in Group 14 for data on this zodiac sign.

The structure ∧ can be associated to a visual impression. The sign drawn here appears on certain types of nautical charts and stands for the light given off by a *lighthouse emitting light flashes.*

Compare with ⚡ in Group 16.

This modern ideogram, first used in the United States, means *danger – radiation from laser emitters.*

This is an **arrow sign**, one of the oldest and most common ideograms. Both ↑ and »→ have been discovered in prehistoric caves and engraved on rocks in the Sahara. An arrow indicates a *specific direction.* It is used to denote direction by the Boy Scouts, as a traffic sign, etc. In certain modern systems it is placed between signs and implies that the sign to the right of an arrow pointing to the right is the *result of,* or *follows logically from,* what is denoted by the sign to the left of the arrow: (a→b).

The arrow is also an ideogram representing the *male sex.* Compare with Ɏ, an inversion of ↑, which is used as the receiving, female sign. Occasionally it has a phallic symbolism, as in ⚲ and ♂.

In modern ideography the arrow is found associated with *snow* and *frost.* See, for example, ⇛, *frosty mist,* a combination of ≡ , *mist,* and ↑.

In the computer world ↑ means *exponentialization* (also drawn ^), i.e., *multiplying the sum by itself.* In physics ↑ is sometimes used to denote the *centers of gravitation.*

This particular arrow sign is a nordic rune called **Tyr**. This Tyr was not only the *god of law and order* but also the *god of victory* in early Germanic mythology. It was an often-used design for the decoration of swords as it was believed to bring luck in battle. This rune was also a symbol of *loyalty*. According to the Anglo-Saxon tradition the same sign was called **Tac** and regarded as the *rune of death*. *Law and order, sword and battle*, and *victory and death* are all ancient Germanic associations with ↑.

This old runic structure is now used freely in Northern and Central Europe as a **fascist symbol**.

This arrow sign turned upside down, ∨, was used in prehistoric times as a graphic symbol for *vulva* or the *vagina*.

Compare with ∇ in Group 22 for *woman*.

This ideogram is used in many modern systems to denote a *flow* or *current*, for example, an *ocean current* on nautical charts and on geographic maps. The number of "feathers" on the arrow often denotes the *relative speed of the current*.

Here we have a common ideogram to denote *movement*. Whereas → is used principally as a sign for *direction*, ⟶ symbolizes *directed movement*. The arrow whose stem is split into several shorter parts illustrates graphically the *idea of a movement*: first a bit, then a little more, etc.

This ideogram appears in different modern systems with the meaning *lift up, get up to, raise*, or *height above sea level*. Inverted, like ⊥ or ⊤, the structure has the opposite significance: *lower, lowered*, or *distance from or to*.

This common modern ideogram denotes *(direction) inward*. The sign denotes a *direction outward* when the arrow points the other way, ⬅].
This sign can also be drawn ⬜→.

This sign is used in the ground-to-air emergency code to signify that a *take-off will be attempted*. The meaning is expressed by combining the sign for *ground*, —— , with ∧ , the sign for a *direction upward*.
Compare with ⊤ above and with the entry sign below.

This sign from the ground-to-air emergency code means *I/we proceed in this direction*. According to other sources, ∧ is a synonym.
⊼ is also an English hobo sign that tells the passing tramp *food is sometimes given here*.

These ideograms mean *moderate turbulence* and *severe turbulence* in some flying contexts.
The sign ⋏, *severe turbulence*, depicts an *airplane*, ⌢, making sudden *upward movements*, ∧ , in the middle of its smooth flight.

The pythagoreans made use of the sign Y, whose vertical line represented *life's path*. The point where the three lines converge represented the *choice between the good* (the right stem) *and the evil* (the left stem).
Compare this with the sign Ⓧ, used in some computer contexts to mean *choose*.
This sign in Christian symbolism is known as the **ypsilon cross**, **Furca**, or the **cross of the robbers** (since the two

robbers crucified on both sides of Christ were, according to certain sources, nailed on crosses of this shape).

This is a sign for *female, woman, receiving inlet* (in electricity), and *mine tunnel*.

Compare with ϒ, an Egyptian hieroglyph for *woman*, or the *female sex*.

Inverted, ⅄, this sign is sometimes used for the *male sex* or *men*, as on toilet doors. "Ladies" is in this case written ⅃.

Compare with ϒ below.

This sign is best understood when thought of as a combination of the arrow sign and the ϒ-sign. It appears in the earliest known rune alphabets and is possibly associated with *moose*. In the Middle Ages clog almanacs used ϒ to denote *holy days related to the Virgin Mary*.

In the family system (see ✷ in Group 41:b), ϒ stands for *man*.

In aerometeorology the same sign means *light icing*.

Nowadays it is most commonly found representing *inlet for antenna* or more specifically the movement downward, ↓, into an appliance.

The inversion of ϒ, that is, ⅄ , is supposed to have been used by Germanic tribes as **Todesrune**, the **rune of death**. In the family system it means *man dies*.

Compare with ☮ in Group 24.

These signs were used in the Swedish Middle Ages **clog al-manacs** to signify the beginning of the *period from March to October*, the summer half-year. It began on 13 April, the day of Tiburtius. This day was also drawn ψ.

Compare with ψ, a sign used by the Euphrates-Tigris cultures, and ψ, found in the Altamira cave.

See also ⟨⟩, for the beginning of the winter half-year.

Refer to ⍤ in Group 5 for more details about the clog almanacs.

This rune from the earliest rune alphabet is associated to *fruit trees*. ✳ in Group 41:b has a similar meaning.

In Anglo-Saxon literature ⟨ is called **pärz**, and is said to mean *secret*, *mystery*, and *initiation*.

This modern ideogram is used in electrical contexts to represent *accumulator*, *battery*, or *power supply*. The longer, vertical line signifies the positive pole. This ideogram is but one of a great many of the same type, such as ⊥ and ⫫.

This is a graph from the U.S. system of hobo signs meaning *here it is*.

It also appears in combination with ⊡ and stands for a danger, as in ⬚, *dangerous neighborhood*, from the same system.

This is one of the many alchemic signs for *potash* or *potassium carbonate*. It was also drawn ⌊⊤⌋. For more information, turn to this sign in Group 3.

This English hobo sign means *there are more tramps on this road*.

This is a prehistoric ideogram that has been adopted and become common in modern ideography. In some meteorological systems it was used to signify *white frost*.

In both the U.S. and Swedish systems of hobo signs it means a *night's shelter here*. The same sign used by English tramps, however, means *invalids live here – show sympathy*.

In other situations this sign can be used to represent an *open vessel*. In its closed form, ◼, it can be found on maps to denote a *big farmhouse* or *small manor house*.

This is an electrical sign for *earth contact* or *earth wire*. On household appliances ⊥ signifies that the *electrical inlet is grounded*.

Compare with the structurally similar and extremely old cave sign ⚲.

A modern ideogram that appears on household appliances and signifies that the appliance is *intended for direct current*.

∿ or ≃ are the corresponding signs for alternating current.

This graph was originally a Semitic symbol, the *Tau cross*. It appears to be associated with *life* and *security*. For more facts, turn to **T** in Group 22.

Compare with ♀ from Group 42, which is similar in structure.

This was one of the signs used in alchemy to denote *borax*. This substance is used in the production of enamel, porcelain, and glass.

4+ is a synonym.

Group 5

Single-axis symmetric, both soft and straight-lined, open signs with crossing lines

Ψ was used in the earliest known runic alphabets but was usually carved Υ. In antiquity this structure was the **staff of Poseidon** (Greece) or **Neptune** (Rome). It was also drawn with the addition of arrowheads as a fish spear, Ψ.

Sometimes it has appeared as an iconic sign on rock carvings and similar pictorial representations. In these instances it meant *paddle*. In the pictorial reproductions of Hell that existed during the Middle Ages the sign Ψ was occasionally used to signify the spears used by the smaller demons or the Devil himself to torture and torment the poor humans. Ψ is related to both the element of water and its opposite, the element of fire. This also implies that it is related to ⚡, which is the gods' primary expression of their power. Compare with ☀ in Group 47.

There are several signs for thunder and lightning, used as staffs in the hands of gods on pictures and hieroglyphic representations. For example, there are Ψ in Group 5; ⚡ from Greece, in Group 11; and ⚔ from the Euphrates-Tigris region. Different types of staff signs are shown in entry ⚕ in Group 41:b.

In the English system of hobo signs Ψ means *work and you'll be given food*.

It can be compared with ♓, the sign for *Pisces*, and with that of the *planet Neptune*, ♆, both of whose structures are similar.

If one elongates the vertical stem of Ψ, it becomes the Greek letter **Psi**. Today the sign is used in many technical and scientific sign systems. It can represent, among other things, *electrostatic current*, *rotation coefficient*, and *psi-function* (e.g., ESP, telepathy, precognition, etc.). It is also drawn ⋎.

The upper sign, the most common graph for the *planet Neptune*, is a staff of Neptune with or without arrowheads and with a crossbar on the vertical bottom line.

In astrology, Ψ is the **mystical planet**. According to Robert Hand, Ψ symbolizes the final and conclusive reality in which all polarities exist at the same time but without any being discernible from another. Ψ is *Nirvana*, the mystical perception of godliness and truth, or nonattachment. Along with Saturn, ♄, it stands for *Maya*, the illusionary reality. In conjunction with Venus, ♀, it denotes *artistic creativity*. Ψ also signifies *self-denial* or the *defeated ego* and *deceitful and secretive activities* such as poisoning. When combined with other planets in a negative way it stands for a withdrawal from the world into drug abuse or mental disorder.

Astronomers consider Ψ worthy of special attention because it is the only planet that does not follow the orbits discovered by Johann Bode. See ♀ in Group 17 for a further description of Bode's law.

According to the graphic symbolism of astrology we find that Ψ is a combination of the crescent of receptivity and personality, ∪, open upward for spirituality, pierced by ⊥, the cross of material existence, showing susceptibility to lower instincts. Alan Oken has defined key characteristics associated with the planet Neptune: 1. The dreamer, artist, musician, film-maker; 2. the great fraud, cheat, swindler; 3. psychic powers; 4. the mystic, spiritualist, and prophet; and 5. universal love.

The planet Neptune is considered to be the planetary ruler of Pisces, ♓, which sign consists of two Neptune graphs joined together. Neptune is also supposed to rule *plants used for the purpose of intoxication*, such as Indian hemp, the coca bush, the opium poppy, the peyote cactus, and the psilocybine mushroom. ♆ also rules such bodily functions as the pineal glands and those parts of the nervous system that are sensitive to psychic impulses and related to the aura.

Everything with boundaries that are in one way or another undefined or unclear is ruled by this planet, for instance, gases, dreams, fantasy, idealism, etc. It is the symbol for *escapism, drug intoxication,* and *glamour,* as well as the symbol of *idealism.*

Neptune is also drawn Ψ , Ψ, and ♁. See two of the entries below.

The planet was first discovered in 1846. Ψ had then already been in use for some time in alchemical contexts.

It sometimes signified *mercury* and sometimes *lime.* In the chemistry of the seventeenth and eighteenth centuries, Ψ was a common sign for *quicklime.* This sign was also used to denote *calcinare,* the process explained at the sign entry ⚬⋏ in Group 18.

This is the sign for *magnesia,* an oxide of the metal magnesium, from the chemistry of the sixteenth century. Its name, *magnesia,* probably stems from the magnetic property of this compound. The Greek word *magenein* means enchant or bewitch.

Compare with the similar Ψ and the synonymous ⚭, both in Group 41:b.

A variation of the Neptune sign used to signify *arsenic* in alchemy and early chemistry. Arsenic was of special import because of its highly poisonous quality and its effectiveness as a medication in different situations. Other signs used for arsenic are collected under ⚥ in Group 42.

A less common variation of the sign for the *planet Neptune*.

A sign used in early chemistry to represent *lead*. Compare with ⵝ from Group 6, which means *alum*. Lead is more commonly drawn as ♄, i.e., using the sign for Saturn.

This is the sign for the *golden number 18* (also written ✳) used in the Middle Ages clog almanacs. The golden number indicated the cycle of the moon in relation to the number of days in a solar year and made it possible to calculate the days of the full and new moons, as well as eclipses. The golden numbers on the clog almanacs are what is left of the old Nordic lunar calendar based on the phases of the moon. With the arrival of Christianity the calendar was changed and restructured according to the solar year. During the Middle Ages, however, the peasants used a calendar that showed both the old lunar calendar and the days of the new solar year.

This sign, by the way, was one of the letters of the alphabet used around the year 1000 in Rumania. It might be that its appearance in Scandinavia was a result of the Vikings' eastward voyages.

This structure appears in modern, technical ideography and stands for *electrical cables, water pipelines, or any other type of connections that cross one another without making contact.*

Compare with +, the sign that represents the opposite idea.

An alchemical sign for *white arsenic.*

One of the signs for *amalgam* used in alchemy and early chemistry. Amalgams are *alloys made by combining mercury with other metals, preferably silver.*

An alchemical sign for *test.*

The anchor form, based on ∪, the symbol of receptivity pointing upward toward the spiritual world, is crowned with the cross of matter, representing the actual and contin-uous existence in the material world. This combination cre-ates the **crux dissimulata**, a Christian symbol of *hope.*

See how this sign is built up by the combination of the old pagan cross ♀ with ∪.

For more information, turn to ⊹ in Group 26.

This sign was used in alchemy and early chemistry to denote *antimony*, a metal that is not found in a pure state in nature. It has long been used in medicine.

This is a **time sign**. According to Kock it was an old Germanic sign for *autumn*. Compare with the similar ♏, the sign of Scorpio, and ≙ with the same meaning.

Cross over the globe, a symbol for *world evangelization*.
For synonyms, see ⌖ in Group 9.

A common alchemical sign for *gravel* or *sand*.

This sign represents the process of *fixation* in alchemy. It was also sometimes drawn Ⅱ. See Part I, "The signs of the alchemists," for data about these processes.

One of the alchemical signs used during the seventeenth century to represent *mercury*. It was also drawn ☿. Other signs used for mercury are collected under ♆ in Group 41:a.

Group 6

Single-axis symmetric, both soft and straight-lined, open signs without crossing lines

This structure appeared in seventeenth-century alchemy. Its meaning is unclear, although it might possibly be *fuse*. It is also found in the English system of hobo signs and means *take this road, it's better.*

An alchemical sign of unknown meaning, possibly, *copper*, in which case it is based on ♀, one of the signs for *Venus*.

One sign used to denote the *soprano clef*, or *treble clef*, in musical notation.

An old alchemical sign for *alum*, which was used, among other things, as an astringent.

This is a very old and common structure. In ancient times, and in antiquity, it was sometimes used for *fire*. In modern times it has been used for *lunar halo*, i.e., the faint and yellow mist that sometimes encircles the moon.

As a pharmaceutical sign it was used to signify *skruppel*, a word derived from Latin and originally meaning a *small stone*. It was also the name given to the smallest coin in the Roman Empire.

A ⟶ B in a geometric context means that A *is a part of* B. Compare this sign with the Egyptian hieroglyph ⟵, meaning *shut up*, *lock in*, or *close in*.

See, for example, ⊣⌂ in Group 53.

A military sign for *machine gun*. The ideograms ⚲ and ⩔ have been used as synonyms. ⋌ is used in Sweden.

This structure, a line culminating in a dot or very small filled circle, is common both in ancient and recent ideography. In a meteorological context ╱ denotes a *coating of ice* or *shards of ice*. Biology has adopted it to signify a *miscarried fetus of unknown sex*. As a military sign, ╱ is sometimes used to mean a *disposable, short-range weapon against tanks*.

The **exclamation mark** is one of the most common modern ideograms. The vertical line, |, denotes *something that is absolute and powerful* (see Group 10). The dot or point, •, represents a *beginning*, an *end*, or *something that is focused*. Taken together they mean that whatever stands immediately before the mark of exclamation is *something incredible or unusual*.

Seriousness is another basic meaning of **!**.

The exclamation mark often appears as an independent ideogram in, for example, comics and advertising. When it is used in the game of chess it means a *good move*.

In other situations **!** can signify something *dangerous* or an *unspecified danger*.

This sign is sometimes used for *plug and socket*.

Compare with ⬙ from the Harappa culture in the Indus Valley around 3000 B.C.

One of the many signs for *mercury* found in early chemistry.

See ☿ in Group 41:a for many other signs for this element.

A sign found on some nautical charts meaning *no bottom reached with sounding*. Inverted, ⁻, the sign is used in musical notation to represent *mezzo-staccato*.

An old Germanic **time sign** for *winter* (Koch). Compare with ∪, *summer*; ♌, *autumn*; and ♉, *spring*, from the same system.

⌢ is synonymous.

A variation of the graph representing the *sign of Sagittarius*. For more information, turn to ♐ in Group 15.

When this sign is vertically positioned, ⥮, it is used on some maps for *coniferous trees*.

A sign from early chemistry for *tartrate*, a *tartaric acid salt*.

There are plenty of synonyms in the systems of alchemy and chemistry. Consult the word index.

This sign has been used in some meteorological systems to signify a *damp mist*. It is a combination of ⦂ , *rain*, and ☰, *mist*. Compare with ⇄ for *frosty mist*.

The sign ≝ is a synonym.

This sign represents the quality, or **quadruplicity**, *cardinal* in astrology. The cardinal signs are those whose cusps coincide with the cardinal points of the zodiac, i.e., Aries, Cancer, Libra, and Capricorn. These four signs are associated to an aggressive and self-assertive nature.

See ◉ in Group 30 and ⌒ in Group 2 for the other quadruplicities.

∧ is also used in typography as a proofreading sign.

This ideogram is common on electrical household appliances and means *on and off control* (a circuit, ○, which is broken, C, but can be re-established again, ❙).

●|o and ◖ are synonyms.

Compare with ☉, *loudspeaker, radio, recorder*, etc., and with ☉, which stands for the connecting switch for a record player.

When ⏻ appears on a TV set it denotes that the set is connected so that it can be switched on or off by remote control.

Sometimes ⓘ and ⏻ appear together to signify the *on* and *off* controls, respectively.

This sign was used in early chemistry to denote *quicklime*.

Compare with ⅄, signifying *lime*, and ⌒, *calcination*, i.e., the process by which one reduces a substance to a fine powder by means of burning with extreme heat.

A very old ideogram for *cave, farm, village,* or *fortress.* It appears, for instance, in the grave of Kivik (see ⛰).

It is sometimes found on modern maps to signify a *cave.* When turned to Ω, it becomes the Greek letter **omega**. In the U.S. system of hobo signs ⊃ means that the *owner is in,* whereas Ϲ stands for the *owner not home.* Compare with ⊃, *keep away, no point in knocking,* from the English hobo system.

In the form Ϙ this sign has been used both as an Egyptian hieroglyph and as a **staff of a god**.

See also ⚲ in Group 42.

This sign, which is common in Western ideography, is used either alone or in combination with other signs.

It represents the *Holy Spirit* in Christianity. According to some Christian sources ⌢ is a stylized dove. Alchemists alternated between ⌢ , ⌢, and ⊖ when signifying the *essence of a substance,* the *spirit,* or *spiritus.*

The earliest known structure similar to it is probably the Egyptian hieroglyph ⌇, for *denial* or *negation.*

This is one of the signs for *acid* in later alchemy.

Synonyms were ⊥, ⬅, and other signs.

The graph for the zodiac sign *Libra,* **the scales**. The sun enters this part of the zodiac sometime around 23 September and exits somewhere near 22 October.

The oldest use of the sign ♎ can be traced back to ancient Greece. Some astrologers interpret this ideogram as a setting sun, which refers to the fact that the sun, at the time of the autumn equinox in the Northern Hemisphere, symbolically sets for the long winter night.

Libra is symbolized by a person holding a common-beam balance, which partly refers to the *autumn equinox* and partly to the personality traits of detachment and objectivity associated with ♎. Compare with the common symbol of justice, a blindfolded person holding a balance, as a sign for impartiality and objectivity.

Compare ♎ as sign for the autumn equinox with ⚖, the sign for the beginning of the winter half-year on medieval clog almanacs.

Libra's sign belongs, together with Gemini, ♊, and Aquarius, ♒, to the **element of air**, ═. The individual characterized by having many planets in air signs will perceive the surrounding world in terms of thought, or through a system of ideas. Such individuals are said to be communicative, easygoing, and intellectual types. See ♊ in Group 46.

♎ is a **cardinal sign**. See ♈ in this group for data about this quadruplicity.

The ruling planet of Libra is Venus, ♀. Both Saturn, ♄, and Jupiter, ♃, are said to be well placed in ♎. Mars, ♂, and the sun, ☉, however, are less favorably placed in ♎.

The signs of Libra, ♎, ♎, or ♎, have been used in alchemy to signify *sublimate*, i.e., the result of a *sublimation*. The **process of sublimation in alchemy** consists of heating up a substance until it is transformed into a gas. Afterward the gas is cooled so that the substance once again becomes solid but without passing through the liquid stage. According to modern chemistry this is an impossibility because every substance that is in gas form must pass through and become a liquid when cooled enough. The liquid state, however, can be very short and pass almost unnoticed. This is particularly the case with mercury chloride, a potent, bacteria-killing poison. The three aforementioned signs therefore also denote *mercury chloride*.

Libra's graph turned upside down, ⤃ , or the signs ⚖ and ⚖, are used in alchemy to denote the process by which a vaporized substance is transformed into a liquid form, the opposite of the process of sublimation: a *precipitation*. This sign has also been used to denote the result of such a process, the *precipitate*.

Group 7

Multi-axis symmetric, soft, open signs with crossing lines

There are almost no Western ideograms in this group. Here are three structures that, because of their form, belong here.

Signs and systems of signs belonging to this group are used, among others, by the Cherokee Indians and the Nsibidi tribe in Africa.

The lowermost sign is used as a logotype by a Swedish construction company. It is also a common structure found as cramp-iron on stone buildings.

Sign for *thunder and lightning* and *divine power* from the Euphrates-Tigris region; the **staff of Adad**.

See also Ψ in Group 5.

Group 8

Multi-axis symmetric, soft, open signs without crossing lines

●

The dot, or the very small, filled circle, is one of the most common Western ideograms. It has been in existence since the time of cave and rock carvings. From time immemorial long rows of dots or points have been used as a way of giving structure to a sign without using lines. As a solitary complement to other structures, the point is younger but still very old. One of our earliest known signs is ⊙, the *sun* sign.

Whether the point is used separate from or in conjunction with other structures it seems to denote something that is of *short duration*, or *small* or *focused*. It also seems to enhance or intensify the meaning. See, for example, **!** and **?**. The dot can also denote a *beginning*, as in ·→, or, as in →·, an *end*, a *goal*.

The dot, the line, the circle segment, and the two spirals constitute the basic elements by which all Western ideograms are designed.

One or more dots are signs associated with *water* and *liquid*. If the signs +, *shoal*, and ‡, *submerged wreck*, used on nautical charts are encircled by points, ⊹ and ⸬⋕⸬, this symbolizes that the items lie on the water's edge. ⊡ is an alchemical sign for *urine* and a meteorological sign for the *ground flooded*.

●●

In Anglo-Saxon meteorology several dots together can mean different types of *rain*.

•̇
•̣ •̣

The ideogram consisting of three dots in triangular form is used in mathematics and geometry with the meaning *consequently, because of*, or *therefore*.

•̇
•̣̇•

The same sign tattooed on the skin between the forefinger and the thumb is known as "hobo dots" in Sweden, and probably has a *protective* significance. Compare with ⊛ in Group 26.

On U.S. maps ∴ can sometimes signify a *ruin*. In other contexts the sign has been used to represent *silver*.

Several points in a triangular form are used in alchemy to represent *sand*. This triangle of dots often was crowned with a cross, like in ⁺ .

Some of the earliest known ideograms in the West consisted of horizontal and vertical rows of dots. Examples have been found on cave walls from prehistoric times. In modern typography . . . denotes *something that is left out*.

The sign ······ , a series of dots in a straight row, indicates the *place where left-out material should be filled in by the imagination or memory*. It is also used to connect two groups of signs and to indicate a *relation* or *correspondence*.

See also ⌒⌒ in Group 14.

One of the signs for *arena*, or *sand* in alchemy and early chemistry. *Sand* was also written ⁺ and otherwise. Note the form ▽, a medieval sign for the element *earth*, and for *stone*.

Note that dotted areas on many maps mean sandy areas.

This sign denotes a *radio beacon* on some nautical charts.

A comic-strip sign that is a symbolic representation of *transmission of radiation* and other similar occurrences. ✳ is a synonym.

This sign is used in some meteorological systems to mean *heavy precipitation falling far from the observation station*. We see the dot used as a sign for *water*, and the parentheses used to indicate a *separateness* or *distance*.

A meteorological sign that means *heavy precipitation falling close to, but not at, the station*. See the sign above.

An ancient Greek variation of the graph for *Pisces*. For more information about the zodiacal sign, turn to ✶ in Group 11. Compare with ‿ in Group 2 and ⛎ in Group 20.

This is an ancient ideogram for *splitting, to split*, or *cleave* that appears in the earliest Chinese writing system and in other very old systems.

Compare with the rune ᛋ, which was also the Hopi symbol for *universal brotherhood*. A brotherhood is in many ways the opposite of a split or cleavage.

When the two lines in the sign above touch each other, , the sign becomes an alchemical symbol for the substance *realgar*. For more information about realgar, turn to ✶ in Group 41:b.

An old alchemical sign for *decoctation* according to a German source.

In modern times the similar ✕ has been used by botanists to denote a *hybrid* or a *result of crossbreeding*, i.e., an individual that is generated from two different species.

Tartar or *tartrate*, i.e., tartaric acid salts used in alchemy. They also appeared as 무, ⚹, and 𝔩𝔩ʔ.

The same sign has been found on rock carvings in South America dating from 300 B.C. It appeared together with ♈ and ☉.

A sign sometimes used in U.S. astronomy to denote a *group of galaxies*.

Compare with ⟋, the sign for a *galaxy*.

One of the graphs for *Aquarius*. For more details concerning this zodiacal sign, turn to ♒ in Group 14.

Group 9

Multi-axis symmetric, straight-lined, open signs with crossing lines

The cross with arms of equal length is an extremely old ideogram used by most cultures. It is also one of the **basic gestalts** in Western ideography (as opposed to the **basic elements**, which are derived entities). The cross is found in every part of the world, in prehistoric caves and engraved on rocks.

In pre-Columbian America the sign seems to have been associated to the the *four points of the compass* and the *weather gods*. In the earliest Chinese ideography it appears as a sign for *perfection* and the most *perfect number – 10*. In astrological symbolism + is the graphic symbol for *matter*, the *earthly life*, the *plane of physical existence*. Compare this with ±, which in early Chinese ideography meant *ground* or *earth*.

+ was used by the alchemists as one of the signs for the *four elements* and their *point of intersection, coniunctio, quinta essentia*, etc. But the cross was much more often used as a sign for *acids* and *vinegar* and *soot* by the alchemists and early chemists.

Semiotically the stem of the cross, the vertical line (see | in Group 10), stands for the *heavenly* or *spiritual*, whereas the transverse beam (see — in Group 10) represents the *material plane of existence*.

The filled cross with arms of equal length, ✚, and the Latin cross, †, whether filled as in ✝ or not, are the symbols most closely associated with the *Western world*. They appear in many Western countries' flags.

In Western ideography the cross, and its opposite, the circle, are the most common basic gestalts and for this reason appear in many different ideographic systems.

Here are some of the meanings of + in different systems: *death, end*, and *beginning* (on coins and medals with reference to inscriptions), *boundary* (maps), *shoal* (maps), *church, chapel* (maps, charts), and *north* (astronomy).

In dualistic systems of signs + represents the positive pole: *plus, positive charge, North Pole, clockwise rotation* (optics), *increase*, and *north of the Equator*.

In the sixteenth century + began to be used in mathematics. The **law of the polarity of meanings of elementary graphs** is well illustrated by +, which is both a sign that *unites*, as in logic, mathematics, and chemistry, and a sign that *separates*, as in numismatics and cartography.

For + as a Christian sign, see † in Group 3.

The sign for the *number 10*, one of the numbers in the **golden series** on the medieval Nordic clog almanacs (see ⵕ in Group 5). Note that ╪ represented the number *10* in the early Chinese ideographic system. Compare with the Latin Χ, which also means *10*.

The diagonal cross with arms of equal length is an extremely old sign.

Like +, it has been found engraved on the walls of prehistoric caves of Europe. In early Chinese ideography it stood for the *number 5*. As an Egyptian hieroglyph it meant *divide, count*, and *break into parts*. Compare this with its use as a sign of multiplication from the beginning of the seventeenth century and the law of the polarity of meanings of elementary graphs.

Χ is ideographically more closely associated with two arrows meeting each other, ⵄ , than to +. The very similar Χ, however, a rune used in some of the old Nordic rune alphabets, is named **gif** or **geba**, and means *gift*, especially a *gift from a chief to a loyal warrior or subject*.

This sign has a wide spectrum of meanings from *confrontation, annulment, cancellation, devoid of sense or meaning, opposition, opposing powers, obstruction,* and *mistake* to *unknown, unfamilar, undecided,* and *unsettled.*

Here are a number of examples of the ways in which ✕ is used: a *crossbreed* between different species or races (in botany and biology), *takes* (chess), *printing error* (printing), *cannot continue* (ground-to-air emergency code), *unknown* (mathematics), *unknown person* (Mr. X), and *road obstruction* (military).

The diagonal cross is sometimes used as a symbol for *Christ* (Greek: Χριστοσ). It also stands for the *number 1,000* in ancient Greece and even represented *Chronos,* the *god of time,* and the *planet Saturn* in Greek and Roman mythology.

When the diagonal cross appears as a closed or filled sign, ✖, it stands for the **cross of St. Andrew** (refer to this sign in Group 28). According to tradition, St. Andrew was too humble to allow himself to be crucified on the same type of cross as Christ.

In everyday use ✕ often indicates that something that is on, or near, ✕ *no longer counts* or is *wrong.* If it appears drawn over other signs, ✕ means that what these signs denote is *cancelled* or *forbidden.* Examples are the road sign ⊗ and the washing sign ⚕, *do not bleach* (from △, *can be bleached*).

In Sweden, ✕ is used by the armed forces on maps to denote that *blasting or other type of destruction has been prepared.*

✕ signified *talc* in seventeenth-century alchemy. As an English hobo sign, it means *don't knock here,* and it sometimes is used as a Swedish **scout sign** of similar meaning: *don't take this road.*

In musical notation ✕ is called **double cross.** See ✚ in Group 11 for more data.

The closed variation, ✖, is found on telephone answering machines indicating the *control for the wiping out of taped messages.*

The combination of the diagonal cross with a vertical line is of special importance in Western ideography. It is the sign for *Jesus Christ* (the initials of the Greek name: Ιεσυσ Χρισ–τοσ). In the form ⚹ it becomes a sign for *Sunday* on clog almanacs (for more details see ⯛ in Group 5); it signifies the *sextile aspect* in astrology, i.e., a 60-degree angle between two planets as seen from the earth; and it is a sign for a *fixed star* in astronomy (compare this with |✳ in botany from Group 3). In Anglo-Saxon tradition, ✳ or ⯛ were runes that stood for *material wealth*.

Other uses: *ammonia* and *ammonium salts* in early chemistry (which were also drawn ✳); *infrequently used* in dictionaries; *snow* in meteorology; *wild growing plants* in botany; *agents accepted* in economy; and *born* in genealogy (a synonym to ☆). If the sign is doubled or tripled it can represent *heavy snowstorms* or *steady snowfall* depending on whether the signs are combined vertically or horizontally.

The same structure, ⊞, appears as a closed sign in Group 27 and means a *conservation area protected by law*.

✳ appears (as does ▯) on modern telephones and signifies special programming facilities.

According to a certain Germanic tradition, taken up by the Nazis, for example, on a ring worn by all SS men, ✳ means *heil, may he live*. The sign was accompanied on the SS ring by the engraved rune Ɯ and a skull.

Two signs for *ammonium salts* used during the seventeenth century. It is also one of the old alchemical signs for the *planet Venus*. Turn to ⊕ in Group 29 for a description of the relation between the number 8 graphically represented by these signs and the planet Venus.

The eight-pointed star was established in the Euphrates-Tigris region 3000 years earlier, as a symbol for the Venus goddess Ischtar. See ✾ in Group 30.

The sign used in seventeenth-century chemistry for *crucible*. It was also drawn ♉ and ♈. In Christian symbolism it is known as the **crutch cross**, the **Jerusalem cross**, or the **cross of the Holy Cross**. For more details, turn to ✚ in Group 28.

This sign was also used for *acids* in alchemy and old chemistry. *Hydrochloric acid*, for example, could be written ✚⊖, where ⊖ signified salt.

The **crossed cross** is a symbol for *world evangelization*. The central cross symbolizes, as it has since the beginning of time, the four points of the compass. The small crosses represent the spread of the Christian faith in all four directions. Examples of synonyms are ✛ and ✚.

Compare with the almost synonymous ✛ in this group.

This sign is known as the **Jerusalem cross**, the **cross of Palestine**, and was used as a symbol for the *kingdom of Jerusalem* after the holy city had been conquered by the crusaders until the Latin kingdom of Jerusalem was defeated by the Islamic mameluks in 1291.

See ✝ in Group 3, and compare with ✩, the symbol for Jerusalem around 400–100 B.C. The symbol was painted or woven in gold on a background of silver.

⊞ sometimes appears as a sign of decoration (in an order or fellowship). See the Jerusalem cross in Group 28.

An early form of the Jerusalem cross was drawn ⊞.

A sign from the U.S. system of hobo signs that means *here people tell you to go to hell*.

A variation of the so-called **anchor cross** in Christian symbolism. The anchor cross is a symbol for *hope*. For further data, see ⚜ in Group 26.

This sign was also used by alchemists to represent *white lead*, which also could be drawn ⇻ because of its association with ♄.

This is known as the **arrow cross**. It is a favorite of fascists because of its meaning, *expansion in all directions*. See ✛ in Group 28.

It is also a military sign for *radar station* or *direction finding station* and, on civil maps, for *monument* or *tower*.

Compare with ⊹ in this group, which has the same basic meaning.

Used in botany to indicate that a plant is *very poisonous*. It stands for *checkmate* in the game of chess (also drawn as ‡ and ⴲ). In mathematics it means *differs from* or *is not the same as*.

The same structure, but turned 90 degrees, was used in early pharmacology on recipes for medications to mean *may it be useful* or *with God's blessing* (usually drawn ⇄) and was called the **invocation cross**. See the synonym ♯ in Group 45.

This structure denotes *great danger*. It is used by botanists to signify that a plant or part of it is *very poisonous*, or *mortal danger*. The tramps and vagrants in England, Sweden, and the United States use it to mean *policeman lives here* or *they call the police*, especially if it is doubled: ‡‡.

In a mathematical context it means *not identical with* (from ≡, *identical with*).

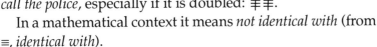

When the above structure is transformed into the sign shown here it loses its association to danger and instead becomes *blessing* and *harmless*. It is a variation of the **pope's cross** and the **Russian Orthodox Church's cross**. See the synonym ⸸ in Group 15.

On nautical charts ⊞ indicates *submerged wreck not dangerous to surface shipping*. Compare with ⊛ for *dangerous wreck at water's edge*.

XX

Sign for *crystallus* in eighteenth-century chemistry. Crystallus is a derivation from a Greek word for ice. It probably signified *crystallization processes* in general or their result.

One of the signs in alchemy and early chemistry for the *essence*. See ⊖ in Group 47 for more signs with this meaning, and consult the word index for still more.

Group 10

Multi-axis symmetric, straight-lined, open signs without crossing lines

The straight line is one of the five **basic elements** in Western ideography.

The straight vertical line stands for *unity, oneness*, the *self* (who am I), the *number 1, authority, power*, the *absolute*, that which is *outstanding*, and *contact between the lower and the higher*.

When it is placed between other signs, | is *demarcating* and *dividing*. In logic, for example, A | B can mean *either* A *or* B *but not both*.

In dualistic systems of meaning | represents the *positive aspect*. In the system for power supply, | means *power on* as opposed to *power off*. | is also an electrical sign denoting *single-phase current*.

The short vertical line also signifies *seriousness* or *danger* (together with !). The traffic sign △ exemplifies this, as does |, used in ground-to-air emergency code to indicate that the *pilot is badly wounded and is in need of a doctor*.

In modern ideography a diagonal line placed over or in another sign symbolizes that what is denoted by the other sign is *forbidden, cancelled*, etc. See, for instance, ⌀, which in certain biological contexts can be used to mean *deceased male*, or the road sign ⊘, which means *no parking*.

The horizontal line represents the *base*, the *earth*, or *land*. Note that in Chinese ideography — has roughly the same spectrum of meaning as | in the West, i.e., denotes the *positive, active, powerful, warm, extrovert*, and *masculine* dimensions of the universe: yang. See ☯ in Group 32.

The short horizontal line is used as an electrical sign to indicate *direct current* or *intended for direct current*.

When — is placed above another sign it *raises* or *increases* that sign's meaning. If placed under another sign it serves to *accentuate* or *multiply* the sign's meaning. If, on the other hand, it appears between two other signs it unites them, as opposed to | , which separates and divides. The latter spectrum of meaning can be most clearly illustrated by the minus sign in mathematics, which links two numbers in a special way, or by o-o for unmarried.

But — can also separate signs. For example, when it appears as a **dash**.

The short horizontal line, especially before or in another sign, *cancels* or *negates* it. For example, in the traffic sign structure $\ominus$, the line cancels the empty circle's endless possibilities for traffic. In logic, chemistry, and mathematics, — is used as the negative sign. It stands for *south* in astronomical and nautical systems, whereas in electrical systems it represents the *negative pole*.

In the now Westernized Chinese yin-yang philosophy the broken line is a symbol for *yin*, the *passive, receptive, material dimension of the universe*. In ground-to-air emergency code –– means *throw down a signalling lantern*.

A series of short horizontal lines placed one after the other in a text indicate *excluded material that should be filled in by memory or imagination*. .... is a synonym. A row of more such lines usually indicates a *relation or correspondence* between groups of other signs.

Two identical, parallel, and vertical lines represent *two complete entities*. An example is $\amalg$, the sign of Gemini and the Latin numeral for 2. In geometry || can mean *parallel with*.

In the U.S. system of hobo signs || stands for *here you can get whatever you want*.

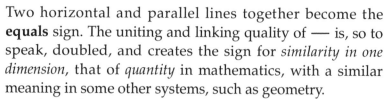

Two horizontal and parallel lines together become the **equals** sign. The uniting and linking quality of — is, so to speak, doubled, and creates the sign for *similarity in one dimension*, that of *quantity* in mathematics, with a similar meaning in some other systems, such as geometry.

= is used in astrology for the *element of air*. This **astrological element**, to which belong the zodiac signs of Libra, ♎, Gemini, ♊, and Aquarius, ♒, is not identical with the corresponding alchemical element, nor is it graphically symbolized the same way. People strongly influenced by one of these signs tend to use their intellect, or their personal system of ideas, as their primary means of recognizing and ordering their environment. In astrology, the opposite of air is water, i.e., experiencing the world primarily through the emotions and feelings.

In the English system of hobo signs = means *here you are given a place to sleep for the night*. In meteorology it can mean *light mist*.

= signifies similarity in one dimension, and ≡ means that the *similarity is so strong that there is no real difference* or *identity exists*. It is interesting that ≡ is used in meteorology to indicate *mist*, i.e., a climatic condition that is evenly milky white, identical.

≡ also represents the *passive intellect* in one system of old psychological signs.

Three identical and parallel lines in a vertical position signify *three units*. It is used in geometry in combination with other signs to mean *is the same as*.

||| can also mean the *active intellect*, sometimes drawn ≋. Compare with the graph ⨯, the *confused intellect*, and the above ≡.

Placed diagonally, ⫽, it tells the U.S. hobo that *this place is not safe*.

Originally an iconic sign for *cannon* and today used to mean *gun*. ıｌı was also used in early chemistry as a sign for *iron*. Iron is usually depicted ♂.

A variation on the theme of three straight lines, one of ten possible combinations that appear in Western writing and ideography. It has no specific meaning. If, however, it appears as Ι, a variation of the single vertical line, it stands for the *emperor, Jesus, connected* (electricity), the *first*, the *only one*, etc.

Sign for *digerere* or *digestio*, i.e., *solution* or the *dissolving of a substance in a liquid at moderate temperatures*. From eighteenth-century chemistry.

Sign for *evaporare* or *evaporatio*, i.e., *evaporate* or *evaporation*, from eighteenth-century chemistry.

A cartographic sign (often military) signifying *bridge*. Compare with)(, *to split or cleave*, and with ═.

This is a computer sign that stands for *separate from*, in expressions like A<>B. The ideogram indicates that A goes in one direction, ←, and B in another, →.

⊵ and ⧣ mean approximately the same thing in mathematics.

In ground-to-air emergency code <> signifies that the *airplane is badly damaged*.

The identical structure, ◇, is a Spanish hobo sign indicating that *there are friends here*. Compare with ⟨⟩, which denotes *universal brotherhood* for the Hopi people in America.

A sign sometimes used for *ice needles* in meteorology. These are also drawn as ╱ .

In chemistry ↔ means *reversible reaction*, and in logic the same sign stands for *equivalence* or that there exists a *dual implication* (i.e., if A then B, and if B then A).

The meaning of this ideogram is self-evident. This specific variation is found in telecommunications and indicates a *squeeze section*. Compare with ✕ and ✳ in Group 9.

A meteorological sign for *frosty mist* in some systems. It is made by combining ≡ for *mist* and ↔ for *ice needles*.

A camera sign for *focus*.
See also ⊖ in Group 47.

A modern ideographic sign (in technical drawings, etc.) indicating *distance* (e.g., between walls).

This sign is known as the **Gamma cross** and is a variation of the cross used in Christian symbolism.
   See **Gamma cross** in the word index for other variations.

A modern ideogram indicating an *increase in pressure* or *high pressure* or *meeting place*.

This sign is known as *footangle*, a common heraldic sign. It is an almost iconic sign representing four nails forged together in such a way that one of the points is always pointing upward when the instrument is placed on the ground. It was a weapon used during the Middle Ages to wound horses and soldiers in the feet.
   Compare with ✛ in Group 9.

One of the graphs for the sign of *Aquarius*. For further details about this sign, turn to ≈ in Group 14.

Fu is a sign in Chinese symbolism for *authority, divine power,* and the *ability to judge between right and wrong.* It is also used in the United States.

Compare with)(, *to split or cleave,* and with ⚓, the Pisces sign, denoting two fish swimming in opposite directions.

Turn to Y in Group 4 for all signs of this type.

A comic-strip sign used to illustrate the *release of energy* or *radiation.* It often is used to illustrate fistfights and explosions. It is also a sign that has been used since antiquity to illustrate the *radiation of light.* Compare with ☼ in Group 14, ☼ in Group 4, and ☼ in Group 8.

Group 11

Multi-axis symmetric, both soft and straight-lined, open signs with crossing lines

A variation of the **anchor cross**. For more details, see ⌘ in Group 26.

A variation of the **crutch cross** found in Christian symbolism. More details are under ┿ in Group 28.
    This sign is also used in alchemy as a sign for *vinegar*.

A variation of the **button cross**. When it is turned 45 degrees it becomes a cross used in musical notation, called a **double cross**. As such it is also drawn ✕, ♯, or ✖ before the note. It indicates that *following note or notes should be played two half-tones higher*. See also ♯ in Group 45.

Found on Greek vases from around 700 B.C. It was also used in certain types of cartography as a sign indicating *stone bottom at the water's edge*. In seventeenth-century alchemy and chemistry, it (and, for instance, ⊹) represented *distilled vinegar* or *acetum*. Note the points, which are signs for *drops of water*.

♓

The most widely used sign for *Pisces*. The sun enters this section of the zodiac around 19 February and leaves it on the spring equinox, around 20 March. It is the last cycle of the moon before the spring equinox. Winter is moving toward spring. There is a promise of life in clear light and cold.

The symbol for Pisces is two fish swimming in opposite directions. The sign of Pisces belongs to the **element of water**, which indicates sensitivity and emotionality. For more details about the astrological elements or triplicities, turn to △ in Group 28.

Pisces belongs to the signs of the **mutable quality** or **quadruplicity**, ⌒, in Group 2. The other signs of this quadruplicity are ♊, ♍, and ♐.

Today the planet Neptune is considered the planetary ruler of Pisces. Jupiter, ♃, however, ruled Pisces until the discovery of Neptune. Sometimes these two planets are said to be co-rulers of Pisces. For more information about Neptune, see ♆ in Group 5.

The planet Mercury, ☿, the principle of intelligence and communication, is said to have its influence distorted when appearing in ♓.

♓ is ideographically related to)(, meaning *to cleave or split*. In terms of astrological symbolism, ♓ shows two crescents of receptivity, ☽, directed outward and held together by the horizontal line of matter. Historically, ♓ consists of two linked Neptune staffs, Ψ, or the staff of Jupiter without barbs.

An ancient Greek variation of the graph for Pisces is drawn ·)(·. Here, the sign for *divided,*)(, is surrounded by two points that symbolize the *element of water.*

These signs are known in Roman mythology as **Jupiter's staff**. Jupiter was the Roman equivalent of the Greek god Zeus and the Germanic god Wuotan or Odin. See 𝕁, Odin's staff, in Group 24.

The **sign for the fish spear**, ♈ or ψ, is the **staff of Poseidon** (Greece) or the **staff of Neptune** (Rome). Jupiter's staff is merely ♈ doubled. If we remove the barbs from Jupiter's staff and turn it 90 degrees then we are left with the most common sign for the zodiacal sign of Pisces. It is not surprising, then, that both Jupiter (according to the earlier tradition from the nineteenth century) and Neptune (according to modern astrology) are the ruling planets of Pisces.

Compare this with the Assyric-Babylonian sign for the staff of Adad, 𝕏. Whatever the variations, these staffs were all associated with *lightning*, *storms*, *thunder*, and the *power to agitate the waters*.

One of the alchemists' signs for *quicklime*. See ψ in Group 5.

One of the alchemists' signs for *mix*. Another was ꝫ. See the latter sign in Group 17.

An alchemical sign for *sal ammoniacus*, or *ammonium salt*.
Synonymous with ⊝x in Group 41:b, and with ⊥ in Group 3.

Group 12

Multi-axis symmetric, both soft and straight-lined, open signs without crossing lines

A sign that since the seventeenth century has been used in mathematics to denote *division*. In medical contexts it is sometimes used to indicate that a patient has *defecated*. In the margin of a letter, the similar ./ means that a *supplement is enclosed*.

Two variations of the **repetition** sign in music.

This sign is sometimes used in mathematics to mean is *approximately equal to*.
    ≃ is synonymous.

A modern ideogram for *meeting place*. It is used in waiting rooms and departure halls in airports, etc.
    Compare with the synonymous ⟩⟨ in Group 10.

These two ideograms, and others very similar to them, appear, for example, on industrial machines. The first, of course, means *tighten* or *press together*. It is roughly synonymous with the sign →|←.

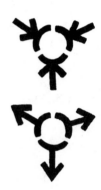

The second sign means *loosen up* or *unscrew*.

Group 13

Asymmetric, soft, open signs with crossing lines

This variation of the **fylfoot** or **swastika** has been found, among other places, on a rune stone in Lund, Sweden. For more details about the swastika, turn to 卐 in Group 15.

The swastika is often called a **tetraskele**, and this variation is a sign for *repeat* in music. The sign for repetition is more usually drawn ·|·, :|:, ⊕, and otherwise.

A Greek variation of the **sauvastika** drawn around 500 B.C.
    For data about the sauvastika as different from the swastika, see 卍 in Group 15.

One of the alchemists' signs for *honey*. See ⚭ in Group 20 for more signs for honey.

This sign appears on pre-Columbian engravings and rock paintings in Arizona. It is known as the **mother and child** or **mother earth**. It also appears on the faces of certain Cretian coins from around 300 B.C. The earliest known examples of this sign are on an Etruscan vase from around 550 B.C.

The ideogram is common along the coasts of Sweden and formed by rows of stones. They are called **virgin dances, Troy fortresses, St. Peter's game, Jerusalem, Jericho, Nineveh**, and **Babylon**.

It is also a common ideogram in many places throughout Europe. One finds it, for instance, in many medieval churches.

Group 14

Asymmetric, soft, open signs without crossing lines

These structures are made up by two of the basic elements of Western ideography: ℗ and ℚ).

Ideographically, ∿ is the sign for *one complete oscillation* or *one whole wave*. If we take the straight line as our starting point, the point of rest, then the wave of a guitar string or the like, when strummed, will move above and below the straight line, graphically ∿ (the sign for *frequency*).

Consequently, ∿ represents all types of *waves* in Western ideography. In musical notation ∿ stands for *grupetto*, i.e., that one should play a group of four notes: the note above, the note itself, the note below, and finish with the note itself again. The sign ∿ stands for a *reversed grupetto*, i.e., one begins with the note under, etc. In logic, ∿ P means that the *opposite of P is true*. ∿ is used in electrical contexts for *alternating current*. It appears in dictionaries for *words that have been referred to earlier* or indicates that a term *is interchangeable with* another. In mathematics ∿ can stand for the *difference between, varies as, is complementary*, etc.

In Spanish and Portuguese writing, ∿ is used over certain letters to indicate a certain pronunciation and is called a **tilde**.

In meteorology ∿ has been or is used to indicate *ice* or a *coating of ice*. The latter is also drawn ⊡ and ∾.

The sign ∾ appears in genealogical contexts and means *baptized*.

Oddly enough, ∿ and ∾ are hardly used as ideograms, although ∿ and ∾ are common.

Although these signs are so basic in Western ideography and are used in so many modern systems, strangely enough they are almost never found in ancient ideography (but see ≃ in Group 18 for a strange medieval use of ∿).

In eighteenth-century chemistry ∿ could mean *solvere*, or *dissolve*, and *solutio*, or *solution*.

When $\sim$ is doubled it stands in mathematics for *approximately the same as*. In the context of electricity $\approx$ means *alternating current* or, in specific situations, *alternating current that is within the audible frequency range*.

Tripled, $\sim$ seems to be humankind's most common ideogram for *water* in general and for *streaming or flowing water* in particular. In the earliest Chinese ideography $\approx$ represented *river* or *stream*. In modern electrical engineering it signifies *three-phased alternating current*, the most common type of current in industrialized countries. This sign in more specialized contexts can also mean *alternating current of a frequency that is above the audible level*.

The above ideogram, but in a vertical position, stands for *steam, liquids that become gases*, etc.

Compare with ⅏, for *drying* in laundry contexts, and the synonym ¦¦ from eighteenth-century chemistry.

This is a sign common in modern systems to denote *distance* and similar concepts. It is also a sign to denote *saintliness* in connection with names of saints.

It is one of the many signs used for *lead* in early chemistry and has long been used for *south*.

S was used by alchemists to denote the *essence* or the *spirit*. V̌ in Group 18 was a synonym. The use of this sign to denote *saintliness* or *holiness* is closely associated with this alchemical use of it.

During the Bronze Age and even earlier, ●● was used as a decorative element. This suggests a certain instinctive feeling for this particular sign's fundamental position as composed of one of the five basic elements in Western ideography in two editions and then connected.

In ancient Greece it was common on vases and amphoras and often signified *water* or the *sea*.

An older variation on the same theme is ◎, found on rock engravings from the Bronze Age in Scania, Sweden. This later sign, however, is much more graphically sophisticated, as you will soon realize if you try to draw it.

See also ∼ and ⌣ in this group.

The **clockwise spiral** (starting from the middle) is strongly associated with *water, power, independent movement,* and *outgoing migrations* of tribes.

Although the other basic elements exist in the earliest ideography, i.e., on the walls of prehistoric caves, in rock carvings, etc., the spiral seems to have come at a later date. One finds it on **discos** from Crete from around 2000 B.C. and as an old symbol for *potential power* in Tibet. It also appears in rock carvings in Utah. Compare with ▭ in Group 16.

The ideogram is primarily a sign illustrating *movement*. In those rock carvings and paintings found in Sweden it often means *potential movement*. Today it appears as a laundry sign for *spin drying*. As isolated ideograms on rock carvings ◎ most probably means *migration* or *tribal wanderings*. The Vikings used it with the meaning *independent movement* (against the sun, waves, and wind when necessary) and eventual *return*. It appeared as a form for the sternposts on their ships.

In ancient Greece ℑ, a similar structure, was used to represent the zodiacal sign *Leo*. This zodiac sign is strongly associated with potential power, strength, etc. See ♌ in Group 50.

⑨ is also related to ⅄ in Group 15.

On nautical charts it sometimes stands for *whirlpool* or *eddy*. The similar ⑨ has been used for over 4000 years as decoration on the clothes of kings, high priests, and gods represented as statues in many different cultures.

Both ⑨ and ⓔ have been used by alchemists for *horse dung*.

In modern times ⑨ and ⓔ are used with a similar meaning in comic strips when *rage*, *pain*, and *curses* are represented. Here these signs are often accompanied by swastikas, exclamation marks, and other symbols of *wrath* and *surprise*.

The mirror image, or inversion, of the above entry symbolizes, like that ideogram, *rotation*. It stands first and foremost for a *counterclockwise rotation* and is therefore related to ⅄ (see Group 15).

This sign appeared in the Euphrates cultures as early as around 2000 B.C., and ⓔ is an Egyptian hieroglyph for *thread* or *measurement*. ⓠ was used in the earliest Chinese ideography with the probable meaning *return* or *homecoming*. The Hopi Indians seem to have given it the same meaning. See ⚬⚬ in this group.

The sign was used by the Phoenicians and as a pattern on Bronze Age jewelry found in Scania, Sweden, dating back to about 1300 B.C. Compare with the hieroglyph ⊓, representing *Egypt*, i.e., that country that one *returns to*, the *homeland*. There is a similar usage in the English system of hobo signs: a *good house for work*, i.e., a place that is worth returning to when one needs food and money.

The sign ↺ is found painted on the walls of houses in Tibet (together with • and ↝), and has perhaps the meaning *home*, the place one returns to.

It can also signify *whirlpool* or *eddy* on nautical charts.

This **staff sign** is sometimes found on the headdresses of kings and gods that appear on old Egyptian stone reliefs and paintings. It is also known as the **augurs' staff**. An **augur** was a Roman religious official whose task was to foretell the future with the help of signs in nature, etc.

Christian symbolism has adopted 𝒫 and used it for their **bishops' croziers**, i.e., the staffs carried by bishops and abbots symbolizing their rank — **baculus pastoralis**, the **shepherd's staff**.

In Egypt the hieroglyph 𝒫 represented the *number 100*.

The **question mark** is similar in structure to the augurs' or soothsayers' staffs. Ideographically, the sign is a combination of the ideogram for a complete wave, $\sim$, stood up in a vertical position, which symbolizes the dimension between the spiritual and the material, i.e., from the possible to what in actual fact exists, and a point or dot below, •, emphasizing the concrete reality.

Semiotically this ideogram can be interpreted as asking: *Which is the one real and concrete fact of all the possible ones* (from the spiritual world above us)? What is the fact down here in this world of matter?

In chess ? means a *bad move*. The question mark is used to indicate an *uncertainty, apprehension,* or *danger* in many different situations, especially in **comic strips** and advertising.

One of the signs for *destillare, distill,* in eighteenth-century chemistry. See ƒ in Group 49 for facts about this process and synonyms. See also the sign ⑤, below.

This structure is used in comic strips and signifies *rotation* and *independent movement*. It is also used to illustrate a *person's state of mind when confronted with a transcendental or in other ways overwhelming reality.*

The sign 🐚 is synonymous for the last meaning.

This structure is closely related to the Celts, the people who populated Western Europe 5000 or 6000 years ago and later were forced west to Britanny, Wales, Scotland, and Ireland by Gauls and Germanic tribes.

Today, the variation ஜ is used to symbolize **Jeune Bretagne**, a separatist movement in the Celtic region of France. The sign is associated with *migrations* and *independent movements.*

Frank Waters, an anthropologist who has studied the Hopi Indians and their culture, writes that the above sign reversed was used by the Hopis in Arizona. It seems to have had a range of meanings centered around the idea of *several returns* or *homecomings.*

Waters has interpreted ஃ as *tribal migration*, cyclical in nature, by a people consisting of a few large tribes or clans.

This sign is known as the **bass clef** or **F-clef** in musical notation. 𝄢 is often used to indicate the *bass control* on radios, tape recorders, and amplifiers. Compare with 𝄞 for treble tone control.

This is the zodiacal sign for *Aquarius*. It is also drawn ♒, ♒, and ♒. It represents both the *period between around 21 January to 18 February each year,* when ☉, the sun, is in ♒

and that part of the zodiac against which ☉ appears during that period. The symbol (the icon) for this section of the zodiac is usually a kneeling man pouring cosmic water out of an urn. This explains the graphic water symbol ∿∿.

Yet despite this symbol, ♒ is not a water sign but an air sign, i.e., ♒ belongs together with ♊ and ♎ to the element of air, ═ (turn to △ in Group 28 for data on the astrological elements). On a psychological level a person characterized by many planets in signs of the air element is very social, cooperative, inventive, intelligent, objective, and humanistic; but all these good traits can become depraved so that superficiality or shallowness, dissociation, and imitation dominate the personality.

The sign ♒ belongs to the quadruplicity of fixed signs (symbolized by ⬤) together with ♉, ♌, and ♏ (see ⬤ in Group 30 for more information concerning quadruplicities). The psychological qualities of the fixed signs are consequence, trustworthiness, endurance, patience, large reserves of energy, and firm goal orientation.

Up until the eighteenth century the planetary system was believed to consist of seven wandering, celestial bodies of which ♄, Saturn, was the outermost, representing the boundaries of time and material existence. ♄ was also believed to rule the signs of Capricorn, ♑, and Aquarius. Nowadays it is the planet Uranus, ♅, that is accepted as the ruling planet of ♒. Turn to ♅ in Group 41:a for further information about Uranus.

Apart from Uranus, the following planets (symbols for the dimensions of the psyche) are supposed to be well placed in ♒: Saturn and ♀, Venus. The sun, however, is not considered well placed in this sign.

According to astrological symbolism the water that Aquarius pours over the earth is the *water of consciousness*. It is the realization that all men and women are brothers and sisters. It is also the *water of intuition*. Aquarius symbolizes the realization of humanity's oneness.

Another fundamental aspect of ♒ is that of communication via every type of media, especially those of intuition, telepathy, and electronics.

In mundane astrology ♒ is associated with the countries of Sweden, Ethiopia, Prussia, Canada, and Poland. It is also linked to the cities of Stockholm, Leningrad, Hamburg, Bremen, Salzburg, and Trent.

The key qualities of individuals born with ⊙ in ♒ are *sociability*, working for *humanitarian ideals and ideas*, a *desire to be on friendly terms with all types of people, intuition*, and *intelligence*.

This sign, found in an English stenography system, means the *previous remark should not be taken seriously*.

Semiotically we see the short vertical line for power and authority curve back and forth, suggesting *unreliability*.

Smoky atmosphere in some U.S. meteorological systems. It is, perhaps, an iconic sign for a factory chimney with smoke blowing away.

One alchemical sign for the process of *distilling*. See ♂ in Group 50.

A variation of the graph for the zodiac sign *Leo*. For more information concerning this sign, turn to ♌ in Group 50. Compare also with ♌, the *moon's north node*.

This is a modern laundry ideogram for *steam* or *evaporation*. Compare with ☰, for *drying of laundry*, and with the old ⧦ in this group.

This asymmetrical line of dots is an ideogram that indicates a *sharing of similar topographic characteristics*. On maps and nautical charts it marks *places that have the same height, depth,* etc. It is also used to denote *paths*, *ways*, and *trails* on maps.
    Compare with ⸺ in Group 8.

This ideogram is the sign for **aum**, the **greeting of peace** in India. It has been used in the West since the 1960s. The ideogram symbolizes the *four states of consciousness*: awake, dreaming, sleeping without dreams, and the transcendental state, *samadhi*, *satori*, or the exteriorized state.
    See also ☙ in Group 20.

This is the most common graph in printed texts for the zodiac sign *Scorpio*. It is also drawn ♏, ♏, and ♏. For more information about Scorpio, turn to ♏ in Group 18.
    In former times ♏ was used in pharmaceutical contexts to signify a *drop* and was an alchemical sign for *transform into liquid*. This process was also symbolized by ♒.

A rune from the earliest runic alphabet. It stood for a j-sound and was associated with a *good annual crop* and with *year*. Notice that the Hopi Indians used it as their symbol for *universal brotherhood*. ᛊ can be seen as the opposite of)(, *to divide or cleave*, with a slight displacement to prevent the sign from being mistaken for a circle, as ().

This rune could also be carved ᚼ, ᚦ , and otherwise.

A sign in alchemy and/or earlier chemistry for *lead*. Lead is usually represented by the Saturn sign, ♄.

See ♂ in Group 49 for other signs signifying lead.

Group 15

Asymmetric, straight-lined, open signs with crossing lines

The **swastika** is a very old ideogram. The first examples are found in Sumeria and earlier cultures that existed in what is now Pakistan about 3000 B.C. Yet it was not until around the year 1000 B.C. that the swastika became a commonly used sign.

Neither the Assyrian-Babylonian nor the Egyptian cultural spheres seem to have used the swastika as a symbol. Most other ancient cultures in Eurasia, however, did use it.

Count Goblet d'Alviella (see bibliography), who conducted research in the distribution and migration of symbols, put forth the theory that certain symbols were mutually exclusive, i.e., they could not appear in the same culture. This was more or less the case with the signs ✛ and ✩ for Jerusalem in Europe during the Middle Ages. According to this theory the same applied to the swastika and the round disc with horizontally spread-out wings and the disc with the four-pointed star (see ⊕ in Group 30). In this case, ⅏ would have been the symbol for the *sun*, the *highest god*, *power*, and *life force*.

The swastika was used before the birth of Christ in China, India, Japan, and Southern Europe. Whether it was used in the Americas, however, is not clear. There are no examples of it on the oldest rock carvings there, and neither the Mayans, the Incas, nor the Aztecs used it. It did, however, appear a couple of hundred years ago among many of the Indian tribes and was probably brought over by the Spanish and Portuguese colonists.

The swastika is often associated with Buddha in India, China, and Japan. In the earliest Chinese symbolism ⅏ was known as **wan** and was a *superlative of the highest degree*. In Japan it was said to be a sign for the *magnificent number 10,000*. In Japan of the Middle Ages 卐 was **manji**, a sign for *enormous luck and protection against evil powers*. In India, according to d'Alviella, the swastika was given its name from *su* = good, and *asti* = to be, with the suffix *ka*. Its arms were angled in a clockwise direction (from the center). The reversed swastika, ⊐⊔, known as **sauvastika**, was associated with *misfortune* and *bad luck*.

The sign was common among the Hittites and in Greece around 1000 B.C. It was used to decorate ceramic pots, vases, coins, and buildings. However, it did not appear in the Nordic countries until after the birth of Christ and then only on a few runic stones, often combined with a cross as in ⚘. The swastika was used in Northern Europe well before that, for instance, in pre-Christian Ireland.

After the birth of Christ, however, 卐 seems to have lost its popularity in most of Europe, with the exception of the Nordic countries, until the nineteenth century – most likely because it became known as a sign representing Buddha and therefore was considered anti-Christian. This disappearance might also have been due to its widespread use in ancient Greece, which was a pagan society. Although it was not common in Europe during this time, it was not totally unknown. It had many different names: **Hakenkreuz** in Germanic princedoms, **fylfot** in England, **Crux gammata** in Rome, and **tetraskelion** or **gammadion** in Greece.

The swastika's spectrum of meaning is centered around *power*, *energy*, and *migration*. It is closely associated with ⚭ and ⚺ in the context of *tribal migrations*. The sign is used in cartography to indicate *electric power stations* and was part of the logotype used by the Swedish company ASEA, now the multinational ABB, producing electrical machinery, until Hitler monopolized 卐 as a national symbol. In the section "The ideographic Struggle in Europe during the 1930s" in Part I you can read more about the way the swastika was introduced and used in Germany. See also ⚡ in Group 34.

The swastika is a common sign in Finland. The victory of the "Whites" during the civil war of 1918 was the victory of the farmers, the middle class, and squires over the Communist workers' movement. 卐 can be seen on the Finnish

Cross of Freedom, a medal created by the winning side in 1918; as a sign for Finnish women's voluntary defense; and on army unit standards.

There is some confusion as to whether the clockwise angled swastika, 卐, or the counter-clockwise angled variation, 卍, is the most positive. Both types have appeared quite regularly in many different contexts, except when the sign is used as an official or national symbol, in which case 卐 is always preferred.

An ancient Greek variation of the **swastika**.

An ancient Greek variation of the **swastika**.

A variation of the **swastika** found on a runic stone from the time of the Norwegian Vikings.

A variation of the **swastika** used in Christian symbolism.

Koch (see bibliography) writes that this is the **sign of the Vehmic Courts**.

Vehmgerichte was a system of *secret tribunals* originating from ancient Germanic criminal law. These courts were especially common in Westphalia during the Middle Ages. Frequent wars had made the normal judiciary system useless. In time the Vehmic Courts began to be abused to obtain personal vengeance, etc., and the princes and governments tried to annihilate them. The last Vehmic tribunal was held in Zell in 1568.

Compare with ✝ in Group 42:a.

Known as the **cross of Christ** in Christian symbolism.

This is the **Russian cross**, the **Greek-Russian cross**, or the **cross of the Russian Orthodox Church**. It was first used by Byzantine artists. When the Roman Empire was divided a few hundred years after the birth of Christ, the eastern empire was named Byzantium.

According to certain sources, the diagonal beam was meant to represent the robber who was crucified on the right side of Christ and ascended to heaven. Another interpretation suggests that the beam was added to the cross of the Greek-Orthodox Church, ✝, and that it symbolized the main saint of Russia, St. Andrew, who was crucified on a diagonal cross.

See also ✝ in Group 3.

This is the most common sign in astrology and astronomy for the zodiacal sign of *Sagittarius*, the *archer*. The sun enters this section of the zodiac (see ◯ in Group 35) around 22 November and exits around 21 December. Sagittarius is symbolized by a being half-horse and half-man, known as a **centaur**, holding a stretched bow, the arrow in place.

The exact age of this graph is difficult to determine. In the form ⚹ it was used already in the natal charts (horoscopes) of ancient Greece. Other signs used for Sagittarius are ↗ and ↗. The sign of the archer is associated with the *projection of self toward new horizons*, both literally (long voyages, new spheres of activities) and metaphorically (deep studies, high ideals, etc.).

Sagittarius's period in the solar year is also the last cycle of the moon before the winter equinox, midwinter, and the longest night (in the Northern Hemisphere). ↗, together with ♈ and ♌, make up the fiery triplicity, the element of fire, △ . See △ in Group 28 for more data about the fiery triplicity.

Persons born with many planets in fiery signs are believed to be characterized by dynamic creativity and a way of perceiving the world through those possibilities they intuitively feel are attainable rather than through their senses (the earthy triplicity), their system of ideas (the airy triplicity), or their emotions (the watery triplicity).

Together with Pisces, ♓, Gemini, ♊, and Virgo, ♍, Sagittarius belongs to the *mutable quadruplicity or quality,* symbolized ⌒

Those individuals who are strongly influenced by the sign of the archer, for example, by the presence of ☉ or one or more of the other planets in ↗, are considered to be flexible, adaptable, and able to learn things easily, and strive for high ideals.

The sign ↗ is ruled by the planet Jupiter, ♃, the psychological principle of expansion. For information about this planet and its symbolism as an astrological sign, see the entry ♃ in Group 17.

Mercury, ☿, is said to be in detriment in ♐. Turn to ☿ in Group 41:a for a description of this particular planet's spectrum of meaning. Two planets that are well placed in ♐ are Venus, ♀, and ☉.

In mundane astrology the cities Cologne, Naples, and Budapest are considered Sagittarian. Countries ruled by ♐ are Arabia, Italy, Spain, and France, especially in Provence.

This is a rune from the earliest Nordic rune alphabet. It was called **naudh**, meaning *misery*.

Runes from the earliest Nordic rune alphabet that were usually carved otherwise.

See ᚠ in Group 16 for more data about this very important rune.

This structure was common and widespread in ancient cultures. It has been found in the prehistoric caves of Western Europe. The signs made up by a combination of three straight lines, like this and the following four entries, are also very common today. Note that seven or eight of the letters of the Western alphabet are made this way and also two of our ten number figures.

This sign is sometimes used in electrical contexts to mean *light socket with switch*. Turned around, it becomes the sign for the *number 4*.

The above sign turned another way becomes the so-called **angled cross** in Christian symbolism.

The above structure need only be changed slightly for it to become one of the signs for *tin* in early chemistry.

Compare with the synonymous ♃ and ♃, used by the alchemists.

See also the similar structure ⇥, which stands for *vitriol*.

This sign is very similar to the above. In earlier alchemy this sign could mean *coagulare*, *coagulate*, or *fixate*.

Finally, we have an example of the same structure in yet another position, found in early chemistry and alchemy, signifying *wax*.

A sign used in early chemistry for *white lead*. This is a white paint made by lead carbonate, known already in antiquity. White lead could also be drawn ✝ and ✠.

An alchemical sign for *flow* or *melt*. This meaning could also be drawn o—₃ and otherwise.

The uppermost sign has been used in some meteorological systems for *high driving snow* or a kind of *light snowstorm*.

The lower, similar sign means *low driving snow*.

Compare with the sign for snowstorm, below.

This ideogram is sometimes used in meteorology to denote a *snowstorm*. It is made up by combining ⊹, the sign for *high driving snow*, and ✳, the sign for *snow*.

This is one of the alchemists' signs for *putreficatio, putrefaction*, the *process of rotting*. The sign ⥮ in Group 17 is synonymous in this respect.

Compare with other signs that denote *strong winds*, like ⚡, ↗, ⚐, and ↻.

This sign has been used in English meteorology to denote *ground partly covered by snow*. The sign for *ground*, □ , has been divided, and the sign for *snow*, ✳, placed in the remaining half, indicating that not all the ground is covered.

Compare with ⊠ for *ground covered by snow*.

Group 16

Asymmetric, straight-lined, open signs without crossing lines

A rune from the earliest runic alphabet. It was most probably called **logr**, meaning *onion* or *water, stream,* or *sea*.

The same structure as the above sign, but in another position, is used today as a **tick** to check and mark off lists, etc. Its meaning: *ready, accounted for, done,* or *wrong, to be corrected,* as when correcting school work, etc. Turned another way, ⌣ , it appears in some English meteorological systems to denote that the *barometric pressure has dropped for the last three hours but has now begun to rise*. The sign's "falling" and "rising" is explained by seeing the horizontal plane as a symbol for time.

A symbol from the U.S. system of hobo signs with the meaning *here they'll rough you up*.

The rune named **ur**, or **uruz**, meaning *strength, sacrificial animal,* and *aurochs,* the now extinct European relative of the American bison or buffalo.

The rune **cher**, or **chör**, associated with *harvest* and a *good year's crop*.
　　See ᛋ in Group 14.

The rune **áss**, *god*, later **óss**, *rapids* or *waterfall*, from the Nordic rune alphabet. It is also carved ᚠ , probably a mixup, and ᚨ.

A similar structure has been found on the neck of a human-shaped figure of a god painted on a rock face in the Sahara and said to be prehistoric. ᚨ is here associated with ⊙. The sign ᚨ stands for *Thursday* in the medieval **clog almanacs**.

In the Viking age ᚨ was associated with the god *Loke*; with the *mouth* and *mouths* in general, whether of rivers or other entities; and with *signals*.

Refer to the following signs and also to ᚠ in this group, which, in the same way as ᚨ , could be drawn ᚠ .

Two variations of the sign for the *golden number 17* in the **clog almanacs**. For more information about the golden numbers and clog almanacs, turn to ᚼ in Group 5.

The rune with the name **fé**, meaning *cattle or livestock*. ᚠ was a Viking Age symbol for *moveable property*. It could be drawn in both ways shown here.

ᚠ is the first sign of the runic alphabet, and ᛩ is the last.

See ᛩ in Group 39, which meant *odal*, i.e., real estate (*odalman* = freeholder).

These signs have been used in meteorology to denote *winds of varying strengths*. The strength of the wind is indicated by the number of short, perpendicular lines according to a simple code. The signs shown here indicate, respectively, *weak wind* and *hurricane*.

Compare with other signs for *weak* and *strong winds:* ↗, ⧏, ↗, and ∂.

This is an international sign used on nautical charts and maps to indicate *tidal stream at high tide*. It can also be drawn with a filled-in arrowhead.

Compare with the sign ↑, which signifies *ebb tide stream*, and with ⤳ and ⋙→, which represent other types of *ocean currents*. Compare also with the signs of the type ↗, which indicate *air currents* or *winds* of certain strengths.

In mathematical ideographic systems, expressions like A ⋛ B can mean A is *less than* B or *greater than* B.

The sign ≠ and others are synonymous.

Compare with the computer sign, <>, in Group 10, meaning *different from in magnitude*.

Signs of this structure, like the very similar sign below, seem to be general symbols for *danger*. This entry was drawn with chalk or scratched into the surface of walls, etc., by Swedish tramps to mean *watch out for a dog!* It also appears as a traffic sign for trains signifying *danger of landslide*.

Similar to a mirror image of N in the Western alphabet, this sign is, in all probability, a basic **gestalt** in Western ideography. With the basic element of the straight line thrice repeated and connected, some ten or more structures can be created, all of which are common in Western ideography. Two of these, ≠ and ⚡, are signs for *danger*. ⚡ is also associated with *energy*, *heat*, and *power*, which all are dangerous.

This structure is seldom seen in the Nordic runic alphabets. Occasionally it is used instead of ⟨ , the **sun rune**, and ↓, the **yew-tree rune**. In the Germanic tradition, ⚡ is the **Sigrune**, i.e., the **rune of victory** (together with ↑ in Group 4). It is strongly associated with *military power, violence, battle, death*, and *war*. See, for instance, 🔣 and ⚡.

⚡ is also a sign for *intense heat*. 🔲, for example, used in industrial engineering, represents an *electric melting oven*.

⚡ is used in some military systems, as in 🔲 for *liaison* and *signal company*. In computer flowcharting ⚡ indicates *communication links*.

In the Japanese **Art of warfare**, a treatise on military strategy from the end of the Middle Ages, ⌐ means *way, path*, or *street*, depending upon the surrounding signs.

⚡ and ⚡ are used in **comic strips** to mean *wrath* and *anger*. The sign is drawn close to the heads of the characters.

This well-known sign, a mirror image of the letter N, is one variation of the **Sigrune**, the **victory rune**.
   See ⚡, above, for more data.

A rune from the earliest runic alphabet whose name means *yew tree*. It is sometimes replaced by the sign ⚡, which in effect is ↾ turned 90 degrees.

From yew the best battle bows were made, and this rune is associated with *defense*.

For more details, turn to ⨎ in Group 34.

Yet another variation of the above entries' type of structure. The sign N is used in mathematics for an unknown number. Doubled it is also a general sign for an *unknown person* in Sweden (Mr. NN). The sign N also represents *north* or *northern*. Compare with S for *south* and + for *north*.

Z , the letter Z, is one of the signs for the highest god in Greek mythology, *Zeus*. In modern physics Z represents the greatest energy, *nuclear power*, in its potential form, *nuclear charge*.

In the English system of hobo signs it is a recommendation to other tramps meaning *present yourselves as former army soldiers*.

When Z appears in a more or less haphazard collection it becomes a "sound iconic" sign for *sleep* used in **comic strips**. It is usually drawn above the character supposed to be sleeping. A row of Zs can also represent a *humming sound*, such as insects or machines would make.

A rune from the earliest Nordic runic alphabet with a name meaning *hail*. It is associated with *accidents* and *misfortune*.

A sign for *cement* or *putty* used in seventeenth-century chemistry.

A seventeenth-century chemical sign for *caustic soda*.

A sign used in some meteorological systems for *lightning without thunder* or *flash of summer lightning*.

Two structures, ⚡ and ↑, both basic gestalts in Western ideography, are combined in this ideogram. The graph for *danger, heat, energy*, ⚡, is joined to the arrow sign, which stands for *directed movement*. It is the Western world's most common ideogram for *lightning, thunder*, and *high voltage electric current*. It is also a general sign for *mythology* in some dictionaries, and for the field of *electricity*.

When it appears in a photographic context (e.g., on cameras), it signifies *flashlight photography*. Turned upside down, ⚡, it is used to indicate *television station* on certain maps.

Compare with ⚡, *radio station*, on some maps.

As a sign for *lightning* it can be a synonym of the ancient sign ♆, Poseidon's or Neptune's staff, with which the god disturbed the seas.

An ideogram for *lightning and thunder* in meteorology.

In the United States ⌐⚡ is a meteorological sign for *thunderstorm of moderate intensity*.

A stylized **triskelion**, Greek for three-leg. See in Group 32.

This sign is associated with *progress* and *competition* and originated in ancient Greece, where it was used on coins.

Nowadays one can find ⚞ on the coat of arms of the Isle of Man, the island between Great Britain and Ireland.

The Isle of Man is inhabited by Celts, and ⚞ is related to ⚬ , an early Celtic sign. For more information, see ⚬ in Group 14.

A similar structure, ⅄, is used in electrical contexts to signify a certain type of *transformer winding*.

For a very similar structure used by a fascist organization, see ⊕ in Group 36.

This sign appears among the Egyptian hieroglyphs and is one of the signs representing *Egypt*. Mirrored and turned 90 degrees, it becomes ⊐, an ideogram for *self* in both early and more modern systems of Chinese writing.

In dictionaries ⊔⊓ is sometimes used to indicate a *compound word*.

Compare with ☰, a sign used on clothes in Ghana called **nkyin nyin**, meaning *transformation of self*.

A sign in the Egyptian hieroglyph system representing the land of *Egypt*. Compare with the synonym ⊔⊓, above. The form is associated with ℗, an ideogram for a *return* or a *homecoming*. Egypt may be considered the country one returns to, the homeland, or the land with reoccurring floods, a prerequisite for its continued existence (〰 for the water from the Nile combined with ℗ for returns).

Note that ▣ in the earliest Chinese writing system meant a *return* or a *coming back*.

A structure similar to the above entry is common in pre-Columbian America, found in what is now Colorado, all over Central America, and even in South America. It is often joined to "the stairs," ⌐⌐ , to become ⌐⌐⌐ .

In most cases this ideogram has a clockwise design, ⊒ , i.e., if one follows the line from the center outward the movement is clockwise. It does, however, sometimes appear the other way, ⊏⊐ , counterclockwise.

Both structures were common as decorative elements in ancient Greece. ⊒ is found, for instance, on a plate with a pictorial representation of the deeds of Jason. The plate can be dated back to around 500 B.C.

Jason was the famous seafaring mythological hero, who among other things set out on the quest to find the golden fleece of the ram, Aries. This myth, as the rows of ram sculptures on the temple in Karnak, Egypt, show, is probably a reference to the beginning of the Aries era around 2350 B.C. See the section "The symbolism of the astrological ages" in Part I for data about these eras.

Since Jason was a famous sea voyager the structure is possibly a combination of ∿∿∿ and ☽, i.e., the ideogram would in this case mean *sea voyages with safe returns* or *ocean travels*.

One of the multitude of signs in alchemy and early chemistry for *iron*. ∅, ⇌, and ♂ are synonymous.

This is an alchemical sign for *reverberating furnace*.
    ♄ is a synonym.

One of the signs for *earthed connection*, *earthed*, or *grounded* in electrical contexts. It is often seen on radios and household appliances, and ⟂ is a synonym.

Compare with ♀ for *suitable reading distance*.

One of the graphs for *Aquarius*. For more details about this zodiac sign, turn to ♒ in Group 14.

This ideogram used in ground-to-air emergency code means *all is well*. The sign is probably derived from the last two letters of the word *well*.

Group 17

Asymmetric, both soft and straight-lined, open signs with crossing lines

♃
♃
♃

This is the sign most commonly used in astronomy and astrology for the *planet Jupiter*. Jupiter moves in the sixth Bodian orbit from the sun (see **Bode's law**), has an orbital time of 12 years, and is the largest planet in the solar system. Jupiter is different from the other planets in that it radiates more energy (of radio-wave frequencies) than it receives from the sun. The Jupiter system with its 14 moons is in a way a *solar system within the solar system*.

It is strongly related to ☉), the sign for potential power. ♃ represents, according to the graphic symbolism of astrology, the personality or soul, ☽ , raised above and supported by the cross of matter, ✚. Through its experiences in the life on earth the soul acquires a wisdom that helps it to understand the universal laws of life.

The key word for ♃ is *expansion*. Jupiter also represents the *establishment*, the *structure of society*, *institutionalized religion*, *authorities*, and *well-meaning government*, as well as *sympathy* and *philanthropy*. When used in psychological astrology Jupiter indicates an *ability to understand and adapt to the established social structure* and the *instinct to expand one's knowledge*, for instance, via studies and travelling.

In the body, ♃ is closely associated with the *liver*, the *hip joints*, and the *pituitary gland*, as well as to the *nourishing processes* in general.

In the family of gods in Greek mythology ♃ represents *Zeus*, the highest of the gods, and his counterpart in Roman mythology, *Jupiter*. Zeus-Jupiter is the *ruler and protector of the home and family life*. On a higher level he is the *protector and ruler of the state and society*. In astrology ♃ is the *greater benefic* while ♀ is the *lesser benefic*, and ♄ is the *greater malefic, bringer of sorrow*, and the *one who deprives*. ♃ is a male planet, well placed in Cancer, ☉, which zodiacal sign is also closely associated with the home and family life. ♃ is the ruling planet of Sagittarius, ♐, and together with ♅,

Neptune, rules over Pisces, ♓. Jupiter's energies have difficulties expressing themselves in ♊, ♍, and ♑.

Due to the fact that a full orbit of Jupiter takes 12 years, ♃ has been used in botany to indicate *perennial plants.* Compare with ☉ and ♂, which signify plants with a life cycle of one year and two years, respectively.

Alchemists have used ♃ and similar signs (see the following four entry signs) to represent *tin, zinc,* and sometimes *electrum,* an alloy of silver and gold.

In cabbalistic mysticism ♃ is the sign of the *Angel Sachiel.*

These are all signs for the god *Zeus,* who played the dominating role in the Greek world of gods. Zeus was the son of Kronos (see ♄) and Ghe (Rhea, see ⊕) and the brother of Poseidon (see ♆) and Hades. He was equipped with the fish spear of thunderbolts. Zeus was the *almighty father* and the *ruler of the forces of weather.*

His counterpart in Roman mythology was *Jupiter.* See ♃ above and ♅ in Group 11.

The graphic symbol for Zeus could also be drawn Ƶ, Z, ∼, and Ƶ. For other possible meanings of these signs, see the following three entries.

A sign for *tin* and for *electrum* (an alloy made of silver and gold) in alchemy and early chemistry. Tin could also be drawn 7 and electrum, ♃.

One of the alchemical signs for *zinc*. ♂ was another sign used in early chemistry to represent *zinc*.

In fact, most of the signs for *Zeus* and for *Jupiter* were at some time or other used by the alchemists to symbolize zinc.

Saturn, the *god of plant growth, harvests, and triumphs*, was the Romans' equivalent to the Greek god Chronos. He was represented with the sign ♄, most likely a development of the sign for Chronos above, ♃.

♄ and ♄ are the most common ideograms for *Saturn*. This planet was already known to exist some 6000 years ago and has, up until the French Revolution at the end of the eighteenth century, represented the outermost boundary of the planetary system and the *measure when calculating long periods of time*.

The planet Saturn uses 29 earth years to orbit the sun and therefore a human lifespan can be measured approximately as two, or at the most three, of this planet's orbits. For this reason it is associated with death and the *Reaper*, the skeleton with the scythe who reaps men and women when their time is up.

Saturn has also become a symbol for *implacable powers*, *restrictions*, and the *relentless structures of the world of matter*.

In astrological symbolism ♄ graphically illustrates the idea that the receptive personality or soul, ☽, as opposed to the spirit, submits to the restrictions of matter, +. In astrology Saturn is known as the *greater malefic* (♂ is the *lesser malefic*), the *bringer of sorrow*, and the *one who takes things away*. But Saturn only brings sorrow and deprivation to those areas of a person's life that are based on illusions and unrealistic expectations. Saturn represents the *unrelenting aspect of reality* that forces the individual to abandon all ideas that are not based on a realistic perception of the material conditions of life.

A child is protected by his or her parents from physical and psychological harm. But for self-fulfillment the child must at some time be freed of this protective shield. Astrologers suggest that the personality protects the self, the spirit, or the true person, in a similar way. Through the imaginations, conceptions, and games of the personality, this inner being is protected until it no longer needs to be protected. Once this stage of development has been reached the outer shell must be broken. The position of Saturn in an individual's natal chart or horoscope reveals the way in which the protective shell is broken, the price that has to be paid for freedom, and the pain that has to be endured during the process of rebirth. If the implications of Saturn are ignored the planet becomes a symbol for *deprivations, inhibitions,* and *hardship.*

♄ has become a sign associated with *duty, responsibility, discipline,* and *work.* In the same way as ♃ signifies *expansion* in the horoscope, ♄ represents the principle of *contraction and consolidation.*

In the outer world Saturn stands for *permanent structures* such as *buildings, heavy machinery,* and *banking* and for *civil servants.* As far as the body is concerned it is associated with the *skeleton and teeth,* the hardest structures in the body and those that support it.

Saturn has long since been perceived as the ruling planet of ♑ and ♒, Capricorn and Aquarius.

Since the discovery of the three extra-Saturnian planets after the end of the Middle Ages, Saturn has had to share its traditional rulership. ♅ has become the ruling planet of ♒. Saturn is considered well placed in ♊ and ♎ and less favorably in ♈ and ♋.

♄ and ♃ often function as opposites in medieval symbolism, where ♄ was associated with *Satan,* the *Tester.*

In alchemy ♄ became the most important sign for *lead.* Botanists have used it to represent *tree-like plants,* i.e., plants

that are not bush-like with life cycles of many years (as opposed to one-year, $\odot$, and two-year, σ, life cycle plants and
to bushes with life cycles of several years, ♃). In this meaning ♄ is synonymous with ♄, ♄, and 5.

The sign used to represent the god *Kronos* or *Chronos* from
Greek mythology. He was the son of Uranus and Ge, the
oldest god and the earth goddess. Chronos castrated his
father with the help of Ge's relatives, the Titans, and by this
act made himself master of heaven and earth.

Chronos was told, however, that one of his children
would revolt against him and take control of his kingdoms.
To prevent this he swallowed all his children except one.
This was Zeus, who tricked his father into swallowing a
stone instead of him. Later, Zeus forced his father to vomit
up his brothers and sisters, after which he forced Chronos
into exile. Although Chronos no longer had any power in
the world of the gods, he remained the *ruler of time.*

Chronos became thereby the *god of fertility and harvest.*
Great festivals were organized in his honor. He is also believed to have been a model for *Father Christmas*, who loves
children and gives presents to those children who have
behaved well.

Chronos was associated, as has already been said, with
the passage of time and the slowest of the then-known planets, *Saturn* (see ♄ in this group). Saturn took so long to orbit
the earth that its cycle, roughly the time span of one human
generation, became a measure of time. The words *chronome-
ter* and *chronology* are derived from Chronos.

A variation among the signs for *Zeus* and/or *Jupiter*. It has
also been used for *steel* in alchemy. σ and Ⓐ were other
signs for *steel*. ♃ could sometimes stand for *tin foil*.

An alchemical sign for *tin oxide*. It is derived from the most common of the alchemists' signs for tin, the Jupiter sign ♃.

This sign comes from an ancient Greek natal chart (horoscope) and probably represented *Chronos*, the *planet Saturn*. Other early signs for Chronos are ∨ᵉ and ∿°.

A sign used in the English and U.S. systems of hobo signs. It means *knock here — if you have what they want then they'll buy* (England) and *stay here* (U.S.).

These two signs represent the *asteroid Ceres*. At the end of the eighteenth century a German astronomer, Johann Bode, discovered that it was possible to calculate the distance of a planet's orbital path from the sun by taking Mercury as 0 and Venus as 3, doubling this number for each new planet, and then adding 4 and dividing by 10. This calculation yielded for Mercury 0.4 and for Venus 0.7. The actual distances from the sun (counted in units of the distance from the earth to the sun) are 0.39 and 0.72, respectively.

There are only three exceptions to **Bode's law** known today: the first is Neptune, ♆, the mystical planet, which has its own individual orbit, and the third is Chiron (see ⚷ in Group 54), while the second is an "empty orbit" between Mars and Jupiter. In the beginning of the eighteenth-century, however, astronomers discovered first one and then a large number of asteroids, i.e., space rocks that vary in size from a diameter of a few meters to over 80 kilometers. Ceres is the largest of the asteroids and the first to have been discovered. It is drawn ⚳ or ⚳. *Ceres* was the name of an *ancient Italian* *goddess of plants and growth*, who later was incorporated in the Roman mythology.

Other important asteroids are Pallas, drawn ⚴, ⚴, or ♀; Juno, drawn ⚵, ♀, or ⚵; and Vesta, drawn ⚶, ⚶, ⚶, or ⚶

In botany ♄ can stand for *weeds*.

A sign sometimes used by alchemists to represent a compound of lead and sulphur, *lead sulphate*. This sign is a combination of ♄ for *lead* and an extra cross from the sign for *sulphur*, ⚴.

♄ can also stand for *lead foil*.

One of the signs for *lime* in early chemistry. Lime was also drawn ♅, ♃, ⊗, ♃, ♃, and ☉.

Quicklime was drawn ⊏ and otherwise.

A sign for *limestone* in early chemistry and late alchemy. See also the entry above.

One of the signs used in alchemy and early chemistry for *arsenic*. The sign ⚶ is one of a couple of synonyms.

For more information on arsenic and alchemy, turn to ♈ in Group 5.

This sign has been used in alchemy to represent *sulphur*. This element was usually drawn ⇴.

See ⇴ in Group 39.

An alchemical sign for *oil*. Usually oil was drawn ⊹. Turn to ⊹ in Group 48 for several synonyms assembled.

A sign used in chess contexts in England for *check!* The dagger, †, is a more common synonym.

An English chess sign for *takes and checks*.

A modern ideogram found, for example, on hi-fi system appliances to denote *loudness*, the *control for reducing the middle range*. It is used at lower volumes to achieve an adequate sound. It sometimes appears drawn in a frame.

Another sign for *band frequency filter* is ≋, meaning *filter that strengthens the middle range*.

This sign, like the above entry, also appears on hi-fi appliances and signifies a *filter that reduces the lower frequency band*. The opposite is ≈, a *filter that reduces the high frequency band*.

This ideogram is used in mathematical and geometrical systems, as well as others, to mean *not similar to*, *not congruent with*, and more. Compare with ≃ for approximate equality or congruence.

An alchemical sign for *vitriol*. For further information about vitriols, turn to ⇗ in Group 18.

Some signs are difficult to place in one group. Does this sign have crossing lines or not? I have chosen to put it in both Group 17 and Group 18. The data, however, are mainly given at the entry in Group 18.

One of the alchemists' signs for *putreficatio*, the *processes of rotting*. ⇇ is a synonym.

See the discussion of alchemy in Part I for more data about *putrefacatio*'s place in the alchemists' strategy.

An alchemical sign for *mix* or *mixture*. ℋ is a synonym.

See also △ in Group 22.

One of the alchemists' **time signs,** meaning *summer*.

A variation of the graphical sign for *Scorpio*. For more information about this zodiac sign, turn to in Group 18.

This variation of the cross is known as a **Roman holy cross**. It has a **swastika** at its center, and it perhaps alludes to the return of Christ or to Christ as a source of energy.

See ⅏ in Group 15 for the meanings of the swastika.

Group 18

Asymmetric, both soft and straight-lined, open signs without crossing lines

The straight line joined to a uniformly curved line to form an open sign is a common structure in Western ideography. It was once used as a sign for the goddess *Aphrodite*, the ancient Greek goddess corresponding to the Roman *Venus*. Aphrodite was also drawn ⌀, ♀, ♀, and ♀.

The same structure is used in a modern electrical context to signify *sliding contact*.

Slightly changed, ∿ becomes ↑, one of the many signs for *mercury* used in alchemy and early chemistry. For synonyms, turn to ♀ in Group 41:a.

Turned 90 degrees the above entry becomes the sign for the *number 2*. In certain meteorological systems 2 can signify *difficult, strong,* or *intensive* when describing weather conditions.

Compare with ♃, the sign for *Zeus* or *Jupiter*, the *god of weather, lightning, and thunder*. See also ☉, the old Greek graph for Leo and for the sun's energy (in Group 50).

In the variation ⟍, the same structure as the above entries stands for *cirro-stratus clouds* in certain meteorological systems.

Turned into a mirror image, the above entries form one of the signs in alchemy for *calcination*. When one calcinated a substance one transformed it into a powder through the application of intense heat. Note here a similarity of meaning with 2 above.

Calcination could also be drawn ♈ and ♅.

One of the signs for a *biennial plant.* Other signs that signify the same idea are ⊙ , ♂, and ⊙ .

Compare with the similar ↓ in musical notation for *soprano clef.*

This rune from the earliest runic alphabet is yet another example of the straight line combined with the circle segment to form an open sign. Its name is believed to have meant *aurochs* and later possibly *slag* or *dross.* According to Eddan, this rune was used as a *help against soot, sorrow, and disputes.*

This is a rune from a later Nordic runic alphabet with a name that most probably meant *boil* or *abscess.* Compare with the rune ⟨ from the earliest runic alphabet, which seems to have had the same name and meaning.

This rune was also used on the medieval **clog calendars** as the sign for *Saturday.* For more information about clog calendars, turn to ⽊ in Group 5.

This last example of an open sign composed by a straight line joined to a uniform curve is from the U.S. system of hobo signs. Its meaning was *here they'll take care of you if you are ill.* Compare with \/, *only the ill are given something,* used in the Swedish system of hobo signs.

A sign for *lapis lazuli* in alchemy. This stone is a dark blue sodium mineral, often used in jewelry, mosaics, etc. It was also the stone used, in former days, to produce *ultramarine,* a rich, deep blue and very expensive paint or coloring pigment.

Compare with ⚡ , similar in structure and found in the U.S. system of hobo signs with the meaning *leave quickly*.

This is the most common ideogram for the *planet Saturn* in print. It also signifies all that this particular planet represents in astronomy and astrology. For more information on Saturn and the Greek god Chronos, turn to ♄ in Group 17. For details as to Saturn's significance in astronomy and astrology, turn to ♄, also in Group 17.

In botany, signs that are in some way related to Saturn, such as ♄, ♄, and ♄, denote that a plant has a *woody stem* or *small bushes with woody stems*.

In cabbalistic mysticism ♄ also appears as a sign for the *angel Cassiel*.

An early chemistry sign for *vitriol*. Vitriols are compounds of sulphur and some metal. They are formed when a metal is dissolved in sulphuric acid and the liquid then is allowed to evaporate. In earlier times sulphuric acid (see ⊕) was made by roasting iron vitriol, ⊞. Vitriol usually referred to *copper sulphate*. Sulphuric acid was often referred to as *vitriol oil*.

Vitriol could also be drawn ⊕+, ⊕+, and otherwise

One of the signs for the god and planet *Zeus/Jupiter*. See ♃ in Group 17 for more data.

Compare with the staff sign 𓏞 from ancient Egyptian pictorial representations.

This well-known structure was already in use in the third century B.C. in India and denoted the *number 3*. � is also the sign in ancient Greece for the measure *drachma*: a *handful*. The drachma was also (and still is) a Greek coin.

The sign for the old measure *ounce*. ꒳ also meant *little* or a *small amount*, and was formerly used in pharmaceutical contexts.

A sign used in early chemistry to denote *alcohol*. It could also be drawn ᵛ̇, with S for *spiritus* or *essence*, the finest and most spiritual substance in wine, that which evaporates first.

Other signs used to represent alcohol were ✡ and, more commonly, ♉.

A sign for *aqua regia* or *aqua regalis*, Latin for king's water. Aqua regia was a mixture of three parts concentrated hydrochloric acid to one part concentrated nitric acid. It was used by the alchemists to dissolve gold. Gold was different from other metals, for it withstood the usual acids and other dissolvants.

King's water was also drawn ⊖.

The **curved arrow** is an extremely old sign found on the walls of prehistoric caves in Western Europe. Today, ↗ is used as a meteorologic and cartographic sign indicating *constant winds*.

The **wavy arrow** is a common sign for *sea currents* on maps and nautical charts, etc. Sea currents are also represented by the signs and ⟫→.

⌁→ is a combination of the sign for *water*, ⌁⌁ , and ↑, the sign for *directed movement*.

A modern ideogram with the basic meaning *mix*. One can find it, for instance, on washing machines, where it signifies *careful treatment, careful wash*, or the *washing of delicate fabrics*.

In old pharmacology *to mix* or *to blend* was represented by the sign ₩.

One of a handful of modern ideograms for *recycling* of cans, bottles, and packaging. These appear on posters advocating recycling, on packages, etc. They usually are composed of two or three curved arrows, more or less stylized. See, for instance, 🜩 (Group 36).

This ideogram is used in some mathematical, geometrical, and other sign systems with the meaning *isomorph* or *congruent*, i.e., *of the same form as*. It can also mean *approximately equal to*. Taking the equals sign, $=$, as a starting point, the upper line is replaced by the sign for a *complete oscillation*, ∿. This implies an equality in one dimension and a variation in another.

Compare with ∿, meaning *frequency*.

In electrical contexts ≅ signifies *alternating current*, which also can be drawn ∿, ≈, and ≋.

∿ often appears in unexpected places, for example, in ɪ̃H̃S̃ , one of the many **Jesus monograms** of the type used at the beginning of the seventeenth century. In Latin the monogram IHS can be interpreted as *I(n) H(oc) S(igno) vinces* =

under this sign you will be victorious; or *I(esus) H(ominem) S(alvator)* = Jesus, Saviour of Men. As ∿ is the sign representing a complete oscillation, it might be that ∿ in ⲓⲏⲋ refers to Christ's defeat and victory, death and resurrection.

A modern ideogram with the basic meaning of *evaporation* or *drying*, from 〰, for *water vapor*.

This ideogram is found on household appliances, etc.

Compare with 〰 in Group 14, which stands for *steam* or *evaporation*.

One sign for *sandstorm* or *duststorm* from U.S. meteorology. Compare with ∂, *cyclone*, and 𝕊, *dust devil*.

Compare also with ≡ for *mist* or *fog* in some meteorological systems.

Known as the **whip**, this sign means, when appearing in the margin of a letter, *supplement or supplements are enclosed*. If it appears with a number, for example, ⅗ , it denotes the number of supplements enclosed.

A slight variation of the above, ⁄ , is a trade and commerce sign meaning *minus* or *with a reduction of*.

Compare these signs with the *repeat* signs in musical notation, :‖ and :‖‖ , and with the sign ∷ used in geometry to denote *proportion*.

One of the many alchemical signs for *mercury*. It was also a sign for the *planet Mercury*, ☿ . For most of the other signs used to represent mercury, turn to ♀ in Group 41:a.

A seldom-used sign for *iron* in alchemy. It was more common to use ♂, the sign for the *planet Mars*.
See the word index for more synonyms.

An alchemical sign for *reverberating furnace*.
⛝ is synonymous.

These are the most common drawn or handwritten graphs for the zodiac sign *Scorpio*. ♏ is more common in printed texts.

The symbol representing this section of the zodiac is a scorpion about to sting its assailant. The graph is believed to have been derived from the Hebrew letter *mem* with the scorpion's tail added. Others suggest that the diagonal, upward-pointing arrow represents Mars, ♂, the sign's ruling planet according to the old astrological tradition. (As is often the case in astrological and other early symbolism, both elements are in fact incorporated in one sign.)

The sun enters the sign of Scorpio around 23 October and exits again around 21 November. Traditionally, ♏ is closely associated with *birth*, the *sexual act*, and *death*. Astrologers consider individuals born with the sun in this sign to be characterized by decisiveness, determination, strong willpower, and, if they are hurt, vindictiveness. They are also believed to have an almost hypnotic power over others by means of their gaze.

According to the old tradition, Mars was the ruling planet. When, however, the remaining three planets had been discovered, astrologers in the West (those in India have chosen not to incorporate ♅, ♆, and ♇ into their system) changed the ruling planet to Pluto. Since ♇ was discovered well into the twentieth century, this rulership is of a very recent origin in comparison with the old one.

The planets ♀ and ☽ are considered badly placed in ♏.

♏ belongs to the **quadruplicity** of fixed signs, which means that those born in this sign are supposed to be consequential, loyal and trustworthy, followers of tradition, and persistent. See ⬤ in Group 30 for more data about the fixed quality.

♏ also belongs to the **triplicity**, or element, water, symbolized ▽. Those born in a sign belonging to the element of water are supposed to be dominated by their feelings, to be very sensitive and reserved, and to have a great sympathy for others. Their feelings dominate their intellect. For further data about the astrological element of water, see △ in Group 28.

The alchemists used ♏ to signify the process of *separation*. See the sections on alchemy in Part I for data about this process.

Group 19

Single-axis symmetric, soft, closed signs with crossing lines

This sign is used in the U.S. system of hobo signs to mean *court of law* or *police station*.

Compare with § from the same system, meaning *here lives a judge*.

The first *Olympic Games* are said to have taken place in the year 776 B.C. in ancient Greece. They were held in honor of Zeus at the foot of the mountain of the gods, Olympus. The event was repeated every four years.

These games ceased to be held sometime during antiquity. In 1893 this old tradition was reestablished by Baron Pierre de Coubertin, and the first Olympic Games in modern times were held in Athens in 1896.

The five circles probably symbolize the *five continents of the world*. Logically, there ought to have been six, as North and South America are counted as separate continents. However, the number five is also related to the planet Venus, ♀ (symbol for the instinct to seek the company of other humans), and thereby to the four-year period between the games. For more details about Venus and the four-year period, see ⊕ in Group 29.

Compare with ⊙⊙, the sign for *married*, and with ⊗, the sign representing the highest form of togetherness, the *community of the Holy Trinity*.

A common design pattern in Nordic ethnic art during the Viking era. This pattern was often carved or painted as a **plaited sign**.

See ⚛ in Group 34 for some signs that often were drawn plaited.

This is the logo of the Japanese car manufacturer *Toyota*. Since there are so few Western signs in this structural group, is shown here as an example of the type of graphs belonging to this group.

Group 20

Single-axis symmetric, soft, closed signs without crossing lines

This sign represents the *moon as a new moon*, i.e., a few days after its conjunction with the sun (☽ ⚹ ☉). In actual fact it is an iconic sign and therefore does not really belong in this dictionary of non-iconic graphic symbols. But owing to its fundamental role in Western ideography — and in astrology, the earliest Western symbol system — it could not be left out without detracting from our understanding of Western ideography.

☽ is first and foremost a general sign for the earth's satellite, the *moon*. It is used as such in astronomy, astrology, and alchemy.

Astrologers, moreover, use it to signify a complex of psychological factors. While the sun, ☉, represents the endless and infinite creative energy that is available to the individual, the moon's function is to give form to this energy and help realize its potential.

For this reason ☽ in astrology symbolizes *all that is receptive in humankind*, the *instinct*, the *subconscious*, the *emotional life*, and the *ability to react*. The key word is *personality*, the inner individual's outer shell that is continually formed and changed by what he or she experiences. ☽ also symbolizes the *mother*, and in a man's horoscope it signifies *women* in general, in particular his *wife* or *partner*.

☽ rules the sign of Cancer, ♋, all those professions that are related to the fields and to food and children, and those associated with the sea or the sea flora and fauna. ☽ is the *female*, or *receptive factor*, of the being.

As a general symbol for the personality, the outer, receptive shell of the inner individual, ☽ is synonymous in the graphic symbolism of astrology with ☽. For example, in ☿ it means that the receptive part of the being, the personality, ∪, is directed upward toward the world of ideas, while the individual, ○, is still linked to the hindrances of the world of matter, +, yet rises above them, i.e., is rational and is not dominated by things and material considerations, but

instead dominates matter thanks to a sensitivity for and re-
ception of higher impulses.

☽ is used in alchemy to represent the metal *silver*. Silver
was also drawn ⏃, ◡, ⏃, and otherwise.

When used in astronomy and in calendars ☽ stands for
the *first phase of the moon* or the *first quarter*, i.e., that period
of the month when those living in the Northern Hemisphere
can see the half moon with its curved side facing right. The
first quarter is sometimes also represented by the sign ◖.
Compare with ●, the sign for the *new moon,* the time when
the moon is not visible at all from the earth because it is too
close to the sun; ○, the *full moon;* and ◑, the *last quarter.*

This sign does not, like the preceding entry, mean the moon
in general, but the *waning moon,* i.e., the *crescent* that can be
seen just before the sun rises for a few days each month. A
very similar sign for the waning moon is ☾, which, together
with the sign for Venus as the *Morning star,* i.e., the goddess
of war, ★, appears on the flags of several countries of
Muslim faith. For more information, turn to ☪ in Group 24.

☾ sometimes represents the *last quarter of the moon,* i.e.,
the moon as a half-moon, seen in the morning with its
curved side to the left in the Northern Hemisphere. It is also
drawn ◑. See ☽ for other signs for the *phases of the moon* in
calendars, etc.

☾ in combination with a star (probably a symbol for the
planet and god Jupiter, who was much worshipped at the
time) was on the coat of arms of the Roman province
Illyricum (roughly today's Yugoslavia) during the reign of
Emperor Hadrian. Around this time, 200-100 B.C., the same
symbol was used on the coat of arms of Constantinople.
This city became the capital of the East Roman Empire,
Byzantium, when the Roman Empire was divided.

A Turkish sultan is said to have used ☾ as his sign around 1100 B.C. After the conquest of Constantinople by the Turks in 1453, ☾ became a symbol for the sultan or emperor of the Turks and thereby for the Ottoman Empire and, later, for Turkey.

It is not likely that the star on the Constantinople coat of arms before the Turkish conquest was drawn as the Venus star, i.e., like ✩ or ✩. It might well have been six-pointed, ✳, like Jupiter's six-pointed staff.

In the twentieth century ☾ has become the main symbol on the flags of many Arab countries and nowadays is a general symbol for the Islamic faith.

❨ is used to symbolize the *Red Crescent*, the organization in the Islamic world that is equivalent to the Red Cross in the West.

This sign was also used to represent the *archangel Gabriel* in cabbalistic mysticism.

The horizontal moon sign, �, signifies the *Arabic League*, a union of Islamic states.

The iconic sign ⌣ represents the *new or waning moon* seen in the region of the Equator and was a symbol for the *moon god Sin*, the *god of vegetation* in the Euphrates culture between 2000 and 1000 B.C. Note that ◡ was also a common sign in the Euphrates culture during the same period. It probably had the same meaning as ⌣.

Compare with ⌢ from the Egyptian hieroglyphic system.

⌣ appears as a **cadence sign** for the *second son*. For more details about the cadence signs, turn to ▰ in Group 22.

This Egyptian hieroglyph may represent the *moon*, although the moon can never be observed in this position from the earth in relation to the horizon (except on those rare occasions when there occurs a partial eclipse and the earth shadows only the lower part of the moon).

In the Hittite hieroglyphic system the similar sign ⌒ signified the *moon* and the *month*.

For those people living near the Equator this iconic sign represents the *new or waning moon together with a planet*, most probably *Venus* as the *Morning or Evening star*. See ⊛ in Group 29.

☻ was common in the Phoenician cultural sphere about 2000 years ago. Today it appears, for instance, on the walls of buildings in Tibet.

Similar in structure are ∪, the **fermata**, a *pause* in musical notation; the U.S. hobo sign ⌒; and ☻ in ॐ, the Indian graph for the greeting of peace, **aum**, where ☻ represents the *state of transcendental consciousness*.

Note that ☻ appears in the Mayans' hieroglyphic system, probably with the same meaning, i.e., *the new or waning moon together with Venus*.

These two graphs are less common variations of the sign for the *planet Pluto*. Pluto is also drawn ♇ and ♀.

The sign's structure is associated with Pluto's orbital path, which is far more elliptic than those of the other planets.

For more information, turn to ♇ in Group 54.

This ideogram is very old. It was a symbol for the *moon god Nannan* and, later, *Sin* in the Euphrates-Tigris region. The sign has most likely been in use from around 2500 B.C. During the Babylonian times it appeared with ❋ and ❋ for the *Venus god* and the *Sun god*, respectively. See these signs in Group 26 and Group 25.

The structurally almost identical ◐ and ◑ appear today in astronomy and almanacs signifying the *first* and *last quarters*, respectively. As a technical engineering sign ◎ is used for a specific type of *compressor*.

This is a cartographic sign that sometimes appears with the meaning *spring* or *well*. It is also drawn ○.

Compare with ◒, *water reservoir*, or *well*.

Note that when ○ is used as a sign for one of the four elements it represents *water*. See, for example, ◬ and ⚲ in Group 24.

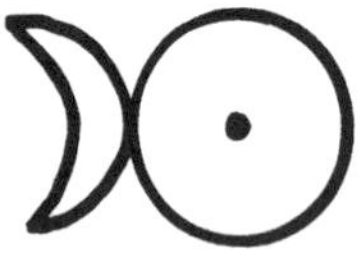

A sign for *platinum*, a metal discovered around the middle of the eighteenth century and proven an element of its own by Scheffer (see bibliography). The sign, used by Scheffer for this new element, is a combination of the sign for *silver*, ☽, and that for *gold*, ☉.

Platinum is gray and shiny, similar to silver. It is resistant to many acids and does not oxidate. Like gold, it is very expensive and has a high density (almost double that of lead), hence ☉.

☉ and ☽☉ are also closely related in that the atom number (number of protons) of gold is 79, whereas that of platinum is 78.

Platinum could also be drawn ♁.

A sign in early chemistry for *water*. In Dalton's chemical sign system from the beginning of the nineteenth century, ○ was the sign for *oxygen*, while ⊙ stood for *hydrogen*. Water is a compound of the elements oxygen and hydrogen.

In the earliest chemistry, i.e., alchemy, water as a substance was represented by ⚥, ▽, and ⊞, while as an element it was often represented by the empty circle in the Middle Ages. In other contexts that were not directly related to chemistry, water could appear as 〰, ○, ∿, or ∿. Compare with ⦂ , ∴, and ∴ for different types of rain.

This is a very modern ideogram for *stereo sound* in radios, tape recorders, TV ads, etc.

This sign appears in nearly all modern-day books and magazines. It stands for *copyright*. The *writer's lawful right to his or her own writings* was not self-evident during the first centuries after the discovery of printing. Books before the time of Gutenberg were hand-written copies of earlier works and were considered the property of, if not the public, then the monastery or center of learning in whose library they were kept. It was not until 1709, in England, and then 1866, through the Bern convention, that the author's right of ownership was almost universally accepted.

○, for *endless possibilities*, is restricted by the letter C, or C, for *copyright*, written within the circle. It illustrates a common mode in Western ideography. See, for example, 50, an international ideogram for the *highest permitted speed* on some public roads.

The **smile sign** or **acid sign**. See the synonymous ☺ in Group 24 for more data.

This sign is used in phonetics to signify a *long sound like that of the u in fur*. The variation ◌ represents a *short o-sound like that in cook*.

In botany this sign may mean *stamen*.

The **heart sign** is as old as ▦, ⋎, ◎ , ⍓, ⛫, ⅄, and ♀. Its meaning for the people living in Europe before the Ice Age, of course, is not known.

Graphically ♡ is related to ⌒, the sign for *fire* and for *flight* in the Middle Ages, and one of the most common signs in Western ideography. It is also related to ⋎, Aries, and to ∞, for *union* or *togetherness*.

It is possible that ♡ began as ♡, an iconic sign for the body's heart. Nowadays, at least in Sweden, ♡ is strongly associated with the *behind* and *defecation*, as it is the sign used to denote a *toilet* for both sexes. On the whole, however, the heart does not appear in any established sign system. It is an anarchistic graph that has yet to find a place in any serious context. It is well known throughout the Western world and signifies *togetherness* or *love*, especially *sexual love, make love,* and *like*.

One sign that is often associated physically to ♡ is ⇻, the arrow, a symbol for *directed energy, flow, penetration, victory,* or *death*. See ♂ in Group 53.

★ and ☆ are other signs that sometimes appear with the heart. The combination stands for *party, togetherness, happiness,* and *favorable opportunity*. It is interesting to note that ◌ is a variation of the Arabic sign for the *number 5*.

The heart sign appears as a symbol in all important cultures. ♡ signifies love in the Christian trilogy of *belief, hope, and love*. It also appears with a religious or "good, positive" meaning among Aztecs, Hindus, Buddhists, Muslims, Jews, Celts, and Taoists.

In ancient Greece the heart sign was related to 𝄞, the *lyre*, attribute of Eros, the god of sexual love (together with the flower) around 600–400 B.C. Later, the attributes of the Greek Eros, his Roman counterpart Amor, and even Cupid (Latin = desire) were changed to the bow and arrow. On a Greek amphora from around 500 B.C. one can see ♡ used as "wreath leaves" placed on the head of Dionysus, the god of wine and feasting. The sign is also used in Africa: see ♥ and ♡. It also appears in early heraldry, for example, on the coat of arms of Magnus Ladulås from the thirteenth century, a Swedish king known for his work to ensure the safety and sanctity of women and to stop the knights' and soldiers' stealing from the peasants.

To find graphical opposites to the symmetric, soft, closed ♡ one has to look for the simplest of those structures that are asymmetric, straight-lined, and open with crossing lines, such as ⚡.

A **heart sign in red** is a symbol for the highest or next highest valued suit of the four suits of the deck of cards. ♥ has appeared in decks of cards since the fifteenth century. Hearts are a symbol for *love, family life,* and *growth*.

It can be added that the biggest bank in the world, the Japanese D.K.B., has chosen the heart sign as its logo in the form ♥.

Diamonds is the suit of cards ranked next lowest in games like whist, bridge, etc. Diamonds are associated with *courage* and *energy*. Turn to ◇ in Group 28, a straight-lined sign that is used for diamonds in some decks and for other meanings.

A sign for *pebbles* (or *mountain crystal*) in alchemy.

This sign is named **xomsa** or **khamsa** (the *number 5*, in Arabic). It is the *hand of Fatima*, the Prophet's favorite daughter. *Khamsa* is a *symbol of good fortune*. It stood for the *support group*, the *blood revenge group*, or the *closest male relatives*, not further than five degrees of relationship from one another. Note that ☆, also closely related to the number 5, is common in the Arab world.

Compare with ⚜, which appears between the arms of the cross on the medal for the Johannites-Maltese Order. Is this an ideographic remain from the crusaders' wars against and final defeat by the Muslims?

This is one of the alchemists' signs for *honey*. Honey was also drawn ◌, ⚥, ㅍ, and in other ways.

This is in fact not an iconic sign, although it is usually thought of as one, because a water drop is spherical in form.

▲ is a modern ideogram that appears on household appliances and machines and signifies that it is *safe against splash* and *can be used outdoors under cover*.

When this sign is doubled, ▲▲, it means that the machine is *waterproof*.

Compare with ▣ for *sprinkle-proof design* and with ⚠ for *rinse-proof design*.

Signs of this form but not filled, ◊, are common in comic strips. They are drawn as three or more "drops" around the head of a character, like ₃°°, to signify *embarrassment* or *fear*.

A variation of the **pointed cross** is the **heraldic dagger**, a very common sign in printed texts.

In typography the sign †, along with ✳, is used as a sign for *note*, i.e., an *amendment to the main text*. In botany the dagger means *poisonous*, in chess, *check!* In timetables it means *Sunday* or *holiday*. In genealogy it is used for *deceased* or *dead*. In dictionaries it indicates an *obsolete word*, and again in botany it may mean a *once cultivated but now wild growing plant*.

This variation of the above sign means *checkmate!* in chess. The *game is over*.

The sign ǂ is a synonym.

Group 21

Single-axis symmetric, straight-lined, closed signs with crossing lines

A sign for *strong fire* or *vigorous heating* in alchemy. It is a combination of △, the sign most commonly representing the element of *fire* in the Middle Ages.

Compare with ⚡ and ⚡⚡ and with ⋀⋀ and ∞, which all have roughly the same meaning.

One of the many signs for *silver* in alchemy. It was also drawn as ☽, ⌣, and ⚬⚬.

Compare with ☖ in Group 22.

The sign in cabbalistic mysticism for *Hagith*, the *fifth of the Olympic spirits* or the *spirit of Venus*.

Compare with the structurally similar ⚘, one of the many signs for *lime* in alchemy.

This design was found on a Norwegian Viking era tapestry. It is believed to have had a religious significance.

For more information, see 井 in Group 27.

This sign is used in computer flow charting to signify *storage in the internal memory*. Compare with ⊂, *online storage*, and with ▽, for *offline storage*.

Group 22

Single-axis symmetric, straight-lined, closed signs without crossing lines

The single-axis symmetric **triangle** can hardly be said to have any meaning in itself; rather, it is a variation of the multi-axis symmetric or equilateral triangle. See △ in Group 28.

Pointed upward it is associated with *fire* and *divine power*. It was used in both the Egyptian and the Hittite hieroglyphic systems. In the latter system △ represented *mu, city*. The ideogram △△ stood for *country* or *kingdom*.

This sign represented the *king* in the Hittite hieroglyphic system. The vertical line, |, signifying *oneness, unique being*, and *authority*, is combined with △ for *power* and *divinity*. Compare with the modern traffic sign composed of an equilateral triangle with a vertical line, ⚠ , which stands for *danger* or *drive carefully*.

The similar ⚠ is used in some Oxford dictionaries for *"words that are likely to cause embarrassment or anger if they are used in the wrong situation"* or *"taboo words."*

The above entry turned upside down is found in some English meteorology, meaning *threatening skies*. Note that the upside down triangle represented the *element of water* in the Middle Ages.

The sign denoted *woman* in prehistoric times and was used by the Sumerians from about 3000 B.C.

Compare with ⩒ for *vulva* or *vagina*, also a prehistoric sign.

The triangle pointing upward, signifying the *element of fire* during the Middle Ages, with a horizontal line added in it, or across it as in ⟁ , became the most common sign for the *element of air*. Air could also be drawn ⩫ and in other ways.

This is the alchemists' most common sign for the *element of earth*. For more information on the elements, turn to in Group 28.

The *earth* element could also be drawn ▽.

In modern times ▽ is used as a computer sign for *offline data storage*. See ☐ in Group 21 for related computer signs.

A sign found on video machines and tape recorders for *eject control*, i.e., the lever or control button one presses to eject the tape. It is synonymous with **II**.

A sign on videotape recorders and other tape recorders. It means *play* or indicates the control button for playing the tape. It is also drawn ▷.

When it appears doubled and is pointing to the right, like ▷▷, it means *fast forward winding* or *image finding*.

An ideogram on radios and other household appliances for *volume control*. Synonymous with **|** and ⌒.

This sign denotes *modem*, MOdulator-DEModulator, and is used both in computer contexts and in tele-engineering. A modem is an appliance that transforms signals from a computer so that they can be sent via telephone lines.

⊞ is one sign for *modulator* and ⊟ is one sign for *demodulator* used in some technical contexts.

One of the alchemists' signs for *mixture*.
   Compare with the alchemists' ⅝ and ⅗ for *mix*.

A modern New Age sign for *crystal*.

An alchemical sign for *strong fire* or *intense heat*. See ⚼ in Group 21 for more signs with this meaning.

This sign has been used for *air* in old chemistry.
   Compare with the more common synonymous sign ⚕ and with △ in this group.

A sign representing the *quincunx* or *inconjunct* aspect in astrology: a 150-degree angle between planets as seen from the earth.
   With this aspect the planets lie in signs of opposite polarity. It is considered a difficult and disharmonic aspect, although not as difficult as ☐ . More common for quincunx is ⚻.

A sign on cameras indicating *zoom*.

A rune from the Nordic runic alphabet with the name **bjarkan**, i.e., the *birch*. It is associated with *new life* and *growth*.

One of the signs from the **Faistos disco** (see ⊛ in Group 26).

The **chevron** structure is one of the earliest ideograms and much later became a common sign in heraldry.

See ∧ in Group 4 for more data on the meaning and for similar signs like ∨, ∧, and ⟨.

One of the many signs for *alcohol* in alchemy. It was also drawn V̌ and ⊶⊙⊦.

Compare with ❖, the modern sign for *narcotics* in pharmaceutical catalogues.

A sign used in some English meteorological systems to denote *ground frozen hard and dry*. ☐ has long been a sign for the *ground*.

Compare with the alchemical sign ⊡ , *urine (liquid on the ground)*; ⊡ in meteorology, representing *flooded ground*; and ⊠ in the same system for *ground covered by snow*.

☐ in Group 21 is structurally somewhat similar.

A sign on video and other tape recorders indicating the *on/off switch for the radio function*.

A Swedish hobo sign for *be careful, angry dogs and/or violent people here.* It is made by combining ∿ , *angry dog,* and ▭ , *violent and brutal house owner.*

Compare with ∿ , *barking dog,* and ▨ , *violent house owner,* from the English system of hobo signs.

One of the signs for *salt alkali* in seventeenth-century chemistry.

These substances were also drawn ⚱ and in other ways.

A sign for *borax* or *tinkal,* from eighteenth-century chemistry. Borax is a white powder used for porcelain enamelling and glass production.

Synonymous signs were ⵣ and 4.

Cadence signs were introduced in heraldry during the sixteenth century and signified the *order in which the sons were born.* ⟅⟆ and ⟆⟇ were signs indicating the *eldest son.* The second, third, and fifth sons, respectively, were indicated by ⌣, ☆, and ○. The remaining cadence signs were iconic. ⚜ indicated the sixth son, and a rose with five petals, the seventh.

This is a common ideogram, originally iconic, for *pushbutton,* found on household appliances to mean function *switched off* and *switched on,* respectively.

See ⏻ in Group 6 for synonyms.

An alchemical sign for *sulphur*. This element was more commonly represented by the triangle of fire with an alchemical cross below, as in and ♀ .

See ♀ in Group 39, where most signs for sulphur are assembled.

Used in technical contexts for *loudspeaker*. On radios and TV sets it denotes the *loudspeaker socket*.

See also ⍋ in Group 4 and ◠◦ in Group 42 from the same context.

This sign occurs on some video or stereo appliances meaning the *balance control of two loudspeakers*.

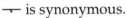 is synonymous.

Compare with ⟳, for *stereo sound from two loudspeakers*.

A sign used in computer flow charting indicating a *manual, offline operation that does not require technical assistance*.

Compare with ▽, *offline data storage*, and ☐ , *backup offline operation*.

An alchemical or old chemistry sign for *flask, bottle*, or *recipient that is not transparent*.

One of the signs for the *asteroid Vesta* in early astronomy. According to Roman mythology, Vesta was the chaste goddess of fire and the home hearth. The sign illustrates the *hearth, Vesta's altar*, above which is the *burning fire*, △ .

Vesta the asteroid is also drawn ⌂ and in other ways.

For more information about asteroids, turn to ♀ in Group 17.

The **pointed cross** or **cross fitchee** has several forms. This type of cross structure originated during the time of the Crusades. The knights brought crosses with them that were designed to be thrust into the ground during worship in their field camps. The pointed cross is associated with *danger*.

A variation of the **cross of St. Anthony**. St. Anthony, a hermit in Egypt, is believed to have chased away a pack of demons with a cross of this type. This cross form is also known as the **Tau cross**, **T-cross**, **Egyptian cross**, and **Crux commissa**. Finally, it is also called the **robbers' cross**, owing to the fact that the robbers crucified next to Christ are believed to have been hung from crosses of this shape, whereas Christ was hung on a Latin cross, †.

The **cross of Philip**, the apostle, is a Latin cross on its side. According to the legend, St. Philip was crucified on a cross in this position. The cross of Phillip appears on the flags of the Nordic countries and, for some reason, only on their flags: ⊞.

The Danish flag, *Dannebrogen*, showing a white cross of Phillip on red, came into use in the fourteenth century and is believed to be the oldest national flag on earth.

This is the standard cross used by the grand master of the Teutonic Crusaders' Order at the battle of Grunwald, Tannenberg, in 1410, against the Poles, where the Teutonic knights were defeated. It was a common cross form on crusader knights' coats of arms during the Middle Ages.

See the crutch cross, ✚, in Group 28.

This type of cross is also called the **Portuguese cross**.

A variation of the **Crux commissa**. See **T**, above.

The **Lorraine cross**. For its historical background, turn to ☩ in Group 3.

In heraldry it is often drawn ⊞.

See also the **threefoil/patriarchal cross**, ✛, in Group 24.

A logo representing *Mouvement populaire francais*, a fascistic movement in France.

This sign is also sometimes used to denote the zodiac sign of *Sagittarius*.

The similar form ↦ is common in geology, logic, and mathematics.

Compare with ♐, the most common sign for *Sagittarius*, and with ⚴, one of the signs used for *iron* in former times.

A sign for *metallum*, or *precious metal*, in the chemistry of the eighteenth century.

See the words *gold*, *silver*, and *platinum* in the word index for synonyms.

Group 23

Single-axis symmetric, both soft and straight-lined, closed
signs with crossing lines

This combination of the **heart sign** and the cross means just what it looks like, i.e., *sorrow*, or *lament*. It appears as a clothes sign in Ghana and is known as **nsoran**.

This sign was used by the alchemists to represent *salt water*. See the word index for different types of water.

One sign for *lime* used in early chemistry. Lime was also drawn ⊤ and ⊡ and in many other ways.

See ⊡ in Group 39 and ⊅ in Group 17 for most of the different signs for lime assembled.

This is the sign for *chrysocolla*, a soldering alloy used with gold.

Compare with ⚒, *fool's gold* or *iron sulphur*, and with ◔, *gold*.

A modern ideogram for *conference*. It is roughly synonymous with ⚹ .

Compare with ∞ and ⊛ , both of which signify *togetherness*.

This is the sign representing *Michaelmas*, the *first day of the Winter half year* in Scandinavia of the Middle Ages, and also, according to the **clog almanacs** (see ♓ in Group 5), the *autumn equinox*. Michaelmas originated from an old Nordic division of the year into two parts: summer and winter half-years.

Compare with the synonym ⚵ in Group 41:b and with the signs for the spring equinox, ♈, ♈, and ♈.

See also ♎ .

This is one of several signs used to symbolize the *art of alchemy*. The sun sign is at the center, surrounded by the four elemental triangles, crowned with the Christian cross, and then placed in the circle, representing the eternal or spiritual dimension and its endless possibilities.

Turn to ⓐ in Group 24 and ⊛ in Group 29 for synonyms.

This is an iconic sign: a picture of an object (which itself is a symbol), the **orb**. The globe was a **symbol of power** used by the Roman emperors. At the top it was provided with a representation of the goddess of victory. This was replaced with the Christian cross by the Byzantine emperors. The sign ⚏ within the circle most probably originates from the conventionalized medieval map of the world, ⊕ .

For more information, look up ⊕ in Group 24.

This entry is the most common graphical symbol of the political theory and practice of *anarchism*.

See the synonymous Ⓐ in Group 24 for more data.

See \W/ in Group 3 for the meaning of the sign inscribed in the circle.

A stylized version of this graph is the logo for the German car manufacturer **Volkswagen Werke**, combining the manufacturer's initials and old symbol structures loaded with positive meaning.

This is the **enneagram**, or "nine graph," a symbol denoting the *essence of being* in cabbalistic mysticism. Through its womb-like form and the number 9 it is associated with the creation of new human beings.

The enneagram also appears in Christian symbolism but with a different structure. See ✿ in Group 27.

Group 24

Single-axis symmetric, both soft and straight-lined, closed
signs without crossing lines

The circle divided in sections by straight lines connected to its center is a common modern ideogram used in the business world, schools, and media to show *given parts of a whole*. ◒ , a cartographic sign, belongs to this group. It means *spring* or *well* (also drawn ◯). Compare with ◨, *water catchment*, in modern fire prevention contexts. ◒ is also used as a meteorological sign to mean *partly overcast*.

If the same sign is divided vertically with the lighter half to the left, ◑, it represents the *last quarter*; the *beginning of the last phase of the moon* before ☽⚯☉ , the new moon; and is synonymous with ☾ , though this last sign more often means the *waning moon*, i.e., the thin crescent of the early morning moon the last couple of days before its disappearance in the light of the sun.

It also appears on some modern household appliances as a sign indicating *on/off switches*. In this case it is synonymous with ●|○ in Group 42, ⏻ in Group 6, and several other signs.

With the dark section to the left, ◐ , it represents the *first quarter*, or the *beginning of the second phase of the moon* at ☽⚯☉ .

The variation ◓ is sometimes used in meteorology to mean *almost clear sky* or *somewhat overcast*.

The upper sign is an eighteenth-century sign with the meaning *mineralia*, the *mineral kingdom*. Other signs of this small system were ⊖, *animalia*, the *animal kingdom*; and ⊕, *vegetabilia*, the *plant kingdom*.

⊕ was one of the signs for *vitriol* in early chemistry. This compound could also be drawn ⊞, ⊕ , and in other ways.

For more information on vitriols, look up ⇗ in Group 18.

An ideogram from the Middle Ages representing a conventionalized *map of the world*. The vertical line signified the *Mediterranean*; the horizontal line to the left represented the *Nile River*; and that to the right, the *Don River*. The right upper section was *Europe*; the left, *Africa*; and the bottom part, *Asia*. In the middle of this last section was *Jerusalem*, indicated by the point.

This ideogram is related to the sign ♁ in Group 23.

This is the **anti-nuclear emblem** or **peace symbol**. It is composed of a Tyr rune, ↑ , lengthened upward, or by the rune Ψ turned upside down. In Germanic countries ⅄ is interpreted as a **Todesrune**, the **rune of death**, or an inverted life rune.

According to some sources ☮ was conceived by placing the signs N and D (for *Nuclear Disarmament*) from the international marine flag signalling system on top of each other and circumscribing the combination with a circle.

Some state that ☮ was invented by Lord Bertrand Russell. S. T. Achen, however, claims that it was designed by G. Holtom at the request of Russell. In any case it was initially used as a rallying sign in 1958 at the first demonstration against Aldermaston (a British research center for the development of nuclear weapons).

The power of this symbol is emphasized by the fact that the South African government, during the 1970s, seriously considered forbidding it. They found it "anti-Christian" and "pro-Communist."

Achen, the late Danish semiotician, wrote that ☮, ironically, was forbidden at times in some of the communist countries.

A circle with several vertical lines was used in some meteorological systems to denote *varying degrees of cloudiness*, the actual degree indicated by the number of lines. Dalton, in his system of signs for chemical substances (nineteenth century), used the similar to represent *soda* or the metal *sodium*.

Another similar sign, , appears as a military sign for *anti-aircraft gun*, the sign being a combination of ○ for the *element of air*, and for *gun* or *cannon*.

This is an international symbol for *anarchism*, the anti-authoritarian underground movement found in cities. It is often seen on the walls of houses, subways, etc., sometimes together with other signs, e.g., in Group 53.

The very similar in Group 23 is a synonym.

Compare with , an old sign for *steel*.

An Egyptian hieroglyph meaning the *underworld* or the *kingdom of death*.

The same structure but upside down has been used as a computer sign meaning *system*. See in this group.

One of the many signs for *lime* in early chemistry. For other signs with the same meaning, look up in Group 17.

A sign representing *magnesium* in early chemistry. This element could also be drawn , , , and in other ways.

This rather iconic sign was first used in the 1980s. It is called the **smile** or **acid sign**, "acid" being a *psychedelic style of music blending American soul and European disco music.*

The music, the sign, and its name, *acid,* are somewhat associated with the pleasure drug *Ecstasy* and to the psychedelic *LSD.*

This sign is also drawn ☺.

An ideogram used in some computer contexts, meaning *symbol has been found.* The ideogram is a combination of 👁, *to see,* and |, for *one entity* or *something definite or absolute,* both placed in the circle of unlimited possibilities.

Dreyfuss (see bibliography) presented these and a large number of other ideograms from computer processing. The latter have not been included in this dictionary because they are not sufficiently well established to remain in their present form.

An ideogram from the seventeenth century representing the *art of alchemy.* This sign can be described as a sign created under the influence of Pythagorean geometry mysticism. It shows symbols for the *four elements* combined in one structure.

See the entry ideogram below and also the word index for other signs for the elements and for the art of alchemy.

A graphical Western representation of a **stupa** from Tibet, a symbol for the *organization of the universe.* It is composed from the bottom up of □ , the *earth element;* ○ , the *element of water;* △ , that of *fire;* ◡ , *air;* and  , representing *ether,* or the *fifth element.*

Compare with ☻, signifying the *state of transcendental consciousness* in the symbols for human states of consciousness under 3☼ in Group 14.

This symbol is used in Ghana as a sign on clothes. It is said to represent the *power or right to inflict capital punishment*. Note that ○ when used in the astrological graphical symbolism signifies *life* or the *spirit of life* and that △ often denotes something *powerful and dangerous*, for instance, divine power. Graphically this ideogram shows the triangle of *divine power* above the empty circle meaning *life*.

A sign from fifteenth-century alchemy for *water*. For most other signs denoting water, look up ○⊙ in Group 20.

Compare with the similar ○◄ for another transparent compound, *glass*.

The sign for the *sun* and *gold* in pre-Christian Greece. Today, the similar structure ◁○ is sometimes used to signify a *loudspeaker*.

The sun and gold were also drawn ℗ , ⊙ , and in other ways.

This sign meant *marcasite, fool's gold,* or *iron sulphate* in alchemy.

Fool's gold was also drawn ♋ .

A graph from the U.S. system of hobo signs meaning *here lives a man with a bad temper.*

Compare with 🏚 from the same system, meaning *dangerous neighborhood*, and with ⊙ from the English hobo system, signifying *Watch out! Here they'll turn you in.*

One of the alchemists' signs for *melting furnace.*

Some of the many synonyms are ⊟ and —⊖— .

A sign for *wind furnace* in alchemy or old chemistry. ♨ was synonymous.

A modern ideogram for *information* or *tourist information*, often presented white in a green square. The sign is, however, mostly presented slightly asymmetrical: ⅰ . Semiotically it is a combination of |, for *one entity, something complete and exceptional*, or a *fact*, placed beneath ○ for *all possibilities.*

Compare with the similar structure **!** , the **exclamation mark**, which expresses the absolute predominating with a point for concentration under it: This is absolute! This is serious!

This sign is found among the Egyptian hieroglyphs. It is also a common sign in modern Western ideography. It has been used in meteorology to signify *dew* and *cumulus clouds.*

Turned upside down, ▽, it could mean *ring around the moon*, also drawn ▽.

Both △ and ▽ are used in physics as signs for *average light intensity.*

∞ is one of the alchemists' signs for *strong fire* or *intense heat*.

See ⟐⟐ in Group 21 for synonymous signs.

Compare ∞ with the old sign for fire, ⟋⟍ .

∽ is one of the alchemists' **time signs**. It was sometimes used for *night*. ♀ was synonymous.

One of the alchemists' signs for *crucible*.

See ⟐ in Group 52 and ♡ below in this group for more data and synonymous signs.

The sign ⌒ placed within a rectangle is a modern ideogram for *water catchment area, storage place for firefighting equipment,* and similar meanings in the context of fire prevention.

Note that ◖, somewhat similar in structure, has been used for *water, spring,* or *well.*

A sign used in seventeenth-century chemistry and alchemy to denote the *melting pot* or *crucible*. This recipient was also drawn ⟨ᐯ⟩, ▽, ✛ , and ⟐.

One of the old chemists' signs for *lead*. Lead is usually drawn ♄, the sign for Saturn.

See ♂ in Group 49 for many synonymous signs.

One of the alchemists' many signs for *mercury*.

See ☿ for most of the signs for mercury assembled in one entry.

The **Celtic cross** or **ring cross**. This type of cross was common in the Scandinavian countries during the Middle Ages. According to Frithiof Dahlby (see bibliography), it was erected where an act of violence had been committed, an accident had occurred, or in front of farmhouses. Today, it is commonly used as a form for gravestones in, for example, Ireland.

A variation of the cross related to the *Lutheran Church*.
   The **Lutheran cross** can also have the form ⬧.
   This cross is a version of the **three-foil cross**.

The **patriarchal cross** is a symbol for the *Roman Catholic Church*. It appears, as is shown here, in the form of a **three-foil cross** (⬧ is a symbol for the Holy Trinity). The patriarchal cross can, however, have other forms.
   In heraldry, for instance, it looks different. The arms are of the same or almost the same length, and it resembles the heraldic version of the cross of Lorraine. See ⬧ in Group 28.

This is the **cross of Golgotha**. It is very similar to the type of cross used on the coat of arms of many a crusader knight.
   See ✝ in Group 22.

This sign is the **Crux gemmata**, a cross decorated with (graphical representations of) precious stones. It is a Christian symbol for the *Christian teaching* and the *12 apostles*.

This is the most common graphical structure representing **Tor's hammer, Mjölner**, a symbol from the Viking era. It appears engraved on stones, or hammered or cast in metal for use as an amulet.

Sign used in computer flow charting meaning *online storage of data*.
    Compare with ▽ for *off-line storage* and ▢ for *storage in internal memory*.

Sign used in computer flow charting for *output to screen* or *display*.

One of the signs for *glass* in the chemistry of the seventeenth century.
    See o— in Group 42 for synonymous signs.

Two variations of the alchemists' sign for *clay*. They are based upon the element signs for ▽, *earth*, or ▽, *water*, and ⅍, *oil* (for the consistency).
    For a similar structure, see ⚶ in Group 30. See also ♀ and ⚶ in Group 41:b, which have similar meanings.

This is **Odin's staff** from a Middle Ages pictorial representation.
    Compare with the staff of Jupiter, ♃, a common sign in Rome, and also with ♃, the staff of Adad, the Babylonian god of thunderstorms and the forces of weather. Note that

the Hittite hieroglyphs for *lightning,* ⚡ , 𝍱 , and 𝍲, were also three-pronged.

The structure ⚡ uppermost on Odin's staff is similar to one of the crowns in the Three Crowns, the symbol on the Swedish national coat of arms. Three is the magic number, God's number, associated with prosperity and power.

The holy number of three appears again in the **fleur de lis,** the **French lily.** It was first used during the twelfth century and then as part of a large *fleur de lis* pattern. Later it was used isolated as an ideogram denoting the *right to rule France (and claims to it whether these were rightful or not).*

Nowadays, ⚜ is widely known as the **international scout sign.**

A sign for the precious fur *ermine,* in heraldry denoting *high rank.*

Compare with ⚛, an extremely ancient symbol for *high (spiritual) rank,* incorporated into Christian symbolism as one of the signs for the Holy Trinity.

Clubs is the suit of the lowest value in an ordinary deck of cards. The symbol is from the fifteenth century. It is associated with *money, wealth, work,* and *luck.*

Compare with the entry below, ♣, for *wood* in alchemy.
See also ⚖ , *pawnshop,* in Group 41:b.

This is the most common sign used in alchemy to denote *wood*. Compare with the symbol for the suit of clubs in a pack of cards, ♣.

Although the alchemists usually drew this sign as it is depicted here, they sometimes used it the other way around.

Spades, originally an iconic sign for a sword (from Greek *spatké* = sword).

This is the symbol on cards of the *next highest suit* in the common deck of playing cards. Spades are associated to *fighting, destiny, logical thinking,* and *death*.

Note that in the ancient **tarot** or **gypsy deck of cards** the symbol for the suit corresponding to spades was an iconic symbol, a picture of a sword.

Compare with ♡ , one of the signs for *cremated* in genealogical contexts.

The signs for diamonds and hearts can be looked up via the word index, and the sign for the suit of clubs is an entry above in this group.

A modern ideogram found on different types of packaging denoting *center of gravity* or *fulcrum*.

⊕ is a synonym.

Compare with ⟶ in Group 40.

A modern ideogram on household appliances indicating a *degree of waterproofness*. It can be found, for instance, on outdoor electrical garden appliances.

See the sign below.

An ideogram found on household appliances indicating a *high degree of waterproofness*. This means that the appliance (e.g., a motor heater or washing machine) can also be used outdoors.

See ♦♦ in Group 20 for nearly synonymous signs.

Both the exclamation mark and the triangle are **warning signs**. ⚠ is a traffic warning sign, but this ideogram is also used, for instance, in Oxford dictionaries to warn for *taboo words*.

See ⚠ in Group 22 for more data.

This is the well-known ideogram found on the flags of Turkey and Pakistan. Positioned in various other ways it appears on several of the Islamic countries' national flags. It is a general symbol for the *Islamic faith*.

The ideogram combines the iconic sign for the *waning moon* and the sign for the *planet Venus* as the Morning star: the **Morning star** and the **Morning crescent**.

The five points of the Venus star represent the *five pillars of Islam*:

Al-Shahadah — the profession of faith: There is no other god but Allah, and Muhammad is his prophet.

As-Salah — the prayer. Five times a day the Muslim kneels and bows to Mecca, putting his forehead to the ground several times and reciting holy prayers.

Az-Zakah — the giving of a certain percentage of one's income to help the poor.

As-Siam — fasting in the month of Ramadan. During this month no food is eaten as long as the sun is over the horizon.

Al-Hadj — the pilgrimage to the holy city, Mecca.

Mecca is the birthplace of the Prophet and the location of the Kaaba, a shrine many centuries older than Islam. Kaaba is a square building, the sides of which measure approximately 10 meters and whose height is approximately 15 meters. The pilgrim walks around this building seven times and then kisses a black stone built into the base of one wall. This stone is the most holy object a Muslim knows. At least once in his lifetime a believer has to go to Mecca to worship in Allah's house, the Kaaba. For a derivation of the relation between ☆ and the planet Venus, look up ✪ in Group 29.

The *crescent moon*, ☽ , was the symbol of *Constantinople*, the capital city of the Eastern Roman Empire, Byzantium. When the Turks, led by Muhammad II, conquered Constantinople in 1453, they also adopted the city's symbol, ☽, but changed it to the *waning moon*, ☾. According to other sources, however, the Turks already used the crescent as their symbol at this time. Now it became the symbol for the *Ottoman-Turkish Empire*. As such it was used until around the end of the eighteenth century.

At the beginning of the nineteenth century a star was added that, at first, was not five-pointed but soon became so.

From the beginning of the twentieth century this symbol began to appear on other Islamic countries' flags.

Group 25

Multi-axis symmetric, soft, closed signs with crossing lines

The Western graph for the number 8 positioned horizontally is a sign to denote the idea of *infinitely great* or *infinity*, often referring to time, distances, or numbers. As far as time is concerned the most common symbol is the snake biting its own tail, or the empty circle, ○. It is as if ∞ represents a double endlessness or *eternity*.

Compare with ☯ in Group 26 and ⬭ below in this group, both of which are similar in structure.

Sometimes the concept of infinity in mathematical systems is expressed by the sign ∝.

This sign appears in genealogy and indicates that a person is *married*. Its basic meaning is *togetherness* or *intimate relation*. It is related to the graphic symbolism of astrology where ○ represents the *spirit of life*, the *human spirit*, or the *real individual*.

The much more modern signs ♀♀ and ♂♂ have the same basic meaning, but also indicate the sex of the two intimately related persons.

The Nsibidi people in Africa use ⅀ to indicate a *married couple*. Note that this ideogram is composed of the common part of two joined circles.

Compare with o-o, *unmarried*, and ○○, *divorced*, both genealogical signs.

In the Swedish system of hobo signs this entry means *here there is nothing to be afraid of, go on begging*. In the English system it recommends the tramp to *tell a moving story*. And in the U.S. system (according to Dreyfuss) it means *here the police treat tramps roughly*. If this is correct, the American hobos probably perceive ⬭ as a sign for handcuffs.

In eighteenth-century chemistry ⬭ was sometimes used for *oleum empyreumaticum*.

Compare also the following entries and ⊛ below.

This is a typographic ideogram used by printers. It means *double exposure.*

Compare with the structurally similar sign below and with ⊙ in Group 20, for *stereo sound.*

Structurally similar to the above entry is ∞. It is not used in any established Western ideographic system, but is much used as a logotype in the business world. In the Japanese treatise *Art of Warfare* it is referred to as a sign for *village.*

Consult the word index for synonyms.

This is a common, ancient, and basic ideogram for a *high spiritual dignity.* ⚛ , which is similar in structure, was already in use around 5000 years ago with the same meaning. In Christian symbolism it represents the *Holy Trinity: Father, Son, and Holy Ghost.* Bishop Theophile of Antioch, who died in A.D. 186, is thought to have been the first to use the concept of the Holy Trinity. This idea is usually drawn ◉, however.

Compare with ∞∞, signifying another type of community and togetherness.

This ideogram is used in electrical contexts and means *fuse.* It illustrates the function of a fuse, i.e., to let a current pass through "a narrow passage," a thin wire of high resistance that is easily burned off so that the current is automatically shut off when the system is overloaded. Fuse can also be drawn ∿ and in other ways.

This sign is used in the Gnostic mystic tradition and is called the **seal of the world**. The philosophy of Gnosticism had its roots in Hellenistic Egypt. Certain Gnostics regarded the Old Testament's God as an evil being who had created an evil world. According to Gnosticism everything physical, material, or earthly is evil, especially the sexual life, which results in the creation of new humans on earth. What a happy bunch they must have been.

This structure is called **St. Hans' cross** or the **Cross of St. John**. It is a magic ideogram from the Viking era or even older. It seems also to have been used in cabbalistic mysticism. Today, it is used as a cartographic and traffic sign to denote a *sight worth seeing*. As a traffic sign it is inserted in the square to denote *ground*: ▦ .

Compare with ⸙ for *prehistoric site*, and with ⌘ in Group 27.

⌘ also appears in pre-Columbian America, where it is associated with ⊞.

This sign was a common structure in classical times in both Greece and Byzantium. It is a common design in Nordic peasant art from the Middle Ages.

In Ghana the similar ✿ is called **nyame dua** and regarded as a symbol for an altar to the heavenly god.

Because the sign is multi-axis symmetric and has eight equal parts it is related to the planet Venus as the goddess of the Morning or Evening star.

See ✪ in Group 29 for the relation between the number 8 and the planet Venus.

This is a symbol for the **Holy Trinity** from Christian symbolism. In this case the symbol is related to **vesica piscis**, ◊, and to ∝ in Group 37.

A modern ideogram representing the *planet earth*. As such it is synonymous with the much older signs ⊕ and ♁.
   A modern synonym is drawn ⊕.

A sign for *silver* in alchemy. Other old signs for silver were ∴, ⌂, ☽, ◠, ◡, �, and ☾.

This is a rather rare ideogram expressing the Western conception of the smallest unit of matter, the *atom*.
   See the two entries below, which are synonymous.

A modern ideogram for the *atom* and thereby also for related phenomena. It is used on many maps for *nuclear reactor*.
   See the entry below for more data.

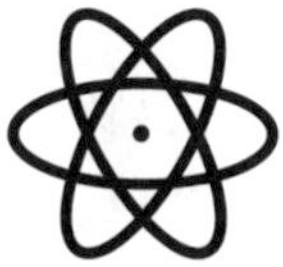

This ideogram was originally a sign for the most recent Western conception of the smallest part of matter, the *atom*. As such it has become a symbol for *uranium, nuclear power plant, nuclear research, nuclear physics*, and *nuclear reactor*.

In this and the two preceding entry signs the ellipses signify the orbits of the *electrons* around the *nucleus*, the point in the center.

Compare with Z , a sign in physics for *nuclear charge*, and with $\bigcirc$, the sign for *galaxy*.

It is interesting that when illustrating the smallest and the largest entities of matter Western ideography uses the same basic sign structure, $\bigcirc$, which is also the structure used to indicate *nothingness* or *zero*.

This is a sign worn on clothes in Ghana, Africa. It means *evil person* according to one source, although it is difficult to imagine that anyone would be happy walking around in clothing decorated with signs of this denotation. A misunderstanding as to its meaning is not unlikely. There is, however, a similarity with the modern ideogram $\bigotimes$ for *nuclear power*, above. Also discernible in this ideogram is the sign structure $\Leftrightarrow$, signifying a *warning* or *threat*, and $\blacklozenge$, used on some medieval Western knights' coats of arms as an *indication of religiosity*. Semiotically analyzed and with known semantically significant elements taken into consideration, this ideogram implies *threat, dangerous power*, and *religious fanaticism*.

This is a variation of the **Coptic cross**. The members of the **Coptic Church** in Egypt, Ethiopia, and a few other countries claim that they practice a more original Christian doctrine or faith than both the Greek Orthodox and the Roman Catholic Churches.

The **star of Ischtar**, i.e., the planet Venus. *Ischtar*, in other countries and times called *Astarte, Aphrodite*, and *Venus*, was a *goddess of war, sex and fertility*.

An eight-pointed star almost always represented this goddess when used in the Near East for a great many centuries before the birth of Christ.

This version of the eight-pointed star was found on a Babylonian seal from around 800 B.C. For its origins, see ⊗ in Group 29.

Today, in the same region where Ischtar/Astarte was worshipped, the star of Venus is often drawn ★ and appears together with ☾ on flags for many or most of the Islamic countries there.

A Phoenician **star of Venus**, symbol for the goddess *Astarte*. See the entry above, ✺, for more data.

During a few centuries around 1000 B.C. this symbol was used in the Euphrates-Tigris region to represent the *sun* and the *sun god*, the *highest power*, or the *highest divinity*. ✺ is often depicted as rising out of ♈︎, one of the signs for the *ram, the sign of Aries*, representing the spring equinox.

The symbol is often in close physical proximity to the ideograms ☽, for the *moon god Sin*, and ✺, for *Ischtar*, as well as with ♈︎, the *staff of the Babylonian sun god Shamash*.

Other sun signs are, for instance, ⊙ , ♀ , ⊕ , and the entry below.

This sign is common in ethnic art in different parts of the world and also in the Nordic countries. The earliest known example of this structure is probably Phoenician. The six-pointed star is believed by many to be a **sun symbol**.

Compare with ⚛ , a **sun cross from Troy**, and the modern Japanese sign for *sunlight*, ⚹ . Note that the six-pointed ✳ in old and ✴ in recent Western ideography represent fixed stars, i.e., suns.

See also the synonymous ⊛ in Group 29.

This ideogram is often designed ✺.

Group 26

Multi-axis symmetric, soft, closed signs without crossing lines

Both the empty and filled circles belong to the oldest ideograms and have been dated to the period immediately after the emergence of the simplest conventionalized representations of humans and animals found on the walls of prehistoric caves and rock faces.

○ is sometimes an iconic sign representing the *sun* and the *moon* (see, for example, ♀). The empty circle also often is used among primitive peoples to indicate openings in the body such as the *eyes* and the *mouth*. It has been in use in ideographic systems of writing for more than 5000 years.

In astrology ○ represents the *eternal, endless, without beginning or end, life itself,* and the *spirit,* as opposed to +, *matter, the physical body,* and *earthly life.* Both graphically and semiotically, ○ and + are almost diametrically opposed.

In today's Western ideography ○ stands for *all possibilities* (within a given system). The circle calls attention to those signs it encircles, and the signs that are placed within it usually illustrate in what way the endless possibilities that the circle represents are limited. See, for instance, the international traffic sign ⑯ .

The empty circle is used in over 50 Western ideographic systems. In astronomy and calendars it indicates the *full moon;* in meteorology, a *clear sky.* As a cartographic sign it stands for *town, community, center of communication;* in electrical contexts, for *measuring instrument* or *electric motor.* It is used in chemistry to denote the all-important element *oxygen.* In the old alchemy it was one of the signs for *alum.* It appears in mechanics and means *center of rotation.* In biology and genealogy it sometimes denotes the *female sex* (□ then indicates the *male sex*). On modern household appliances, such as videotape recorders, it indicates *power switch.*

According to the law of the polarity of meanings of elementary graphs, ○ ought to also mean the opposite of all possibilities, or all time. That is indeed the case. It is often used to mean *prohibition,* i.e., *no possibility* whatsoever, for example, when prohibiting the use of bicycles or the playing of football, etc. The activity prohibited is often indicated by alphabetical signs outside ○. In some of the systems of hobo signs ○ means *here you get nothing*.

An empty circle that is considerably smaller than most of the other signs in a given ideographic system has a spectrum of meaning that focuses on the idea of something *small* or *weak*. It often means *small part of a larger unit that is divided into equal parts*. Thus it is used to represent *degrees* when measuring temperature and when dividing a circle. ○ is used in music and phonetics to indicate *weak tones* and *toneless sounds*, and in some meteorology it has been used for *low intensity* about weather conditions.

This sign is the indispensable **point** or **dot**, a basic element in Western ideography together with ℗ , ☺ , — , and ⌒ .
  For more information about this sign, turn to Group 8.

This structure, the **filled circle**, the **disc**, or the **globe**, seems to be older than ○. It is, perhaps, the most common of the non-iconic signs chiselled or hollowed out in Nordic rock carvings. ● is found among the Egyptian hieroglyphs, in Japanese Buddhist symbolism, and in India (for example, on the brows of women to indicate that they are married).
  ● is used in astronomy and calendars to denote the *new moon* (☽ ⁄ ☉) and in meteorology it sometimes stands for *cloudy* weather or *overcast sky*. As a cartographic sign it indicates *communities*, *towns*, or *centers* of communication. In early chemistry it was used for *coal*. On video appliances it denotes the *recording control*, as does ◉.

The vertical **oval** or **ellipse** is, from a graphic point of view, an advanced sign, a combination of the basic elements ☺ and ☺. It means *nothing, zero,* or *absence.*

◊ is the opposite of ○, *all, eternity, all time,* or *all possibilities.* See the law of the polarity of meanings of elementary graphs in Part I.

Note how the structure has been used in the ideogram ⚛ to represent *electrons,* one of the smallest units of matter, almost totally lacking measurable weight. As ⬭ it is a modern U.S. sign sometimes used to denote one of the largest entities of matter in the universe, a *galaxy* with its millions of sun systems.

When the longitudinal axis is diagonal, the above structure is used to denote *tones* as the main **note sign** in the Western system of musical notation.

It is also used as a sign for *galaxy* in some astronomical systems.

A modern sign used, for instance, in mathematical systems for *infinite, infinitely great sum or number,* or *indefinite number.* In some mathematical systems $\propto$ is synonymous.

See also the synonymous ∞ in Group 25 and the structurally not too dissimilar ⧀ for married.

Two **zero signs** placed together are used in Austria to denote a *toilet.*

Compare with the synonymous ♡.

In botany 00 can mean *indefinite number of stamens* (more than 20).

The circle with a point at its center is very old. This ideogram seems to have been used in every cultural sphere on earth. Wherever it appears, it has the same meaning: the *sun* or something that is closely associated with the sun, such as *hydrogen* (in Dalton's nineteenth-century chemistry). It means *sunshine* in meteorology, *gold* in alchemy, *annual plant* in botany (one sun cycle), *driving wheel* on locomotives as a railway ideogram, and *here live bad-tempered people* in both the English and U.S. systems of hobo signs.

The sun sign is one of the oldest gestalts in Western ideography. See "The basic ideographic structures" in Part I.

The scholars of the Middle Ages, who in their narrow-minded authoritarian belief system confused the roles of the earth and the sun in the universe, used ⊙ as a sign for the *earth surrounded by the great ocean*. For a sign with a similar meaning, see ⊕ in Group 24.

In cabbalistic mysticism, the *archangel Michael* was related to the *sun and the day of the sun, Sunday*. ⊙ was the sign used to represent the archangel.

When ⊙ is not used in direct association to the sun or gold, in modern ideography it most often indicates a center. This is the case in cartography and blueprints of different types. In the same way the Swedish boy scouts use it to mean *I have gone home* (the center for a child is home). The sign ◎ is used similarly by boy scouts in England. It is said to be engraved on the gravestone in Kenya of Robert Baden-Powell, the founder of Scouting.

Although ⊙ is found in practically every type of culture and in all periods of history, there are exceptions. In Babylon, for example, the sun was indicated by the ideogram ✸, a four-pointed star with wavy radiation lines emanating from its center. In other regions the sun was represented by a disc with outstretched wings on either side. Count d'Alviella claimed, in his famous book on the migration of symbols throughout the world, that both ancient Indian signs such as ⚓ and pre-Columbian American signs such as ✪, the three-leg ⅄ , and the swastika were *sun symbols*.

In esoteric astrology ⊙ represents the *creative spark of divine consciousness* that exists in every individual and links him or her to the source and origins of life, so that he or she is also a co-creator of the world. This is the *conscious self*. In astrological psychology ⊙ stands for the *desire to live* and the *energy of life*. This life energy is "colored" by the zodiac sign in which ⊙ is passing at the moment of an individual's birth.

In the body ⊙ symbolizes the *heart*, the *blood circulation*, and the *backbone*. As a symbol for important people in an individual's life it represents *people in positions of authority, men in general*, and *world and religious leaders*. It is also related to the *father*. ⊙ rules ♌, the zodiac sign *Leo*. See Group 50.

Other *sun symbols* are ♇, ⊕, ⊗, ☼, and ♄ .

This sign is associated with ⊙ and with the idea of the sun as a center, and as a source of light and energy. It is used on maps to indicate different types of *centers from which energy and/or communication emanate*: *central station, lighthouse, post office, transformer station, telegraph and telephone station*, and *pushbutton* (for light, power, etc.).

This structure is similar to the entry above and was used as a chemical sign by Dalton at the beginning of the nineteenth century to denote *lime*. It has also been used to represent *gold* in trading contexts, and it is an astronomical sign for *planetary nebula*, i.e., a *cloud of gases and dust in a planetary system*.

In the Japanese treatise *Art of Warfare*, ⊙ stands for *dwelling place* or *camp*.

This is another of the earliest ideograms used by humans in this cycle of civilization. It is associated with something *divine* or *powerful*. Later, ◎ has been used in Buddhist art to indicate *charisma*, the *emanation of spiritual power from a person*, the **halo**. As a halo it has also been used in Christian symbolism, although the ancient sun symbol ⊕ is more common for that purpose.

In accordance with the law of polarity of meanings of elementary graphs, this sign has also been used as an *anti-Semitic symbol* (compare with ✡). At the Fourth Lateran Council in 1215 it was decided that Jews should wear high pointed hats to distinguish them from others. Some years later the yellow ring was invented for the same purpose. Note that when ◎ is used as a halo in Buddhism it is usually yellow or orange.

Written instructions as to how the yellow ring was to be worn on clothes still exist, for example, from Reichstadt Frankfurt in 1452.

A few modern uses of this sign: *calm* in meteorology, *temporary runway* in aviation, *I have gone home* in the English system of boy scout signs, *here they give you food and money* in the English system of hobo signs, and *here all is fine* in the Swedish system of hobo signs.

This sign, or a similar one with more concentric circles like the entry below, is often found on Nordic rock carvings. It has also been found on cliff paintings in the Sahara and in other places. In all these cases ◎ is closely associated to ●, ⊕, and 𝜃𝜃 (see the section "The development of sign structures through the ages" in Part I).

The similar sign **adinkirahane**, ⊕ or ◎ , used on clothes in Ghana, means the *highest*, the *best*, or the *king*.

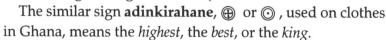

This sign is the most common of the non-iconic signs in use today to represent a *target*. A similar sign has been found on the brow of a statue representing an Indian priest king, dated back to around 3000 B.C.

In 1576 the planetary system was represented, following Copernicus's theory, by a similar structure made up of eight concentric circles.

This ideogram is used on some machines meaning *automatic operation* or *automatic function*. Compare with the following entry.

In botany this sign is used to represent an *indefinite number of petals*. When used as a meteorological sign it means *heat haze* or *dry haze*. In computer flow charting it can stand for *automatically operated keyboard*.

On instrument panels and machines this ideogram can indicate that a function is *manually operated*.

Compare with the two preceding entries, which are relatively antonymous.

A sign in alchemy for *caput mortuum*, the *skull, death's head*, the *epitomy of decline and decay*, or *nigredo*. It is the starting point for the alchemical work of transforming man/the impure or base metal into pure gold, ⊙ , spirit.

This sign appears, for instance, as a shield sign in a painting on a Greek vase from around 500 B.C.

Compare with the synonymous ⊙ below in this group.

A protecting sign for *invaluable cultural relic* or *culturally valuable building or monument,* used to protect against bombing, etc., and called the **Roerich sign** after its creator. It was introduced after international conferences held during the 1930s. It has, however, seldom been used, as witness the enormous cultural devastations by bombing during World War II. The structure is associated with a sign worn by deaf persons, to protect them in traffic.

Compare with ∴ in Group 8.

This sign is used, along with ♂ and ②, in botany to indicate *biennial plants.* In the English system of hobo signs it means *danger, here they'll try to get you arrested.*

When the points are placed vertically, ⊙ , we find it used in alchemy, alternating with ⊕ and others, to denote *sea salt.*

One of the alchemists' signs for *nigredo* or *caput mortuum.* See the entry ⊙ above for more data.

In eighteenth-century chemistry this sign was used for *residuum, rest,* or *residue.*

The Hopis in Arizona have long used an identical sign in their ideography.

This sign is an example of the type of sign succeeding the early chemical signs for the basic elements around 1800. The sign ⊙ stood for *mercury,* ⊙ for *aluminium earth* (an important substance in printing and the production of colors, also used as an antiseptic), and ⊙ represented *gold.*

The most common sign for *mercury* in early chemistry was ☿, and for *gold,* ⊙ .

It is common to find identical ideograms in different parts of the world that, according to today's prevailing theories, have had no earlier connections with one another. Such is the case with this sign, found both in pre-Columbian Central America (in Aztec symbols representing the world), on sword-hilts from the Bronze Age in the Nordic countries, and on the Phaistos disco.

Compare with ⊛ below in this group.

The Phaistos disco resembles a small grammophone record made of burned clay, about 15 centimeters in diameter, with an ideographic script running in a spiral on either side. There are about 120 signs in approximately 30 groups on each side. It was found at the excavations of a prehistoric town on the island of Crete. It is approximately 4000 years old. Other ideograms on this disc are ⟫ and ✳.

The **ring cross** or **sun wheel** was a common symbol in the Nordic countries and can still be seen on ancient slabs and in many churches. It was also common in pre-Columbian America and throughout a large part of the Mediterranean region about 3500 years ago. For more information, see ⊕ in Group 29.

This particular version of the sign is also sometimes called the **Celtic cross**, although this name usually is used for a Latin cross with this structure at the center. Today, it is used as a logo by some new fascist organizations. According to d'Alviella, 卐 , ✛, and ⊛ are all *sun symbols and* it is most probably their association to power and to older times (it was better before, when the social structure was more rigid and equality almost nonexistent) that attracts these groups. Both Nordiska Rikspartiet in Södermanland, Sweden, and Jeune Nation in France use this sign. It is also used in Christian symbolism to denote *nimbus* or *halo* and as the **consecration cross**.

One of the Bronze Age altars from around 1000 B.C., found in Scania, Sweden, has this form. It also appears on Nordic rock carvings, and in ancient Egypt.

A sign from a Bronze Age altar in the Toulouse museum. , , and  also appear on this altar.

This sign appears in both the Mayan and the Egyptian hieroglyphic systems. In the latter,  probably meant *city*.

One of the symbols for the *four evangelists* used, for instance, in gothic architecture and in churches.

See also the similar structure  in Group 29.

A seventeenth-century alchemical sign for *oil*. Oil was also drawn ♂, ⊕, as two of the entries below, and in many other ways. Three golden circular forms is also an old sign for *pawnbrokers* and *money-lenders*, still used today in the business world. A common sign for *pawn shop* is ☖. Note that ∴ is the sign for *silver* used in some modern mining contexts and a sign for *rain* in meteorology.

Compare with ♣, **clubs**, and ⚇ , one of the signs for *silver* in alchemy.

This sign means *here you can get food and money* in both the Swedish and English hobo systems. In Sweden the same meaning could also be drawn ⁛.

Sign from eighteenth-century chemistry for *oleum essentiale*, or *essential oil*. These oils were volatile liquids with distinct odor or flavor, pressed or distilled from flowers, fruits, or other plant parts.

Compare with the entry ⚇ above.

This is a blessed sign that appears, among other places, in the early symbolism of **Buddha's footprints** in India. In the West ⚶ is a symbol for the *hexachord*, a series of four tones and one semitone, or six notes, and for *harmonics* in general.

One of the many signs for *silver* in alchemy. Silver was also drawn ☽, ⚎ , ⌒, and otherwise.

Look up the entry ◇ in Group 25 for these and three more old signs for silver assembled.

One of the alchemists' signs for *distilled oil*, or *oleum destil-latum*. See ⚊ in Group 42 and ⚇ in this group for more signs for *oil*.

This prehistoric sign was found on one of the walls in the Marsoulas cave. Some 10,000 years later this same sign appears on the trousers of a hangman about to execute someone in a sixteenth-century Flemish painting.

Two common signs for **asterisk** used in typography. The asterisk is used as a sign for footnotes, i.e., short comments and explanations or references to sources of information relevant to the main text of a book or magazine article, added by the writer and put at the bottom of the pages. As a sign for footnotes the asterisk is sometimes replaced by the dagger, †. In astrological contexts the asterisk can signify the *sextile aspect*; in botany it has been used for a *subspecies*; in books about mushroom picking and mushroom flora one asterisk close to the name of the mushroom usually means that it is *edible*, while two such signs mean that a mushroom is *good*, and three, that it is *very tasty*. In musical notation an asterisk indicates that the *pedal* should be used when playing the piano.

Finally, asterisks can be used in texts to indicate words left out, although three full stops is the more common ideogram for this use. Note that "asterisk" comes from the Greek word *asterikos*, meaning a small star.

Nsoroma, an *adinkira print* on clothes from Ghana. This sign's meaning: *Like the stars, I am one of the children of the Highest One, and rest in God trusting not only in myself.*

Like ✳ the sign ✪ is a *sun symbol.* Note the six points, which characterize all signs for fixed stars, i.e., faraway suns.

The same sign has been used in the United States by the armed forces to indicate *windmill* or *mill* on maps.

Another sign from the Phaistos disco (see ⊛ in this group). The **eight-pointed star** is an ancient symbol for the *Venus goddess* or the *planet Venus* as either the *Morning star* or the *Evening star,* but not both.

See ⊛ in Group 29 for an explanation of this.

Similar signs, but with more or less "petals," have long been used in ethnic art and decoration all over the Western and Eastern world and as symbols and logotypes. Most common are 6, 8, or 12 petals. A symbol of this type used by the Japanese emperor has 16 petals. This number was also used in the Euphrates culture around 2000 B.C. The symbol appears with 12 petals on a procession relief in Persepolis dated back to around 500 B.C., on a bronze mirror from about 200 B.C. in China, and on a war painting from Benin in sixteenth-century Africa. Finally, this type of sign with 13 petals has been found on a box engraved with runes found in England and dating from around the seventh century.

This sign is known as an **Ethiopian emblem**. This is the only version of a three-pointed star the author of this work has ever seen. Otherwise the **caltrap,** ᚼ, is about as structurally similar a sign as can be found, and just as strange looking.

The number 3 is considered to be a very *holy or divine number* in most cultures and religions. This entry has been found on the robe of an Indian priest-king from a statuette dated back to around 3000 B.C. In Christian contexts is used as a symbol for the *Holy Trinity*. As such it is often placed within a circle or used in church architecture and windows.

For the Christian history of this ideogram, turn to ⊛ in Group 25.

From the prince of Byblos's seal and the period 3000 to 2000 B.C. Byblos was a coastal city in old Phoenicia (modern-day Lebanon). In antiquity there was a famous Aphrodite temple in the city. Its inhabitants were good shipbuilders, and opposite Byblos in the Mediterranean lay Cyprus, the "island of Aphrodite," also well known for its Aphrodite temples. Aphrodite was the same Venus deity as the old Astarte and the still older Ischtar.

The sign ⊂⊃ appears in the Egyptian hieroglyphic system. Much later, and drawn vertically, it became a symbol for Christ, **vesica piscis** (literally, the air bladder of a fish). This sign is also a symbol of *virginity* or *purity*. It often appears in a **mandorla**, i.e., is surrounded by a radiating aurelia, or gloria, as in ◊ . The cabbalistic mystics used ◊ to signify *innocence*.

Compare with its graphic opposite, †, and you will see that the antographity corresponds to an antonymity of the same scope, the latter ideogram denoting *sin*, *guilt*, and *loss of innocence*.

In modern meteorology this structure can mean *clear air* or *extremely good visibility*. In some U.S. meteorology, however, this structure turned 90 degrees, ⊂⊃ , can stand for *visibility reduced by smoke.* The law of the polarity of meanings of elementary graphs seems to be at work here.

A **camera sign** found on the light aperture control to indicate a setting suitable for photographing in *hazy or cloudy weather.*

A **camera sign** found on the aperture control to indicate a setting suitable for photographing in *sunlight.*

This sign appears on a picture of Tlaloc, the god of rain, found in Mexico and dated back to around 500 B.C. It is similar to the **Eastern star**, Venus as the goddess of fertility and war.

For a description of this sign's relation to the planet Venus, see ⊛ in Group 29. See also ☆ and ☾ .

Compare with the European ★ and the U.S. ✪ in Group 30.

An **adinkira** print on garments worn in Ghana and meaning *jealousy.* ✸ is a modern ideogram that can have the same meaning in comic strips (see Group 44). See also ♡ and ♡ .

An **adinkira** print symbol on clothes from Ghana, **nyame dua**, meaning *holy place*. Compare with ⊕ , a Bronze Age sign found on altars, and with ✾ from Group 25. *Nyame dua* is also drawn ✾, which is identical to an old Swedish ethnic art design.

This is known as the **anchored cross**, because it is said that the ends of the cross arms are similar in shape to the flukes of an anchor. But they also are rather similar in shape to ♈ or ♈ , the ancient symbols representing *Aries, rebirth, new beginnings,* and *growth.*

In Rome during the third century the Christians were persecuted to such an extent that they dared not use the cross as their symbol. (Compare this with the way Hitler forbade the use of political and ideological symbols other than ⚡ once he was in power.) This led to the creation of the **crux dissimulata**, i.e., the **disguised or dissimilar cross**. The intention was that no non-Christian would recognize the crux dissimulata as a Christian rallying symbol and object of worship. For this reason the anchor form ⚓ was often used.

See ⚓ in Group 5.

A sign for *glass flask* or *glass bottle* in alchemy. ◊ in Group 22 had the similar but not identical meaning of *not transparent flask.*

Compare with ⧖ , composed of identical elements, meaning *hour.*

Sign for the **star of the Venus goddess**, or **Ischtar's star**, during the Babylonian reign in the Euphrates-Tigris region.

Refer to ⊛ in Group 29 for the relation between the planet and goddess of Venus and the **eight-pointed star**.

When Iraq (the modern name for the Euphrates-Tigris region) achieved its independence in 1921, this particular **Venus star** was used on their flag. After the revolution of 1958 a new flag was created with three Venus stars of the type ★ on it.

See the following entry for more facts.

This is one of the ideograms for Ischtar, queen of the heavens; heavenly mother of all borne by women; sister of the highest of the Babylonian gods, the sun god Shamash; the goddess of sexual pleasures; and the only real woman god in Babylon and Assyria (all other female gods were but shadows of their male god consorts).

Ischtar is also the god of childbirth and as such is often depicted with a child in her arms. Being the only real woman god in the Near East for a couple of millennia, up to the time when the new ideology of Christianity expanded into the Mediterranean region, she is in fact Virgin Mary, or rather, the Holy Virgin is what is left of Ischtar (Astarte, Aphrodite) after Christianity's takeover.

Astarte was the Greek form of the Semitic name Astarit (Hebrew Astoret) for the queen of the heavens. In the temples of Ischtar, she being the goddess of fertility and thus also of sexual pleasures, girls and women served the believers under surveillance by eunuchs.

Ischtar was, however, also the goddess of hunting and warfare. Since in the skies she was symbolized by Venus, she was both the fertility goddess of the Evening star and the war goddess of the Morning star.

This graphic representation of Venus is from Babylonia around 2000 B.C. The two sets of four arms or points of the star sign, one behind the other, refer to the exactiy eight years it took for either of Venus's two appearances (the Morning star and the Evening star) to return to the same sign of the zodiac and the same place in that sign.

See above for more data.

Group 27

Multi-axis symmetric, straight-lined, closed signs with crossing lines

Both the square and the cross with equal arms are related to the *earth*, the *ground*, and the *land*. Logically, a combination of the two ought to strengthen this association. We discover, however, that such a graphic structure hardly has been used in Western ideography. It appears only as a sign for *contact* in some electrical contexts and as *help center for wounded* in certain military systems.

Not so in Chinese and Japanese ideography, where this entry sign actually means *field* or *ground*.

Some Western countries' flags, though, have crosses. Since the flags have rectangular form they come very close to this structure. And, of course, a national flag is a symbol for a people's ownership of land.

This is one of the signs representing *water* in alchemy. To see most of the water signs assembled, look up ∞ in Group 20.

This structure is found on the walls of many West European caves and also in pre-Columbian Peru. Its meaning is unknown.

Compare with ＃ and others in Group 45.

An ancient Germanic sign with the name **eye of fire** (according to Koch). It was also an alchemical sign for the *four elements*: ▽, water; ▽̶, earth; △ , fire; and △̶ , air. Other signs for the four elements of alchemy are ⊕ and ⌀.

If we turn the above entry sign 45 degrees, to ⊠, it becomes a **station sign** used in astronomy and astrology. Seen from the earth the planets sometimes move forward and sometimes backward through the zodiac. When the planets change direction the impression for a short while is that they are *standing still*. It is in this position they are said to be *in station*.

In alchemy and old chemistry ⊠ was one of the **time signs** and stood for *month*. As such it could also be drawn ⊠.

See ∑ in Group 40 and ℘ in Group 42 for more time signs.

This structure is an alchemical **time sign** for *year*.

Compare with the above sign entries.

This is a design of a *board used for games,* carved in wood and found in a Viking grave in Uppland, Sweden. It was called **hnefatafl**.

Here we have the sign for *sun, fixed star,* and for *snow,* ✳ , the iconic sign for the six-pointed crystal that is created when water freezes. This sign is written inside a square, representing the *ground*. We find it sometimes used in meteorology meaning the *ground is covered by snow*.

Compare with ⊡ , which denotes *wet ground* or *urine,* and with ⊡ , for *flooded ground*. See also ♨ in Group 39.

An alchemical sign for *warm or hot water*, made up by ▽ for the *element of water* and ✳ for a *star* or *sun: extreme heat*.
    See ∞ in Group 20 for more signs for water.

An open cross within a closed one is a typical structure in Greece and the Near East about 1000 B.C. It appears to have been related to the *weather*; the *four winds* that brought rain in the West, the East, and pre-Columbian America; and the *four points of the compass*. + is associated with the *ground*, the *fields*, and the *earth*. Via the weather, the cross is associated with the *sun* and often appears together with the sun sign, as in the Indian ideogram ⊶ and the Peruvian sun cross ⊹ from pre-Columbian times. The cross was also an attribute of the Greek sun god Apollo hundreds of years before the Christian era.
    See ⊹, the restoration cross, found in fifteenth-century heraldry, for a possible remainder of the ancient relationship between + and ⊙ .

A rune from the earliest rune alphabet. Its name propably meant *day*. It was also carved ◊ , ☓ , and, ᛞ . It was associated with *light, breakthrough,* and *success.*

A **time sign** for *hour* in alchemy and early chemistry. Hour was also drawn ᚡ , ⧖, and ⧗ , all probably conventionalized representations of sand-glasses or hourglasses.

Design found in Norway on a piece of tapestry from the Viking era. Other non-iconic signs found on the same tapestry are ⌂ and ⌐⌐⌐.

Compare with ⌘ in Group 25.

An ideogram used in the English system of hobo signs meaning *here people are afraid of tramps*. It is structurally similar to ⌸, *cubic*, and ⌹ , *improve register*.

Compare with ⌹ , *cowards, they give only in order to get rid of you*, used in the U.S. system of hobo signs.

A variation of the **Maltese cross**. See ✛ in Group 28 for more data.

In England, this sign is, or has been, used as the logotype for the *British motor vehicle inspection*.

See ⚛ in Group 34 for this sign's history.

This **triceps** means *divine power*. According to the Anglo-Saxon tradition it was originally a Nordic sign. We can see that it is similar to the preceding entry sign, with the addition of equilateral triangles at the end of each arm.

The giant Japanese *Mitsubishi Group* has taken this sign as their logotype.

Compare with ⚙ , which is composed of two triceps of this type joined in a circle and is used as the logo for a radio and appliance sales chain.

The **pentagram** or **pentacle** belongs to the group of some 20 basic gestalts in Western ideography. Despite the fact that ☆ consists of five straight lines it is still a single entity, a holistic design. It is quite unlikely that this design was discovered by chance. Here are other gestalts with which to compare it: ○, △, □, +, ↑, ☺, ∨, ⚐ , and ₀₀₀ .

The pentagram was probably discovered as a result of astronomical research in the Euphrates-Tigris region about 6000 years ago. For a derivation of this sign, see ⊛ in Group 29.

Isolated pentagrams have been found on broken fragments of pot sherds in Palestine, at levels dating from around 4000 B.C. It was a common sign among the Sumerians around 2700 B.C. Some of those who have conducted research of symbols believe ☆ was used by the Sumerians as a cosmic symbol representing the four corners of the earth and the vault of the heavens. This, however, seems a bit far-fetched. The sign + would have been better suited for this particular interpretation. After the Sumerian time there is also no clear evidence as to what the pentagram might have meant. It is not until the sign appears in Pythagorean mysticism that it has a defined meaning: it is said to symbolize the *human being*. The points of ☆ represent the head, arms, and legs of the body. Yet this interpretation seems to underestimate the intelligence and knowledge of the Pythagoreans. They did, however, use the sign widely and are believed to have used this sign in their letters to one another as a wish of good health around 400 B.C.

What we do know with all certainty is that ☆ played an important role as a sign on the official seal of the *city of Jerusalem* during the period 300–150 B.C.

The pentagram has been called **Solomon's seal** or **Solomon's shield** in medieval Jewish mysticism.

The five-pointed star also had already appeared in pre-Columbian America, although not in the form of the pentagram, but as ✧, which shows that the high cultures existing at that time — in the same way as, for example, the Mayan culture — had not succeeded in discovering the design ☆ despite their advanced knowledge of the timing of the appearances of the Morning star and the Evening star.

After the Sumerian epoch in the Euphrates-Tigris region, the Venus goddess seems to have been symbolized by ✳, the **eight-pointed star**. The pentagram fell out of use and did not appear in this region until some 1,000 years later.

Count Goblet d'Alviella suggested in his book *La migration des Symboles* (see bibliography) at the end of the nineteenth century that certain graphic symbols for powerful entities exclude each other. Thus, ✳ for Venus as the goddess of fertility and war excludes the sign ☆. The two do not appear simultaneously in the same political, economic, and cultural spheres. The same applies (an example from d'Alviella) for the sun god symbolized by 卐 and by the winged globe, ∞⊃ . We could refer to this as the law of the graphic exclusivity of dominating symbols of power.

The pentagram is sometimes known as the **Eastern star** and is apparently then identical with the **Morning star** and the planet Venus as the war goddess Ischtar or Astarte. Note that ☆ is very popular with the military. All officers in modern armies have a number of five-pointed stars on their uniforms. These stars are also found painted on the sides of tanks and fighter planes in the United States, the U.S.S.R., and China. See ☆ in Group 28.

In Western ideography it appears on some of the coats of arms of the crusader knights. During the Middle Ages, however, ☆ began to be associated with *magic* and the *Devil*. It was used in Nordic countries, where it was drawn on doors and walls as *protection against trolls and evil*. When the sign is turned so that two of its ends are pointing upward, like ⛥, it represents the *Devil*.

Today ⭐ is mainly used as a sign signifying a *favorable opportunity* (for example, in sale advertisements), *parties,* and a *spirit of togetherness.* In comic strips, however, it has retained its old association to warfare in that it is used to indicate the *mental state resulting from a blow to the head* (to "see stars") or the *pain resulting from a blow or injury.*

In the Japanese *Art of Warfare,* ⭐ stands for *forts and fortresses,* as does ⬡.

For ⭐ as a plaited sign, turn to Group 34.

As a *cadence sign* ⭐ stands for the *third son* (see ⏤ in Group 22).

The sign ⭐ is not used in modern Western ideographic systems. The filled or the empty variation, ☆, however, is occasionally found in fire prevention contexts, as a sign indicating a source of light on nautical charts, and for unpostmarked stamps in philately.

The **hexagram** is based on the gestalt △. The earliest examples found are dated back to around 800–600 B.C. If it had been designed by a process of random experimentation with the graphic element △, the hexagram would have been created long before ⭐ . Present historical facts, however, state that ✡ appeared at least 3000 years later than ⭐.

During antiquity ✡ was a symbol for the *Jewish kingdom.* When this kingdom was conquered in A.D. 70, and, in fact, already some 100 years before that, the Jewish people began to spread throughout the world, as did the symbol ✡.

The hexagram is sometimes known as the **shield of David** or the **Magen David**. According to the late Danish semiotician S.T. Achen, the Muslims refer to ✡ as **Solomon's seal**, whereas E. Zehren points out that the sign on **Solomon's seal** was ⭐. The hexagram is frequently used in the magic formulas in the ancient book of witchcraft, *The Key of Solomon.*

✡ was first and foremost used by alchemists in the Middle Ages as a general symbol representing the *art of alchemy*
and secondly as a sign for ▽, *water*, and △ , *fire*. Together,
these two signs formed the symbol for *fire water* or the *essence*, or *spiritus*, in wine: *alcohol*. It was also the sign for the
quintessence, the *fifth element*. See the synonym ♀ in Group 50.

In some alchemical contexts, however, ✡ was used to
mean *drink!*

The Jews in Europe used ✡ during the Middle Ages on
their banners and prayer shawls. When they were repressed
by the Church and the princes, however, a pointed hat and,
later, a yellow ring, were used to distinguish them, not ✡.

The hexagram became more popular during the nineteenth century and was used to decorate newly built syna-
gogues. The founders of the Zionist movement adopted the
hexagram as a rallying symbol in their attempts to create a
Jewish national state in Palestine.

On November 9, 1938, at the orders of Heydrich, the hexagram combined with the color yellow, earlier used to distinguish the Jews, was introduced to mark all those of Jewish
birth.

✡ in blue has appeared on the flag of Israel since 1948.

It is interesting to note that ▓ also appeared in pre-Columbian America. In Uxmal, Central America, ▓ is found on a
cliff engraving from around 1000 B.C. The "trailing" or
"hanging" elements, ▦ , remind one of similar structures
from the Phoenician cultural sphere around the Mediterranean during antiquity. This American version of ✡ was
plaited.

The hexagram, plaited and red, is used as a symbol for the
Magen David Adom, a humanitarian organization similar to
the Red Cross.

✡ is hardly used in modern ideography except as a sign
for motors with certain characteristics in electrical engineering. The "empty" hexagram, without crossing lines, or the

filled version, ✦, is never used in Western ideography except as a form for a **policeman's badge** in Iceland and in certain states in the United States (the **sheriff's star**). (As a form of a policeman's badge ★ is also common in the United States.)

The ideogram for *marital love* among the Nsibidi people of Ghana, Africa. Note the eight-pointed star, the Venus star.

Compare with ☿ in another African system, also representing *marital love*, and with ⚭ for *married* in genealogy.

The **heptagram**, a seven-pointed star, is an obvious development of ✰. The number seven is well known in Western symbolism. The traditional seven planets (the wandering celestial bodies as opposed to the fixed stars) were associated with seven *celestial spheres*, thus the old expression "to be in seventh heaven." The diatonic scale has seven tones: do, re, mi, fa, so, la, ti. All through the Old Testament are examples of the significance of the *number 7*.

The four phases of the moon took 29 days, i.e., a little more than 7 days each. The menstruation cycle of women is 28 days, which is 4 times 7. God created the world in 6 days and rested on the seventh, the day of the Sabbath. Seven years is the length of each of the four phases of the planet Saturn, ♄, in relation to its position in the birth chart or horoscope: separating square, opposition, approaching square, and conjunction.

For a derivation of the 7-day week and the names of the days, turn to ✹ in Group 29.

This octagram has been frequently used as a decorative element in many countries and epochs.

In the Japanese *Art of Warfare* it stands for *fort* or *fortresses*.

Another heptagram, called the **mystical star** according to Gnostic tradition.

The **octagram of creation** according to the Gnostic tradition. It is related to the planet Venus as the goddess of fertility.

This design has also been used in the Nordic countries as an **invocation of magic** and a **protecting ideogram** carved into doors and walls.

An **enneagram**, or **nine-pointed star**. This enneagram is not drawn in one continous line but as three triangles on top of one another.

This ideogram is used in Christian symbolism to indicate the *nine gifts of the spirit*: *love, happiness, peace, patience, leniency, benevolence, trustworthiness, meekness or gentleness,* and *temperance.*

See also ⊖ in Group 23, also called an enneagram.

✿ inscribed in a triangle is the symbol for the revived Order of the Temple Knights, which has lodges in all Scandinavian countries. In their symbol, however, ✿ is plaited.

See ✛ in Group 28 for facts about the medieval Order of the Temple Knights.

The **cross of endlessness** is, quite logically, considered to be a symbol for *eternity*. As such, ⊠ is synonymous with ◯ and ∞.

Compare with ⌘ and ♯.

Structure used by the Nazis in their Germanic symbolism. ⊕ was often used together with ⅏ and ↑.

See ⋇ in Group 9 for more data.

One of the alchemists' signs for *stones* or *pebbles*.

See ⟊ in Group 39 for a synonym.

A very recent modern graffiti sign used by youths in Sweden, with unknown meaning. It is also drawn ⊗.

Group 28

Multi-axis symmetric, straight-lined, closed signs without crossing lines

The equilateral triangle (as the single-axis symmetric triangle, △) is newer than ↑, ˅, +, and ○, but older than, for
example, the pentagram and the swastika. △ seems hardly
to have been used in the prehistoric age, i.e., it is not seen on
old rock carvings and cave paintings.

△ is first and foremost associated with the *holy, divine
number of 3*. It is through the tension of opposites that the
new is created, the third. Philosophically, the thesis gives
rise to its antithesis, and these two together create a synthe-
sis (Hegel, Marx, Mao). Graphically, we can exemplify it
with the opposites + and ○ , which when synthesized become ⊕. Xenocrates, who died in 324 B.C., stated that △ was
a symbol for *God*. In Christian symbolism it stands for the
Holy Trinity.

It is also a symbol for *power* and, as such, related to *danger*.
But according to the law of the polarity of meanings of the
elementary graphs, it also means *success, prosperity*, and
safety. The Hittites used it to mean *well, good*, or *healthy*.

As is often the case with basic gestalts the two meanings
are sometimes united in the same sign occurrence. This is
the case when △ is used as a traffic sign, where it indicates
danger or a *threat*, but also *safety* for those who observe the
sign.

In astrology it represents the most positive of the aspects,
the *trine*, or the angle of 120 degrees between planets, and
also the *astrological element of fire*.

The astrological elements are organized in the so-called
triplicities, a dividing of the zodiac signs into four groups of
three: fire, △; earth, ⊕; air, = ; and water, ▽. The *fire signs*
are Aries, ♈; Leo, ♌; and Sagittarius, ♐.

The astrological elements are symbols for four different
ways of relating to and understanding the world the individual lives in. Individuals mainly influenced by the element
of fire relate to people and things in terms of the opportunities these might mean for themselves and their lives.

According to the trend in modern astrology toward Jungian psychoanalysis, one or more of these perceptionary elements are dominant in an individual, while the others are
linked to the subconscious complex called the *shadow,* a
person of the same sex characterized by despicable and
contemptuous qualities. The shadow is often symbolized
by Saturn, ♄, in the birth chart. The other most important
complex of this type is *animus,* an ideal personality of the
opposite sex that is subconsciously projected onto suitable
persons of the opposite sex, leading to love affairs of the
type, "it is as if we had known each other all our lives,
although we have only known each other a week."

Signs that belong to the same element lie in the aspect △,
trine, to one another. This creates a basis for harmony,
approachability, and understanding.

Both in Tibet and in European alchemy △ signified the
element of fire. With a line added, ⟁ or ⟁ , it was transformed into the alchemical symbol for the *element of air.* (See
▽ below for a similar change of meaning.)

The system of traffic signs is one of the most common
modern ideographic systems. In this △ is a general sign for
danger. What is dangerous is signified by other signs within
the triangle. ▲ is used as a standard sign on the dashboard
of cars for warning lights. It also appears as a warning triangle to be folded out and placed on the road when a car is
stopped on a highway. On medicine packaging ▲ means a
drug that can slow down reactions.

△ is used in some 40 modern ideographic systems. It is
used in the ground-to-air emergency code to mean it is *probably safe to land here.* In botany it means *evergreen perennials.*
It appears as a tele-engineering sign for *telephone* and in meteorology can signify *hail.* Philatelists use it to indicate that
*enough of the envelope is left to show the whole postmark together
with the stamp.* It is used in physics to indicate a *lowering of*

the freezing point or a *lowering of the temperature.* Chemists, however, use it to mean *warming up* (as did the alchemists).

In cartography △ sometimes stands for *natural gas,* while ▲ in the same context can stand for *oil* or *oil well,* all these denotations connected to the element of fire.

When the above entry sign is turned 90 degrees to the right, to ▷, we find it used on flags of several nations.

With its point downward the triangle adopts a negative spectrum of meaning. In alchemy it represents *water,* the *passive element.* With a line, ▽ or ⩒, it becomes the *element of earth.* In both the U.S. and English systems of hobo signs it means *no good: too many have been here.* As a traffic sign it means the passive *yield,* or *give way to crossing traffic.*

Even in the astrological system of elements ▽ stands for *water,* and in certain meteorological systems it is used to denote a *rain shower,* although it is more common to use the single-axis symmetric triangle, ▽, for this meaning.

The **eye of the dragon,** according to Koch (see bibliography), is an ancient Germanic sign. We can analyze this sign as a combination of ▽ for *threat* and Y for the *choice between good and evil.*

Compare with ⊗, an old sign for *phosphorus,* a highly poisonous and inflammable substance.

The **square** in a horizontal-vertical position is an expression of the two dimensions that constitute a surface. □ means *land, field, ground,* or the *element earth*. The Egyptians used it in their system of hieroglyphs, where it is supposed to have meant *realization* or *materialization*. In the Orient, as in the West, □ symbolizes *land* or *ground*.

For the alchemists this square represented *salt*. Salt was often produced by letting sea water evaporate on the ground. Even in modern meteorology □ can represent the *ground*. The sign placed within the square indicates the weather's effect on the ground, as in ⊠, *snow-covered*.

The ground-to-air emergency code also relates this structure to the ground or the land: *compass and map are needed*. Two other examples of its association to the ground or land are the use of □ and ■ on maps for *farm* or *farmhouse*.

In astrology □ signifies the most difficult and tense aspect that can occur between two planets in a natal chart. This aspect is called the *square*, the *angle of 90 degrees*.

Botanists sometimes use it to denote the *male* individual of dioecious plants (in which case ○ stands for the *female*). In military contexts the sign can be used for *private soldiers*.

The filled square, ■ , appears on videotape recorders for the *control for interrupting recording or play*.

Last, it should be mentioned that squares with lines in them occur in garments to indicate how the garment should be treated in washing. Thus, for instance, ⦀ means that the *garment can be drip-dried*.

The square within a square has a different spectrum of meaning than ☐ . It means *keep, retain, keep inside,* or *close in.* When used as an English **boy scout sign** it means *wait here.* In some cartographical systems it stands for *fortress* (see the word index for synonyms).

It can also represent a *manhole,* as it does in electrical engineering. A manhole is an opening to a lower, closed space or room where lines can be checked and repaired.

On electrical household appliances it means that they are better isolated than usual. The sign 回 indicates *appliances that can use both grounded and non-grounded sockets or outlets.*

Diagonally placed, ◈, this sign signifies a *tank trap* in some military systems. In heraldry, ◈ can appear high on a woman's coat of arms showing that she is *divorced.* (∞ and ⌀ have the same meaning in a genealogical context.) Note that ◇ was the shape of a woman's coat of arms when noble ladies were allowed to have their own coats of arms at the end of the Middle Ages, around the year 1500.

The diagonally placed square has no particular spectrum of meaning as far as we know. It was engraved in the cave of Marsoulas in prehistoric times, but there are no clues as to what it might have meant.

The sign is the symbol for the *suit of diamonds* in a pack of cards. Diamonds are usually associated with *courage* and *daring.* The English hobos made use of ◇ to mean *here live generous people, but behave well, show them respect, and take nothing for granted.*

In meteorology it can sometimes signify *clear air* and in chemistry, *soft soap.* It has been used in biological contexts for an *individual of unknown or unclear sex.*

Compare with ♀ , one of the alchemists' signs for *sulphur* and also one of the signs for the *asteroid Pallas.*

A **rhombus** with its longest axis placed vertically was some-times used for *soap* in alchemy.

◊ is also an **early form of note sign** in music, a sign for *tone*, later replaced by the well-known ○.

A **rhombus,** its longest axis placed horizontally, was some-times used during the seventeenth century to mean *anti-mony* or *antimonite*. This substance was also drawn ♉ and ♂.

The sign is now used in computer flow charting. It indicates *conditions for a program step that are based on* >, <, *or* =.

A **time sign** for *autumn* in old Germanic systems.

Compare with the synonymous ♏ in Group 5 and other time signs.

These ideograms were put into use at the beginning of the 1970s in medical bulletins, prescriptions, and drug cata-logues. The uppermost means *danger for habituation* and is applicable to amphetamines (drugs that stimulate the central nervous system) and drugs with the opposite effect, like the opiates morphine and heroin and similar drugs (narcotics).

The lower sign means *weak stimulants or depressants, but some risk for habituation*. This sign applies to barbiturates and similar drugs, i.e., the most common sleeping pills, tranquil-izers (e.g., Valium), and sedatives.

This structure is used in the context of modern architecture and communications. As a sign in computer flow charting ⊿ means *sorting*.

With the square placed diagonally it becomes an Indian **yantra structure**. Yantras are visual structures linked to subconscious psychological complexes. Meditating over a yantra is considered to help when one is trying to reach higher levels of consciousness, i.e., ⌣ in 𝟛 in Group 14.

Thus, it likely is psychological considerations and not chance that made Germany's (and Europe's) currently biggest bank, *Deutsche Bank*, adopt the yantra structure ⊿ in the form ▨ as its logotype.

This is a medieval ideogram representing the *four elements*. Compare with the sign entry below, of which it is the central part.

This symbol has been used to represent the elements in astrology, alchemy, and philosophy. At the top are the triangles representing the elements of *air* and *fire*, and at the bottom are the triangles for the elements *earth* and *water*.

See the word index for other **element symbols**.

During the seventeenth century this structure was used as a pattern for the *natal chart* (often now somewhat misleadingly called the horoscope). The triangles between the inner and outer horizontal-vertical squares correspond to the *12 houses* (see the word index for definitions). The name and date of birth of the individual was written in the inner square.

Compare with natal chart patterns from other times, such as ⊕ and ⼢⼣ . For a modern pattern for the birth or natal chart, the zodiac circle, look up ◯ in Group 35.

This is a modern ideogram that signifies a *nature preserve protected by law*. It can be found on road signs. For the spectrum of meaning of the central sign structure, look up ✳ in Group 9.

In the same system there is also the sign ⊞ , indicating a *sight worth seeing, either from a cultural or a scenic point of view*.

The horizontal rectangle is found in some 20 ideographic systems and denotes an *enclosed space, tank,* or *closed room.* Since   often signifies *heat*, it follows that ⬛ means *heat oven* in some technical contexts.

As a genealogical sign ▭ means *buried.*

The meaning of this sign is further clarified when we compare it with ▭ , an Egyptian hieroglyph signifying *dwelling* or *house.*

In the English and Swedish systems of hobo signs   means *danger, people living here will try to have you arrested,* and the *owner of this house is a brute*, respectively. See ▥ in Group 22 and ▧ in Group 34, both of which have a similar meaning.

▭ is also used in computer flow charting. It indicates a *certain group of program instructions* or a *secondary process.*

The vertically positioned or standing rectangle is very seldom used in Western ideography. It is used doubled, though. ‖ and ∥ are found on video appliances, meaning *control button for pause.*

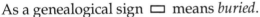

The regular **pentagon** is a uniform, five-sided structure closely associated with the *planet Venus,* ♀. The Venus goddess was in ancient times both a war and a fertility divinity. The promoters of the Christian ideology sought to suppress the sexual pleasure aspects of this ancient goddess. Therefore, they had to carefully retain all the rest of what the goddess stood for, lest they create disobedience and ideological havoc. Consequently, they were more than happy to retain the aggressive and warmongering aspect: Venus as the goddess of warfare and sacrifice. From the sixteenth century until the eighteenth century the pentagon, as a structure closely associated with the pagan goddess through the celestial movements of the planet Venus, was common as a basic design for fortresses. Reminiscences of this are still to be found today, as, for example, in the U.S. Pentagon complex in Arlington, Virginia, a military headquarters, although not a fortress in the usual sense of the word.

If one plots the position of the planet Venus in the zodiac when it first appears as the Morning or Evening star after a period of invisibility (at ♀ ☌ ☉), then waits until ♀ disappears again, then repeats the procedure the next time Venus reappears either as the Morning or the Evening star and does this for a period of 1,460 days (i.e., exactly four years), if a line is drawn between each of the positions, from the first to the second, etc., the design revealed when all the points have been joined together is that of an exactly regular pentagon.

For this reason ⬠ is closely associated with ✩ in Group 27. It is thereby also related to ☆ , an ideogram widely used by armed forces both in the West and in the East (in fact over the whole planet). For a more detailed description of the relation between ⬠ and ♀, read the entry ⨂ in Group 29.

⬠ seems to be used in very few, if any, of the established Western ideographic systems. Compare this with the fact that the structure △ is used in over 40 different systems.

The regular **hexagon**, a uniform, six-sided, geometrical design, is used in Western ideography in the contexts of chemistry and electricity and in engineering to represent a *flow restriction*.

The substance *benzene* is a very important compound in aromatic organic chemistry, i.e., the field of chemistry working with compounds based upon carbon. Benzene is used as a dissolvant when producing pharmaceutical products. It is a poisonous and extremely flammable substance that is extracted from coal tar.

Different models for the benzene molecule have long been designed to try to explain the chemical properties of benzene. It was the German Friedrich August Kekule von Stradonitz who, because of a dream he had in 1865, devised the best model to date, which happened to have the form ◯. This has, since then, become a universally accepted model of the chemical structure of benzene.

The **four-pointed star**, or **sun star**, denotes, according to Koch (see bibliography), a *serious and solemn warning*.

Compare with ⊕, the logotype for *NATO*. In this logotype ✧ was combined with ⅙, the symbol used by the recently defeated German Wehrmacht. (NATO was formed in 1949.) But the Americans straightened out the Hakenkreuz a bit, to ⅄.

In the Euphrates-Tigris region ✧ in the form ✳ represented the *highest god*, the *sun god Shamash*.

Note also that ✧ in the form ⊕ is the logotype of the biggest bank in the United States, *Citicorp*.

The **five-pointed star without crossing lines** is one of the most common and important Western ideograms. It is used in the flags of some 35 countries. Its first appearance on a national flag is believed to have been in 1777, when the United States of America declared itself an independent country.

This star is also the *most widely used military symbol* and is found on the tanks and fighter jets of all the superpowers, as well as in the armed forces of all other countries on uniforms, etc. It is, in this particular use, related to ⬡, in this group, and to ☆ , the sign for the *planet Venus as the Morning star* and the *goddess of war*. For nearly all armed forces on this planet the golden five-pointed star without crossing lines is the symbol *par préférence* of military rank and power. For its origins and a description of its relation to ♀ , look up ⊛ in Group 29.

The five-pointed star is also a *symbol of ideologies* and appears together with other structures to denote different creeds and belief systems: with the hammer and sickle it represents *communism*; with palm leaves, *Scientology*; with the half-moon, *Islam*; with a T-sign inside the star, *Tupamaros* (the now-defeated socialist city guerillas in Uruguay). With crossing lines, as ☆ in the sign ⬬, it represents the *Bahai religion*. These are just a few of the ideologies using the five-pointed Venus star as their logotypes.

☆ has several other uses. It denotes the *Bethlehem star*. It is sometimes a sign to indicate an *especially good quality product or achievement* (recall the five-pointed gold and silver stars that were used in the lower grades at school). Philatelists use it to mean a *stamp that has not been postmarked*.

It is also a *sign of protection* associated with *security* and *safety*. ★, for example, indicates *emergency exits* and *storage spaces for safety equipment*.

☆ can also appear alone, doubled, or multiplied several times to denote *varying degrees of coldness in a freezer*. It would have been more logical in this case to use the six-pointed star because of its relation to crystallized water; ☆ has no direct relation to the idea of coldness.

This sign is associated with *law and order* and is found used as a **police badge** and **sheriff's star** in several states (✩, however, is more common). On gravestones it is commonly used to indicate the *date of birth*.

As a *cadence sign* it denotes the *third son*.

☆ is a sign for the *Eastern star* (along with ✪ and ★). The Eastern star is the planet Venus when it appears as the Morning star. The Bethlehem star is often drawn ★. It was this star that the three wise men, the Magi, saw and followed to Bethlehem when Jesus was born. The Bethlehem star is a typical Christmas symbol, as is the eight-pointed Venus star.

There is a theory propagated by certain researchers of symbolism that the star observed by the wise men was, in reality, several planets and/or distant suns that conjugated at the time of Jesus' birth (a few years before the beginning of our present chronology). But those who study the night skies and different conjunctions know that it is extremely rare for such a phenomenon to be mistaken for a single star, and even if this in fact was the case, the stars would have been distinguishable a few hours before and after the conjunction.

Whether the South and Central American cultures ever were able to plot Venus' movements we do not know, but they, too, had a five-pointed star, albeit lacking in graphical precision: ✮.

Although ☆ is quite common in the Western culture it is used in a relatively small number of modern sign systems, including philately and some simple cartography, where it represents *centers of communication* and *towns*. It is also used on some nautical charts to signify *sources of light* and *lighthouses*.

In the world of comic strips only some ten non-iconic ideograms are used. ☆ is one of them. *Pain in a part of the body* is marked by such signs with or without some ⸓ and/or ⸓ in between them: ⸓⸓⸓.

☆ is also used in this way, but not so commonly.

This variation of the five-pointed star is common in heraldry and relatively common in military contexts, especially on uniforms. It has no special significance, though.

In heraldry it is called **mullet**, the rowel of a spur. Note, however, that in French heraldry the mullet is a six-pointed star.

The **two-axis, symmetric six-pointed star without crossing lines** is often a sign for *fixed stars* (as opposed to the planets — wandering stars) and especially for the *pole star*. Compare with ✕ in Group 9, which has the same meaning.

With two of its rays or points horizontally lengthened, i.e., as ✶, it appears as a symbol for *coniunctio* in esoteric alchemy. See the section "Esoteric alchemy" in Part I.

The star sign's six rays are associated with the six-pointed structure of crystallized water. This sign, therefore, is indirectly related to the *North Pole* and the pole star.

✶ is also used as a genealogical sign. When found on gravestones it indicates the *date of birth*. This sign stands for the *beginning of earthly life* in the same way as † symbolizes its end. Synonymous in this respect are ☆ and ✷. Note that neither the four-pointed nor the seven-pointed or eight-pointed stars are used for this purpose; for indicating birthdates, only the signs for Venus and the pole star (or some other sun) will do.

Strange as it may sound, the **regular six-pointed star with-out crossing lines** is almost never used in Western ideo-graphic systems. It is, however, used in some U.S. states as a form for **policemen's badges**, connoting *law and order*.

The **eight-pointed star** is a very old symbol for ♀, the *planet Venus*. See ⊛ in Group 29.

It is hardly used in any of the established Western ideo-graphic systems, but is, on the other hand, very common as a *Christmas star* or the *star of Bethlehem*.

This star, but with a square in its middle, ✵, can be seen on a painting from the fifteenth or sixteenth century, a por-trait of Vlad, the Pole Piercer, more commonly known as Count Dracula (from the Rumanian *draculu* = devil). Vlad was prince of Valakia, the southern part of what is now Rumania, and tried to rule its several million inhabitants and fight off his enemies at the same time, as he had to with-stand constant pressure from the Hungarians in the north and the Ottoman Turks in the south. But he surely also con-sidered it his duty to defend Christianity, ✛, against the Ottoman Turks, ☾, the latter having recently conquered the capital of the Eastern Roman Empire, Constantinople, taking over its symbol, ⌣, and renaming this mighty Christian metropolis, which for more than 1000 years had withstood all attacks, Istanbul.

Vlad was well known for his cruelty. At one time he or-dered all of the tens of thousands of poor Turkish peasants living in Valakia to be murdered. The Muslim Turks proba-bly had an eight-pointed Venus star on their banners as well as the crescent, just as today they use ★, also a symbol for Venus as the Morning star, the goddess of activity and fight-ing. Note also that the square in ✵ is a symbol for *land*, the fief to be defended against the enemies.

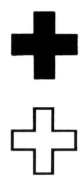

The filled or closed cross with short arms of equal length was a common sign in ancient Greece, in pre-Columbian America, and in the Near East approximately 1000 years before the birth of Christ. But crosses were already used in the Euphrates-Tigris region around 1500 B.C. They first seem to have been wheel crosses with four spokes, which in time lost their rim and became real crosses, albeit with rounded outer edges on the arms as a legacy from their past history of close contact with the wheel's rim. These early crosses were like the four-spoked wheels of the sun god and power symbols, and had nothing to do with torture.

The Romans were a cruel and barbaric race, whatever you may have learned in school and however efficiently you may have been able to deafen yourself to the screams of terror and agony of the women and children burned, chewed upon by starved crocodiles and lions, and carefully pierced on poles to die slowly in the Coliseum for the pleasure of the populace of stinking Rome. The ruling patricians had ordered the use of T-crosses as racks for torturing workers (slaves, often prisoners of war) and peasants not willing to obey the whims of their masters, while they reserved for themselves the right to die quickly by decapitation with the help of a sharp sword in the hands of an expert, for those among them who happened to make a faux pas. The origin of the word *cross* is the Latin word *crux*, from the verb *cruciare,* meaning to torture. When the successful new ideology of Christianity began to spread, the worship of masochistic suffering also spread, and the promoters of apostles and would-be saints competed in devising ugly past deaths for their protégés — the immensely sought-after prize being the honor of having a torture rack named after them (like the cross of St. Peter, the cross of St. Andrew, the cross of St. Phillip, etc.)

The **Greek cross**, however, with its short, broad arms, was never a suitable torture rack but a close descendant of the four-spoked wheel crosses, the ancient and worshipped symbol for divinity in the Euphrates-Tigris and Syrian regions. The sun god of these regions was symbolized in two ways: by the four-spoked wheel, with or without two spread wings on either side, and by the four-pointed star sign, with or without a circle around it, ✳. From which of these two four-armed symbols the first real so-called Greek crosses evolved we do not know, but we know that the sign ✚ appears together with ✳ — a symbol representing the *horned divinity of fertility, sexual pleasures, hunting, and warfare* that was associated with the planet Venus — on a Babylonian seal from around 1500 B.C.

Since we now in some detail have explored the origin of the symbol *par préférence* for the Western way of life, let us proceed to today's uses of the cross other than as symbol for masochistic suffering and torture.

In the United States ✚ has been used as a meteorological sign to denote a *mixing of air masses*. Note the relation of this use of the cross sign to the Hopi sign + and its probable meaning, the *four winds or corners of the earth*.

Apart from being named the Greek cross, this sign entry is also called **St. George's cross**. This version of the cross is also the logotype adopted by the *Red Cross*, established as an international organization in 1863 at the Geneva convention, the first serious attempt to agree on laws to, at least cosmetically, check the insane activity of warfare. St. George's cross was common on the shields and standards used by the crusaders around the year 1100. Today it can be seen on the flags of Greece and Switzerland.

The **cross of St. Andrew** was the sign used for the Scottish flag before Scotland's union with England. The **Union Jack,** today's British flag, is a combination of the English St. George's cross (white), the Scottish cross of St. Andrew (white and red), and the Irish cross of St. Patrick (red).

The cross of St. Andrew in the second and common form of it, ✖ (surrounded by five-pointed stars), was also the symbol for the Southern states during the American Civil War, the Confederate battle flag.

✖ is a modern ideogram printed on bottles, packages, etc., that means *harmful* or *corroding chemical.*

This form of cross is sometimes called **St. George's cross** (like ✚ in an above entry). St. George was a Christian officer in the Roman army who came to Lydia, where he discovered that the people were being terrorized by a dragon. This dragon subsisted on human flesh and had at that time just demanded the king's daughter as his next meal. George killed the dragon, but was then beheaded by the king because he had persuaded the queen to convert to the Christian faith. The crusaders were so impressed by this exhibition of passivity and humility on the part of an expert warrior that they chose George as their saint and protector.

The medals of various orders often carry St. George's cross.

In alchemy ⊹ has sometimes been used to signify *arsenic,* also drawn ♂ and otherwise. See ♂ in Group 54 for more signs for arsenic.

Compare with ✚ in Group 30.

A variation of the **arrow cross** used by the *Hungarian fascists* during the 1930s and 1940s. In other forms the arrow cross is said to have been used as a rallying sign for the Magyarian tribes about the time that they arrived in the region now called Hungary, around the year 1000.

The root meaning of the arrow cross is *expansion in all directions*, thus it is a symbol denoting *expansion*. In this it is synonymous with all the Christian crosses used to represent world evangelization, an expression of the expansion of the doctrines of the Christian faith in all directions. Examples of these crosses are ⊹ and ⊹.

For other meanings of the arrow cross, look up ⊹ in Group 9.

The **Maltese cross,** or **cross of promise**, is related to the Sovereign Ex-territorial State St. John of Jerusalem, Rhodes, and Malta Supreme Military Hospital Order. The order runs an activity in many countries similar to that of the Red Cross and has diplomatic representation in several of the world's major cities.

This cross form is used on the Maltese merchant marine flag. It is also the form used for the most important medals in many countries.

The eight points of the cross symbolize the *eight qualities of a knight: loyalty, piety, generosity, courage, honor and glory, contempt of death, helpfulness,* and *reverence for the Church.*

This cross is also found on the seal of the Order of Knight Templars. The order was inaugurated by eight knights in 1118, who in the presence of the patriarch of Jerusalem vowed, among other things, to defend pilgrims travelling to the holy city.

This combination of a Maltese cross and St. George's cross is sometimes called a **Greek cross**. In this structural group of graphs there are no less than three different cross designs called Greek crosses. This type of cross was quite common in Scandinavia during the Viking era, for which one of the reasons might be the great export of young Vikings from Sweden to Miklagård (Constantinople), during the centuries around A.D. 800, for service in the guard protecting the Byzantine emperor and his glorious city at the Golden Horn.

The **crutch cross** is sometimes interpreted as the joining together of four **Tau crosses** (see **T** in Group 22). This ideogram has been used, for example, by the *anti-Nazi party led by Dollfuss in Austria* during the 1930s. It was also very common in Portugal, at least before the revolution against the old fascist regime in the 1970s.

This fascist symbol was taken up by the murderous ultrasocialists in Kampuchea (Cambodia), the Khmer Rouge. They used it on their banners during the Communist revolution in Cambodia and at the siege and fall of its capital, Phnom Penh, in 1975.

Compare with ✝ in Group 22, a battle sign frequently used by crusader knights and by the knights of the Teutonic Order occupying the northern part of what is now Poland and the land on the east coast of the Baltic.

A version of the **cross of Lorraine** or **Lothringenkreuz**, conventionalized for heraldic uses as a coat of arms symbol and order medal.

See the common cross of Lorraine, ✝, in Group 3 for more data.

An almost identical but often much smaller and filled version of this sign, , has been used in cabbalistic mysticism to represent a *holy name*. Today, it is used by the pope, archbishops, and bishops, placed immediately before their signatures on documents.

The **Jerusalem cross**. In gold on a silvery background, it was the banner used to represent the *Crusaders' Kingdom of Jerusalem*. Nowadays the Jerusalem cross appears on, among other places, the medal of the Order of the Holy Sepulchre, which is presented by the pope.

For more data, see ⌗ in Group 9.

Group 29

Multi-axis symmetric, both soft and straight-lined, closed signs with crossing lines

The **wheel cross, sun cross**, or **Wuotan's (Odin's) cross**. ⊕ is a structure that first began to appear when humankind was on the threshold of the Bronze Age. It is common on rock carvings and it appears in ancient Egypt, China, pre-Columbian America, and the Near East.

From the facts available it seems as if ⊕ is associated with the wheel, not so much with its invention as with its revolutionary effect on the existing society. In ancient China this sign was associated with *thunder, power, energy, head*, and *respect*. In ancient Babylon it symbolized the *sun god, Shamash*, and appeared in the form ⊛ .

When the first ideographic writing systems were developed, ⊕ was included. It appears in the earliest systems of writing used by the Egyptians, Hittites, Cretians, Greeks, Etruscans, and Romans.

In ancient Greece it signified a *sphere* or *globe*. It was also used as a *natal chart pattern* in ancient astrology. In modern astrology it is the sign for the *planet earth*, the astrological *element earth*, and *Fortuna, the Part of Fortune*, an important position in the natal chart related to progress and hindrances in the material aspect of an individual's life. (Compare with ⊹ in Group 39.) In astronomy it is also used as a symbol for the *planet earth* and is synonymous with ♁ .

It is easy to trace a shift in this sign's meaning over time. In earliest times ⊕ was a symbol for the *highest power*, for the *sun* and its counterpart, the *king*. It represented power and control. This meaning changed so that ⊕ more and more adopted the meaning of + , i.e., the *earth*, the *land*, and the *points of the compass*.

The Christian Church has followed its tradition faithfully and included this ancient pagan sign among the crosses of its symbolism. ⊕ is known as the **Gamma cross**, the **Roman Catholic cross**, the **consecration cross**, and the **inauguration cross**. At the inauguration of a church, the bishop, using blessed water or oil, draws the wheel cross at 12 different places on the church walls.

Its use as a **halo** or **gloria**, i.e., the *spiritual power or energy that holy people emanate*, suggests a return to its original meaning as a sign of power.

During the Middle Ages the alchemists used ⊕ to signify *copper alloys* (from the Venus sign, ♀, which also means copper) and sometimes for *yleaster*, possibly *stardust* or *meteorite iron*.

It appears in about 15 modern ideographic systems. In certain U.S. meteorological systems it has been used to indicate that *visibility is worsened by fog or dust*. Some English meteorological systems use it to mean a *solar halo*, i.e., a ring around the sun. It is often related to *visibility* and *signalling* in modern ideography.

In all three systems of hobo signs (U.S., English, and Swedish) we find that ⊕, ⊗, or ⊕ mean *here you will find food, work, and/or money; generous people.*

In the wheel cross, when the cross is placed diagonally in the circle, there occurs a noticeable change of meaning. In this case the cancelling and neutralizing characteristics of the diagonal cross come into play. Some of the potentialities of the empty circle, which represents all possibilities, are cancelled. See ⊗, the traffic sign that *limits the possibilities as to where a vehicle can be parked*, and ⊗, used in printing to signify that a *type is damaged or faulty* (the possibility of setting the text is in this way cancelled).

The Swedish military uses ✕ on maps when marking permanent constructions like bridges to be *prepared for destruction*. When the object or installation has been *blown up*, a circle, ○, is drawn around ✕.

When the cross appears within a circle but free from it, i.e., not touching the circumference, a new spectrum of meaning prevails. It becomes a positive sign, a *plus*, and the circle now signifies a *closed unit*. In the English system of hobo signs it means *here you will get a day's work*. In a technical context it can mean *rising pressure* (in a tank or something similar). An arrow can be added to denote a directed movement, ⊕→, whereupon it becomes a chemical sign for *positive ions*. Even without the arrow it can denote positive ions, though. As a sign in physics ⊕ signifies a *proton* or *positron*, i.e., a small, positively charged unit in the atom.

⊕ can sometimes be given the same meaning as ⊕ and in such instances should be viewed as a stylized version of ⊕ .

Note that ⊕ was the **shield of the god of dawn** for the Aztecs.

See also ⑨ in Group 32.

A sign sometimes used by alchemists to denote *saffron*.

This ideogram is, among other things, a *sun symbol*. It has been found on seals from Mohenjo-Daro from around 3000 B.C.

The **sun wheel**, ⊛ , was the Gauls' most used beneficial amulet. The Gauls were the Celtic tribes living in what is now the French-speaking region of Europe. Christian symbolism adopted the form, changing it slightly so that it became a **Christ monogram** drawn within a circle: ⊛ .

The circle divided into six equal parts, with another circle in its center, ⊛ , is the **Tibetan world symbol**, the **world**

wheel. The outer rim is further divided into 12 parts in the same way as the Western zodiac circle. The inner circle band is divided into a light half and a dark half, which suggests that the wheel also symbolizes the same idea of the *unity of opposites* as does the Chinese **yin-yang sign, ⬤** . In Japan, ⊗ is considered to be a sign with positive connotations.

This sign is not, however, widely used in modern ideography except as an electrical sign for a specific type of *electric motor*.

The alchemists sometimes used it to denote *malachite*, an emerald-green mineral containing copper used, among other things, for the production of coloring pigment.

It is also worth noting that the Celts used ⊗ as the attribute of *Taranis, the god of thunder*. In this use the sign is equivalent to the staff carried by Zeus or Jupiter, ⚡, the **staff of thunder and lightning**.

A sign from eighteenth-century chemistry for *sapo, soap*, or *soft soap*. These were compounds of fatty acids with sodium (soap) or potassium (soft soap).

They were included in the pharmacopoeias of the times as detergents and medicines for external use.

A structure used in alchemical contexts as a general sign for the *art of alchemy*. Rudolf Steiner adopted this sign and now it is closely associated with *Steiner's anthroposophy*. The symbol is also found engraved on rock faces around 1000 B.C. in Uxmal, Central America (refer to the section on "Ancient American ideograms" in Part I).

Today, it is used as an electrical sign for *windings of certain types*.

For similar structures, turn to ⊛ in Group 23 and ⊛ in Group 30. See also ✢ in Group 27.

The **weekday heptagram**. In ancient times the seven-day week was not used. In the kingdom that existed along the shores of the Nile from 3000–2000 B.C. a ten-day week was used. The ten-day week was prevalent in both Egypt and Greece until after the death of Jesus and even in Asia Minor and the Euphrates-Tigris region. A remnant of this method of dividing time is found in the astrological **decanates**, a division of the zodiac signs into three parts of ten degrees, or days, each with a certain planet as ruler.

At the beginning of the first millennium B.C. in Assyria a five-day week was used. In ancient Israel they used a seven-day week, but it is difficult to calculate just how long this method of dividing time had been in use.

It was with the adoption and widespread use of the seven-day week throughout the Hellenistic world of mixed cultures that this heptagram was created. If we arrange the planets known at that time in order of the length of their orbital time around the earth, the result is the following: the moon, Mercury, Venus, the sun, Mars, Jupiter, and Saturn. If we place them in this order around the points of the heptagram and then take a pen and follow the lines as if we were drawing a heptagram, we discover the planets that correspond to each of the seven weekdays: ⊙, *Sunday*; ☽, *Monday*; ♂, *Tuesday*, Tyr's day — Mars' day, mardi; ☿, *Wednesday* (Wuotan's or Odin's day in the Nordic countries — *mercredi*, Mercury's day, in Latin countries); ♃, *Thursday* (Tor's day — *jovedi*, Jupiter's day, in Latin countries); ♀ , *Friday* (Freja's day in the Nordic countries — Venus' day, *vendredi*, in Latin countries); ♄, *Saturday*, Saturn's day (*lördag* – *lögare* day, bathing and washing day, in the Nordic countries).

The **pentagram within a circle**. This ideogram has no meaning by itself. A filled version of the sign, ⊛ , is used as a
symbol of *war* in the United States and appears on tanks and
fighter jets.

This sign can be called a **design-iconic symbol** for the
planet Venus. This planet is the only one in our system that
can clearly be identified with a graphic structure unambiguously derived from a plotting of its astronomical movements in space.

As the orbit of ♀, Venus, is closer to the sun than is the
earth's, it is never seen more than 48 degrees from ☉, i.e.,
♀ is visible as the Morning or Evening star in the immediate
vicinity of ☉. This means that Venus can only be seen from
earth just before sunrise in the morning or just after sunset
in the evening. During a period of 247 days, ♀ is visible as
the Evening star. Then Venus comes too close to the sun to
be visible from earth.

♀ remains invisible for 14 days, to reappear as the Morning star, Phosphoros, immediately before ☉ rises in the east
(the Eastern star, ⊛). For 245 days we can see ♀ each morning at dawn before it again disappears into the sun's light by
getting too close to the sun. The planet is now invisible for
78 days. On the 79th evening it appears again in the west
immediately after the setting of ☉. Venus is now the
Evening star, Hesperos, Aphrodite, the goddess of beauty,
fertility, sex, and peace.

If one knows the ecliptic (see ♌ in Group 38) and can pinpoint the present position of the planets in relation to the
constellations of fixed stars in the zodiac (see ◯ in Group
35), it is possible to mark the exact place in the 360 degrees
of the zodiac where the Morning star first appears shortly
before sunrise after a period of invisibility.

If we do this, wait for the Morning star to appear again
584 days later (the synodic orbital time of ♀) and mark its
position in the zodiac, and then repeat this process until we

have five positions of ♀ as the Morning star, we will find that exactly eight years plus one day have passed. If we then draw a line from the first point marked to the second point marked, then to the third, and so on, we end up with a pentagram.

The following lines are taken from Zehren (see "An annotated bibliography" in Part I).

"It was only the planet Venus that possessed the five-pointed star sign. Not one of the innumerable stars above us can by its orbit recreate this sign. . . .

"Moreover, the points of the pentagram pointed to five different groups of stars or constellations which were easy to remember; each had a given name. . . . It was only later discovered that the five points moved slowly throughout the vault of heaven as if they were hands of a giant clock. . . . Over a period of four years each point of the pentagram was displaced one day, a 365th part of the zodiac circle. . . . After 1460 solar years the 'hands' stood at their original places. This unit of 1460 years is the *Egyptian 'Sothis year'* and belongs not only to the god Seth-Sirius but, much more importantly, to the goddess Sothis. And this goddess was no other than . . . Venus herself.

"The space of time between the first appearance of the planet Venus and its reappearance at the same place is exactly 1,460 days, i.e., four solar years, which was the calendar used in antiquity by the Greeks to measure the Olympiades (which is also the time interval between the modern Olympic Games).

"But after 1,460 days Venus becomes the Morning star if it was first the Evening star and vice-versa."

The pentagon, ◯ (see Group 28), also can be produced by the above procedure, with the difference that one takes into account Venus's first appearance irrespective of whether it is as the Morning or the Evening star.

Among those peoples who do not know that the two appearances represent one planet, we thus get two gods or divine powers, both related to the number 8. The reason for this is that ♀ is visible in one of its two appearances during a period of 245–247 days, which is equivalent to eight cycles of the moon. It was possible to see the brightest star in the heavens together with the new moon (or waning moon) eight times before it eventually was swallowed by the sun, i.e., made invisible by the sun's light.

Later, when those peoples had learned to draw a map of the ecliptic (the zodiac), it became possible to draw ☆, and then the two divinities got another close association to the number 8: it took eight years for ♀ as one of the two gods to complete a full cycle of the zodiac and return to its initial starting point.

It was only when humans realized that the Morning star and the Evening star were the same planet that the pentagon, ⬠, and the four-year period could be linked to ♀.

The Akkadians were the first to realize this. Inanna, the Sumerian queen of the heavens and the daughter of the moon, was given another role by the Semitic Akkadians. She was called Ischtar, the queen of the heavens, goddess of war but also of divine beauty and peace.

There were three highest divinities in the Euphrates-Tigris region. Their symbols can be seen in almost every ancient mythological representation. They are ⊕, the *sun god;* ☽, the *moon god;* and ✳, *Inanna, Ischtar,* or *Astarte.*

Yet despite the fact that the true nature of ♀ had been discovered and established in the Euphrates-Tigris region, the barbaric priests and medicine men of the Greek tribes continued to believe that the Morning and Evening stars were two separate entities. The differences between the corresponding two divinities were more accentuated than in other cultures, and these differences crystallized with the overall development of their civilization into Athena, the

Morning star and goddess of hunt and battle, and Aphrodite the Evening goddess of love. It was not until 400 B.C. (about 1500 years after the Sumerians) that the Greeks discovered the unity of ☆ and ✸. Diogenes Laertius writes: "and it is believed that he [Parmenides, 400 B.C.] realized, as the first, that the Evening and Morning stars were the same star, which Favorinus relates to us in his fifth book of 'Worthwhile thoughts.' Others claim that it was Pythagoras."

Throughout history we find that always one of Venus's two aspects has been overemphasized, and this has occurred in nearly all cultural spheres. The planet ♀ as goddess for *hunt, battle,* and *the new day* is symbolized by the sign for the *waning moon* or the *dying snake,* ☾, and the design-iconic ideogram for ♀, namely, ☆. Instead of ☪ we sometimes find ☽. No comparable graphic symbol for ♀ that illustrates the divine qualities of *beauty, peace, love making,* and *sexuality* of Venus as the Evening star seems ever to have existed.

But if we return to the Euphrates-Tigris region we find that Ischtar, the goddess of war, fertility, and sexuality, somewhere between 2000 and 1000 B.C. began to be symbolized by the symbol ✺, in which one four-pointed star structure is placed behind another. The Morning and Evening stars were then graphically united and, most probably, also in the existing body of astronomical knowledge.

Even after the Greeks realized that there was only one star, they continued to overemphasize one of its appearances. It was Athena, the goddess of war and of the war-like and slave-holding Athens, who predominated at the cost of Aphrodite. In the later *Odyssey,* Aphrodite is hardly mentioned.

It has continued in this vein. The planet ♀ as the Morning star, ☪ , has given us a symbol of war *par préférence:* ☆. The other ancient Venus symbol, the rosette with eight petals,

✻, is rarely seen. And ☽, the planet as Aphrodite, the Evening star, together with the *young bull, the new moon*, is never used.

Last, we should mention that ✻, ✻, and ✻ all represented a *divinity of fertility* and not only a *goddess of war and sexual pleasures*. The most illustrative symbol for this particular quality must be a young woman with her child. When a new ideology discovers that it cannot wipe out an ancient and well-established ideological structure, almost as impossible to get rid of as is the brightest star in the sky of planet earth, it can adopt this structure (if you can't beat them, join them) and attempt to change its meaning by giving the symbol new meanings.

This is only partially possible, though. The new ideological establishment can try to emphasize and encourage those elements that agree with the new ideology and at the same time suppress those that do not. The ardent advocates of the Christian ideology thus approved of fertility, but disapproved of its relation to sexual pleasures and tried to suppress this aspect of fertility, though not fertility as such.

As a result we still have, after 2000 years of ideological domination by the Christian faith, a holy female god, an Inanna, a goddess of fertility, but a very strange one, one who has managed to bear the best earthly fruit of all — a human child — but without having engaged in un-Christian lustful and lecherous activities with a man. The Morning star continues to be a goddess and central role player in the lives of the peoples around the Mediterranean, but as the chaste *Virgin Mary*, a goddess in an ideology that emphasizes suffering, warfare, death, and martyrdom much more than intimate sexual relations, sensuality, and love between men and women.

Those 2000 years have been characterized by the conflict between high but often stupid ideals and a hateful practice, the conflict between the two fish bound together and forever trying to swim in different directions, by the sign of Pisces, by Jesus. From this comes the whore and madonna complex and the worship of the *virgin vulva*, ⬭ (see Group 44), which, instead of being a symbol for lecherous intimacy and pleasure, has been turned into a symbol for Jesus, for torture, for the degradation of one human by another, for the crucifixion of the son of the Venus goddess.

What, then, will happen in the New Age? Will ♀ as ★ finally be pushed into the background? Will ⬭ regain its original meaning, and the aspect ✳ of ♀ dominate from now on?

The author of this work is happy to state that this, in fact, is how it looks today.

This sign has been used in astronomy to denote the *sun's mass*. Dalton used it in his chemical system created in 1808 to denote *magnesium*. See the word index for synonyms.

In India, 4000 years ago, this structure was regarded as a holy sign. It is also found on Japanese Buddha statues from the eighth century. The Christian Church has added ⊛ to its symbolism as a *Christ monogram*, sometimes with an added outer circle suggesting the idea of eternity: ⊛.

In modern ideography it appears as a sign for *siren*.

Refer to ⊛ in this group for a description of the relation between the number 8 and other holy signs with positive connotations.

A modern ideogram for the *planet earth*. The synonymous ⊕ is more common. The lines in the circle symbolize the imaginary lines of longitude and latitude.

Compare with ⊕ and ♁, both of which have the same meaning but are a couple thousand years older.

This is a sign meaning *boil* according to an old German treatise. Semiotically the ideogram can be analyzed as △ for *fire* (the heat necessary for boiling), ▽ for the *water* to be boiled, and a dot or point in the center from the sign for the sun, ⊙. The dot or point is used to stress the heating aspect and to distinguish the ideogram from the common representation of alcohol (*fire-water*, as the Native Americans used to say) in alchemy by the hexagram.

A symbol for the *four evangelists* in Gothic church architecture. More common is ◎ in Group 26.

Dr. Timothy Leary, a professor at Harvard University during the 1960s who was fired due to his experiments with LSD and his belief that this drug was a positive stimulant that could be used for expanding awareness of subconscious structures and aspects of the world not perceived in a normal consciousness state, has propagated the sign ⊗ as a symbol for the *League for Spiritual Discovery*, or *LSD*.

An ethnic art design from eighteenth-century East Gotaland in Sweden. These designs were common in ethnic decorative art in many regions and epochs.

Compare with ✿ and ❁, also common decorative designs used for thousands of years in ethnic art.

Group 30

Multi-axis symmetric, both soft and straight-lined, closed signs without crossing lines

The circle divided by a horizontal line is a structure often found on rock carvings. In early Chinese calligraphy it represented the *sun* (earliest ⊙). In the Greek alphabet it is used to signify the letter *theta*, it is used in at least ten different ideographic systems of natural science, and it is a symbol in the "science fiction" religion Scientology for the *individual human spirit*.

The alchemists used it to denote *salt* (more usually drawn ⊙ or ⊖). In a **system of the four elements** that is Spanish in origin, we find ⊖ meaning *water* (the others are ⊕ , *earth*, ⊙ , *fire*, and ○ , *air*).

This sign is generally associated with the idea of something *absolute*, e.g., *absolute time, absolute temperature, absolute center*, etc. With regard to this ⊖ can be said to be synonymous with | and | . In other modern systems ⊖ is used to mean *stop* or *end*.

The circle divided into two equal parts along a vertical line is an ancient sign of the alphabets used in antiquity in the Near East. The alchemists used it to signify *nitrogen*, or *saltpeter*. Among the Hittites ⊕ and ⊕ were closely associated with the idea of *lightning*.

In his nineteenth-century system for the chemical elements John Dalton used ⊕ for nitrogen.

When the line in the circle is horizontal but does not touch the circumference the sign becomes a *negative unit* or *something negative in a closed room* or, as a traffic symbol, a sign for *stop*, ⊜ , *one-way traffic only*. ⊖ can also represent a *negative ion*.

Falling pressure (in a tank) and *negative pole* are other related meanings of this sign.

The sign ⓘ is found on modern household appliances and indicates the *on and off switch* (the same knob or button). It is synonymous with (ᵕ) , ◑ , •ᴼ, and ∞.

This is a sign indicating *unsympathetic and irritable people* in the English system of hobo signs. In the Swedish system it means *be careful — otherwise they'll call the police.*

Compare with ⊙ used by U.S. hobos and meaning *people here will try to get you arrested.*

In eighteenth-century chemistry, and also in some alchemical contexts, this sign stands for *sal alcalinus,* or *alkaline salt,* i.e., salts of alkali, foremost of potassium and sodium.

Formerly all compounds that could be dissolved in less than 500 parts of water were called *salts.*

In some meteorological contexts this sign was used to indicate *sky obscured by mist, smoke, dust, or something similar.*

Compare with ◌◌ and ⌢ᵂ, both of which have a similar meaning.

This sign structure is found on Nordic Bronze Age altars and in prehistoric Egypt. ⊕ is also a heraldic sign known as the **mirror**. As a Bronze Age symbol it was most probably a sun symbol.

In eighteenth-century chemistry this sign was used for *saccharum*, or *sugar*.

Compare with the **Mayan cross**, ⊹, and with ⊛, found in ancient Troy and made up of five sun signs and an arrow cross.

A triangle drawn within a circle is rarely found in modern ideography. In earlier times, however, it was more popular. See, for example, ⊕, which represented the elements in an alchemical context, and △ as a symbol for the Christian idea of *three-in-one*, the *Holy Trinity*.

Compare with ⟁ and ⟁ , both of which denote the Holy Trinity, and with ▲, *feu de roie*, which was perhaps some kind of fireworks in the seventeenth century.

In modern ideography we find the identical structure ⊘ used as a road sign and on office machines and household appliances to mean *stop*.

A sign for *phosphorus* used in early chemistry. Phosphorus was usually drawn ⋏.

Structurally similar is ⊛ , *choose!* See ⊛ in Group 24. Compare also with ⊛.

This is an internationally recognized warning sign, usually red or black on a yellow background, meaning *dangerous radioactivity*.

It is also common in computing contexts indicating that there is an *external memory* or *offline memory storage*. In this case it originates from an iconic sign for the magnetic tape cassettes used for storing data from large computer systems.

For related structures with similar meanings turn to ⚝ and ♣ , both in this group.

This is an example of several similar structures that some centuries ago were drawn on barns and houses to pacify evil powers, ward off misfortune, and bring good fortune. This version has also been used as a *protection against lightning*.

See the related structure ⚹ in Group 27.

The sign for the *Eastern star*, i.e., the *planet Venus*, ♀, as the Morning star. It is quite common among the tribal peoples in Africa and the Americas, and drawn both with and without a surrounding circle. For its historical background and origins, see ☆ in Group 27 and ⊛ in Group 29.

This particular version was found on a photograph of the Apache chief Geronimo, who lived during the nineteenth century. The sign was on his headgear. Compare with ✻ found on the headgear of the cruel Vlad, Count Dracula, on a fifteenth-century painting. In both cases the star associates to ♀ in its role as a war divinity.

Note that in the United States a rather similar ideogram has been used on fighter jets and tanks.

This modern ideogram is used as a warning for *microwave radiation*. It appears on household appliances. Refer to ♣ in this group for another radiation warning sign.

A Christian symbol used in Spain to represent the *Holy Trinity*.

See ♧ in Group 26 for history and synonyms of signs for the Holy Trinity.

A sign (corresponding to the Hebraic letter **koph**) used in cabbalistic mysticism. ⚠ was also used in eighteenth-century chemistry as a sign for *phlogiston*.

The phlogiston theory flowered between 1650 and 1850. Phlogiston was considered to be a substance that existed in different proportions in other substances, a kind of fixed fire showing up and disappearing when a substance burned. Phlogiston was thought to be the element of fire in its pure dormant form (note that △ is the alchemical sign for fire). Coal was believed to contain a large quantity of phlogiston because of the great amount of heat it produced while burning. All metals were thought to contain phlogiston as well as something that is now called metal oxides. A whole theory was developed that corresponds closely to the modern understanding of the combustion process. It succeeded in explaining the principles of this process just as well as the modern theory. It was, however, more complicated because it presupposed the existence of phlogiston.

In eighteenth-century chemistry phlogiston could also be drawn ⚹. In the same time and system △ was also used for *resina*, or *resin*.

Compare with ⚴ . See also the similar signs ▽ and ▼ in Group 24.

A Christian symbol for the *Holy Trinity*. It is composed by △, the sign for *divinity*, *power*, and *fire*, and ☒, for *holiness* and *prosperity*. Moreover, each side of the ideogram depicts ∿, a sign in Christian symbolism for the *Holy Ghost or Spirit*. This latter sign was also used in alchemy and signified the *spirit* or *spiritus*, the *essence of a substance*.

As a meteorological sign △ signifies *ice granules, hail, frozen raindrops*. Compare with ▽, *rain*, and ✳ , ⚹ , and ⊠ , representing *ice* and *snow*. ⋀ from Group 6 is graphically similar.

Points often represent water in Western ideography. It might be that this ideogram has been drawn incorrectly. It would have been more logical to use the sign ▽, *water*, than △ , *fire*.

This is a modern ideogram warning for *dangerous radiation, radioactivity*. It is used on appliances to warn and in other ways. Compare with ⚠ in this group, which is also a warning sign for radiation, and with ☼-, a warning sign for laser radiation.

See ☢ in this group.

This ideogram is found both in earlier and present-day systems. In the earliest system of Chinese writing 甶 meant *village* (an iconic sign for the central field and well). In alchemy it meant *urine*. As a meteorological sign ⊡ signifies that the *ground is wet* (⊡ means *flooded ground*). Placed diagonally, it was sometimes used by alchemists to mean *sulphur*, although it was more usual to represent sulphur with ⇡ or ⇡ .

In the U.S. system of hobo signs ⊡ and similar structures are signs for *danger*. See, for example, ⊡ , *water is dangerous to drink*; ⊡ , *dangerous neighborhood*; and ⊡ , *here lives a man with a bad temper*.

When used in connection with fire protection it has signified the whereabouts of a *police station*. In military contexts it has been used for *vehicle driver* and *orderly*.

The similar ⊡ is a road sign from the 1980s meaning *road to take for trucks with dangerous cargo*.

This structure resembles the above but is inverted and diagonally placed. It is found in heraldry as a symbol for *religiosity* on coats of arms.

The sign ⊡ is common in modern ideography. It is used on videotape recorders indicating the *switch for record*. If we look at this more closely, however, we discover ● denotes *record* and that ☐ stands for *stop*. Both ⊡ and ● occur on appliances. The similar structures ⊙ and ⊙ denote *switch for recording with reduced noise*.

⊡ is also used in astrology to denote the *fixed qualities or signs*, the *fixed quadruplicity*. The **quadruplicities** or **qualities** divide the zodiac into three groups of four signs each. The signs that begin with the cardinal points — Aries,

♈, Cancer, ♋ , Libra, ♎ , and Capricorn, ♑ — are known as the **cardinal signs** and symbolized by ⋀ , a symbol of radiation. Individuals who have many planets or important ones in any one of these signs in their nativity are believed to be more *enterprising, creative, self-assertive,* and *independent* than other nativities.

Those signs that follow immediately after a cardinal sign in the zodiac — Taurus, ♉ , Leo, ♌ , Scorpio, ♏ , and Aquarius, ♒ — are known as the **fixed signs**. They are symbolized by ◉. Persons stamped with *fixed qualities* can be recognized by such characteristics as *consequential behavior, loyalty, trustworthiness, respect for traditions, patience, endurance,* and *goal orientation.*

The final group, the signs that follow after the fixed signs and appear just before the cardinal signs, is known as the **mutable signs**. These are symbolized by ⌒. The signs are Gemini, ♊ , Virgo, ♍ , Sagittarius, ♐ , and Pisces, ♓. The keywords for those personalities that are "colored" by these signs are *adaptability, ability to make a little go a long way, flexibility with words when in company, ease to learn new things,* and *ability to understand both parties in conflicts.*

▢ , similar to this sign, is used as a washing sign to indicate *tumble-drying* or *can be tumble-dried.* ⊠ means the opposite.

As an electrical sign it means *understation with rotating machines.*

This sign has been used in U.S. meteorology to mean *extremely good visibility.* This meaning is also drawn ○ and ◖.

Compare with ◇ for *soap* and *clean air.* See also ◖ in Group 26.

This is the **Mantuan cross**. The version here shown is **Eiser-nas Kreuz**, the **iron cross**, a German Order medal. The order was inaugurated by King Friedrich Wilhelm III of Prussia in the year 1813, intended to unite and encourage his people in their fight against Napoleon's French armies. This cross is used by Germany on its navy flags. During the First World War it appeared as a *battle sign* on the sides of German tanks, fighter aircraft, etc. It has also been used as a *fascist* symbol, for example, in France. This type of cross was used on the Portuguese flag, on Portuguese fighter jets, etc., during the period of fascism that ended with the revolution in 1974.

This is the **restoration cross**, a pierced cross from the fifteenth century, used in heraldry and on coins (Henry VI of England). Compare with ⊹, a variation found in twelfth-century Peru and probably an **Inca sign for the sun**.

Structurally, it is identical with ⊹, the symbol used by the Mayan people for their *fire god*. See also ⊕ , found on an ancient burial pot found in Argentina.

This is the **St. Birgitta cross** with five precious stones depicted, representing the five wounds of Christ.

The threefoil sign is an ancient symbol for *holiness* and *divinity*. See ♤ . It was adopted in the Christian symbolism and given a Christian meaning.

For a history of this sign, look up ⊛ in Group 25. The **threefoil cross** is also known as the **cross of Lazarus**.

The sign for *hour* in French alchemy during the seventeenth century. X and ⋈ were other graphs the alchemists used for *hour*.

A modern ideogram for *time* in general. It is related to 8 above.

This is a seventeenth-century chemistry sign for *auripigmentum*, or *orpiment, arsenic sulphide*.
    It was also drawn ⊂⊃ .

A **Venus star** with eight points found in a temple near Jericho, in northern Canaan. Herod, after his retirement, beautified the town and lived here until his death. This mosaic is dated to around 300 B.C.
    Compare with ✳, an eight-pointed star from pre-Columbian Peru, possibly also a Venus symbol, although the sun cross or wheel cross in its middle makes its association to Venus doubtful. For more information on the relation of the eight-pointed star signs and Venus, look up ⊛ in Group 29.

An eight-pointed star sign found on a Greek vase from the fifth century B.C. It is possibly synonymous with Venus stars as ✳ . See the entry above.

Group 31

Asymmetric, soft signs with crossing lines

This is an ideogram from a caster found in Hissarlik, Turkey, considered the place where ancient Homerian Troy was situated. It is believed to date from around 2000 B.C. According to d'Alviella (see bibliography in Part I) it is most probably a **sun symbol**. For more information, see 卐 in Group 15.

This ideogram is a graphic model of the current theory of the *organization of matter on the microcosmic level*. The point in the middle denotes the nucleus of the atom, and the ovals indicate the orbital paths of the invisible electrons. The model is presented in an imagined three-dimensional space (suggested by the asymmetry). The sign is a symbol for *uranium, nuclear power, nuclear physics*, and related areas. Compare with ✖, a sign from eighteenth-century Africa. See the synonymous but more common ✖ and ⚛ in Group 25.

Group 32

Asymmetric, soft signs without crossing lines

This is a Japanese equivalent to European nobility's heraldic coats of arms. It shows the *spiral of potential energy*. It is called the **seed of life** or the **seed of the universe**.

The Tibetan symbol for the *origins of the universe* shows a **seed of the universe** rotating clockwise in the *spiral of potential energy*. (See ◉ in Group 14.) The same structure, ◉ , is also the coat of arms of the Aztec god Quetzlcoatl, the feathered snake, most probably a chief from another culture arriving in the Aztec empires around the year A.D. 700. He introduced a new body of knowledge and art and is believed to have discouraged the practice of human sacrifice. He accepted offerings of snakes and butterflies though. According to the legend he came from the west, was a white man, and wore a beard. According to Aztec astrology he was to return at the beginning of the sixteenth century. Queztlcoatl is associated with the planet Venus as the Morning star. See ⊕ in Group 29.

When the Spaniards arrived at the beginning of the sixteenth century, King Montezuma and his court believed them to be forerunners or attendants of the god Quetzlcoatl. As a result of this mistake the king and his guards were cruelly murdered in the name of the Christian God.

For the sake of comparison Huitzilopochtlis' coat of arms is also shown. He was the Aztecs' *war god* and demanded human sacrifice. Note the number of the "seeds," five, and compare with ⊛, one of the signs of the Venus goddess of war in Group 29.

An ancient Chinese symbol for the *universe* that has become integrated in Western ideography. illustrates the two opposing dimensions that give the world its dynamics: *yin* and *yang*. Yin represents the *passive, receiving, recipient, malleable, matter* and is symbolized by the broken horizontal line, --. Yang represents *energy, activity, warmth, spirit* and is symbolized by an unbroken short horizontal line, —. (In Chinese symbolism — in most cases carries the same meanings as | does in Western ideography.)

There exists nothing that is totally yin or all yang. This fact is symbolized by the presence of a smaller circle in each half in the other half's color.

Structurally ◑ and S are the closest related Western signs. As far as the spectrum of meaning is concerned ⊕ is rather synonymous, being a common sign for the *uniting of opposite elements* for the alchemists.

A Japanese heraldic sign found on a Samurai coat of arms in which two "seeds of the universe" rotate counterclockwise.

This symbol from Japanese Samurai heraldry is also an old Shintoist symbol for the *universe* named **tomoye**.

Another symbol from the heraldry of the Japanese Samurai. Compare with ⋏⋎ , used as a sign on clothes worn in Ghana, Africa, meaning *I am afraid of nothing but God*.

According to d'Alviella (see bibliography in Part I) such structural similarities exemplify how symbol structures are spread via trade.

An ideogram common in Scandinavia in the Viking era. Both this and its mirror image were used on Celtic vessels before the birth of Christ and in many other areas.

There is a structurally similar Mayan hieroglyph, ⊕ , but it has six "spokes." What it meant is unknown but it is similar to an Aztec sign meaning *day*. By the seven spokes in this ideogram it can be associated with ✳, the weekday heptagram.

⊛ can also be seen as an iconic sign for a *millstone* and is used on cameras as a sign indicating *minimal light aperture*. Compare it in this use with ◯ for *maximal light aperture*.

This is a structurally advanced ideogram, combining three of the basic elements and the series. It is an invention from the twentieth century, first used in the world of comic strips and advertising, meaning *thoughts* or *inner dialogue*. What is being thought is written in the largest of the **thought bubbles**.

A modern ideogram, but probably much older than the above entry. It is drawn around words or sentences that are *spoken*. Again it is used most often in the world of comic strips, schoolbooks, brochures, and advertising.

The type of signs most closely related as far as meaning is concerned is **speech bands**, i.e., signs that begin at the

mouth of figures drawn on paper and reliefs in the ancient Indian civilizations of Mexico. These speech bands
have been most readily used by the Aztecs, who drew them
like ᴧᴧᴧ .

Compare with 𝕊𝕜, a detail from the door of the church of
Rogelösa, Sweden, from the twelfth century.

This ideogram is from the world of comic strips. The sign is
drawn around written words close to the mouths of characters, signifying that the character is not speaking normally
for everyone close by to hear, ◯, nor is thinking them, ꜟ°°°,
but *speaks in a low voice* or *whispers* to keep what is said a
secret.

See also ♧ in Group 34.

This sign structure is uncommon because it is closed. Since
it is very difficult to draw it probably had magical significance. It is often found on vessels and representations from
the Bronze Age. This instance is found on a rock carving
from Scania, Sweden.

See ◉◉ in Group 14 for the spectrum of meaning of the
basic sign structure.

This structure is called the **spiral of life** and was found in
the remnants of an old temple from the Bronze Age in Ireland. The sign is drawn in one single line without beginning
or end. Compare with ⚬⚬ , an old Celtic sign that was used
in pre-Columbian America and in Greece and neighboring
countries in antiquity.

See also ◉◉ in Group 14.

Signs of this type are called **triskelion, three-leg**. This one is from a shield that was used as a prize at competitions in Athens around 500 B.C.

    See ⚡ and 卍.

Symbols of this type are called **triquetras**, which is Latin for three-cornered. This sign is a symbol for the *Holy Trinity* in Christian symbolism. The design builds upon the ancient sign for holiness, ⚭ , and the cabbalistic symbol for purity and innocence, ◖. Since one of the symbols for Jesus is a fish, one may also interpret this triquetra as a **Jesus symbol** composed by three conventionalized, plaited fish. See ∝ in Group 37.

This is a plaited version of ✠ , the **St. Hans' cross** or **cross of St. John**.

    See this cross in Group 25.

This old Egyptian hieroglyph was, like most of the other ones, later used in other Western systems. In alchemy it meant *still*, *retort*, *alembic*. Of course, it could also be used to indicate the activity of *distilling*. *Still*, or *alembic*, was also drawn ◯ and ✕ .

Since a couple of centuries before the birth of Christ this and similar signs have meant the *sun*, the *disc of the sun*, and *gold* for the alchemists. Compare with the most common of the signs for the sun and for gold, ☉ , and with ⚥, with the same meaning.

The alchemists' sign for *marcasite,* or *fool's gold,* an almost golden compound of iron and sulphur. Marcasite was also drawn 𝄪.

This is a sign for the letter or sound *yod* in the Hebrew alphabet. This letter is the first one in the Hebrew name for God, *Jahweh.*

The sign is sometimes used in Christian symbolism, and recently has been used in some U.S. comic strips to indicate *holy fire, Holy Spirit, drops of holy fire.*

Group 33

Asymmetric, straight-lined, closed signs with crossing lines

For the meaning of this sign, turn to ⚡ in Group 34.

Note that this sign is simply an asymmetrical distortion of the structurally similar rune ᛗ.

This swastika has been found in pre-Columbian America. ⊹ was found on an antique vessel in what is now Peru.

卍 , a swastika from a Japanese Buddha statue is from about the same time as this entry — around the year A.D. 760.

A sign meaning *cubic* in some systems of geometry. ⌸ is rarely used. Compare with ⌸, *improve register*, a proofreading sign from the United States.

Group 34

Asymmetric, straight-lined, closed signs without crossing lines

A modern ideogram found on radios, televisions, and amplifiers. It indicates the *volume control*. The sign is "sound iconic" in the same way as ➜, meaning the same thing.

A sign used in computer flow charting to indicate either *output* or *input*, i.e., that *at this point in the program data is either put in or taken out via the keyboard, the screen, or another device.* See also ⊂, *online data storage,* and ◯, *the output is shown on the screen.*

In a genealogical context, this sign means *buried*. It is also drawn as ⛊. It is structurally similar to the Egyptian hieroglyph ◁.

When found drawn with chalk or scratched into the surface of a wall outside a house, this sign means *the owner or those that live here are cruel people.* It is used in the English hobo system. Sweden uses ▭ for the same meaning. ▨ is found in both the English and U.S. systems and means *bad-tempered people and/or dogs.* Compare with the structurally similar Egyptian hieroglyph, ⬭ .

This sign has been used to signify *coagulatio,* the result before the last step in the alchemical process. For more information, turn to the sections on alchemy in Part I.
    Compare with ⊕ , which is structurally similar.

A sign found in computer flow charting indicating *manual input* via an online connected keyboard.

Compare with ▽ , which means *manual offline operation without mechanical assistance*.

Turn to ▽ in Group 22 for *storage of input*.

A sign found on videotape recorders, telephone answering machines, and other similar devices signifying the *switch for the removal of the tape*. Synonymous with ⏏.

An ideogram for *color control* on televisions and videotape recorders. Synonymous with ⦿ and other signs.

Fascists in all parts of the world have in one way or another been fascinated by ⚡, the ideogram for *lightning*. As this sign is a symbol for the s-sound in the runic alphabet it has become associated in Germanic countries with *sun, strength, battle, victory*, etc. See ⚡ in Group 16.

The sign ⚡ appeared on the uniforms worn by certain South Vietnamese troops before the Communist seizure of power.

In Germany, this sign is known as the *Sig-rune ähnlich*, i.e., similar to the victory rune, **⚡**. This variation is called *Donnerkeil, thunderbolt*. It has been used by the Dutch Nazi party and one of the two English Nazi parties.

The original form is **⟨** in Group 16, the rune for *yew tree*, from the earliest runic alphabet. Because of its long growing period, it was used to make the battle bow, the most dangerous weapon during the Viking era.

Note that the rune **⟨** is sometimes carved **⚡**, the old sign for *battle, victory*, and *danger*.

Hitler's Nazi party was, in its early days, subject to violence and resistance in the form of fights, the breaking up of meetings, etc. As a result, the *Schutz Staffeln, SS*, were formed. They were protection units that fought against other political groups, preferably the Communists.

Compare with **卌**, *cooling system with several levels*, in Group 52, and **⊡** below.

Sign on an SS ring. See **И** in Group 16, and **✳** in Group 9.

This form of the swastika, the closed, diagonally postioned, square-formed variation, was the emblem used by Nazism and the men around Hitler. It was in 1920 that the swastika was officially recognized and used in the party banner.

It had already appeared earlier in the twentieth century as an anti-Semitic and uniting symbol in Germany and Austria. For other variations of the swastika, its names, and historical background, turn to **卐** in Group 15.

The swastika form is associated with *the sun* and *power*. The swastika moving in a clockwise direction is related to the form and also to its meaning, *reincarnation, return,* etc. ⚡ symbolizes, therefore, *national reincarnation*. The American Nazi party uses the same sign but with a circle at its center: ⚡.

In China we find the form 卐 as a *superlative* in general terms and as a sign for the *magnificent number 10,000*. Compare with the staff of god used in the Euphrates-Tigris cultures and ancient Egypt, ‿◯‿, which in Egypt had a corresponding function and among other things illustrated the *magnificent number 10,000,000*.

This and similar structures are common in a modern technical context. ⚡ signifies *heat* and ▭, *closed space*. Therefore ▭ represents in certain systems *storage cupboard, melting oven, cooler* (heat is fed into a cold space), etc.

See the corresponding meaning in ⚡, *cooling system with several levels*, in Group 52.

A plaited sign to denote *success* and *protection against evil forces*. It is found on a Sumerian seal and on a picture stone found in Gotaland, Sweden, dating from the early part of the Viking era.

It is an interesting fact that plaited signs are often considered peculiar in some way and have magic qualities. The following signs are examples found in a plaited form: ⌘, ✿, △, and the sign below.

The plaited pentagram has been a *protective sign against evil powers* in the Western world and in Japan. It is found in the Nordic countries drawn on the doors of barns and rest houses to ward off the occult and to invoke the aid of protecting forces. The sign ⦾ has a similar meaning today.

The plaited pentagram appears in the stonemason's emblem on the Moroccan banner.

See also ☆ in Group 27. Even the hexagram can appear plaited.

A modern ideogram used in comic strips and advertising. The sign is drawn around the written word or sentence and symbolises that it is spoken. It is drawn next to a person's mouth or a speaker and symbolizes *human speech heard through an electronic medium* such as a telephone or radio, or *human speech under extreme circumstances* such as anger, fear, or irritation.

Compare with ◯, the sign for *normal speech*, and ₒ₀° for *thoughts*.

Group 35

Asymmetric, both soft and straight-lined, closed signs with crossing lines

The **zodiac**, the **ecliptic**, the **via solis**, or the **way of the sun** is the orbit in the celestial skies along which the sun moves around the earth (from a geocentric reference point). It is known as the ecliptic because it is along this path, at the points where it intersects the earth's equatorial plane, that eclipses occur. The ecliptic inclines about 24 degrees in relation to the earth's equatorial plane.

The zodiac is a belt with a width of about 9 degrees of arc on either side of the ecliptic, i.e., the belt where the planets can be seen during their movement around the earth.

The signs of the zodiac start at the spring equinox around 21 March. Most of the zodiac signs are named after constellations of fixed stars. Nowadays, however, the constellations do not lie in connection to the signs they are associated with but approximately 30 degrees away. For facts about this, see "The symbolism of the astrological ages" in Part I.

This zodiac circle is also a common birth chart (horoscope) pattern. The division of the houses has the degrees of the signs for reference. The positions of the planets, the ascendant, and the GC are given. See ⊠ in Group 28 for other horoscope patterns.

A modern ideogram for *frequency*. It is a combination of the sign for a *complete wave* or *oscillation*, $\sim$, and the straight line.

This ideogram is used by several *theosophic societies*. See ◉ in Group 29 for more details. The ideogram is a combination of the ancient Egyptian sign ☥, a staff of god and a symbol for life and rebirth. This sign is placed at the center of the star of the two opposites, ✡ , which is in turn placed in the circle of eternity. The whole structure is then crowned with the

fylfot, which is here associated with the *continual rebirth of metempsychosis*.

See also the alchemical sign ⊛ in Group 23.

The fylfot rotating counterclockwise (following one of the lines from the center gives this movement) is known in India as *sauvastika*, the bringer of misfortune. See 卍 in Group 15 for more data.

Group 36

Asymmetric, both soft and straight-lined, closed signs without crossing lines

A modern ideogram for a *continuously increasing variable*. It is used on household appliances and is synonymous with ◿ and ❗.

An ideogram for *color intensity control* on TVs. It is sometimes drawn ⦂. Compare with the structurally similar ◑ for *contrast control*, the control of lightness and darkness on TV screens.

This is one of the signs used to mean an item *can be recycled*. The sign ♺ is synonymous.

This sign is believed to be one of the alchemists' signs for *honey*. See ⚭ in Group 20 for more signs with this meaning.

A sign used in computer program flow charting to mean *paper document*. Refer also to the sign below.

A sign used in computer flow charting to indicate *punched tape*. See the above sign.

A sign for *coating of ice* in meteorology. This is a thin coating of ice created by the falling of supercooled or freezing rain.

We see the *ground*, □, covered by *ice*, ∿ .

A sign used in the Swedish and English systems of hobo signs. In Sweden it means *bad-tempered people live here,* and in England it indicates that *here people are dangerous and/or there are dogs.*

Compare with ▦ from the U.S. system of hobo signs, meaning *here lives a dangerous dog.*

Both ▭ in Group 28 and ▨ in Group 22 have similar structures and mean approximately the same.

An alchemical sign for *gold-leaf* or *gold-foil,* i.e., gold that has been pressed so thin that it can float on the breath. Gold was the only metal that could be hammered out to such extreme thinness.

Compare with ⊙ and ♄ for *gold.*

This is a combination of one of the alchemical signs for *gold,* ♄ , and the sign for *silver,* ☽ . Its meaning is *electrum,* i.e., an *alloy of gold and silver.*

Compare with the structurally similar ⵙ⊙, which uses the same components, the sign for the *sun* and for *gold,* ⊙ , and the half-moon for *silver,* ☽, and stands for *platinum.*

Electrum was also drawn ⫲ .

An ideogram found on fuses used in electrical circuits meaning *stiff fuse*, i.e., a fuse that can bear short, strong charges
when household machines are switched on, sudden strong
charges that would burn out normal fuses.

Here the sign for *potential energy*, ℮ , is combined with a
straight line to an iconic sign for the very slow animal, the
snail.

In this ideogram used on clothes in Ghana we see one of the
most common ideograms representing the *Eastern star*, the
planet *Venus*, ★, the *Morning star*, and indirectly a new start
to the day combined with the sign ☼, representing a *rotation*
or *an independent movement*. It means *Sesa woruban: I change
or transform my life* or *change in life*.

This sign is the logo for *Afrikaaner Weerstandsbeweging*, a
white organization in South Africa opposed to ending the
policy of apartheid.

Compare with ⚇ in Group 14.

Group 37

Single-axis, symmetric, soft, both open and closed signs with one or more crossing lines

This sign is an italic form of the *first letter, alpha,* in the Greek alphabet. It is used in dozens of technical and scientific systems. English lawyers often mark their folders with this sign to indicate that the *case is closed.*

In Christian symbolism ∝, the stylized *fish,* is a symbol for *Jesus.* The word *fish* in Greek is a combination of the initial letters of the name *Jesus Christ, Son of God, Savior.* Compare with ◊, another Jesus symbol. For further information, see Group 26.

These ideograms are structurally identical to the signs above. But owing to the fact that the open ends have been elongated it looks different. ⊝ has been used in alchemy to represent *calcinated copper,* i.e., *copper oxide in powder form* produced by heating copper intensely.

Turn to ⌒, *calcinate,* and the synonyms ♀, ♀, and ⊕∈.

Turned as ⌇ it becomes another sign for *sulphur.* Sulphur is usually drawn as ♄.

One of several alchemical signs for *salt derived from alkali metals,* which is also drawn as ⊠, ♀, and ⊟.

A sign used in English meteorology signifying *dust devils,* i.e., whirlpools of wind that lift up dust and chaff, or miniature tornadoes. Compare with ∂, the U.S. sign for *tornado.* Within the U.S. system of hobo signs ⧢ denotes *judge lives here.*

This sign is used in telecommunications and electronics to mean *inductance*, i.e., the ideogram is related to the generation of electricity by allowing a coiled conductor to move in a magnetic field or letting the magnetic field move close to the conductor. It can also be drawn as -m-.

The sign used in alchemy for the substance *realgar*. For further information, see ⌀ in Group 41:b.
   In alchemy ⌀ denotes *smoke*.

An alchemical sign denoting *potassium hydrogen tartrate*.

An alchemical sign for *hydrochloric acid*. Compare with ←⊕ for *nitric acid* and with ← denoting *acid*. See also ⊕ in Group 30.

Group 38

Single-axis symmetric, soft, both open and closed signs
without crossing lines

This sign represents the *moon* in the Egyptian hieroglyphic writing system. The alchemists have used it to mean the *moon* and, turned this way, ☽ , to mean *silver*.

Compare with 𓋳, the Egyptian hieroglyph for *gold*, and with the similar structure ⋈ for *mirage, illusion*.

These are four common variations of graphs for the *sign of the bull, Taurus*. The first is the most common. Taurus is that part of the ecliptic (see ♌ in this group) that begins where the sun stands around 20 April, and ends where it stands around 20 May. Taurus, ♉ , is also a **time sign** representing that part of the year when ☉ moves in this part of the ecliptic or zodiac.

Taurus belongs, together with ♌, ♏, and ♒, to the **fixed quadruplicity**, symbolized by the sign ◉. See this sign in Group 30 for more information about the quadruplicities.

Together with ♍ and ♑ Taurus belongs to the *earth element*, drawn ⊕ . This means, according to astrologers, that individuals strongly influenced by ♉ — for instance, by having ☉ , ☽ , and other planets in this sign — will be characterized by a certain *deliberateness, slowness, relentlessness, perseverance, sensuality*, and a general *tendency toward things and relationships that are palpably material rather than abstract* like ideas and thoughts.

For more details on the triplicities, i.e., elements, turn to △ in Group 28.

The planet Venus, ♀ (see ⊕ in Group 29), is the planetary ruler of ♉. The moon, ☽, and Jupiter, ♃, are also considered well placed in ♉, whereas ♂ and ♅ are poorly placed in this sign.

♉ is also thought to have been the zodiac sign that had the dominating influence on the cultural development on the earth from about 4500 B.C. until 2350 B.C. It was during this period that humankind began to root itself in fixed dwelling places and to develop farming techniques. Before this era humankind had mainly made its living by fishing and hunting.

In alchemy ♉ was sometimes used to signify the metal *bismuth*.

The same sign structure as the above discussed, but upside down, has been used freely in alchemy and early chemistry. ☊ represented *salt alkali* and *cobalt*.

This sign means *variation* in astronomy. The moon's variation is the moon's periodically accelerated orbital speed caused by the fact that the sun's gravitational pull sometimes works against and sometimes with the orbital movement of the moon around the earth.

According to Koch (see bibliography in Part I) this is an early Germanic **time sign** for the season of *spring*. The other signs in this particular system are ᔑ, summer, ♏, autumn, and ╥, winter.

Compare with ♈, the graph for *Aries, the ram,* and that period of the year that begins at the spring equinox.

The almost identical ♉ is mentioned in one source as one of the alchemists' signs for *smoke*.

The sun, the moon, and all the planets (seem to) move around the earth in a belt that is at most 18 degrees wide. This belt is known as the **zodiac** (see ◯ in Group 35). The middle of the belt is known as the **ecliptic**, or the "way of the sun."

The movement of the moon around the earth follows an orbit that is slightly slanting in relation to the ecliptic. On each of its revolutions around the earth the moon cuts the ecliptic at two places. The point where the moon cuts the ecliptic from south to north is known as the *moon's north node* or *caput draconis*, the *dragon's head*.

These signs for the north node have different forms but are, nevertheless, similar to one another.

These nodes take 18 years to move one full revolution through the zodiac. The 18-year cycles are important both in astronomy, as they make **eclipses** possible to predict, and in human life, as they correspond to the age when individuals are allowed to marry, manage their own bank accounts, drive cars, etc.

The sign in the middle of those shown here is the graph for the north node as it was drawn in a Greek natal chart more than 2,000 years ago.

According to astrology ☊ is a symbol for *gifts* and *resources made available to the individual without them having been consciously sought*. It is also associated with *blood relations* and *contacts with people of the opposite sex that lead to childbirth*.

These two graphs are different signs for the *moon's south node*. See the above entry for data about the nodes of the moon. According to astrology the south node in the natal chart is associated with *sacrifices* and *efforts that life demands without giving anything in return*. Both the north and south nodes are associated with *blood ties* and *contacts with people of the opposite sex that lead to childbirth*.

For the alchemists ʊ meant *precipitation*, often through a *deposit*.

This meaning was also expressed by ⥑.

A sign found in cartography to indicate a *lighthouse* on maps and nautical charts. Lighthouses are also represented by ✳, ⌁, ⊙, and some other signs.

The alchemists freely borrowed signs from astrology. ⌢ was used by alchemists during the seventeenth century to signify *sublimation* or *sublimate*. The sign ⌐ had the same meaning.

The **sublimation** was a process whereby a substance was heated until it transformed into steam or gas. Then it was cooled to let it become solid directly, without first going through the stage of being fluid (an impossibility according to modern physics, but if the fluid stage was short enough it could give the impression of being nonexistent).

In modern ideography this sign is used on TV sets and stereos to mean *tape recorder* or *video*. It can also be drawn ⌣.

Here is an alchemical sign meaning *rubber, resin*.

See also the synonymous ♀ in Group 39.

An old chemical sign for *zinc*. Other signs for zinc were ⚵, ⚵, ♄, and ⌗.

This sign structure appears in eighteenth- and nineteenth-century chemistry. It probably was used to represent *zinc oxide*.

Compare with ♀, a sign for the *planet Pluto*. See also ◯, a modern sign for *brake, brakes*, and the structurally similar ©.

This sign was carved on large stone slabs used to build a grave chamber in Kivik, Sweden. Its meaning is unknown, but it appears with ⊕ in this Bronze Age grave.

Signs like ◉ are similar in structure. This one has been found on an idol from pre-Columbian America.

o—ᴣ is an alchemical sign for *flow, something molten*. The same idea was also drawn ⅋ and otherwise.

A sign for *argentum auratum,* propably *gilded silver,* in eighteenth-century chemistry. Composed by parts of ☉, *gold*, and the moon sign for silver.

One of the alchemists' many signs for *vinegar*.
See ♉ for most of the vinegar signs shown together.

One of the alchemists' signs for *realgar*.
See ♋ for further information on realgar.
Compare with ᨓ for *fire* and with ⊷ in Group 42.

The upward pointing triangle to denote the element of fire in alchemy during the Middle Ages became the *hot and humid element of air* with a horizontal bar added across it.

The air element was also drawn △ and =.

This sign has also been used in modern times as a meteorological sign for *frozen rain*, i.e., *hail*.

A sign for *lapis stone*, from eighteenth-century chemistry. It was probably often used for *galmeja*, the *carbonate of zinc*.

Stone was also drawn ⛢ in alchemy and old chemistry.

Among the substances most fascinating the alchemists besides gold, silver, mercury, and arsenic were sulphur and phosphorus. This sign is the most commonly used for *sulphur*. In the symbolism of the Middle Ages the upward pointing triangle was the sign for the element of fire. Sulphur was associated with Hell, and Hell with the Underworld. This is the reason for the arrow pointing down to the underworld. A horizontal bar has been added to the arrow to make a cross. The alchemists tried to include the form of the cross in most of their sign structures.

The signs ⚴ and ⚴ have been used to represent the *asteroid Pallas*, more usually drawn ⚴. See ⚴ in Group 17 for more information about the asteroids.

⚴ is the most common sign for *sulphur* in alchemy. Sulphur was also drawn ♈, ⌨, ⚴, ♀, ⚴, ♉, and ♋, and otherwise.

Group 39

Single-axis symmetric, straight-lined, both open and closed
signs with crossing lines

An alchemical sign for *pyrophorus,* which probably was a *compound with phosphorus* and a very *inflammable substance.* This sign was used in eighteenth-century chemistry.

The sign for the element of *fire,* △ , but without the downward pointing arrow or the cross of the sign for sulphur. Instead a cross has been added to its top. This combination of graphs became the most common symbol for *phosphorus,* a substance that is closely associated with fire.

Phosphorus was also drawn .

As phosphorus was not discovered until 1669,  is in fact a chemical rather than an alchemical sign.

Compare with the sign  above and the sign  below in this group.

Another variation of the sign for *phosphorus* in eighteenth-century chemistry. For more signs for phosphorus, see  in Group 30.

See also  in this group.

A sign for *terra silicea* in eighteenth-century chemistry. **Terra** together with different qualifying words denoted different types of soil and substances with earth-like qualities and consistencies.

The sign  is based on the alchemical sign for the *element of earth,* 🜃, below.

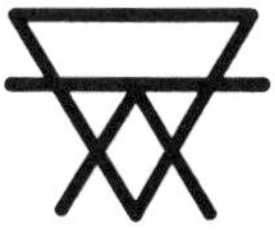

The most common of the alchemists' signs for the *element of earth*. This element was also drawn ▽.

Rubber, a sign from the chemistry of the eighteenth century. See also ⚹ in Group 41:b.

A sign for the *asteroid Pallas*. This asteroid was also drawn ⚴ and ⚴.

For more information on the asteroids, turn to ♀ in Group 17 and ⚴ in this group.

One of the signs for *sulphur* in early chemistry and alchemy. Sulphur was more commonly drawn ⚴ and ⚴.

See the sign directly above for synonyms.

This is a rarely used astrological sign to denote the *part of the spirit*. ⊽ corresponds to ⊕, *Fortuna* (see the word index).

It has been suggested that the Arabs introduced this sign during the Middle Ages. ⊕ and ⊽ were calculated from the positions of ☉, ☽, and the ascendant.

The **part of the cross** is another of these **Arabian parts** in the birth chart (horoscope), associated with disease and death. The position of the cross was calculated from the positions of ♄, ♂, and the ascendant. The **part of the heart**, finally, was associated with love and relationships. Its position was calculated from the positions of ☉, ♀, and the ascendant.

According to Robert Hand (see bibliography in Part I) the Arabian parts originate from ancient Greece despite being called Arabian parts.

Compare with ♁ below, similar in both structure and meaning.

The alchemists believed that a simple substance could be transmuted into a more precious one through the addition of an enzyme-like substance known as *lapis philosophorum*, the *stone of the wise*, an *elixir*.

This substance could transform other substances without itself being changed. It was sometimes drawn ♁. A more sophisticated variation of the graphic symbol for the *philosophers' stone* was 🜍. See this sign in Group 53.

This is a sign from eighteenth-century chemistry for *metallum sulphuratum*, a *compound of a metal and sulphur*.

Other signs for this type of compound were ☿ , ♃ , ⚕ , ⚥ , and ⚥ .

One of the meteorological signs for *hail*, *soft hail*.

Compare with △ for *ice granules*, △ for *small hail*, and ✳ for *snow*.

A meteorological sign for *snow showers*, *squalls*.

Compare with ✳ above and with the sign for *rain showers*, ▽̇ .

Variations of the sign believed to mean *disordered intellect* or *confused mental state*. Its origin is unknown.

Compare with ||| or ≋, which stand for the *active intellect*. Refer also to the structurally similar ⋏ in Group 40, meaning *men in battle*.

An old pharmacology sign meaning *blend, mix*.

A variation of the graph for *Sagittarius*.

For more information about this sign, turn to ↗ in Group 15.

A sign for *stone* in alchemy and early chemistry. The same structure but turned on its side, ⊟, is used in the English system of hobo signs and means *here live working people — talk a lot*.

Stone was also drawn ⍱.

The sign for *friendship between men* in the system of **family signs**.

See also ✳ in Group 41:b, Υ in Group 4, and Ͷ in this group.

A sign used to denote *talc* in early chemistry and alchemy.

Signs for *lime* or *limestone* in early chemistry.

Lime was also drawn as Ψ, Ⴧ, ℟, ⊘, and otherwise.

A sign for *tartar*, i.e., *tartaric acid salt*, used in eighteenth-century chemistry.

It is also drawn as ↙.

Tartaric acid was commonly used by alchemists and chemists. It was drawn in many ways. Two of them were ⅉⅈ and ൠ.

See the word index for synonyms.

A sign for *salt alkali* used in both early chemistry and alchemy. Salt was also drawn as □ and ⊕.

Salt alkali was common *table salt,* or *natrium chloride.* Like *elixir, alchemy,* and *algebra,* the word *alkali* is of Arabian origin. The alkali metals were sodium and potassium.

For other signs for salt, see ⅜ in Group 41:b.

One of the early chemical and alchemical signs for *amalgam* or an *alloy of mercury and silver.*

Amalgam was also drawn ⌗ , 大 , and otherwise.

One of the many **Christ monograms**. It is built up by a cross above the letters A and Ω, alpha and omega, the first and last letters of the Greek alphabet. Its meaning is *Christ as the first and the last.*

A sign to denote *buried* in genealogy. Other signs with the same meaning are ⊐ and ⌒.

The rune **madr,** *man* or *human,* from the earliest Nordic rune alphabet.

The rune **odal** signifying *real estate, nonmovable property*. See
⟨ in Group 16 for **fä** (cattle), i.e., *movable or personal property*.
    The rune ⟨ is the first in the **futark**, the rune alphabet, and
⟨ is the last.

According to a German source this is an old sign for *camphor*.

One of the signs for the *asteroid Juno*. For more information
on asteroids, turn to ⟨ in this group and ⟨ in Group 17.
    In astrology this asteroid is associated with marriage and
sexual relationships.
    Juno can also be drawn ⟨ and ⟨.

Poseidon, the ruler of water, thunder, and earthquakes in
Greek mythology in antiquity. He has the **trident** as his
attribute.
    This particular sign is a trident from a Greek amphora.
Compare with ⟨, a hieroglyph for *lightning, great power,*
and *domination* in the Hittite system. The signs ⟨ and ⟨
also had this meaning.
    See ⟨ in Group 3.

An ideogram used in modern cargo handling. It is printed
on the packing and means *protect from the cold* or *may not
freeze*.
    If the sign structure at the top had been ⟨, the sign for
snow, or ⟨, *ice*, its meaning would have been even clearer.
    Compare with the structurally similar ⟨ in Group 42.

Group 40

Single-axis symmetric, straight-lined, both open and closed
signs without crossing lines

This is one of the world's oldest ideograms. It has been found on the walls of the Trois frères cave in France. It was probably drawn some 10,000 years ago. In the Nordic runic alphabet ϸ is a sign for a sound that is no longer used. The name of this rune is associated with *giants, titans*. On the Middle Ages clog almanacs (see ⵜ in Group 5) it meant *Wednesday*; that is, the day of the greatest of the Viking gods, Wuotan or Odin.

The sign is associated with the words *turs, ogres*, and *ass* (the ass gods — especially Tor, the chief enemy of the giants). Later it was associated with *cataract*, i.e., it is an expression of *power*. Other signs for power are ϴ , ϟ , and ⌁.

Compare with ϸ, which stands for 5 in the set of golden numbers (see ⵜ).

See also the rune ᚠ in Group 16.

A modern ideogram found on stereos indicating the *balance control for two sound channels*. It is synonymous with ◣◢. Compare with ▣ in Group 24, *balancing of weight*.

This sign is found on videotape recorders and ordinary tape recorders indicating the *eject control*.

Synonymous with the more common ⏏.

A common sign for *woman* in both modern and ancient ideography. The corresponding sign for *man* is ⌐ or ⵜ.

See ⵜ in Group 41:b in the so-called **family system**.

Upside down, ∇, it becomes the sign for *woman dies* or *dead woman* in the family system.

The ideogram for *intercourse, sexual intercourse* used in the family system.

　　See ✳ in Group 41:b.

　　Compare with ▭o in Group 42, which has approximately the same meaning.

A less common variation of the graph for *Sagittarius*. For more information about this zodiac sign, turn to ♐ in Group 15.

An ideogram for *fast movement*, e.g., on household appliances like tape recorders. *Normal speed* in the same context is drawn —▷.

　　See ⌒○ in Group 54 for a sign with approximately the same meaning in another context.

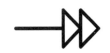

Mars-saffran from seventeenth-century chemistry. Compare with ⚶ , an ideogram that is about 3,500 years old, found on rock carvings in France.

The first letter in the Western alphabet and thereby an ideogram representing the *best, first, excellent marks, good physique* (A-team, A-child, etc.), a *beginning*, a *start*.

　　See Ⓐ in Group 24.

　　Compare with the structurally similar ᴀ or ✕, a *disordered state of mind*.

This is a sign used in the U.S. system of hobo signs meaning *here lives a man with a gun.*

The Virgin Mary is a remnant of a divinity much worshipped in antiquity in the countries of the Middle East and the shores of the Mediterranean. She was a fertility and activity goddess and not in the least chaste and was related to the planet Venus. Christianity took her over and made her a virgin.

Many of the holy days, or holidays, in the West are related to this fertility goddess. This was the case during the Middle Ages in Sweden before the acceptance of the Lutheran teaching at the beginning of the sixteenth century. These teachings (and their acceptance) represented in a way the final rejection of female divinity and a total acceptance of male superiority, patriarchalism, and, yes, stupidity, for lack of psychological balance in the ideological systems of Northern Europe.

This was one of the signs for Virgin Mary used on clog almanacs (see ⵋ in Group 5) to denote *holidays* such as the *Annunciation Day*, etc.

The sign is structurally similar to ⩊ , which means *mountain* in the earliest Chinese system of writing.

Compare with ⩊, the sign for *fire* in the same Chinese system.

A sign from the **family system** (see ✳ in Group 41:b) meaning *men fighting* (originating from ⵙ for *man*).

Compare with ⵅ, a *disordered state of mind.*

Soufre des philosophes, or the *wise man's sulphur,* was used in seventeenth-century chemistry.
Compare with ♁, the most common sign for sulphur.

This is a **time sign** used in alchemy for *week.*
Compare with ⊠ for *month* and other time signs.

One of the alchemists' signs for *honey.*
See ♋ in Group 20 for more signs with this meaning.

This is the sign in alchemy for *rock salt.* See the word index for synonyms.

In eighteenth-century chemistry this sign was used for *magnes.* It might refer to a *magnet* since *magnes lapis* (magnet stone) meant magnet, and since the structure has two "terminals."

One of the alchemists' many signs for *lye.*
See 4 in Group 53 for more data.

A sign for *tartar, tartrate*, i.e., *salts of tartaric acid*, used in seventeenth-century chemistry. The sign ♊ is one of the very many synonyms.

For the other signs, turn to ⅋ in Group 8.

A seventeenth-century alchemical sign for *water*. Water was also drawn ⊞, ⚮, and, later, ∞.

ͳ is the earliest form of **musical note** in the West, dating from about the end of the Middle Ages. Compare with the sign ♀ for the *asteroid Pallas*, with ◊ for *soap*, and with today's musical *note* sign, ♪ .

Turned upside down, ♣, this sign was used as an ideogram by the Sumerians around 3000 B.C.

◊ is a sign from the Swedish system of hobo signs meaning *here you'll meet resistance*.

Turned upside down, ◊, we find it used in the U.S. hobo system meaning *prepare to defend yourself*.

Turned on its side, ◇—, this same structure was one of the alchemists' many signs for *salt, rock salt*. The sign ◻H is one synonym.

This sign has been used for *alum* in seventeenth-century chemistry. Alum was also drawn ͳ and ○.

Compare this ideogram with 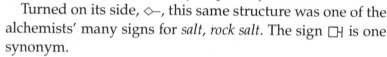 , which is an ancient Egyptian hieroglyph. The roots of alchemy are found in ancient Egypt, and especially in Alexandria where the Nile enters the Mediterranean.

This is a boy scout sign meaning a *letter in this direction.*

Compare with the Spanish scouting sign ⊜→ for *drinkable water in this direction.*

This ideogram depicts a successively bigger quantity of something. It is used on some sound equipment and appliances for *volume control, sound volume.*

Synonyms are, for instance, ◁ and ◠ .

Group 41:a

Single-axis symmetric, both soft and straight-lined, both open and closed signs with straight lines (right-angled crossing lines only)

This is our planet's ideogram, the sign for the *earth*, or *the planet Tellus*. It has been found on a Cyprian coin from around 500 B.C.

It is similar to the so-called **orb**, used by Middle Ages rulers to symbolize their control over a part of the earth. See ♁ in Group 23.

Compare with the structurally similar graph representing our nearest planetary neighbor in space, Venus, and with the astrological sign for the element of *earth*, ⊕. Compare also with the sign for *earth* = *ground*, ☐.

In alchemy and early chemistry ♁ was used for *antimony*, an element similar to arsenic (see ♈ in Group 5), blue-white to silver-white, which was once used as a medicament and for bronzing, for alloys, etc.

In alchemy this sign has also been used for *cinnabar*, i.e., *red mercury sulphide*, an important coloring substance. Today it is used on maps to indicate a *chapel, rectory*, etc.

A "filled-in" version of this sign, ♁, is used in military contexts to denote the *officer in command*. The ordinary ♁ can also mean commanding officer.

An ideogram from seventeenth-century alchemy for *cinnabar*, i.e., *red mercuric sulphide, vermilion*. Cinnabar was also drawn ♁ and ⅃.

See ♀ below in this group.

A cartographic sign for *mosque*. The sign ☿ is synonymous.

Compare with ⚝ mentioned in the last paragraph of the entry below.

This ideogram is probably a **sun cross** and likely has had such meanings as *sun, sunlight, warmth,* or *solar energy.* It is about 4,000 years old and was found at excavations of the ancient city of Troy on Crete.

If one removes the cross we are left with ⊰⊱, a common sign in Japan for *sunlight* and *stars.*

Compare ⊰⊱ with ✳ found on a clay cylinder in the Euphrates-Tigris region.

This is the sign for *Venus, the planet,* our closest neighbor in the planetary system apart from the moon. In ancient Greece the sign for this planet was drawn ♀ and φ. Here the planet was associated with Aphrodite and Athena. In the Roman Empire it was associated with Venus, in the Phoenician Empire to Astarte, and earlier in the Euphrates-Tigris region to Inanna and, later, Ischtar. The sign representing all three, Ischtar-Inanna-Astarte, is the **eight-pointed star,** ✳.

The planet Venus appears to us on earth as either the *Morning star* alone or together with the waning moon, ☾, or as the *Evening star,* alone or with the crescent of the new moon visible. Venus is the only planet that is unambiguously associated to one and only one graphic structure, ☆. If one plots Venus' movements in the zodiac during exactly eight years, this structure is the result. See ⊕ in Group 29 for further data in this respect.

The planet ♀ was worshipped by all peoples and cultures of antiquity as the *divinity of fertility,* the *goddess of war, beauty, and love.* In its role as the goddess of war and fertility it is associated with the Morning star. In its role as the divinity of sexual love it is associated with the Evening star. In the cradle of our culture, ancient Greece, it was not realized until around 500 B.C. that these two stars were one and the same.

The astrologers consider ♀ (together with ♃, *Jupiter*) to be a *benefactor*, its influence in the birth chart being positive.

As a horoscope symbol Venus represents the *drive for togetherness*, the *aesthetic drive*, and *sensuality*. The planet ♀ is the ruler of ♉, Taurus, and ♎, Libra. It is not considered well placed in ♈, Aries, and ♏, Scorpio.

The planet Venus has always been linked in the West to the *female sex, woman*, and to the female in biology, botany, medicine, and other natural sciences. Lately it has been adopted by the *women's liberation movement* in the form ♀.

Since antiquity it can also be found related to the metal *copper*. Today we can see this in the logotype for STORA (once Stora Kopparbergs Inc.). The Venus sign is used in cartography on maps to indicate a *copper mine*.

The background for this is that the island of Cyprus in antiquity was a great exporter of copper. It also happened to be one place where the goddess Astarte or Ischtar was especially worshipped. Consequently, when the sign for the planet associated with this goddess of fertility was established as ♀ it also became associated to this *island of copper* (*cuprum* in Latin, from which the island's name, Cyprus, is derived).

The day of Venus is Friday, the day of Freja, the fertility goddess in the Nordic countries. In Latin countries Friday is *vendredi*, referring to Venus. Refer to the weekday heptagram, ✳, in Group 29.

The use of this sign, however, has not always been consistent. During the eighteenth century it was sometimes used to signify *mercury*. In cabbalistic mysticism it sometimes represented the *archangel Anael*.

A sign from eighteenth-century chemistry meaning *cuprum auratum*, which might have meant *gilded copper*. From ♀ for *copper* and ☉ for *gold*.

A sign from alchemy for *calcinated copper*, or *copper oxide*. From the sign ♀ for *copper*. Refer to ⌒ in Group 18 for the process of calcination.
    See ꟽ in Group 37 for synonymous signs.

The relation between the planet Venus and the metal copper is the reason for this sign's use by alchemists for *brass*, an alloy of copper, ♀, and zinc, ♃.

In eighteenth-century chemistry this was a sign for *pulversiare*, or *pulverize*, and for *pulvis*, Latin for *powder*.
    See ꟽ in Group 37 for more data.

A slightly archaic sign for the *asteroid Juno*.
    For more information on the asteroids, turn to ⚵ in Group 17.

These two structures are prehistoric signs found on the rock carvings in Valais, Switzerland. What they meant is not known and they have not yet been used in modern ideography. The general rule otherwise is that all signs that were

in use 3,000–4,000 years ago are now used in one way or
another but with new meanings.

Compare them with the modern ideogram ⸮ for *suitable
reading distance.*

One of the graphs for the *planet Pluto.* This planet is usually
drawn ♇ .

For more information on Pluto, turn to ♇ in Group 54.

Another, but even more unusual, sign for this planet is
◎.

This is the sign for the *planet Mercury.* Its orbit is the one
closest to the sun in our planetary system. Mercury rotates
around the sun four times while the earth makes one revolution. Its closeness to the sun accounts for this speed;
otherwise, ☿ would fall into the sun. Mercury is about the
same size as the moon.

This closeness also means that Mercury is never seen
more than 28 degrees from ☉, which in turn means that it
can only be seen at specific times and then only after the sun
has set or immediately before the sun rises.

In ancient Greece the sign for Mercury was drawn ☿. In
Greece Mercury was represented by *Hermes,* the quick-
footed *messenger of the gods,* often pictured with wings at his
ankles. Hermes, and later the Roman god Mercury, were
symbolized by the **caduceus, the staff of the snake,** ☤. The
staff of the snake has become a *symbol for trade and communications.* This caduceus, or snake staff, has been mixed
up with the **Aesculapii staff,** with only one snake, a symbol
for the *art of healing or medicine.*

The messenger of the Greek gods, Hermes, was identified
in the Roman Empire with *Mercury, the god of merchants and
also thieves.*

In astrological psychology Mercury stands for the *intellect* and, on a more fundamental level, for the *processes of symbolism*. All our knowledge of the world reaches us via symbols and signs. These symbols are collections of similar nerve impulses. When these nerve impulses reach different parts of the brain then different "ingredients" of our reality can be identified: light patterns, sound, odors, tastes, etc. Every sensory perception is a sign created in the brain that, most of the time, relates to some outer physical reality.

The position of ☿ in the natal chart, or horoscope, indicates the character of the individual's intellect, his or her inventiveness and communication ability, and the functioning of his or her nervous system.

Those who are lucky enough to be born with a well-placed ☿ , according to astrologers, have a *good linguistic ability*, are *fast thinkers*, and *like to communicate*. They are said to have a *well-developed ability to convince others* as well as a *good memory* for even the minutest details.

If ☿ is less well placed it can give *restlessness, inconsistent behavior*, and *superficiality*.

In mundane astrology Mercury stands for business, letter writing, short journeys, gossip between neighbors, school and university, technical and natural science institutions, printing, publishing companies, publishers, and all those people who are in one way or another working in these fields.

Anatomically it stands for the *nervous system, the organs of vision and speech*, and *the hands*, all considered in this case as instruments of the intellect.

Mercury is the ruling planet of ♊, Gemini, and ♍, Virgo. The planet is considered not very well placed in ♐, Sagittarius, and ♓, Pisces.

In alchemy all that was volatile, i.e., all that could be sublimated (♒) or distilled (♌), was sometimes referred to as mercury (via a transference from the sublimated white, poisonous compound *mercuric chloride*). But normally and most commonly ☿ was used to represent *mercury*. Alchemists were always very much interested in this fluid metal (close to gold, mercury having the atom number 80, gold having 79). Mercury could dissolve other metals and combine itself with them into *amalgams*, ⚶. The alchemists produced mercury by roasting cinnabar (see ☖ and ⚴ in this group).

Mercury is poisonous, and thus the sign for it has often been used in pharmacology to mean *dangerous poison*.

Hermes was, contrary to the other Greek gods, both male and female, a *hermaphrodite*. For this reason the sign has been used both in biology and botany to mean *double-sexed*.

As a weekday sign it stands for *Wednesday*. See ⊛ in Group 29 for a derivation of the planets' days.

In the Germanic countries this day is known as Odin's or Wuotan's day, in Anglo-Saxon countries as Wednesday. In Latin countries it is known as the day of Mercury.

The hermaphroditic character of Mercury (what interested the alchemists was this uniting of opposites) has given it a special position in the field of alchemy. Apart from meaning mercury and compounds with mercury it could also be used to signify the *coniunctio*, or uniting of opposites, in esoteric alchemy. (Refer to the section "Esoteric alchemy" in Part I.) Also note its appearance in ⚕, the philosopher's or wise man's stone (for more data, see ⚵ in Group 39).

As to the age of this sign's structure, it is believed to be about 3,000 years. Compare with ☿ found on a Babylonian clay cylinder.

Mercury was also drawn ☿, ☿, and ☿. These three signs together with ☖ could also mean *minium, red lead, red lead oxide*, or *cinnabar*, i.e., the substance used by alchemists to produce mercury.

One of the signs used in early chemistry to denote *alcohol* or *wine spirit*.

This is a sign from alchemy whose meaning is unknown. It was associated with ♉, the sign of Taurus, which for the alchemists meant congelation.

See "The signs of the alchemists" in Part I.

One of the 20 or so signs for *mercury* and *mercuric compounds* used in alchemy and early chemistry. See ☿ in this group.

Mercury was produced by roasting red mercuric sulphide, or cinnabar.

A variation of the sign for *mercury* in alchemy. Note the similarity to the Mercury sign ☿.

Other signs to denote mercury and compounds of mercury are ♈, ☿, ſ, ⊹, ♌, Ψ, ⊖, ☉, and ⚕.

The old sign for the *planet Mars*, ♂, also a sign for *iron*, became, with a horizontal bar added to it, the sign for a compound of iron and sulphur, *ferrohydrosulphate*.

This sign was used both in alchemy and in early chemistry.

Placed horizontally, ⊶, the sign represents the metal *magnesium*.

Compare with ♀, the sign for *sulphur*.

Pointed diagonally upward, ♂, the sign was used for *chalybs*, or *steel*, in eighteenth-century chemistry. See ⚙ in Group 41:b for more signs for steel.

The sun sign, ⊙, with the sign for the planet earth, ♁, placed over it creates the ideogram for *chaos* and *confusion* and appears in a chemistry textbook written in the year 1728.

Semiotically we see matter, ♁, dominating the spirit, ⊙, by being placed above it, meaning that materialistic considerations are allowed to take precedence, resulting in chaos.

Turned the other way, ♀, it means *perfection, quinta essentia*. See ♌ in Group 54.

This structure used in early chemistry means *precipitate*. Compare with the synonym ⯝ .

One of the signs for *glass* in early chemistry and alchemy.

Glass could also be drawn ⫭ and o-o (the latter also represented arsenic).

A sign from alchemy for *sulphur, brimstone, black sulphur,* or *black mercuric sulphide*. The sign ♒ is a synonym.

A sign used in early chemistry and alchemy for *arsenic sulphate*. The sign is a combination of ♁ for *sulphur* and o-o for *arsenic*.

One of the synonyms was ↑.

See ♒ in Group 41:b and the next entry.

A sign for *phlogiston* in eighteenth-century chemistry. See ⟁ in Group 30 for data on phlogiston.

The sign ⟁ was also used for *resin* and *resinous drugs* in old pharmacology.

A sign for the *fourth Olympic spirit* in some cabbalistic mysticist contexts.

A sign from old chemistry for *cuprum arsenicatum*, i.e., a *compound of copper, ♀, and ⟁, arsenic.*

The most common sign for the *planet Uranus*. This graph for Uranus is based on the letter H from the name of Sir William Herschel, the discoverer of this planet.

The discovery of ♅ occurred at approximately the same time as one of the greatest upheavals in the present cycle of human history, the French Revolution. Before this the planetary system's outer limit, which had also marked the outer limit of the human life and the material existence, had been for many thousands of years ♄, Saturn, Kronos. Before the French Revolution it was taken for granted that there existed a higher class of human beings, the aristocracy, appointed by the gods to rule over the lower classes.

The discovery of this planet came as a shock in the fields of both astronomy and astrology, the latter not recovering until the twentieth century. Even today, astrologers in India refuse to acknowledge the existence of the three outer planets.

As a result this planet has come to symbolize *total and sudden change or upheaval, unpredictability, modern science, anarchy,* and *the destruction of an established order.*

The planet Uranus is encircled by half a dozen moons. It differentiates itself from the other planets in our system by the fact that its rotational axis lies almost parallel with the sun's equatorial plane. It is the third largest planet after ♃ and ♄. Its volume would contain 50 earths and it takes 84 years to circle the sun.

In esoteric astrology ♅ is related to the *sexual mores of society.* These mores are said to become almost antithetic after 42 years, that is, after half an orbit of ♅.

In the earlier astrological system ♄ was the ruler of Capricorn, ♑, and Aquarius, ♒. Nowadays ♅ is considered the ruling planet for these zodiac signs. Uranus is also considered to be badly placed in ♌, Leo.

According to astrological psychology those people who are powerfully influenced by ♅ —for instance, by having several planets in ♒ or where ♅ is in close contact with either ☉ or ☽ — are characterized by being *highly individualistic* and *unwilling to be dominated by society's rules and conventions.* They are also supposed to have a *well-developed sixth sense,* as well as having *high humanistic ideals.* They often work to better society and humankind.

Physiologically ♅ rules the *electric impulses* in the nervous system.

In mundane astrology Uranus rules over astrologers, occultists, inventors, and those who are connected to aviation, spacecraft, electronics, and modern scientific breakthroughs. Such things as computers, electronics, and space technology are all ruled by this planet.

The keywords for ♅ are: 1. *intuition, inspiration, "the sixth sense"*; 2. the *breaking of old ideologies, ideas, and structures*; 3. *bohemians, hippies, dropouts,* and *anarchists*; 4. *revolution and humanism*; and 5. an *energy that is directed toward attaining higher consciousness.*

The planet Uranus is also drawn ♅ , ♁, and ♁ .

It is sometimes used as a military sign to denote a *howitzer,* a heavy long-range gun or cannon.

A sign in alchemy for *tartrate.* See ♄ in Group 39 for more information and synonymous signs.

This is a sign from eighteenth-century chemistry for *mercurius sulphuratus,* a *compound of mercury and sulphur,* or *cinnabar* (see the word index for the many synonymous signs).

Arsenicum sulphuratum, or *auripigmentum, realgar,* in eighteenth-century chemistry. See ♼ in Group 41:b for more data.

Antimonium sulphuratum in eighteenth-century chemistry.
♨ has also been used to represent *steel* in alchemical contexts.

  Refer to the word index for other symbols for steel.

Ferrum sulphuratum, or *pyrite*, in eighteenth-century chemistry. It is a *compound of iron and sulphur.*

A sign for the *element of air* in some cabbalistic mysticist
contexts. Compare with ♒, the sign for the *element of water*
in the same context.

The sign of the spirit above the divine triangle crowned with
the cross of Christ makes this a *Trinity symbol.* The same idea
was also drawn ♨, ♨, and ♨.

  See ⊕ in Group 25 for data about the concept of the *Holy
Trinity.*

A Latin cross with a stylized crown—a *symbol of victory* in
Christian symbolism.

One of the signs that the U.S. *Ku Klux Klan* uses. Like other secret societies, the Ku Klux Klan uses its own symbols, although they (like the garb with the hoods) have their roots in Spanish Catholic symbolism. The Klan was created after the U.S. Civil War by some of the defeated white southerners with the intention of keeping control over the recently freed slaves. The Klan ultimately developed into a reactionary petit bourgeois organization, their spear aimed at all that was new, humanistic, and liberal.

Compare with ⚓, a sign on maps and nautical charts for *lighthouse*.

See also ✳ for information concerning a similar organization in Europe 500 years ago.

A sign for a *safe campsite with fresh water*, used in the U.S. system of hobo signs.

Here are three signs from the Middle Ages. They are found in some cabbalistic mysticist contexts on magical amulet seals and represent the fixed stars *Algol*, *Antares*, and *Sirius*.

For other signs of this type, see Groups 41:b, 47, 53, and 54.

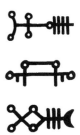

Group 41:b

Single-axis symmetric, both soft and straight-lined, both open and closed signs with crossing lines (at least one crossing line that is not at right angles or not straight-lined)

This is one of the oldest ideograms we know. Round stones have been found with this structure inscribed on them in red in the Mas d'Azil cave. Ⴔ also appears in several ancient alphabets such as the rune alphabet, in which, for a short period of time, it stood for the m-sound instead of ᛗ.

Compare with the sign ♀ in Group 42 and with the following sign entry.

A modern ideogram to denote *loudspeaker, radio, speech recording machine, telephone answering machine,* etc. ⌀ can also signify (the plug-in for) a *record player.*

Compare with ☒ and ⊲ , both denoting *loudspeaker,* and with (⏻), indicating an *on and off switch* for electricity.

A sign for *manganese* or *magnesium* used in eighteenth-century chemistry. These two metals were thought to be the same element. It was not until the end of the eighteenth century that Carl Scheele could prove them to be different elements.

Manganese has the atomic number of 25 (iron, ♂, has 26) and is found as manganese oxide in nature. It is used primarily as an alloy with iron in order to produce a special steel.

This sign was also used for *magnesia,* which is the oxide of manganese and was very much used by alchemists and chemists for various purposes.

Signs for magnesia at different times and in different systems have been ♂, O+ , (⑀), and (⊙).

This sign represents *nitric acid,* also from eighteenth-century chemistry. Other signs for nitric acid are ε–O , ⌗ , and ▽ .

Compare with the following structurally identical sign.

The sign ♀ was used in old pharmacology and had the meaning a *dose of medicine*, a *large pill*.

♀ has been found, for example, together with ●, ⊛, and ⊞, on a Buddha statue from Japan from around A.D. 760.

In Europe it also stood for *bolus*, a *clay containing iron oxide* that was formerly used by chemists in order to make pills, when milling cloth, as a coloring substance, and in the purification of oils.

In old chemistry and in alchemy the sign was used for *orichalcum*, a *golden metal alloy*.

In alchemy, finally, it has sometimes been used for *dissolvant*.

Compare with ♀ in Group 42, which is structurally similar; with ♀ in this group; and with ▽, a sign in alchemy for *clay*.

Atrament or *red vitriol*, a *salt of copper and sulphuric acid* used in seventeenth-century chemistry.

The sign is made up by combining the sign ⊕, for *sulphuric acid*, and ♀, *copper*.

Compare with ⊕+ below, which is structurally similar.

This sign stands for *blue vitriol*, a *copper sulphate*, one of the most important salts of copper and sulphuric acid. The sign originates, like the above entry, from seventeenth-century chemistry.

See ⊕+ above for a derivation of its graphical structure.

Compare with the structurally similar ♀ below. Note that ⊕ was one of the signs used by alchemists for *sulphur*.

For more information about vitriols and other ways of drawing them, turn to ⅁ in Group 18.

This sign is known as the **Egyptian cross** or **Coptic cross** in Christian symbolism. It is closely related to *crux ansata*, ♀, which in turn originates from the ancient Egyptian hieroglyph ♀, **ankh.**

For more information, turn to ♀ in Group 42.

The **Celtic cross**. For information on the Celtic cross turn to ⊕ in Group 24.

Compare with the **Lutheran cross**, ⊹; with ⊕, signifying *oil* in alchemy; and with ⊕ in Group 26.

One of the signs used to represent *tin* in early chemistry. Tin was usually drawn with the Jupiter sign, ♃, but could also be drawn as ♃ and ♃ .

Structurally similar is ♆, the sign for the *planet Neptune.*

A sign for *sal ammoniacus* or *ammonium salt* from eighteenth-century chemistry.

This sign from eighteenth-century chemistry stood for *terra ponderosa*, Latin for heavy soil. ♅ probably denoted *ponderosa salita*, i.e., *chlorine barium.*

Sign for *hepar calcis* from eighteenth-century chemistry. Based on Ψ for *lime*.

A sign for *hepar magnesiae* from eighteenth-century chemistry.

Sign for *hepar terraepond* from eighteenth-century chemistry. The Latin word *hepar* means liver.

This sign meant *potassium carbonate* for the alchemists and early chemists.

One of the alchemists' signs for *wood*. The sign ⚹ was a much more common synonym.

The sign for *aqua regia*, or *king's water*, in alchemy and early chemistry.
　　See ♑ in Group 18 for more data about this strong solvent and blend of acids.
　　Compare with the structurally similar ⊷ in Group 37.

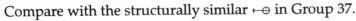

This is a sign from India for *Hindu, Hinduism*. It is used as ☾ is used to denote Islam and Indians of the Muslim faith.

A sign from alchemy meaning *melting oven* and *forge*. This meaning could also be drawn ⊟ and otherwise. See the word index.

    Compare with –⊖– for *fuse, melt together* from eighteenth-century chemistry.

A sign for *salt*, or *sodium chloride*, found in alchemy and early chemistry. Compare with the structurally similar sign used to indicate a *mosque* on maps, ⚲.

    Salt was also drawn ⊙, ⊕, □, ⊖, and otherwise.

Crocus veneris, or *calcinated copper*, possibly a sign for yellow copper oxide. A seventeenth-century chemistry sign.

    Refer to the structurally similar sign in this group, ⊙∈, and the more or less synonymous signs ϶, ♀, and ⚯.

A variation of the sign for the *planet Mercury*, for the metal *mercury*, and for *poison* in early chemistry.

    For more information, turn to ☿ in Group 41:a.

Like the entry above, another variation of the sign for *Mercury*.

In some cabbalistic mysticist contexts ⴕ was used to signify the *archangel Raphael*.

Graphically, this particular Mercury sign is closely associated to the old variation ☿.

The **staff of Mercurius** was sometimes mistaken for the **staff of Aesculape,** the latter having only one snake, which means that Mercury has also been used in many countries as the **emblem of medicine.**

Compare with the **Phoenician staff** sign ϙ.

Western ideography contains a large number of staff signs, i.e., graphic structures depicted as if they were staffs or tools used by the gods and goddesses in mythological representations. Below are the most common of these staff signs: ⸮, the **augur's staff** (and the Christian **bishop's crosier**); 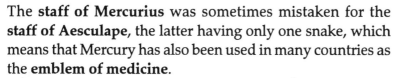, the staff borne by the Babylonian god of thunder and the weather, **Adad's staff;** ⚒, the staff of the Germanic father of the gods, **Wuotan's or Odin's staff;** ♆, the staff of the Greek father of the gods, the **staff of Zeus,** which corresponds to the Romans' **staff of Jupiter;** ♆, the **staff of Neptune;** ⚡, **Tor's hammer, Mjölner;** ᷳ, which was among other uses held by the Sumerian Venus goddess. Finally, there is ☥, the **ankh staff** from ancient Egypt.

In ancient Egypt there were also two other staffs used as **symbols of power:** ⸮ and ⸮. A third staff, ⸮, represented *gold, fortune,* and *riches.* Compare ⸮ with the sign ⌒c , the sign for the *god Zeus /planet Jupiter.*

Caduceus, the **staff of the snake,** here shown in two of its variations. The staff is the attribute of Hermes (Greece) and Mercurius (Rome). It has, on account of this, become a symbol for *trade and communication.* On old Swedish maps ⚕ was used to indicate a *marketplace.*

This sign structure has been used in Western ideography since ancient times. In ancient Greece it was the sign for *Ares, the war god,* interpreted by many as an iconic sign for the shield and spear.

It can also be seen as ○ for the *spirit of the individual,* possessed (pierced) by the arrow, the symbol for the idea of *directed movement* or *action,* a symbol representing the *ability to take action, goal-orientation, masculinity.*

Compare with ♂, the ancient and modern sign for the planet Mars and for Mars, the Roman god of war.

In electrical contexts ∅ means *ampere meter,* or *ammeter,* while in geology it is used to represent a *flat, scored rock,* the arrow indicating the direction of the ice flow — the flow being the cause of the scratches in the rock's surface.

This ancient ideogram also appears in the U.S. system of hobo signs meaning *useless to go in this direction.* Compare with ○→ from the same system, which means *go this way.*

A sign found in the Swedish system of hobo signs meaning *here live unfriendly people.* It is also used in the U.S. system, where it means *leave this place quickly!*

Carbo, or *coal,* a sign from eighteenth-century chemistry. Compare with ⚶ below.

This sign has been used in geometrical contexts to indicate an *angle*. In astronomy it represents the *inclination of the ecliptic*. (For more information on the ecliptic, turn to ⬡ in Group 35.)

⟨ is sometimes be used in astrology to signify the *ascendant*, i.e., the zodiacal degree of a sign that rises over the eastern horizon at the time of birth of an indivdual (*ascendere* is Latin for rise).

Compare with 🜨, found in a prehistoric cave in France, as well as with the ancient Egyptian hieroglyph 𓏤.

A sign for *steel* in early chemistry. Steel was also drawn ♃⊢ and ♂.

It is similar in structure to the symbol of *anarchism*, Ⓐ .

One of the signs in medieval alchemy for *glass*.

Most of the synonymous signs are assembled in the entry o— in Group 42.

This is a sign from alchemy representing *black sulphur, brimstone, black mercury*.

For more information, turn to ♁ in Group 41:a.

Compare this sign with the structurally similar sign above, ♀.

This sign stands for *gummi-resina,* or *rubber,* and was used in eighteenth-century chemistry.

Compare with ♀ for *rubber* in Group 39.

A sign for *argilla,* or *clay,* from eighteenth-century chemistry.

Clay was also drawn ▽ and ▽. See this last sign in Group 24 for a derivation of the sign's graphical structure.

This is the ideogram for *realgar,* a *compound of sulphur and arsenic,* a ruby-red paste used in the production of glass, small shot, signal lights, grounding paint for ships' hulls, etc. It was a substance that the alchemists worked continuously with during the Middle Ages.

Note that sulphur could be drawn ⊗ and arsenic, o-o, which two signs are combined in this particular sign.

Realgar was also drawn ʃ, ♉, ♉, and Χ.

A modern ideogram for *lesbian love, love between women.* First common in the second half of the twentieth century.

Compare with ∞ for *togetherness, marriage* and with ♂ for *male homosexual love.*

A structure from the English system of hobo signs meaning *fruit trees in the garden.*

Compare with ⚹, a sign from the earliest Chinese writing system signifying *winter.* Compare also with ♎, the sign for the *autumn equinox* used on the clog almanacs, and with the similar ♉ above.

A sign from alchemy for *arsenic sulphate*, a *compound of sulphur and arsenic*. The basic structure o-o stands for *arsenic*.
Synonyms are ⚭, ⚯, o=o, and more.

A medieval Nordic sign for *Michaelmas*, the *first day of the winter half of the year*, the *autumn equinox*. It was used on the clog almanacs (see ⯝ in Group 5).
Compare with ⚭ in Group 23, which is synonymous.
See also the sign for the spring equinox, ♈, ♈, and ♃ below.

This is the sign for the *Annunciation Day*, the *spring equinox*, used on the clog almanacs (see ⚯).
Compare with ♈ and ♈ denoting the beginning of the *summer half of the year* during the Middle Ages.
The Annunciation Day was also represented by the sign ⊎. See also the above entry.

One of the signs in early chemistry for *acetum*, or *vinegar*.
Vinegar was also drawn ♯, ✝, ✢, and ⊹.

One of the many alchemical signs for the *planet Mercury* and for *mercury*.
For more data, see ☿ in Group 41:a.
Compare with the structurally similar ⚯ for *amalgamates*, i.e., alloys with mercury.

This sign is said to have been used on the coat of arms of the Medici family and thus comes from Italy of the Middle Ages. The Medicis were extremely rich and great lenders of money. For this reason ⚏ and ⚏ have become symbols for *pawnshops, pawnbrokers.*

The sign ⚏ signifies *oil* in certain alchemical contexts.

Compare also with ♣, the sign for the suit of clubs in the most common deck of playing cards. Note that clubs often are associated with money.

This sign has been used in cabbalistic contexts for *Phul, the spirit of the moon,* the *seventh Olympic spirit.* It has been included here as an example of a whole series of similar signs used, for instance, in the book of magic called **Salomo's Key.**

A sign meaning a *family.* It is a combination of ⌊, *woman,* ⌉, *man,* and ⚸, *woman with child.*

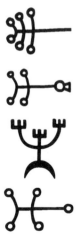

These four signs are from medieval **magic amulet seals.** They stand for the **fixed stars** or distant suns *Polaris, Algorab, Spica,* and *Procyon,* respectively. All of them originate from cabbalistic mysticist contexts.

Look up **fixed star** in the word index for other star signs in the system.

Group 42

Single-axis symmetric, both soft and straight-lined, both open and closed signs without crossing lines

Although this and the next entry are extremely old ideograms they are still used widely in the Western ideography of today. ⚲ is a **staff sign** (see ⚕ in Group 41:b for all such signs) that was used from about 2500 B.C. in the Euphrates-Tigris region. The Egyptians used it to represent the *number 10,000,000.* ⚲ also may have been a general sign for *greatness* and *power.*

This variation of the entry structure above is used in modern ideography for *microphone,* e.g., on telephone answering machines and other household appliances. As a military sign it is used to denote an *outpost.*

An ancient ideogram used in the earliest Chinese writing, this meant the *sunrise, a new day.*

Much later in Western astronomy it had the same meaning but was also used to denote the *lower edge of the disc of the sun.* The horizontal line signifies *the land, the horizon,* and ☉ is the universal ideogram for the *sun.*

Alchemists used ⚯ to signify *day.*

Note that in the Bliss system ⚲ was used to mean *day.* Bliss used the same structure, but turned upside down, to denote *night.*

This sign appears in several prehistoric European caves. Its meaning is unknown but probably is related to that of the above ideogram, ☉ .

Compare with ⏚, the sign for *grounded contact* in electricity.

This is a sign for *aurum fulminans* in eighteenth-century chemistry. *Aurum* is Latin for gold, and *fulminans* means shining or flashing: *flashing gold*.

The sun sign ☉ also stands for *gold*.

Here we have another age-old ideogram. In ancient Greece this sign represented the *goddess Aphrodite*, the *principle of beauty*, and *sexual love*. As a sign for Aphrodite (and maybe her predecessors Astarte and Ischtar) it was also drawn ♀ , ∿ , and ♀ .

At the end of the Middle Ages this sign was sometimes used by the alchemists to signify *night*. The sign could also stand for *copper* although for this meaning it was usually drawn ♀.

The sign ♀ is commonly used in modern technical, electrical, and military systems.

The similar ○ can be found on household appliances indicating the *(outlet for) record player*. Compare the structurally similar ⊘ in Group 41:b.

Sometimes ♀ is used on maps to indicate a *mine*.

In medieval alchemy ⚬̸ sometimes stood for *day*. The ideogram means *conjunction* in astronomy and astrology, i.e., that two celestial bodies lie on the same longitude as seen from the earth. Compare with ☍ for *opposition*.

With the circle filled, ⚫̸, it can be used as an astronomical sign for an *eclipse of the sun*, which makes sense when one realizes that such an eclipse is a conjunction of the sun and the moon.

Vertically placed, ⬇, it sometimes appears as a military sign for *sentinel*, and as ⬇ it can stand for a *private soldier*.

When drawn with a very small, filled circle (i.e., a point), ⟋, it has been used as a meteorological sign to indicate a *coating of ice* or *ice needles*.

In certain biological contexts, ⏐ means an *aborted fetus of unknown sex*.

The sign structure ⟋ was used for *night* by the alchemists.

A sign for *glass* used in late medieval alchemy.

Glass was also drawn ☒☒, o-o, and ♇.

A variation of the sign for the *planet Venus*, the goddess associated with it, *Aphrodite*, and the metal *copper*.

See ♀ in this group and ♀ in Group 41:a for more information. Refer also to the entry below.

The ancient Egyptian **staff sign** or god staff **ankh**, which is also believed to be the hieroglyph used to symbolize *reproduction* and *sexual union*. According to other sources ☥ means *life* and *zest for life*. The best summary of its meaning is *future life*, *life after death*.

Hathor, who was both the goddess of the zest for life and the goddess of death, carried ♀ and gave life with it. This contradictory character in many ways corresponds to the Venus goddesses Inanna, Ischtar, Astarte, and Aphrodite. For a derivation of the relation between ♀, ✳, and ♀, see ⊕ in Group 29.

The hieroglyph ♀ is sometimes called **key of the Nile**. The symbol is associated with Imkotep (living around 3000 B.C.), physician for the pharaoh's family. Long after his death Imkotep was made the god of medicine or healing in Egypt. That is why this symbol is used as the logotype for a multinational pharmaceutical manufacturer.

The same sign structure, but with the closed element filled in, ♀, has been found in Peru used by the Mochica culture around the seventh century.

The above entry sign was adopted by Christian symbolism and given the name **crux ansata** or **Coptic cross**. The *crux ansata*, or handlebar cross, was also drawn ♀.

Compare with ♀ in Group 41:b and also with ♀ in this group.

This sign has also been used to represent *copper* during the seventeenth and eighteenth centuries instead of the more common ♀.

A variation of the **anchor cross** or **crux dissimulata** in Christian symbolism. Compare with the above ♀.

Look up ⚓ in Group 30 for more information about the **crux dissimulata**.

It is interesting to note that a variation of the structure that later became the **crux dissimulata** already existed around the year 2000 B.C. on the seal belonging to the prince of Byblos. Byblos was a Phoenician city in what is now Lebanon. This **staff sign** shows the sun, ⊙, placed on a staff of power.

Here is one of the most common graphic combinations in Western ideography: the circle and the arrow. This particular variation has been found on the walls of the Niaux cave in France and is most probably more than 10,000 years old.

A seldom used sign for the *planet Uranus* (see ♅ in Group 41:a). Uranus is also drawn as ⚷, which has an entry below in this group.

This sign has also been used to signify *morning*, showing the disc of the sun rising. With the arrow pointing downward it represented *evening*.

The same sign structure as the above entry but diagonally positioned is one of the most common ideograms in our Western culture. It stands for the *planet Mars*, which in ancient Greece was drawn ⚣.

In Greece, the planet and god were known as *Ares*. In the Roman Empire, however, Ares became Mars. Quite early on there arose a relation between this sign and the metal used for weapons, *iron*.

For those who know where to look, the planet Mars can be observed as a reddish star in the zodiac. Space probes from the earth have shown that Mars is a stone desert, its atmosphere being very thin. No life, in earthly terms, has been found, but from the space probe *Viking* in 1976 photographs were taken showing three pyramids, roughly three times the size of the Kheops pyramid in Egypt. Two of them lay in ruins.

The planet Venus, ♀, was in earlier times associated with a common goddess of fertility, war, sex, and peace. This was true of nearly all known ancient cultures around the Mediterranean. But from about 2400 B.C. until 250 B.C. this Venus goddess was gradually replaced by masculine divinities.

In astrology the planet Mars is referred to as a *malefic*, i.e., an evil planet, together with Saturn, ♄. Saturn was the great malefic and   the *lesser malefic*. In psychological astrology Mars represents such traits of character as *self-assertion, aggressivity*, and *the ego*, i.e., the urge to distinguish oneself as a unique individual. As all religions in theory are ultimately searching for a union with the universe, yoga, a return to God, it is no wonder that   has been looked upon as something evil. Its function in the human being is in direct opposition to the objective of religion. It is to separate oneself, to individualize oneself.

This planet   is the earth's closest neighbor in the planetary system outward from the sun. Mars has many similarities with ⊕, the earth. The days of both planets are approximately 24 hours long. The inclination of their axes of rotation is almost the same, which means that   also has four seasons. These seasons, however, are longer, as Mars' rotation around the sun takes nearly double the time of an earth year, 687 days.

This, together with the fact that the range of temperature on   is similar to that of the earth, means that it is the only planet in our system that could be colonized in the future. Such a colonization would depend on whether suitable micro-organisms could be introduced to break down minerals into water so that plants could be grown to create an atmosphere rich in oxygen.

As the planet Venus, ♀, the moon's daughter, symbolizes the female principle, , the *sun's son*, symbolizes the *masculine principle*. In the biological sciences this sign has been used to represent the *male* of plants and animals.

The two signs ruled by Venus, ♎ and ♉, lie directly opposite those ruled by Mars, ♈, and ♏. In the birth chart (horoscope) is not well placed in ♉ and ♎. It is, on the other hand, a positive attribute when appearing in ♈ and ♏ and is also considered well placed in ♌ and ♑.

The planet is associated with the astrological element of fire, △. According to astrological symbolism, the sign ruled by Mars, ♈, is a representation of humankind's first stage of development, when individuals became aware of themselves as individuals, separate from the human collective. This newly discovered individuality is like a toy for the individual influenced by , and he uses it whenever he is given the opportunity.

In its aspect of fire, symbolizes the *zest for life*. A human being needs an adequate amount of to have *courage, physical energy*, and *independence of mind and actions* to be able to meet life's difficulties and trials. When appears in such signs as Pisces, ♓, and Taurus, ♉, in the birth chart of the individual it is considered to correlate with problems in this area. When, on the other hand, its influence is too strong, for instance, when there are too many planets in ♈, ♌, or ♐, the fire sign, the worst characteristics of the Martian principle are embodied: *cruelty, selfishness, lust for war*, and *a desire for total dominance*.

This planet, however, is not only a symbol for *the warrior, the murderer*, and *the slave owner* but also for *the surgeon* who heals and *the hunter* who brings home food.

On the physiological level Mars represents *the blood, the outer sex organs, the adrenal glands, the muscle tissue*, and *the nose.* The professions ruled by this planet are the military ones and those that have to do with cutting or piercing, such as butcher, surgeon, and carpenter.

In early astrology Mars ruled both ♈ and ♏, but after the discovery of the three outer planets it became related primarily to the first. Mars was replaced with Pluto as the ruler of ♏.

Among the weekdays Mars represents *Tuesday,* the day of Mars in Latin countries. Refer to the weekday heptagram, ✹, in Group 29.

In alchemy Mars has always been related to the metal *iron.* As a result this sign is often used on maps to indicate an *iron mine.* As Mars takes a little less than two years to circle the sun, in botany the Mars sign has come to represent *plants with a two-year growing cycle* (together with the ideograms ⊙, ⊙⊙, and ②).

The Mars sign has also been used in early chemistry to represent *zinc,* although this metal is more often found represented with one of the symbols for Jupiter, ♃, ⚃, or ♃.

The sign has also been used to signify *morning,* like ♂ above in this group.

In the U.S. system of hobo signs, and in the Boy Scout sign systems of certain countries, it means *go this way.*

With the circle filled, ♂, it is used in military contexts to denote a *grenade thrower* or *mortar.*

A variation of the sign for *iron* in alchemy. It is a combination of the sign ⇅ for *cannon* or *iron* and for *iron.*

A sign for the *planet Uranus*. The sign for this planet is usually drawn ♅. See ♅ in Group 41:a for further information regarding this planet and its role in the most common of the symbol systems.

⛢ has also been used to signify *morning*, consisting of the sign for the sun, ☉, and its rising, ↑.

With the arrow pointing downward it signifies *evening*.

It is also used in modern military ideography as a sign for *machine gun* or *machine-gun placement*.

Placed diagonally, ♂, it is a sign from eighteenth-century chemistry to denote *ferrum auratum*, a *yellow iron compound*. The sign is composed by for iron and ☉ for gold.

A variation of the sign for *iron* in alchemy.

A variation of the sign for *iron* used in alchemy and early chemistry. Other signs used to represent iron are ı|ı, ‡, ⟋, ⟋, and ⌀.

The sign for Mars with a double arrow is an early chemistry sign for *steel*. Steel was also drawn ♃ and Ⓐ.

A less common sign for the *asteroid Pallas*. Pallas is also drawn ♠ and ♀.

For more information on the asteroids, turn to ♀ in Group 17.

These are partly iconic signs for *comets*.

In alchemy they have been used to denote *gold*, probably as a result of the relation to the Egyptian hieroglyph for gold, ⟨⟩ . Gold is usually represented with the sun sign ☉.

In modern military contexts ⚸ stands for *searchlight*.

Due to the fact that comets are rare occurrences, these and similar signs have also been adopted and used in dictionaries and lexicography in general to mean that a word is *rarely used*.

This sign structure is sometimes used to indicate an *inn* on maps and a *mosque* on nautical charts. Mosque is also drawn ⚚ and ♁.

Turned around to ♀ or ⚲ it was used by the alchemists to signify *calcinated copper*, or *copper oxide*. This substance, however, is more commonly drawn ⊕⚹ and otherwise.

A sign in alchemy for *nitric acid*. This acid was also drawn ▽ and ♯. Compare with ⊷ for *hydrochloric acid*.

The prefix ⟵ was commonly used to indicate an *acid*. One added it, for example, to the sign for *sulphur*, ⟵♃, which gave one the sign for *sulphuric acid*.

The sign ⌒ is an old one in alchemy for *fire*. With ⟵ added to the sign the etching and burning qualities of acids were symbolized.

A seldom used sign for the *planet Mars* in alchemy.

In cabbalistic mysticism this sign was a symbol for the *angel Samael*.

For facts about Mars, see above in this group.

A rare variation of the sign for the *planet Neptune*. Other rare signs for it are ♁ and ♆.

See ♆ in Group 5 for more information about Neptune.

According to a German source this is an old sign for *coal*.

Compare with ♒ in Group 41:b.

A sign used in early chemistry for the substance *antimony*. Antimony, a basic element similar to arsenic, was used among other things as a medicament.

Antimony could also be drawn ♁, ♆, and ◇.

For antimony oxide, turn to ♅ in Group 53.

One of the signs for *Vesta, the asteroid,* and for the *Roman god-dess Vesta.*

   See ⌂ in Group 42 for more data on Vesta.

This was a sign for *zinc* in eighteenth-century chemistry. Zinc was usually represented by one of the signs for Jupiter in alchemy and old chemistry.

This sign is sometimes used on geological maps to denote a *volcano.*

An ideogram for *mating, pairing* used in biology. The sign is based on a system where □ represents the male and ○ the female.

   The sign o‑o has a similar semiotic and graphic structure and appears in genealogical contexts for *unmarried.*

A less common sign for the *planet Neptune.* Refer to ♆ above in this group for further reference.

An ideogram used in technical engineering to signify *photo sensitivity*, a *lens sensitive to light*.

The sign ▣⁺ represents the light projector part of this "electric eye," used, for example, for closing and opening doors automatically.

A sign for the *earth element* used in cabbalistic mysticist contexts.

The other three elements in this particular system are drawn ᵕ for *water*, ⵜ for *air*, and ☼ for *fire*.

An ideogram that represents a *woman with child*, from the sign ⵜ for *woman*. This sign is part of the so-called **family system**.

For more information, turn to ✳ in Group 41:b.

An ideogram for *pregnant woman*. Refer to the ideogram above for further references.

This sign is used in meteorology to indicate *rain showers*. Compare with the structurally similar △, for *ice grains* or *small, frozen raindrops*.

Compare also the Egyptian hieroglyph ៣ for *rain*, a combination of ⌐, *heaven*, and ⌇⌇⌇, *water*.

A sign for *camphor* in early chemistry. Camphor was used as a medicament. One of its uses was to cause convulsions and unconsciousness in schizophrenics or severely depressed patients during the nineteenth century, before the psychiatrists started to induce convulsions and unconsciousness by means of heavy doses of insulin or very strong electric shocks to the brain.

A modern ideogram on stereo sound equipment and radios that indicates the *selector* or *outlet for tape recorders*. It is also drawn ⌒⌒.
 Compare with ⊤, *socket for connecting the antenna*, and ◁, *outlet for loudspeakers*.

This is a sign used in early chemistry to denote the metal *nickel*. Compare with ʒ, which could sometimes signify *arsenic* but was more commonly used to signify *nickel*.

A variation of the sign for *arsenic* in alchemy. Arsenic was also drawn ⊥, ♉, ⳨, o‑o, +⌒, ʒ, and ♋.

One of the signs for *sulphur* used in alchemy. The most common sign for sulphur was ♄.

This type of structure—small circles connected by straight lines—is very old. It has been found in ancient China and on Nordic rock carvings.

In China, these structures are signs for different *constellations of stars*. In cabbalistic mysticist contexts a similar structure is used to picture the *stars*, *sound*, and *mathematical expression*.

Structures of this type are also common in modern electronics and telecommunications.

For graphical similarity see, for instance, ⚛ in Group 41:b.

This is a sign for the process of *purification* in alchemy. ♈ in Group 2 is synonymous.

For data about this process, see the sections on alchemy in Part I.

A sign for *eau de vie*, i.e., *wine spirit*, *alcohol*, used in early chemistry. Wine spirit was also drawn ⚭, ♯, and ѵ.

See the structurally similar signs ♈ for *clay* and ♒ for *oil*.

An eighteenth-century chemistry sign for *magnetic iron*. It is also used to mean *rising*. Used for the latter meaning it is possibly identical with ♌, signifying the *moon's northern node*.

Turned upside down, ♈, it meant *setting*. For more information about the nodes of the moon, turn to ♌ in Group 38.

A sign for *oil* in general and for *olive oil* in particular, used in alchemy.

See the entry below and the word index for the many synonyms.

Two signs for *oil* used in alchemy.

An ideogram for the *on and off switch* on electrical household appliances.

The signs ⦶, ⏻, and ◐, among some others, mean the same.

This sign has been used in meteorology to signify a *smoky atmosphere*. The sign is synonymous, as is ⊖.

A Phoenician **staff sign** that is several thousand years old. For more information on the different types of staff signs refer to in Group 41:b.

was adopted by alchemists and used in ideograms such as (see this sign in Group 53).

The alchemists considered and to be synonymous.

This sign means *melting, digestion* in alchemy.
    The sign ♌ was a synonym. For more data see the section "The signs of the alchemists" in Part I.

An alchemical sign for *spirit* or *soul*.
    See ⚎ in Group 6.

This is a very ancient ideographic structure. It is common in prehistoric cave paintings in Western Europe. It is also similar to ᚦ, the rune associated with giants, from the earliest Nordic rune alphabet.
    The sign is also found in the suit of golden numbers on the clog almanacs, signifying the *number 5*. For more information on the clog almanacs, turn to ᚼ in Group 5.

Today, the above entry's sign structure is still used, but turned 90 degrees to ⌓. It has been used for *dew* in meteorology; most likely this use is based upon the sign as iconic for the *rising sun*.
    On nautical charts it is sometimes used to signify *permanent navigation mark* without regard to its form.
    Compare with the 5,000-year-old staff of god, ⚕, from the Euphrates-Tigris region and with similar signs from the beginning of this group. Refer also to ⛎ for *halo around the moon*.

A sign for *aurora borealis*, or *Northern lights*, in certain meteorological systems.

Compare with the graphically similar ⍩, which is an Egyptian hieroglyph, said to have meant *woman*, and the hieroglyph 𓈍 for *gold*.

The sign ⍨ , for *holiday* in the Nordic countries during the Middle Ages, is structurally closely related to △.

One of the signs in alchemy for *soap* or *soft soap*. This meaning could also be drawn ◊ .

An ideogram for *fundere* or *io fusio*, i.e., *melt together* or *fuse*, from eighteenth-century chemistry.

Compare with ─⊖─ for *melting oven* in Group 41:b.

An eighteenth-century ideogram used in chemistry to signify *year*.

In botany, for instance, ⊙ is used to mean the same. In alchemy ▦ was a synonym.

Compare with other **time signs** like ⊠ for *month*, ⟋ for *day*, and ⧖ or ⧗ for *hour*.

A modern ideogram that has been used for *plug and socket* in electrical contexts. Compare with the 4,500-year-old sign ⍖ from the Harappa culture in India.

One of the signs for *wood* in alchemy, also used for *sulphite* in early chemistry.

Compare with **clubs**, ♣, and with the synonymous ♣. The alchemists usually drew the sign for *wood* this way.

One of the signs for *horse dung* used by the alchemists.

Synonymous were the signs ℮, ☺, ♈, and ⌇ .

In genealogy ▽ is used to mean *cremated*. The signs ⚱ and ⚱ are synonymous.

Compare with **spades**, ♠, the card suit associated with death.

One of the signs for the *asteroid Vesta*. The signs ⚶, ⚶, and ⌁ are synonymous.

Compare with the Egyptian hieroglyph ▱, which has a similar structure.

For more information on asteroids and other signs for them, turn to ⚳ in Group 17.

Vesta was the goddess of fire and of the chastely life of the domestic hearth in ancient Rome. The signs ◡, ∼, △, and ⌒ all signify *fire*.

A sign used in the U.S. system of hobo signs. It means *here it is dangerous*.

Compare with ⌐ for *here it is*. Refer also to ⊙, which in the same system means *here lives a bad-tempered man*.

A sign from the English system of hobo signs. It means *here lives a kind man*. Note the divine number of 3 and the friendly sunrays.

Compare with ∴ , a protective sign; V▴▴ , for *here lives a gentle woman who is easily moved to sympathy*; and ⊙ , *danger, people here will try to have you arrested*.

A sign from the U.S. system of hobo signs that means *poisonous water*.

Compare with the entry 🏠 above.

Group 43

Multi-axis symmetric, soft, both open and closed signs with crossing lines

Signs with the structural characteristics of this group seem hardly to have been used in Western ideography. Oddly enough, one of the very few signs used means *mirage*.

A mirage is a hot air phenomenon that occurs in deserts and at sea. Distant objects and landscapes can appear to be close, and there are those who say they have even seen things not known to exist.

One well-known mirage phenomenon is the *fata morgana*, seen off the coasts of southern Italy.

The same structure as above but placed vertically is an old British sign for *dead flat*, the *widest part of a ship's hull*. Dead flat could also be drawn ⋈.

This sign is a combination of the common part of two partly joined circles. Compare with ⵣ found in an African sign system meaning *married couple* or *wedlocked love*.

According to E. Zehren (see bibliography in Part I) ⵣ is an **ing rune**, a divine sign used by the Germanic tribes the Ingveons, Cimbrians, and Teutons. It is also an ideogram for the *moon god* that graphically unites the new and the waning moon, ☾ and ☽.

This sign depicting two spirals is used in electrical and technological contexts to signify a *transformer*, i.e., an appliance that uses an incoming current and electrical inductance to produce an outgoing current with a higher or lower voltage.

The signs ⌇ and ⸺ are synonymous.

Group 44

Multi-axis symmetric, soft, both open and closed signs
without crossing lines

Structures composed by small round and filled circles are some of the oldest ideograms of humankind. They are commonly found, for example, on the Nordic rock carvings and are known as **bowl hollows**.

Three such small forms placed in a triangular form is a common sign in modern Western ideography. These signs sometimes appear on maps to indicate *ruins* or *sights worth seeing*. Tatooed on the upper side of the hand between the thumb and the forefinger they are known as **hobo spots** and probably have a protective function in much the same way as the similar Roerich sign ⊛ (Group 26).

In meteorology ⸪ has been used for *rain*. In modern mining technology it stands for *silver* (compare with ⚷ for *pawnbroker*, and with ♣ for *clubs*).

In mathematics and geometry it means *therefore, as a result, consequently*.

See also Group 8 for similar signs.

◯ is an ideogram for *brakes* depicting a wheel and its brakeshoes. The sign, however, means *brakes* and *braking* in general.

In British meteorology ⦿ has been used to mean a *downpour in sight but not directly over the weather station*.

When the arches of the outer circle are turned around,)●(, the sign indicates that a *downpour is in sight but far from the weather station*.

A modern ideogram signifying *radiation* or *radiation source*. It is used, for example, in the sign ⚠ from Group 30.

Other signs with the same meaning are ⁙ and ⁜ .

Compare with the ancient Egyptian way of symbolizing the *radiation from the sun*, ⤋, and with the sign ☢ in Group 30, similar both in structure and meaning.

One of the many signs used to represent *gold* by the alchemists. Other signs with the same meaning are ♀, ☉ , and
☉ .
    An identical structure is found on the helmet of a holy
statue found in Peru and dating from pre-Columbian times.
    Structurally similar is the sign for the *element of fire*, ☼ ,
used both in cabbalistic mysticist and in alchemical contexts.
    Compare with ☉ , similar in structure and meaning *radio
beacon*.

A modern ideogram used in comic strips. Placed around the
head of a cartoon figure it indicates that the person in question is *confused, in a difficult situation*, etc. The sign illustrates
the graphic idea of (warm or cold) *sweating*.
    Compare with ☀ in Group 54.

Biohazard warning, a U.S. sign that warns against *biologically
dangerous substances*.
    The signs ☢ and ☣ have similar meanings.

This is one of the alchemists' signs for *sal ammoniacus*, or *ammonium salt*.
    Synonymous are the signs)(, ⊥, and ⊖x.

This ideogram is from the famous stele of Naram-Sin from around 2300 B.C. An Akkadian king can be seen worshipping this structure, an **eight-pointed Venus star** with radiation flowing from it in the form of five wavy lines between each of the star's eight points.

See ⊕ in Group 29 for a derivation of this mathematics.

The sign ◊, **vesica piscis**, the **fish bladder**, or the **mystical almond** was adopted by Christian symbolism from pagan symbolism. Christianity implanted more and more of its worship of virginity in ◊, and it eventually became a sign to denote *purity* and *virginity*.

That is why ◊ in modern times has been used in meteorology to signify *exceptionally clear air* or *excellent visibility*.

In accordance with the law of the polarity of meanings of elementary graphs it has also been used in the same meteorological context in the United States to indicate that *visibility is impaired by smoke*.

The **mandorla** is a sort of almond-shaped **halo** or **nimbus** that is often combined with the old symbol of virginity, ◊. In Christian symbolism the combination symbolizes the *purity and virginity of Christ*.

The mandorla has also been used in cabbalistic mysticism.

See ∝ in Group 37 and compare with the symbol for *the Holy Trinity*, ☖.

Group 45

Multi-axis symmetric, straight-lined, both open and closed signs with crossing lines

About 4,000 years ago ♯ was used as a script sign in Elam at the Persian Gulf. Later it was adopted by the alchemists and given the meaning *lead* (the metal was usually represented with the sign for Saturn, ♄).

In alchemy this sign was sometimes used also for *spiritus*, or *alcohol*.

In music it signifies a suggestion to *raise a half tone*. See ♯ in Group 51.

In the pharmacology of former times it was drawn on recipes and meant *Take in God's name*, ℞, or *May this be good for you*. This **invocation cross** was followed by the name of the drug and the prescribed dose.

It is also used as a sign in the game of chess meaning *checks*, *takes*, or *moves to*. In mathematics it can mean *creates a completely ordered field*. As a geometrical sign ♯ means *equal to* and *parallel*.

There is a stylized asymmetrical version, **#**, often used on different types of paper forms. When **#** is followed by a number the sign is short for *number*.

The most up-to-date use of **#** is on telephones, where it appears on a button. With this, and with another button marked ✳, the telephone can be programmed in various ways.

Stylized this way by the alchemists, the above entry structure was used for *lead*, although this metal usually was represented by the sign for Saturn.

Like the above entry, a sign for *lead* in alchemy.

A rune called **ingz**, associated with *fertility*, from one of the runic alphabets.

The rune ᛪ in Group 27 is synonymous.

This structure has been used in alchemy to denote *aqua fortis*, or *nitric acid*, as ⌗ was used to differentiate between gold and silver. It dissolved silver, but not gold.

In other alchemical contexts it has meant *amalgam*, i.e., an alloy with mercury. Compare with the synonymous ⚱.

In the U.S. system of hobo signs ⌗ means *prison*.

The same basic structure as the above, but slightly enlarged, is used in both the English and Swedish systems of hobo signs to mean *avoid this place*.

Compare with the U.S. hobo sign ⌗ above and with *##* meaning *a crime has been comitted here so the place is not safe for strangers*.

In heraldic contexts this pattern repeated so as to cover a given area signifies the color *black*.

In China this sign has been used, from the earliest Chinese writing to the modern day, to signify the *Empire of the Middle*, i.e., *China*. China was formerly regarded by the Chinese as the only civilized country. All the others were inhabited by barbarians.

China was situated between heaven and the underworld; therefore the Empire of the Middle.

The only use that 中 seems to have in the West at present is in geometry, where it stands for a *quadrangle*. What a waste of such a simple and beautiful structure.

There are, however, similar signs. For example: 申 from a protective device made of clay for an Indian woman's genitals; ⊕ for *Buddhist temple* on some nautical charts; ⊠ for *temple*, again on nautical charts; ⏑, with several different meanings in a wide variety of modern technical systems; and ≠ in mathematics signifying *not equal to.*

A sign for *iron vitriol, iron sulphate* in alchemy.
    See ⋝ in Group 18 for more information on vitriols.
    Roasting iron vitriol was an early method of producing *sulphuric acid,* ⩗ .
    Compare with the similar ⟠ for *ink.*

The **square cross**. The filled-in square represents the earth with its four corners (note that ▢ was often used in earlier times to mean *the earth, the land* and *the element of earth*), and the cross clearly represents Christ and his teaching. Therefore ✚ is a symbol for *world evangelization,* the *spreading of the holy gospel.*
    The signs ✚ and † are synonymous.

A sign for *potassium carbonate* used in late alchemy and early chemistry.

A variation of a rune-sign.
    See ⋈ in Group 27 for more information.

In the earliest known Chinese writing this ideogram represented *yin and yang*, i.e., the fundamental dualism of reality. Compare with the more advanced form expressing the same philosophical approach, ⑤, in Group 32.

In the West this sign has long been an ideogram for the *number 10* (from the Latin X). It has also signified an *hourglass* and has, as a result, been associated with *time* and *hour*. As a **time sign** X is synonymous with ⚔.

It is interesting to note that in the earliest Chinese writing the number 10 was drawn +, that is, with the most important of all symbols for the Western philosophical approach: + = 10 in the system X, whereas X = 10 in the system +.

Alembic, distillation flask, or *still* in alchemy and early chemistry.

The signs ◌ and ◌ are synonymous.

An alembic was made of glass and XX was also one of the alchemists' signs for *glass*. This compound was also drawn ♈ and in many other ways.

A variation of the sign for the **arrow cross**. This sign is a favorite among fascists since it denotes an *expansion* in all four cardinal points.

✛ is also used in cartography. On some maps it signifies a *monument* or a *tower*.

Refer to ✛ in Group 9 for more information. See also ✛ in Group 28.

Group 46

Multi-axis symmetric, straight-lined, both open and closed signs without crossing lines

I

The **Roman numeral for 1**, which is also used in the English-speaking world to signify *I* (I am), symbolizes the *singular, individual, imperator* (i.e., *emperor*), *Jesus*—in fact, most persons who are considered to be unique.

In connection with electric switches it means *power on, electricity on*. (I is used as an opposite to 0 both in electronics and mathematics.)

See also | in Group 10, a less pronounced symbol for the same idea.

II

The **Roman numeral for 2**. This is the graph for the zodiac sign *Gemini*. See below.

Turned 90 degrees, ⊨ is used in musical notation for the C-clef. In an elongated form, ⊨, called **brevis**, it means *concerns two notes*.

This is the most common of the graphs for the *sign of Gemini*, or *the twins*. In ancient Greece this graph was drawn =, and around the year 1500, ⊐⊏ was used. Today, ⵊ is one common variation.

The sign of Gemini is both that part of the ecliptic that the sun, ☉ , enters around 21 May and exits around 21 June, at the midsummer equinox, and the period of the solar year when the sun is in that part of the ecliptic.

The Latin name for Ⅱ is *Gemini*, and Ⅱ together with Libra, ♎, and Aquarius, ♒, belongs to the astrological element of air, represented by the sign =. In astrological psychology those with many planets in signs of the air element are characterized by *perceiving the world around them primarily in terms of thoughts, of their intellects*. This means that such an individual fits his or her experiences into a pre-existing framework of ideas. This framework can be based on what the person has learned from books, teachings, or conversations, or it may have been slowly and painstakingly built up by his or her own mental process. Whichever the case, the existence of this framework is important in that the person strongly influenced by this element will show a tendency to always search for a logical pattern in his or her experiences, a pattern that fits in with the pre-existing structure of ideas.

In astrology the opposite of the element of air is not the earth element, as in alchemy, but water, an astrological symbol for the emotions. It is the emotional component of the psyche that is sometimes less than well developed.

There are two ways (∇ and $=$ in astrological symbolism) of experiencing life that often exclude each other. Persons dominated by the element of emotions, ∇, often perceive and experience in a totally subjective, even illogical way, and at an intimate level. Persons dominated by the element of thought, $=$, often are unbiased and detached, sometimes so much so that they seem impersonal.

Individuals born in air signs are characterized by *a highly developed intellect; an ability to be objective; a love of culture, civilization, and refinement;* and *an appreciation for and maintaining of principles.*

The air types often show *a fear of being enclosed or caught in a deeper emotional relationship* (or in fact any relationship). Gemini types detest when people come to them with emotional demands and detest being "owned" by someone, more so than other signs. *Change* and *adaptability* are keywords for individuals with many planets in $\mathrm{I\!I}$.

The sign of Gemini belongs to the mutable quality, symbolized by $\frown$. Look up ◉ in Group 30 for facts about the astrological qualities or quadruplicities.

Mercury, $\mathrm{\breve{y}}$, is the ruling planet for $\mathrm{I\!I}$, Gemini, being the lord of *thought, trade,* and *communication.* The planet Saturn, $\mathrm{\breve{5}}$, a symbol for *stability, structure, discipline,* and *inhibition,* is considered to be well placed in $\mathrm{I\!I}$, whereas Jupiter, $\mathrm{2\!\!+}$, the symbol for *expansiveness,* is considered to not have enough scope in Gemini.

The graphic symbol for Gemini, ♊, represents the *dualism* that the intellect signifies, i.e., the intellect creates a subject that perceives an object (out of the primary, the undivided). On the positive side, the two pillars of ♊ are also two terminals in the outer world and therefore symbolize the *exchange of messages*. A keyword for ♊ is *ideas* and the communication of them. *Change* and *changeability* are other keywords.

Anatomically the sign of Gemini rules *the hands* and *the arms*. In mundane astrology ♊ is considered to rule, among others, the countries of the United States and Belgium, and cities like London and San Francisco are Gemini cities.

In that part of esoteric astrology in which the signs of the zodiac represent stages in the development of humankind, the first, ♈, represents the discovery of the land, and the second, ♉, the cultivation of it. Next ♊ communicates with other individuals and groups so that the best products produced by the different groups can be exchanged for others for the benefit of everyone involved.

In alchemy ♊ was used for the process of *fixation* (see the section "The signs of the alchemists" in Part I). Fixation was also drawn ♇.

A sign used in heraldry, called **caltrap**. The caltrap was four nails or points of steel fused together so that when three of them rested on the ground, the fourth pointed upward. Caltraps were very effective weapons against cavalry and soldiers with poor shoes. They were spread out all over the ground in the path of attacking enemy forces.

Compare ⅄ with the graphically similar arrow cross, ⊹.

An ideogram found on computer keyboards that indicates *hexadecimal numbers*. In the same way as our normal counting system is based on 10 and has 10 figures, the binary system (having only 2 figures, 0 and 1) is based on 2, and the hexadecimal system is based on 16 (and has 16 figures or signs: 0, 1, 2, 3, 4, 5, 6, 7, 8, 9, A, B, C, D, E, and F).

The sign for hexadecimal numbers can also be drawn Ⴒ.

A sign used in cartography to indicate a *fort* or *fortress*.

See the entry ☆ below for further references.

This sign was used in early chemistry and late alchemy for *ink*.

Compare with ⊞ for *vitriol of Mars*, or *red iron sulfate*.

One of the signs used in cartography to mean *fort* or *fortress*. Note that the form ⬠, the pentagon, is associated with ♀, ☆ (of which it is the central part), and war.

See ⬠ in Group 28 and the synonymous ✧ above.

Group 47

Multi-axis symmetric, both soft and straight-lined, both open and closed signs with crossing lines

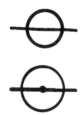

Yet another of humankind's earliest ideograms. It has been found, among other places, on the rock paintings in the inner Sahara. It has also been used in many of the earliest systems of writing.

In alchemy, it was used as a sign for *spiritus,* the *spirit,* and therefore for *the essence, the finest, the most precious.* Alcohol, for example, was the spirit in wine. *Spiritus,* or spirit, was also drawn ⏜ and ≏ .

In early astronomy ⊖ stood for the *zenith of the sun,* while ⊖ represented the *sun's center.*

In a geological context ⊖ means a *flat, grooved rock face.* (If the sign appears with an arrow as Ø in a geological context, it denotes the *direction of the movement of the ice* that grooved the rock.)

In modern times the most common use of this extremely ancient ideogram is in technical contexts, where one of its most common meanings is *(open) valve.*

On ships it is a main part of the **Plimsoll mark** (see ⊖ in Group 53).

On cameras it is sometimes used to indicate the *focal plane* or *film plane.* Compare with →|←, which stands for *focus.*

The sign ϕ is **phi**, the twenty-first letter of the Greek alphabet.

In a vertical position this sign is occasionally used in Western ideography. It is much more common leaning slightly to the right.

The sign Ø is part of the Danish and Norwegian alphabets, signifying a vowel sounding like a combination of the *u* in *fur,* and the *oo* in *foot.*

It is also common in computer programs and stands for *zero,* as it does in the mathematical theory of sets.

It sometimes means *diameter* and in other contexts *mean* or *average* number. As a biological sign it has been used to signify a *dead female* (a combination of ╱, *abolished*, and ○ , *female*). Compare its use here with the use of ⊗, below in this group.

In its vertical position, φ, it represents the *number 15* of golden numbers on the clog almanacs (for information about the almanacs see ♓ in Group 5).

The sign φ was used in the oldest Chinese calligraphy with the same meaning as 中 has today, i.e., the *Empire of the Middle*.

Compare ⌀ with the very similar sign ⌀, for the Greek god of warfare and action, Ares.

Turned this way, ◌, the structure appears in the U.S. system of hobo signs with the meaning *a good road to follow*.

A sign for one of the most important *iron ores, red iron oxide, bloodstone,* or *haematite*. It was used by the alchemists.

Compare with the graphically similar ⊹, which is an entry below in this group.

This is a sign for a purification process in alchemy whereby one purified a substance by heating it to white-hot, by *burning out* all impurities.

It was probably often used by the alchemists interchangeably with the sign ⚔, below in this group.

A sign for *wax* and *oil* in alchemy. See also the entry sign ⊕ below, which was a synonym.

With the circle filled in, ⊕, it becomes a Christian symbol for *world evangelization*, the *spreading of the holy gospel* all over the world. In this respect it is synonymous with ✝ and ✚ and others.

The sign ⊕ is rarely seen although the graphically similar ⊕ is very common.

In alchemy this entry sign was sometimes used to signify *oil* or *wax*. In early chemistry it denoted *crystalline copper acetate*. Swedish hobos used it to mean *no money here but one can get food*.

In musical notation sign it signifies the *end of a passage that is to be repeated*, a **repeat sign**.

In mining contexts it has been used to indicate an *abandoned mine shaft*, with the circle signifying the entrance hole and the cross over it signifying that it is not valid, or abolished. In cargo handling the sign ⊕ on packing sometimes signifies the *center of gravity*. Compare with the synonymous ⊞.

The above entry sign structure turned 45 degrees signifies *total clearance, zero position* when found on a key on modern office machines. When one presses this key the machine deletes all stored data and is ready to begin anew.

It is amusing to compare this meaning of ⊗ with that given by the alchemists to ⊗ during the seventeenth century: *keep, preserve*. This is an illustration of the *law of the polarity of meanings of elementary graphs*.

Another example of this pair of opposites, *clear away – preserve*, can be found in the **family system** (see ✳ in Group 41:b), in which ⊗ means *child dies*.

The meaning *burn out*, by making white-hot, given to ⊗ by some of the alchemists summarizes both opposites in that this process means that the burned-out metal or compound gets rid of impurities while at the same time the essence is kept or preserved.

In its use as a modern washing information sign on clothes ⊗ also has a meaning that comprehends the opposites *remove – preserve*, albeit indirectly: it means *cannot be dry-cleaned.* By dry-cleaning a garment one removes the dirt and preserves the garment at the same time, and both these meanings lie behind the information presented, i.e., that the garment will not stand up to dry-cleaning.

During the eighteenth century natural scientists sometimes used this sign to signify the *oxygen principle*. The element oxygen was not discovered until the 1770s although it makes up roughly half of the mass of this planet's surface layers of rock and soil.

In old marine technology and navigation it appeared as a sign for the *widest section of a ship, dead flat.* Here ⊗ is related to ⊕ for the *center of gravity.*

A **Coptic cross with four nails** from Christian symbolism. Note that *crux ansata,* ♀, is often called a Coptic cross.

The **Coptic cross** ♀ is closely related to the ancient Egyptian hieroglyph ☥. The Coptic church is older than both the Roman Catholic and Greek Catholic churches and is found primarily in Egypt and Ethiopia.

This sign is an ideogram from India. The Hindu god Vishnu in his form of Vishnarupa incarnates the whole universe. Vishnu holds this sign in one of his four hands (the upper right one).

This is a modern ideogram used on garments to indicate that they *cannot take tumble drying.* It is composed by ▢, meaning *rotating machine* in electrical contexts, and ✕, meaning *abolishing* or *not valid* when drawn over another ideogram.

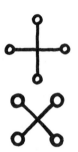

One of the alchemists' many signs for *argent vif* (French for living silver), or *mercury*. Mercury was commonly drawn with the sign ☿ for Mercurius, the god, and Mercury, the planet.

Other synonyms were ♀, ⚏, ☿, and ☿̣.

With the small circles filled, as +, or as shown here, the sign was called the **button cross** in Christian symbolism.

This structure turned 45 degrees to ✖ was a sign for *crucible* or *melting pot* according to an old German source.

See +⃛ in Group 9 for synonyms.

This type of structure is common on Bronze Age objects found in different parts of the world. The sign has also been found on Nordic rock carvings. Some researchers consider it to be a sun symbol but this is contradicted by the fact that the well-known and more common sun symbol, ⊕, appears on the same rock carvings. Furthermore the sun cross, -⃛-, is one of the most important signs apart from ☀ found engraved on an old gold horn in Slesvig, Denmark.

Our only clues as to its meaning, and they are weak ones, are that ∪ in rare instances is used as a sign for *fire* or *flames* in Western ideography and that Ψ signifies the *staff of Poseidon or Neptune* as well as the spear used by devils to torture humans in the flames of hell.

These signs signified *saffron yellow copper, calcinated copper, crocus veneris* and were used in seventeenth-century alchemy. This substance was also drawn ←o and ⊕←.

Compare with ↕, Mars-saffron.

It is structurally similar to o-o, a common sign for *glass* and for *arsenic*, and to the sign entry below.

This sign meant *acidum arsenici,* or *arsenic acid,* in alchemy and early chemistry. The sign is composed by o-o for *arsenic* and ⊹ for *acid.*

A sign for *acetic acid* or *wine vinegar.* Other signs for these substances in alchemy and early chemistry were ⊹, ⨯, ✢, and ♄.

Note that the very similar ♯ meant *spiritus,* or *alcohol* for the alchemists.

An ideogram for an *important part of the body* according to an old German source. The same source states that ✡ was synonymous.

Group 48

Multi-axis symmetric, both soft and straight-lined, both open and closed signs without crossing lines

A sign for *wax* in alchemy. It was probably used to signify *oil* as well.

Wax and oil were also drawn ⊕, ⊕, ⊷, ƶ, ⅋ , ꬵ, and 4.

The same structure as that of the above entry sign is used in computer contexts to indicate *hexadecimal numbers*.

For more information see ⊓ in Group 46.

One of the many signs in alchemy for *olive oil* and *wax*. See ⊹ above, where many synonymous signs can be seen.

The sign ⊽⊽ is still another synonym.

In Christian symbolism this ideogram is known as the **lily cross.**

A common ideogram on household appliances indicating the *increase/decrease control*. It is also used to indicate the control for *automatic adjustment of picture quality* on TVs.

Signs for control buttons for increasing or decreasing volume, intensity, etc., can also be drawn ◁, ▰▰▰, and ⌐.

The entry sign below is another synonym.

A modern ideogram signifying the *volume control* on household appliances such as TVs, stereos, etc.

See the above entry, ✕✕, for some synonyms.

This sign was used by some alchemists to mean *grind, crush, mill*.

This is the same structure as the above entry sign, but turned 90 degrees. It is a Japanese sign for *sunlight, sun,* and *stars*.

In the West we see ✕✕ used on cameras as a sign for the *light adjustment*.

It has been used in cartography as a sign for *water mill*.

This ideogram is the most common for the *sun, sunshine,* and *light* in general. It is used in meteorology, on cameras, and on household appliances like TV sets for *light adjustment control* or *brightness control*.

Compare with the ancient sun sign ☉.

A **sun cross** found in Slesvig, Denmark, on a golden horn from the Bronze Age. The ideogram is composed by the sign + (nowadays known as the Christian button cross) and ☉, the universal sun sign.

See also ✳, found in pre-Columbian Peru, and ☼, which has been used to signify a *mill* on some maps.

This ideogram has been used in cabbalistic contexts for *fire*. To see the other element signs in the system turn to ♧ in Group 42.

In other contexts fire can be drawn △ and ⌒ and in many other ways.

This is a sign from the English system of hobo signs meaning *here lives a kind woman*. We see a combination of a modern sun sign and the structure ∴, meaning *protection* and *material wealth*.

This is a U.S. ideogram with unknown meaning, although it is a combination of the age-old sun sign ⊙ and the modern Western sun sign ☼, which would make the sign very strongly associated with the sun and/or sunshine.

The almost identical ☼, however, has been used for *mill* on some U.S. maps.

This structure has been used in alchemy to signify both *glass* and *arsenic*, which is understandable as arsenic is a main component in glass manufacturing.

In a genealogical context o-o means *unmarried*. Compare with ⊙ for *married*.

Refer to o◄ for other ways of representing *glass*. Turn to ⚲ in Group 42 for all the different signs for *arsenic*.

This is the same structure as that of the above sign turned to a vertical position. It has been used both for *nickel* and for *calcinated copper* in alchemy. *Nickel* was also drawn ⚲.

For other ways of representing *calcinated copper* see ⚥ in Group 47.

This is one of the most important signs in astrology and astronomy. It means *opposition*, i.e., that two planets lie immediately opposite one another, as seen from the earth. The moon is full when the sun, ☉, and the moon, ☽, are in opposition to each other. This relation is drawn ☉ ⚯ ☽.

The same sign as the above entry, but with the circles filled, ●●, denotes an *eclipse of the moon* in astronomy. This phenomenon means that the opposition of the sun and the moon (the full moon) is exact so that the shadow from the earth covers the surface of the moon.

Usually, when the moon is full, it moves either slightly above or below the earth's orbit around the sun and therefore is not shadowed by the earth.

A ●● occurs when that longitude in the ecliptic (see ◯ in Group 35) where the moon is in exact opposition to the sun is also one of the **moon's nodes**, ☋ and ☊.

For more facts in this respect, look up ☊ in Group 38.

This is a chess sign that means a *short castling* — simplified, the king and the closest of the castles move together, the king ending in the cornermost position.

A *long castling* is drawn o-o-o.

A genealogical sign for *divorced*. It is synonymous with the sign ⚲.

Compare with ⚭ for *married*.

Divorce is also drawn ◈ in heraldry. Turn to this sign in Group 28 for more data.

One of the alchemists' signs for *year*. The sign is a synonym.

For more time signs, look up **time signs** in the word index.

The well-known ideogram for *percent*, or *number per hundred*, belongs to this structural group. This ideogram's brother, ‰, *per thousand*, however, belongs to Group 54.

This **time sign** meant *hour* for the alchemists.

See ⵝ in Group 27 for more signs with this meaning.

A variation of the graph for the zodiac sign of *Gemini*. The most common graph is ♊. It can be found in Group 46 along with other synonymous variations.

Group 49

Asymmetric, soft, both open and closed signs with crossing lines

This sign is the first letter in the Greek alphabet, **alpha**, written in italic form. In the hieroglyphic system of ancient Egypt ⴖ was a sign for *thread* or *yarn* and *measurement*.

  For ⴖ as a symmetric sign structure, see ∝ in Group 37.

These signs denote *distillation*, i.e., the process of heating a liquid until it boils and evaporates and then letting the steam or gas come into contact with a cold surface, causing it to condense and become liquid again. This was one of the most important processes in alchemy.

  Distillation was also drawn ♂, ♌, and ♍.

A somewhat iconic sign used in electrical contexts to represent *coils, windings* in transformers, electrical motors, instruments, etc. It is also a sign for an *inductor*.

  For more data in this respect, see ∾∾∾ and other signs in Group 37.

A sign found in comic strips signifying a *mental state of confusion* due to drugs, a shock, etc. It is placed above the head of the figure and often found together with several ✩.

  The sign ۞ is sometimes used synonymously in the same contexts.

Ampersand, meaning *and*. It is used in logotypes, company names, and commerce. It originates from the Latin *et* meaning *and*, the two letters *e* and *t* having been joined together.

  Turned as if viewed in a mirror, to ⅋, it becomes the sign for an old weight measurement, roughly a *pound*.

One of the most common signs in musical notation. It is also often used in many different contexts to symbolize *music in general*. In musical notation 𝄞 is the **G-clef**.

The sign 𝄞 is often used to indicate the *treble tones register* or *filter* on stereos and TVs, or the "sharpness" of the sounds.

Compare with ℣, which is often used in the corresponding ways and contexts for bass tone register control.

There exist lots of signs for old measurements. Structurally, most of them belong to this group. It is not meaningful to include them all here, but one should know that those old signs used for measurements and currencies before the decimalization often are asymmetric and drawn with curved and crossing lines.

The structure shown here is the old sign for *penge*.

One of the signs for the war god *Ares*, representing the power of violence and warfare in ancient Greece. It was also drawn ⇘.

Ares was not very visibly worshipped in ancient Greece. He just existed. In the Roman Empire, however, Ares' counterpart, Mars, ♂, was one of the empire's most important divinities after Jupiter.

Compare ⌀ with ⚢, found on a rock carving in Bohuslän, Sweden.

An alchemical sign for *lead*. It was probably given this meaning owing to a confusion of signs. ⌀ is very similar to ⌀, the Ares or Mars sign, which also signifies *iron*. Lead was usually represented by the sign for Saturn, ♄.

Lead could also be drawn S, ℈, ▽, ♯, and otherwise.

The most common graph for the zodiac sign *Virgo, the Virgin*. The sun enters this sign around 23 August, and exits around 23 September. It is not only a symbol for this part of the solar year (a period of time) but also for that part of the zodiac that the sun moves through during the stated period (a part of space).

The iconic symbol for the sign of Virgo is often a picture of a female angel holding an ear of corn in her hand.

In esoteric astrology each sign represents a special era in the development of humankind. The sign ♍ follows ♌, where the individual engages in asserting his or her independence. ♌ is often preoccupied in giving orders to others. Leo is only slightly aware of those people who carry out the orders. Thirty degrees farther on we find the sign of *Libra*, the sign that symbolizes a perfect working partnership. Leo is blinded by his or her own power and unmindful concerning the interaction necessary to make people work well together. He or she is also ignorant about what is demanded of a socially mature individual. Before ♌ can attain peace of mind through the understanding of the Other that comes with ♎ he or she has to learn how to receive orders and serve others. The individual must learn to become the receiving partner rather than the one who demands. This learning is what happens in ♍.

Humankind (or the individual) in ♍ arrives in this life with all of ♌'s creative potential, but unlike ♌, who without inhibitions sends out vibrations into the world, ♍ is totally absorbed by an ongoing interpretation and appraisal of other people's reactions to his or her self-expression. It is important for this type of person that no one, especially him- or herself, should be hurt. ♍ is often aware of all those forms that an idea can take, but is continuously wondering which one of them is the best. Before doing anything, he or she studies all the details from every possible angle and tries to reach an understanding of the problem from all points of view. This is ♍'s weakness. His or her active intellect approaches each new aspect as separate and therefore creates new aspects to think about. Before he or she realizes what has happened and can control the situation, he or she has already lost sight of the original idea.

Discrimination is the keyword for ♍, who easily can perceive even the minutest differences.

Virgo is still unaware of the whole spectrum of human relations. ♌ expressed the spectrum of order-giving, and ♍ takes the other direction and becomes the one who obeys and receives orders. It is only in ♎ that the process of give and take is completed and a balance is achieved, and it is in Aquarius, ♒ , finally, that the individual (humankind) becomes whole, complete.

The individual who has ☉ in ♍ is usually very eager to be of use in life. He or she finds pleasure in precision and usefulness.

The sign of Virgo is of the negative polarity. ♍ belongs to the earth element (symbolized graphically by ⊕) together with ♉, Taurus, and ♑, Capricorn. This element is related to the senses and sensual perception as the primary way of perceiving the environment. The element ⊕ is considered in astrological symbolism to denote *good sense*, an effective approach in matters material, which is the opposite of the fire signs' capacity for fantastical visions and their highly developed intuition. This characteristic of ♍ often means that he or she "is unable to see the forest for the trees." Despite the fact that the earth signs are excellent at collecting facts they often lose sight of the relations and connections between them and their real meaning.

Virgo belongs to the group of signs known as mutable, symbolized by ⌒. For a concise description of this quality or quadruplicity, turn to ◉ in Group 30.

On the physiologic and anatomical plane ♍ rules *the intestines* and *the stomach*. Physical and psychical stresses in life are first and foremost felt by this type of individual (i.e., those who have ⊙ in ♍ or several planets in that sign) in the stomach and intestines.

In mundane astrology ♍ is associated with Turkey, Brazil, and the West Indies. The cities Paris, Athens, Boston, Corinth, and Jerusalem are said to be related to this sign.

The ruling planet is Mercury, ☿. Saturn is said to be well placed in this sign, whereas Jupiter's energies have difficulties in expression in Virgo.

A zodiacal and psychological opposite of this earthbound, practical, and factual individual are some persons born in the sign of *Pisces*, ♓, since they are so sensitive, idealistic, and believing.

In alchemy, ♍ is used to represent the process of *distillation*, one of the processes used to remove impurities and isolate the purest part of the substances the alchemists worked with.

This structure is a sign for *juice* or *sap*, used by some of the alchemists. The entry sign below is a synonym.

A variation of the above entry sign.

Group 50

Asymmetric, soft, both open and closed signs without crossing lines

A sign for *retort*, or *distillery tube*. It also symbolized the process of *distillation*. A retort was a glass vessel with a long, tapering, down-angled neck or beak used for heating up liquids and letting the gas out via the beak into a cooled flask for condensation.

Retort was also drawn ☌ and ⚹ in alchemy.

The process of distillation could be drawn ♋ and was sometimes symbolized with the sign for the sign of Virgo, ♍.

The graph for *Leo*, the zodiacal sign. In earlier times ♌ and, later, ♌ were also used to represent this zodiacal sign.

The sun, ☉, enters this sign around 23 July, and exits around 22 August. As with all the signs of the zodiac, ♌ stands for both the part of space through which ☉ passes during this time and the time period itself.

Leo belongs to the fiery triplicity, or the element of fire, △, together with the signs of Sagittarius, ♐, and Aries, ♈. The individuals strongly influenced by or born in this sign are characterized by relying on their intuition when relating to the outside world. In astrology the psychological opposite of △ is not, as would be expected, ▽, the element of water, but that of earth, ⊕. Earth signs attempt to understand all they see and come into contact with via its material facts as perceived by their sense organs, whereas the fire signs relate to the world in terms of its potentialities and possibilities. As far as the earth element is concerned, the fire element is unrealistic, dissolute, and fantasizing.

The individuals born in a fire sign have a strong need to mythologize their experiences and relate them to an inner world of fairy tales, rather than to the facts of the world of matter we live in. They are often attracted to the fields of theater and film. If an individual has ☉ in ♌ (or several planets in ♌ or ♐ or ♈) he or she will seek a dramatic life and will quite happily create the necessary excitement in his or her inner world if it is missing in real life.

Leo belongs to the fixed quality or quadruplicity, symbolized by ⬤. For data about this quadruplicity look up that sign in Group 30.

The element △ together with the quality ⬤ are believed to give individuals strongly influenced by ♌ *a need or desire to rule and order others around*, which in extreme cases (as with the Leos Napoleon and Mussolini) can have disastrous consequences.

In most cultures the lion is used as a symbol of power. In the Roman Empire, Christians were torn apart and eaten by lions in the Coliseum, an allegorical expression of the way in which the Roman Empire defeated and consumed enemies of the state.

Leo is a fixed sign and thus wants to stabilize what has already happened (the inheritance) but also desires to leave his or her imprint on the world (♌ is a positive, masculine sign).

Keywords for ♌ are *confidence, warmth, love, protection,* and *creativity*. But so also are *vanity, dictatorial tendencies, extravagance,* and *egoism*.

The following countries are associated with this sign in mundane astrology: France, Italy, and Rumania. The Alpine regions of Europe are considered to belong to ♌'s sphere. The cities of Prague, Bombay, Damascus, Chicago, Philadelphia, and Los Angeles are closely related to the sign of the lion.

Leo's ruling planet is ☉. Mars, ♂, is well placed in Leo. But the energies of Saturn, ♄, and of Neptune, ♆, have difficulties expressing themselves in this sign.

Anatomically ♌ rules *the heart* and *the spine*.

In alchemy ♌ was used to denote the process of *digestion*.

A variation of ideogram for the zodiac sign *Leo*. See ♌ above for facts about this sign.

This structure has also been used by some alchemists to mean *dissolve* or *solution*. Note that ∿ had the same meaning when used by chemists in the eighteenth century.

A meteorological sign used in the United States to indicate *hurricane* or *tornado*.

Compare with ⚐ for *dust devils* and other signs for strong winds.

The well-known sign for *paragraph*, sometimes used as a general sign for *law* and / or *bureaucracy*. As a biological sign it can mean a *typical specimen of a species*.

§ is used in typography to mean *section* or *paragraph*. ¶ is synonymous in this respect.

This two-part sign is the most common for the zodiac sign of *Cancer*, which in earlier times was often called the sign of the crab.

The sun, ☉, enters this part of the ecliptic around 22 June and exits around 23 July. This means that ♋ is a sign for both that month-long period of each year and that part of space. The crab begins at midsummer in the Northern Hemisphere and is the zodiacal sign most closely associated with summer.

Together with the zodiac signs Scorpio, ♏, and Pisces, ♓, Cancer belongs to the astrological element of water, ▽. In astrological symbolism water stands for feelings. The individual born in this sign uses his or her feelings to come to terms with the environment. There is nothing more important for an individual in a water sign than personal relations

and human values. They are prepared to sacrifice everything to retain a relationship and will create a crisis, even if
they have to pay a high price, to achieve the necessary reaction or response from their partner.

The feelings are the "air" the Cancer person breathes. In
the world of feelings there are no well-defined boundaries
between this and that, me and them. Instead everything is
one huge sea of waves in which strict and well-defined
differences are impossible to maintain.

The water signs are symbolized by three cold-blooded
animals: crabs (or crayfish), scorpions, and fish. When they
appear in dreams they are often associated with the instinctive, unconscious energies that lie close to the very roots of
human nature and at the same time are far from the rational,
sensible thinking and acting.

♋ belongs, together with Libra, ♎, Capricorn, ♑, and
Aries, ♈, to the cardinal quality or quadruplicity symbolized by ∧. For more information on the cardinal quadruplicity, look up ⬤ in Group 30.

According to astrologers the home and family are more
important for individuals with ☉ in ♋ than for others.
Their symbol is the crab or the crayfish, an animal that has a
hard shell, but that is soft and sensitive inside. Keywords for
this type of individual are *sensitivity to all feelings and emotions, concern for other persons' needs, very responsive, very much
for home and family*, and *an understanding of all human states of
mind*.

The keywords for the negative aspect of this sign are *a
tendency to become hysterical and irritable, a tendency to nourish
ungrounded fears*, and *an exaggerated and almost blind love for
one's own group*.

The moon, ☽, is this sign's ruling planet. In astrological
symbolism the moon is related to the home, the family,
emotional life, the feminine aspect of the psyche, and the
subconscious. The moon also symbolizes receptivity and

responsiveness. It covers all those aspects that also characterize individuals born in ♋.

The facts that ♋ is a water sign, that it is cardinal, and that it is negative mean that the sign has an emotional, self-inhibiting, and passive tendency that comes into conflict with the basically enterprising spirit.

Anatomically ♋ rules *the breast or chest, the female sexual organs, the stomach* and *the digestive system* in general.

In mundane astrology the sign of the crab is associated with Scotland, Holland, New Zealand, and most of Africa, as well as parts of the United States. The cities ruled by Cancer are Amsterdam, Venice, Stockholm, New York, Constantinople, and Milan.

Both Jupiter, ♃, and Mercury, ☿, are considered well placed in this sign. The energies symbolized by Saturn, ♄, and Mars, ♂, however, do not have ease of expression in this sign.

In alchemy ♋ is related to the *process of dissolution,* i.e., a process by which a substance is dissolved in a liquid like an acid.

This is a sign form used in alchemy for *aurum cum caloric,* or *gold plus heat,* maybe *molten gold.* Similar to ☉ for *gold.*

One of the many signs for *silver* in alchemy. Silver was also drawn ☾, ⟁, ⌒, etc.

See ✧ in Group 25 for more synonyms.

The sign for the *salpeter flower*, a flower-like precipitation of saltpeter, e.g., on damp walls. The sign was used by the alchemists of the Middle Ages.

An ideogram found on some nautical charts representing a *sound signal sent out from under the water*.

This is one of the many signs for *gold* used in alchemy. Gold was usually drawn with the sun sign ☉, but ☌, ♀, ⊙, ◎, ⌀, and others were also used.

Another sign for *gold* in alchemy. See the above entry sign for most of the synonyms.

The ancient structure ⚥ has been found both in pre-Columbian America and in Bronze Age Europe. In Europe it is especially associated with the Celtic tribes.

In this variation, ⚥, it appears in modern times in France as a sign for *Jeune Bretagne*, a separatist movement in the Celtic part of Bretagne.

The basic symbol ⚥ is associated with *migrations* or *independent movements of tribes or clans*. For more information look up this symbol in Group 14.

One of the alchemists' signs for *lead*, which was more usually represented with the sign for Saturn, ♄.

For most other signs for lead assembled, look up ♂ in
Group 49.

This is a modern ideogram, first used in the world of comic
strips. Drawn above the head of a figure it symbolizes the
moment of death, or *passing out*. The same or similar structures, used in the same way, can also indicate the *sudden
realization that a cherished idea is an illusion.*

An Egyptian hieroglyph for the *sun god, his arrival and victory
over darkness.* This sign has also been used in Christian symbolism.

Today it is used by subcultures using illicit drugs as a
general symbol for *altered or higher states of awareness*, e.g., in
association with the use of LSD.

Compare with ⊚ from computer technology contexts
and with ⊕ from the same contexts, indicating that a symbol has been found.

A variation of the graph for the *planet Mercury* from ancient
Greece (where the planet was associated with the *messenger
of the gods, Hermes*).

Mercury is usually drawn as ☿. For facts about the god
and the planet, see this entry sign in Group 41:a.

Group 51

Asymmetric, straight-lined, both open and closed signs with crossing lines

This is a common ideogram in modern Western systems. As a sign used in trade and commerce it means *number*. It is also common on computer printouts.

In musical notation it is called a **sharp** and indicates that one should *raise a half tone*. (Another similar sign, ♮ , *cancels the raised half tone;* ♭ indicates that the *tone should be lowered*.)

The sign # has also been used in early chemistry to denote *air*.

In medicine the sign is sometimes used to indicate a *fracture*, i.e., a *broken bone*.

Compare with ☒, an Egyptian hieroglyph.

A sign used in both the Swedish and U.S. systems of hobo signs. It means a *crime has been committed so the place is not safe for strangers*. This meaning is also drawn # and ▦.

These last ideograms can be found in Group 45.

A sign for a *general pause* in musical notation. It means a *long pause* or *pause for all parts* in a musical work.

One of the signs for *Hermes*, the *messenger of the gods* in Greek mythology, forerunner to the Roman *Mercurius* (☿).

Other signs used for the hermaphrodite Hermes are ☿̑ and ♀̣.

This is a sign from alchemy meaning *put in wind furnace*. The ideogram ⅔ in Group 53 is a synonym.

A sign for *borax* or *tinkal*, a substance used, among other things, for enamelling and in the manufacturing of glass and porcelain. It was used in both alchemy and early chemistry.

One of the alchemists' many signs for *arsenic*. Refer to ⚥ in Group 42 for other signs to denote arsenic.

Nitrogenous air, i.e., *nitreous gases* like *nitrogen dioxide*, was represented by this ideogram in eighteenth-century chemistry.

The structure is a combination of △, for the *element of air*, and the vertical line in ⊕ for *nitrogen*.

These signs represent the astrological aspect *sesqui-quadrate*, which separates two planets in the zodiac by *four-and-a-half signs* or an *angle of 135 degrees*.

The sign ⊡ is a combination of the sign ∟ indicating 45 degrees (half of a square, 90 degrees) and the sign □ for a *square* or *right angle*.

This aspect is considered to be a weak and slightly disharmonious aspect in the birth chart or horoscope.

This is a straight-lined variation of the common graph for the *sign of Virgo*, the *Virgin*, ♍. For data on this zodiac sign, look it up in Group 49.

This and the following two entry signs have been used in cabbalistic mysticist contexts for the spirits of three planets.

This sign symbolizes *Arathron*, the *first Olympic spirit*, the *spirit of Saturn*.

 The *second Olympic spirit, Bethor, the spirit of Jupiter.* See the entry signs above and below.

 The sign for *Phalec*, the *third Olympic spirit*, the *spirit of Mars.* See the two entries above.

 This is a Greek variation of the **fylfot** or the **sauvastika** form. It was found on an amphora from around 500 B.C.

Group 52

Asymmetric, straight-lined, both open and closed signs
without crossing lines

This very basic ideographic structure is found as a rune from the earliest known rune alphabet. Its name (probably) meant *happiness*.

The same structure as that of the above entry sign is used in prosody, cartography, and other modern ideographic systems. These ideograms signify *points in time or space from which distances or rhythms are measured, distance reference points, rhythm reference points.*

Signs like these are used in meteorology to indicate *winds of different strengths*. The strength of the wind is shown by the number of bars on the side of the arrow. The signs shown here denote *weak winds* and *storm*, respectively.

The signs ╱ and ╱ in Group 16 have the same meaning.

Some other signs representing winds are ╱, §, and ϱ.

A sign for *Ares*, the *god of war and devastation* in ancient Greece. Ares had the children Deimos and Phobos (Horror and Fear) and their sister Eris (Discord). He was later adopted by the Romans under the name Mars. For this reason the two moons of Mars are known as Phobos and Deimos.

For other signs for Ares, look up ♂ in Group 49.

A sign for *aqua fortis*, or *nitric acid*, used in alchemy and early chemistry. Here we can decipher the alchemical sign for the element of water, ▽, with an F added for *fortis*, Latin for strong. Aqua fortis, or the strong water, was the only acid the alchemists knew that could dissolve silver, but not gold, and it was used accordingly. When platinum was discovered alchemy already had given way to modern chemistry, but nitric acid cannot dissolve platinum either.

Nitric acid was also drawn ε—⊕, #, and otherwise.

A sign for *crucible*, or *melting pot*, used in old chemistry. A crucible was a small but strong bowl in which metals could be melted.

Crucible was also drawn ⊹, ♡, and otherwise.

This sign is a rune from the Nordic runic alphabet. It was called **raido**, which meant a *raid*, a *riding*, a *journey*.

On the clog almanacs ᚱ was a sign for *Friday*. (Look up ᚼ in Group 5 for data about the clog almanacs.)

In modern times ᚱ is used on road signs and maps in Scandinavia for *Old Norse relics or monuments*.

A **Celtic swastika** from a ceremonial shield made of gold found in England.

A sign used by Swedish hobos meaning *generous woman* or *here lives a woman whose sympathy is easily aroused.*
    Compare with the synonymous ⬠ₐ₄₄ in Group 34 and with ꝑₐ₄₄ for *kind woman, tell moving story* from the U.S. system of hobo signs.

This is an ideogram for *mirror* that is sometimes used in modern physics and optics.
    Compare with the heraldic sign for a mirror, ⊕ .

A modern sign used in architecture for a part of an "electric eye," i.e., a device used to automatically open and close doors that sends a light beam across an opening to a light-sensitive lens on the other side.
    See ↘○ in Group 42.

A Swedish boy scout sign meaning *letter within three paces in the direction of the arrow.*

A modern sign for *tent camp,* used, for instance, when mapping mountain climbing expeditions.

Group 53

Asymmetric, both soft and straight-lined, both open and closed signs with crossing lines

An ideogram used both in the British and the Swedish systems of hobo signs with the meaning *go on in this direction*.

Note the similarity with the Ares sign from ancient Greece, ♂.

A symbol used to denote the *plug-in for a record player* on sound equipment like stereos.

The sign ◯ is synonymous.

This is a sign for *antimony oxide* from late alchemy and early chemistry.

Note that the very similar old sign for the planet earth, ♁, was also used to denote the substance antimony.

A sign used in early chemistry for *sulphuric acid*. Derived from the sign for sulphur, ⊕.

A more common sign for sulphuric acid was ⚶ combined with a prefix, ←, for acid, to ⊷.

See ⊢⊕ in Group 42 for more signs for acids.

A sign from eighteenth-century chemistry for *argentum cuprofoetum, a compound of copper and silver*.

The ideogram is drawn by combining ♀ for copper and ☽ for silver.

This sign from eighteenth-century chemistry signified *orical-chum argentatum*. The ideogram is composed by ♀ for orical-chum and ☽ for silver.

The sign for *house occupiers, squatters.* This is a modern ideogram used by members of a youth movement in Germanic countries who occupy evacuated houses. The group is involved in continuous fighting with the police, the authorities, and the construction firms who are demolishing habitable houses in cities' central areas in order to build new high-rises on the lots.

This sign is closely associated with Ⓐ in Group 24.

A sign from botany, but not much in use currently, representing *hermaphrodite, double-sexed plants.* Derived from ♂ for *male sex* and ♀ for *female sex.*

Formerly it was more common to use the sign for the hermaphrodite god, Hermes, or Mercury, ☿, to represent this type of plant.

This is a recent ideogram denoting *male homosexual love.*

Compare with ♀♀ in Group 41:b and with ⊙ in Group 25.

A sign used in eighteenth-century chemistry for *sal sedativus,* or *calming salt,* probably the same as *sal sedativum, boric acid,* which was widely used as an antiseptic.

This is a sign used by some of the alchemists for *horse dung*. Look up ♀ in Group 42 for synonyms.

Most of the **Christ monograms** used in Christian symbolism belong to this structural group. The monograms usually are composed by the initials of Christ in their Greek form: PX (corresponding to RK in the latin alphabet). Here, the X has been turned 45 degrees to form a cross.

A **Christ monogram**: P and X. See the above entry.

A **Christ monogram**: P and X. See the above entry.

A **Christ monogram**: P and X and a cross. See the above entry.

A **Christ monogram** combined with the Greek letters α, alpha, and ω, omega, the first and last letters of the Greek alphabet. A symbol for *Christ as the first and the last*.

A **Christ monogram** combined with △, the symbol of divinity and of the Holy Trinity. Its meaning: *Christ is the center of the Holy Trinity.*

A **Christ monogram**. See the above entry.

This sign was formerly used in pharmacology and similar contexts. When used nowadays it indicates that the drug or medicine prescribed is not delivered without a prescription from a certified physician, i.e., *only a certified physician may prescribe this medicine.*

Formerly this sign was written on the prescriptions and meant *to be taken, prescribed, recipe.*

See ♯, the invocation cross, in Group 45.

In astrological symbolism ℞ or ℞ are signs for a *retrograde movement*. As seen from earth the planets move primarily in the same direction as the sun, but it does happen that a planet seems to come to a halt and then begins to move backward. This apparent reversal of movement is called retrogradation. Many astrologists claim that a retrograde planet in an individual's birth chart (horoscope) symbolizes *tendencies or energies inherited from previous incarnations.*

This ideogram is known as the **Plimsoll mark** (after its inventor, the British civil servant Plimsoll, living in the latter half of the nineteenth century, who took a great interest in the safety of cargo ships). It was introduced in 1870 and painted on the sides of ships by the water line.

The letters stood for different parts of the oceans with their different concentrations of salt, i.e., different ability to make ships float. WNA, for example, denoted winter freeboard in the North Atlantic. The upper edge of each line indicated the allowed freeboard.

One of the many alchemical signs for *sulphur*. Sulphur was usually drawn ♁. See this sign in Group 39.

A sign for *alkali* or *lye* used in both alchemy and early chemistry. It was also used to represent *ammoniac*. Lye was also drawn ⊽ .

Alkali were the *hydroxides of alkaline metals* such as sodium and potassium (e.g., soda, or sodium hydroxide).

This ideogram was a symbol for the *Polish resistance movement during World War II, Polsky Walski*. The sign is composed by the anchor sign, the symbol for hope *par préférence*, and a P for Poland.

One of the alchemists' signs for the *quintessence*.
Look up ♃ in Group 50 for more data.

This is one of the signs for *process in wind furnace* in alchemy.
The sign ⚗ in Group 51 is a synonym.

This is a **time sign** used by the alchemists, meaning *spring*.
Look up this word in the word index for synonyms.

A sign used in late alchemy and early chemistry for *cinnabar*.
See ☿ for more data on cinnabar.
This sign was probably also used as a synonym to ȝȝ
below.

This sign from early chemistry signified *filtrate* or *strain*.
Compare with the entry sign ȝȝ above.

A sign from eighteenth-century chemistry meaning *stannum
sulphuratum, aurum musivum,* a *compound of tin and sulphur.*
The strange thing is that the ideogram is composed by the
sign for the philosopher's stone, ☋, and the Jupiter sign for
tin (*stannum* in Latin). One would rather have expected the
common sign for sulphur, ♄, and the Jupiter sign.

This is a sign from eighteenth-century chemistry for *sulphuric acid*. It is composed by joining the most common sign for sulphur, ⇪, and the prefix ↤ for acid.

The sign ⊕ in this group is a synonym. For further synonyms, see the word index.

A sign for *rubber* used in early chemistry.

There are a couple of synonyms. Look them up with the help of the word index.

In this structural group there is a whole series of signs that all denote *measures*, *measurements*, or *standards* of some kind. They are not very enlightening semiotically, and therefore are not listed here. But two examples are given: £ is the sign that was used to represent the *pound sterling*, the *British currency*: $ is the **dollar sign**, the *U.S. currency*.

This structure is used both as one of the graphs for the *U.S. currency* and as a structure used in computer programs. When $ is placed after the name of a variable in the programming language BASIC, it indicates that it contains a *text*, a *string of letters* and not figures.

In other computer languages $ can stand in front of a string of figures, and then it means that the string consists of hexadecimal numerals.

For data on the hexadecimal system, see ⊓ in Group 46.

This ideogram is often used to represent *alternating current* and sometimes for *frequency*. With the former meaning ∿ is synonymous with ≃ , ≈ , and ≋, whereas *frequency* can also be drawn as ∿.

Note that ∿ is the sign for *a complete oscillation*.

An ideogram used in geology to represent *twisted mountain formations*.

The Nsibidi people in Ghana, Africa, use the same structure to indicate a situation where *two witnesses contradict each other, and one is telling the truth* (the straight line).

The sign for *Ophiel*, the *sixth Olympic spirit*, the *spirit of Mercurius*. It has been used in cabbalistic mysticist contexts.

A sign used in cabbalistic mysticist contexts to represent the *element of water*.

For the other elements in this system, turn to ⚯ in Group 42.

This is a modern sign for *sexual love*. How modern it is cannot readily be determined. It might have been used already at the end of the nineteenth-century, in the romantic years around the turn of the century, or even earlier than that.

The ideogram is, however, composed of the sign of the heart (for *liking* and *community* and *the part of the body below the stomach*) and the arrow of Cupid or Eros.

For more data, look up ♡ in Group 20 and ❀ in Group 2.

A Middle Ages **magic amulet seal** to denote the *Pleiades*, a *constellation of fixed stars or suns* found in the direction of the end of the star sign Taurus (not to be confused with the zodiac sign with the same name).

A **magic amulet seal** representing the *fixed star Deneb Algedi*. See the above sign entry, and also **fixed star** in the word index.

A **magic amulet seal** representing the *fixed star Alphecca*. See the above sign entry.

A variation of the graph for the Greek god *Zeus*. In the context of alchemy the metals *tin, zinc,* and *electrum* were often signified by the sign for Zeus or Jupiter.

For more information on Zeus, look up ♃ in Group 17.

These entries are two variations of common graphs for the *sign of Capricorn*. The sun, ☉, enters this part of the zodiac around 21 December and exits around 20 January. Consequently, Capricorn, or the *sign of the goat*, signifies both the time period each year when the sun moves through this part of the ecliptic and the part of space against which this movement can be seen from the earth.

In the Scandinavian or Nordic countries, Christmas is a Christian adaptation of an old Nordic new year feast (celebrating the longest night and the return of the sun with offerings of gifts to one another and pagan sacrificial rites).

This was an astrologically important happening, being the winter solstice.

This point in the solar year marked the end of the old and the beginning of the new solar year. The first moon, or month, of the new year was that of Capricorn. That is the reason why even today one of the most common Christmas symbols in Scandinavia is a goat made of straw, the *Julbock*, a symbol of the zodiac sign of the goat. This is a remnant of the old polytheistic religion that was replaced around the year A.D. 1000 by Christianity in a violent overthrowing of the old order (almost all treasures from the so-called Viking Age found buried in the fields are from these revolutionary years).

The sign ♑ belongs to the cardinal quality or quadruplicity together with ♈, Aries, ♋, Cancer, and ♎, Libra. These four have in common the fact that they mark the beginning of a new season, a new relation of light and darkness. The cardinal signs, symbolized by ∧, are the instigators of activity, initiators motivated by an inner ambition.

The sign ♑ belongs, together with Virgo, ♍, and Taurus, ♉, to the astrological *element of earth*, ⊕. This means that ♑, according to astrologers, is characterized by being practical, having good common sense and "both feet on the ground." The earthy individual relates to the world via the senses (instead of ideas, air, ═; intuitively perceived potentialities, fire, △; or emotions, water, ▽). For more information on the astrological element of earth, look up ♍ in Group 49.

The sign ♑ is symbolized by the mountain goat, an animal found high up in the Alps, fearlessly climbing but with a sure footing. The Capricorn individual uses, in the same way, all possible resources to reach the top.

Astrologers claim that Capricorn types are creatures of habit who find it difficult to change a way of living once it has been established.

The keywords for Capricorn individuals are *ambition, realism, hard work,* and *ability to find constructive solutions to problems encountered.*

Anatomically Capricorn represents the *knees,* but also the hardest of the bodily structures, those that give stability and firmness to the flesh.

In mundane astrology ♑ represents permanent structures such as the state, large firms, bureaucratic organizations, etc. The ruling planet of Capricorn is ♄, Saturn. This planet since ancient times has been associated with permanent structures: the teeth and the skeleton in the human body; discipline, duty, responsibility, and self-discipline in individual psychology; and buildings and construction work and earth-moving equipment in everyday living.

The planet ♂ is considered well placed in ♑, and so is ☿. The moon, ☽, and Jupiter, ♃, however, have difficulties expressing their energies in this sign.

In mundane astrology ♑ is the ruler of such countries as Albania, Greece (certain parts), Bulgaria, Afghanistan, Mexico, and India. Capricorn cities are Oxford, Brussels, New Delhi, and Port Said. Hindus and Jews are considered to be closely related to ♑.

The sign ♑ was used in alchemy to denote *fermentatio,* i.e., the *process of fermentation.*

A sign for the alchemists' *lapis philosophorum,* the *stone of wisdom,* the *goal of the alchemical process.* In this sign are combined the signs for the three most important substances used by the alchemist: sulphur, 🜍, salt, ⊖, and mercury, ☿. Above the signs for these three substances is the symbol

-☥-, a sign originating in ancient Egyptian symbolism, signifying the *human consciousness* and *spirit*.

For more information refer to the section "Esoteric alchemy" in Part I. *Lapis philosophorum* was also drawn 🜃.

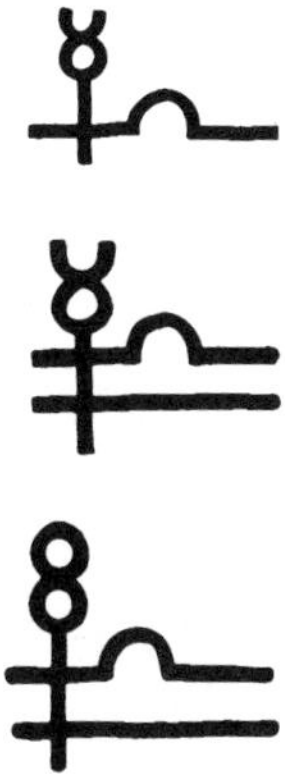

These signs, or ♎, the Libra sign, were used in alchemy to denote a *sublimate,* i.e., the *result of sublimation*.

They also stood for *mercury chloride,* the substance that the alchemists could most easily sublimate.

For more information about the process of sublimation, look up ♎ in Group 6, or read the sections on alchemy in Part I.

Compare with ☿ for mercury.

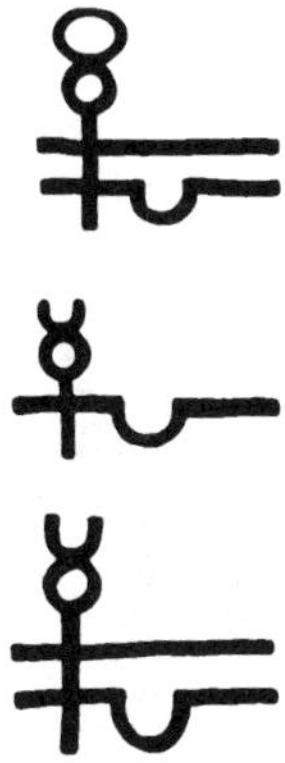

These signs, or ⩡, the Libra graph turned upside down, were used in alchemy to denote the process in which a vaporized substance was transformed into a liquid form, *precipitation*. The signs were also used to signify the result of such a process: the *precipitate*.

See also ☿♎ above.

Group 54

Asymmetric, both soft and straight-lined, both open and closed signs without crossing lines

A **flat** or **lowering sign** used in the system of musical notation. If it is placed before a note it indicates that this note's sound frequency *should be lowered a half tone.*

Compare with the corresponding sign for *rise a half tone,* # , ♯ , or ✕.

Signs called **notes** in the system of musical notation. ♩ represents a half-note, a tone that has a specific length. A whole note is drawn ○; a fourth part of a note, ♩ ; an eighth part of a note, ♪; a sixteenth part of a note, ♪ ; a thirty-second part of a note, ♪ ; and so on.

This sign signified *iron filings* in early chemistry (or old alchemy). It is derived from ♂ for *iron* with three points added signifying the filings.

A sign used in seventeenth-century alchemy to denote *magnesia*, a substance that probably was the metal magnesium's oxide (the metal was not yet discovered) or some similar substance.

One of the many signs for *arsenic* in alchemy. This substance was also drawn ⵙ, +ⵎ, and o-o.

For other ways of symbolizing arsenic, see the sign below and ⚥ in Group 42.

Like the above sign entry, another of the alchemists' signs for *arsenic*.

Quinta essentia, the fifth element, besides fire, water, earth, and air—the element that is necessary to explain the diversity and multiplicity of life, *the ether*, the best (*the quintessence*). The alchemists also used this sign for the same meaning. The idea of a fifth element came from the Pythagoreans. The Chinese also counted five elements. For them, metal was the fifth element.

This is one of the most recent ideograms in Western ideography. ♆ is the sign used to represent the *planet Chiron*, discovered in the 1970s. Chiron's orbit lies between those of Saturn and Uranus. Its orbital period is 51 years.

The astrologers who have accepted the existence of this new planet (whose longitudinal positions are given in most of the reliable ephemerides) believe it to be related to the sign of Sagittarius, ♐, and have characterized it as a *teacher and faith-healer*, whatever the latter word combination can mean.

Another of the alchemists' many signs for *mercury*. For synonymous signs, look up ╬ in Group 47, or consult the word index.

‰ is the well-known ideogram for *per thousand*, or *per-millage*.

Compare with ⚹, which is structurally similar, and with ⁄ in Group 18. ⬤₀, which signifies the *on and off switch* on electric and electronic appliances and machines, is also similar.

This sign is one of a kind used to represent *constellations of fixed stars* in Chinese and other cultural spheres. The type of sign that we call **stars** appeared for the first time in the Phoenician and Babylonian cultures.

The cabbalists also used this type of sign to denote constellations of the fixed stars. See the sign entry below.

Medieval **magic amulet seals** to denote the fixed stars *Arcturus* and *Regulus*, respectively. These structures have been used in cabbalistic mysticist contexts.

For more signs for fixed stars or constellations, look up **fixed star** in the word index.

This is a sign from eighteenth-century chemistry for *alcali volatile*, or *ammonia*.

Ammonia was also drawn ⚹ and ✳, and otherwise.

One of the most common graphs for the *sign of Cancer*. Strictly defined it should not be in this group at all (according to the rule that all straight lines that in one end become curved are regarded as soft elements in this book).

For more information about this sign, look up ♋ in Group 50.

A sign in genealogy for *divorced*. This meaning could also be drawn o|o.

For associated data, look up this last sign in Group 48.

This ideogram is in reality a combination of two graphs, ♂ for *day*, and ♀ for *night,* respectively. This ideogram and its components were used by the alchemists as **time signs**.

For other time signs and for synonyms consult the word index.

A Spanish boy scout sign for *drinkable water in this direction.* The ideogram is a combination of the sign for *water,* ≋, placed within the circle of all possibilities, with an arrow added to indicate the direction of the available possibilities drawn within the circle.

A Spanish boy scout sign for *this water is dangerous to drink.* Compare with the above sign entry. The water sign has been placed within the triangle of power, signifying a danger. This sort of ideography is frequently used by those who design our traffic signs.

This sign belongs to the so-called **family system** and means a *childbirth, child is born.*
 For other signs in this system, look up ※ in Group 41:b.

A sign from the **family system**. It means *mother with child.*

A sign used in early chemistry to represent *lye, sodium hydroxide.*
 For more information, turn to 4~ in Group 53.

According to one source this is a sign used in alchemy and early chemistry for *gold.* This is probably due to a misunderstanding. The alchemists and early chemists usually drew gold with the age-old sign ⊙ or the medieval signs ♄ and ♀.

A sign found in the U.S. system of hobo signs, meaning *say nothing, don't talk at all.*
 Compare with the similar sign ⊡/ from the same system, with the meaning *in this town there is alcohol* (from the time of Prohibition).
 ◊ is also found in seventeenth-century alchemy, said to mean *laton* (French), a word that does not exist in modern French dictionaries.

These two sign entries are from the U.S. system of hobo signs and mean *here one can sleep in the barn*.
    Compare with ⌒ used in the British system of hobo signs for a *good haystack/barn for a night's sleep*.

This is a sign from the U.S. system of hobo signs meaning *thieves in the neighborhood*.

$$\frac{2}{10}$$

Alinea, a typographical sign formerly used in printed texts that indicated a *text corresponding to the beginning of a new train of thought*.

Variations of typographical signs used in early literature indicating a *text corresponding to the beginning of a new train of thought*, a **paragraph sign**.
    See the above entry sign, which is synonymous.

A variation of the sign for *Hermes*, the *messenger of the gods* in Greek mythology, corresponding to the Roman Mercurius.
    Hermes was also drawn as ⚵, ☿, and otherwise.
    For more data on Hermes, look up ⚵ in Group 51.

This is a rune from Britain and the Middle Ages that does not exist in any of the Nordic rune alphabets.

However, Shepherd (see bibliography in Part I) suggests it was a sign for *fehe*, which means love.

Compare with the first rune in the Nordic rune alphabets, named **fé**, ᚠ, in Group 16.

The most common graph for the *planet Pluto*. This planet is also symbolized by ♀, ◎, and ♉.

According to Bode's law (see ♃ in Group 17), the ninth planet of the sun should orbit at a distance of about 40 earth-sun distances from ☉. Bode formulated his law in the eighteenth century. But ♉ was not discovered until 1930. Pluto was found to orbit at approximately the right distance from the sun. But the planet's orbit is much more elliptic than those of the other known planets. Therefore, it sometimes takes only 13 years to move through one of the signs of the zodiac, while at other times it takes 31 years to move through one of the zodiac's 30-degree divisions of the ecliptic. Pluto's orbit inclines at 17 degrees relative to the ecliptic (see ♌ in Group 38 for more information concerning the ecliptic).

In theory Pluto was discovered around the year 1905 by Percival Lowell, a U.S. astronomer. The graph for the planet is based upon his initials.

Using mathematics and astronomical calculations Lowell predicted that a planet, with a small diameter, would orbit at a distance of approximately 40 earth-sun distances and that this planet's orbital period would be approximately 282 years. The actual orbital period of Pluto is 242 years. Apart from this discrepancy, Lowell's predictions were quite right.

Most of this planet's physical characteristics are unknown, but it is supposed to have a surface temperature of minus 200 degrees Celsius.

In astrological symbolism ♇ represents *death and rebirth, total transformation, atomic energy, ruthlessness, dictatorships, large organizations,* and *competition.* Astrologers in the West claim Pluto to be the ruling planet of Scorpio, ♏; the sign formerly was thought to be ruled by Mars.

The U.S. astrologer Alan Oken suggests that ♇ is merely a higher octave of ♂. Mars breaks down form, he claims, but ♇ transforms its very atomic structure.

The planet ♂ is also the aggressive and emotional energy behind wars. The planet ♇ represents the ultimate destruction, the atom bomb. ♂ signifies the passion in sexuality; ♇ represents the orgasm. ♂ is the anger that makes the soldier pull the trigger. ♇ is the force that separates the soul from the body, Oken says.

The astrological significance of a planet is affected by the situations of human societies at the time of the planet's discovery. When ♇ was discovered in 1930, the criminals had the upper hand in the United States thanks to the stupid prohibition of alcoholic beverages. Fascist regimes were appearing in Italy, Germany, and the Soviet Union. This time in the present cycle of human civilization was also the beginning of the nuclear age and signalled the first tremors of the Great Depression. At that time ♇ was passing through the sign of Cancer, ♋. At the time of the final translation of this symbols dictionary into English, Pluto is leaving the sign it rules, Scorpio, and entering Sagittarius, the sign of the archer projecting his arrow to distant futures.

This planet is named after the Roman god Pluto, guardian of the underworld and the god of the kingdom of death. Hades was the parallel god for the Greeks, and the underworld was later called Hades, after its ruler. In Greek mythology, however, Hades was also the ruler over riches and buried treasures, and it is from this that the word *plutocracy* is derived, meaning a regime in which the rich rule the masses.

We can add that a lot of astrologers believe it to be significant that ♇ was discovered on the longitude of 20 degrees Cancer and that the first atom bomb on earth in this cycle of civilization was detonated at the exact moment when the planet ♃, Saturn, reached this longitude.

Mundane astrology has not yet associated ♇ to specific countries and cities. Pluto is, however, supposed to rule over *those who work underground*, for instance, in mines or subways, but also those who, figuratively speaking, work underground, such as mafiosi, terrorists, etc. The planet ♇ is also associated with *espionage, detective work*, and *faithhealing*.

In conclusion it should be mentioned that most astrologers agree that ♇ is associated with the workings of the *deepest, subconscious psychic processes* in humans.

A modern ideogram that indicates the *most suitable reading distance from a lamp*. (The actual distance is given in number of centimeters.)

Compare with ⏚ for *contact, grounded, ground wire*.

Ancient graphs for *Kronos*, the Greek god. This divinity, in the form of the Roman god Saturn, is closely associated to ♑, the zodiac sign of Capricorn. We can see that these old graphs for the god and planet Saturn structurally are very close to the graphs for Capricorn.

Kronos was also drawn ♃ and otherwise.

For more information on Kronos, turn to ♄ in Group 17.

Two variations of graphs for the *planet Saturn* and also used for the element *lead*. Saturn is usually represented by the sign ♄.

For other lead signs, turn to ♂ in Group 49. For graphs for Saturn, look up ♄ in Group 17.

These two signs sometimes appear in cartography signifying *radio station*.

A lexicographic sign found in dictionaries to indicate that a specific term belongs to the *field of electricity*.

The ideogram commonly used to signify electricity is ⚡, but in lexicography it is, oddly enough, mostly used for mythological terms and concepts.

This sign is an old version of the graph for the god *Zeus/Jupiter*.

For more information concerning this divinity, look up ♃ in Group 17.

These are modern ideograms used in the world of comic strips. Drawn close to a figure or structure they indicate that the entity *suddenly has come to a halt* after having travelled at a high speed.

Like the above entry signs, this one is from the world of comic strips. It, or part of it, is drawn around the heads of figures, and signifies *jealous rage, inhibited rage* and the like.

The sign 🏵 in Group 26 is somewhat synonymous.

There is an old Viking-era saying, expressed in beautiful alliteration, which states that nothing in this world is lasting, but that the most lasting is *dom* over *dod* man, i.e., posterity's judgment of a dead man's use of his life.

I would like to finish this project with a sign from the world of comic strips. Some persons might consider it neither established enough in Western ideography nor used in contexts serious enough for it to be included here. But it is nevertheless well known to millions of teenagers and, recently, grownups in the West: the **Phantom's good sign**. This sign is a swastika variation. The basic meaning of the swastika, *independent energy* and *movement*, has been combined with the monogram of Christ, ☧: *Go for it with all-embracing goodwill!*

Part III: Word Index

ability to react 224
absolute 146
absolute and powerful 123
accidents 192
accounted for 188
accumulator 110
acetum 154
acid 126, 142
acid sign 230, 255
active 146
active intellect 148
Age of Gemini 41
Age of Pisces 42
Age of Taurus 41
agents accepted 141
air 148, 240, 312, 504
airplane 108
airplane is badly damaged 150
alchemy 51
alcohol 213, 241, 301, 415, 450, 464, 476
alkaline salt 343
all is well 196
all that in one way or another exists 103
all that is receptive in humankind 224
all that lacks existence 103
almighty father 199
almost clear sky 252
alternating current 167
alum 122
amalgam 118
amendment to the main text 233
American hobo signs 63
ammonia 141
ammonium salt 99, 156, 426, 461
ammonium salts 141
Amor 92, 231
anarchism 249, 254
Anchor cross 143, 154, 439
anchored cross 289
and 103
anger 191
angled cross 184
ankh 46, 438
anti-aircraft gun 254
anti-nuclear emblem 253
antimony 119
Anu 94
apprehension 170

approximately equal to 158
approximately the same as 167
Aquarius 38, 171, 172–173
Arabic League 226
archangel Gabriel 226
archer 182
arena 133
Aries 38
arrow cross 143, 323
arsenic 116, 204, 449
arsenic, white 118
art of alchemy 249, 255, 301
Art of Warfare 267
artistic creativity 115
ash 98
áss 189
assimilating 86
Astarte 271
asteroid Ceres 203
asteroid Juno 99
asteroid Vesta 243
atom 269-270
aum 227
aurochs 188
authority 146, 152
autumn equinox 127
average light intensity 257

Babylon 163
bad luck 179
bad move 170
balance control 243
band frequency filter 205
baptized 166
base 146
basic elements 12, 92
basic elements of Western ideography 86
bass control 171
battery 110
battle 97, 191, 367
battle against tuberculosis 96
be careful, angry dogs and/or
       violent people here 242
because of 132
beginning 132, 138
beginning of the last phase of the moon 252
beginning of the second phase of the
       moon 252

behind 230
benevolence 303
Bern convention 229
big farmhouse 111
birch 241
bjarkan 241
black hand 28
blessing 144
blood banner 66
blood revenge group 232
blown up 329
die Blutfahne 66
boat 86
Bode's law 203, 532
boil 88, 102
borax 112, 242
born 141
bottle 243
boundary 138
bowl 88
braces 90
break into parts 139
breakthrough 296
bridge 149
Bronze Age 41
brought close together 86
Buddha 178
burial 94
burn 98
button cross 154

cadence sign 226
calcinare 116
calcination 125
can be used outdoors under cover 233
cancel 146
cancelled 100
Cancer 38, 498
cannon 149
cannot continue 140
Capricorn 38, 520
caput mortuum 56
cardinal 125
cardinal signs 91
Catena aurea Homeri 58
cattle 189
caustic soda 193
cave 126

celestial spheres 302
Celtic cross 68, 259, 282
cement 193
centaur 39, 182
center of gravity 262
centers of gravitation 106
certain types of high, thin clouds 87
changes to 103
chapel 138
check! 205, 233
checkmate 143
checkmate! 233
chemistry 51
cher 188
chevron 102, 241
chör 188
Christian teaching 259
Chronos 38, 140, 202–203
chrysocolla 248
church 138
cinis 98
circle 10
cirlce segment 12
city 30, 238
city of Jerusalem 298
clay 260
cleave 134, 149, 155, 175
clockwise rotation 139
close in 123
closest male relatives 232
clubs 261
coagulare 184
coagulate 184
coagulation 57
coating of ice 123, 166
coatings of ice 123
combustion 98
coming back 194
communication links 191
competition 194
complementary 166
complete oscillation 166
compound word 194
compressor 228
conference 248
coniferous trees 124
coniunctio 138
connected 149

conscience 86
consecration cross 282, 328
consequently 132
control for reducing the middle range 205
copper 41
copper alloys 329
Coptic Church 270
Coptic cross 270, 439
copyright 229
coquere 88
count 139
counterclockwise rotation 169
country 238
courage 232
court of law 220
cremated 262
crescendo 104
crescent 225
croix de Lorraine 95
cross 10
cross fitchee 244
cross of Christ 181
cross of endlessness 304
cross of Golgatha 259
cross of Lorraine 324
cross of Palestine 142
cross of Peter 46
cross of Philip 47, 244
cross of the Russian Orthodox Church 181
cross of St. Andrew 140, 322
cross of St. Anthony 244
Cross of St. John 268
cross of the archangels 95
cross of the Evangelists 95
cross of the Holy Cross 142
cross of the patriarch 46
cross of the pope 46, 96
cross of the robbers 108
cross of the Russian Orthodox Church 46
crossbreed 140
crossed cross 142
crucible 142, 258
crutch cross 142, 154, 324
Crux commissa 244
crux dissimulata 118, 439
Crux Gammata 48, 179
Crux gemmata 259
crystal 240

crystallization processes 144
crystallus 144
cumulus clouds 257
cuneiform writing 23
Cupid 92, 231
current 107
curses 169
cusp 37

damp mist 125
danger 146, 170, 190, 193
danger – angry dog 105
danger – radiation from laser emitters 106
danger of landslide 190
dangerous 123
dangerous neighborhood 110
dangerous power 270
dangerous radioactivity 345
Danish flag, Dannebrogen 244
dead 94, 233
death 94, 97, 138, 191
deceased 233
deceased male 146
decoctation 135
decrease in volume 104
defeated ego 115
defecated 158
defecation 230
defense 192
degree of waterproofness 262
demarcating 146
demodulator 239
denial 126
derived from 103
destillare 170
destiny 262
Devil 299
dew 257
died in battle 97
difference between 166
different from in magnitude 190
differs from 143
digerere 149
digestio 149
diminuendo 104
Dionysus 231
direct current 146
directed movement 107, 193

direction 107
direction of movement 87
disordered intellect 394
display 260
dissolvant 425
dissolve 166, 498
distance 134, 151, 167
distance from or to 107
distill 170
distillary tube 496
distillation 56, 490, 494, 496
distillation flask 467
distilled oil 285
distilled vinegar 154
distilling 173, 360
divide 139, 175
dividing 146
divine power 130, 152, 238, 297
division 158
don't knock here 140
don't take this road 140
done 188
dot 132
double cross 140, 154
double exposure 267
double quintile 36
drink! 301
drop 174
drug intoxication 116
drying 167
drying of laundry 174
dual implication 150

earth 133, 146, 239, 294, 296, 312, 328, 408
earth contact 111
earth element 448
earth wire 111
earthed connection 196
earthly life 138
Eastern Hemisphere 97
Eastern star 299
ebullire 88
Ecstasy 255
eddy 169
effect 105
Egypt 195
Egyptian cross 46, 244
Egyptian hieroglyphs 22–23

eikon 7
eight-pointed star 299
eighth house 37
Eiserne Front 67
either 146
eject control 239
electric melting oven 191
electric power stations 179
electrical inlet 111
electricity 193
electrum 199
element earth 328
element of air 127, 238
element of earth 239
element of fire 238
element of water 296
eleventh house 37
elixir 52
emotional life 224
emperor 149
end 132, 138
energy 105, 179, 193, 232, 328
English hobo signs 62
enneagram 250, 303
equals 148, 214
equivalence 150
Erhardt Brigade 64
ermine 261
Eros 92, 231
escapism 116
Esoteric alchemy 52, 56–58
essence 144, 167, 301
essence of a substance 126
essence of being 250
eternity 266
etheric oil 98
Eurasia 97
evangelization of the world 95
evaporare 149
evaporate 149
evaporatio 149
evaporation 149, 174
Evening star 43
evil person 270
exclamation mark 123
exiled Cubans 96
expansion in all directions 143
exponential 12

exponentialization 106
external memory 345
extreme heat 296
extrovert 146
eye of fire 294

faculty of reason 86
family life 231
farm 126
fasces 67
fast forward 102
fast forward winding 239
Father 267
favorable opportunity 300
female 109
fermata 89, 227
field 294
fields 296
fifth element 301
fifth house 37
fifth of the Olympic spirits 236
fighting 262
fire 87, 122, 238, 301, 312, 486
fire fighting equipment 86
fire-water 339
first 149, 228
first day of the Winter half year 249
first house 37
first phase of the moon 225
first point 37
first quarter 225, 252
fish 38
five 139
five continents of the world 220
five pillars of Islam 263
five-pointed star 10
fixate 184
fixation 119
fixed star 97, 141, 295
flash of summer lightning 193
flashlight photography 193
flask 243
fleur de lis 261
flow 107, 184
focus 150
focused 132
follows logically from 106
food is sometimes given here 108

fool's gold 256
footangle 151
footprints of Buddha 48
forbidden 146
fort 303
fortress 126
forts and fortresses 300
Fortuna, the Part of Fortune 328
fortune 429
four elements 138, 255, 294
four evangelists 95
four points of the compass 138, 296
four winds 296
four-year period 45
four-spoked wheel 41
fourth house 37
French lily 261
frequency 166
frost 103, 106
frosty mist 150
fruit trees 110
fulcrum 262
fuse 267
fylfot 48, 179, 373

game is over 233
Gamma cross 151, 328
gammadion 48, 179
Ge 202
geba 139
Gemini 38, 470
gentleness 303
get up to 107
gif 139
gift 139
given parts of a whole 252
glass 260
globe 328
glyfein 22
Gnosticism 268, 303
goal 132
god 189
god of fertility and harvest 202
god of law and order 107
god of sexual love 231
god of time 140
god of vegetation 226
god of victory 107

goddess of war, sex and fertility 271
gold 256, 277, 281, 360, 429, 445, 461,
        501, 530
gold plus heat 500
gold-foil 377
gold-leaf 377
golden (Aries) fleece 41
golden chain of Homer 58, 96
golden fleece of the ram 91
golden metal alloy 425
golden number 17 189
golden number 18 117
Golgata cross 95
good annual crop 175
good haystack for the night 86
good move 123
good year's crop 188
grand master of the Teutonic Crusaders'
        Order 245
gravel 119
great danger 143
greater benefic 198
greater than 103, 190
Greek cross 320, 324
Greek Orthodox Church 96
Greek-Russian cross 181
ground 241, 268, 294, 296
ground flooded 132
ground frozen hard and dry 241
ground partly covered by snow 185
grounded 111, 310, 437, 534
group has or desires a peaceful relation 102
group is in conflict 102
growth 231, 241
grupetto 166
guilt 94
gun 149

Hagith 236
hail 192
Hakenkreuz 179
half parallels 56
half quintile 36
half-sextile 36
hand of Fatima 232
happiness 303
harmless 144
harvest 188

has died 94
have not understood 104
head 328
heart sign 230
heart, red 231
heat 193
heavy snowstorms 141
height above sea level 107
heptagram 302
heraldic dagger 233
here it is 110
here lives a dangerous dog 377
here lives a man with a bad temper 257
here people are afraid of tramps 297
here people tell you to go to hell 142
here they'll rough you up 188
here you are given a place to sleep for the
        night 148
here you can get whatever you want 147
here you will find food, work and/or
        money 329
here you will get a day's work 330
Hermes 92
hexagram 300
hieroglyph 22
hieros 22
high degree of waterproofness 263
high driving snow 185
high pressure 151
high rank 261
high spiritual dignity 267
high voltage electric current 193
higher reason 86
highest divinity 271
highest god 178
highest power 271
highest priest 96
highest teacher 96
hindrance to be overcome 97
hnefatafl 295
hobo signs 59–63
holiday 233
holiness 167
Holy Ghost 267
Holy Spirit 126
Holy Trinity 267, 269
homecoming 169, 194
honey 162, 232

hope 118, 143
horse 104
horse dung 169
hour 296
human being 298
humming sound 192
hurricane 190
hybrid 135
hydrochloric acid 142

ice 166
ice needles 150
icon 7
idea of a movement 107
idealism 116
identical with 143
identity exists 148
ideographic system of writing 72
image finding 239
Imperial Fascists 67
in station 295
inaugural cross 46
inauguration cross 328
incinerare 98
inconjunct 36, 240
increase 139
increase in pressure 151
independent movement 168, 171
independent movements 171
indication of relogiosity 270
infinitely great 266
infinity 266
information 257
inlet for antenna 104, 109
instinct 224
intelligence 173
intended for direct current 111
intense heat 191, 240, 258
interchangeable with 166
intimate relation 266
intuition 173
invalids live here – show sympathy 111
invocation cross 143
invocation of magic 303
iron 41, 97, 149, 195, 216, 440
Iron front 67
iron sulphate 256
is 43

is a part of 123
is not the same as 143
is the same as 148
Ischtar 271
Islamic faith 263

Jason 41
Jericho 163
Jerusalem 163
Jerusalem cross 142, 325
Jesus Christ 38, 140, 149, 207, 214, 215,
     244, 287, 396, 514, 515
Jeune Nation 68
Jewish kingdom 300
Jupiter 35, 198–199, 202, 212, 535

kaen 102
Kan cross 48
kaun 102
keep away – no use knocking 86
keep away, no point in knocking 126
Key of Solomon, The 301
key of the Nile 439
khamsa 232
king 238
kingdom 238
kingdom of death 254
kingdom of Jerusalem 142
Kronos 202

ladder of transmigration 96
lament 248
land 146, 294
lapis philosophorum 52, 57
large-scale power industries 45
last quarter 252
last quarter of the moon 225
last quarters 228
Latin cross 46, 94
lead 117, 167, 175, 201, 204, 258
lead foil 204
lead sulphate 204
lead, white 143, 184
leniency 303
Leo 38, 496
less than 103, 190
lesser benefic 198
liaison 191

Libra 38, 126
lictor bundle 69
lictors 69
life 256
life force 178
life's path 108
lift up 107
light 296
light icing 109
light mist 148
light snowstorm 185
light socket with switch 183
lighthouse emitting light flashes 106
lightning 193, 261
lightning without thunder 193
like 230
lime 204, 248, 254
limestone 204
limits the possibilities as to where
      a vehicle can be parked 329
liquid 132
liquids that become gases 167
livestock 189
lock in 123
logical thinking 262
logr 188
Loke 189
loosen up 159
Lothringenkreuz 324
loudspeaker 243
loudness 205
love 230-231, 303
low driving snow 185
lower 107
lowered 107
loyalty 107
LSD 255
luck 261
lunar halo 122
Lutheran Church 259
Lutheran cross 259
lyre 92, 231

machine gun 123
Magen David 300
Magen David Adom 301
magic 299
magnesia 116

magnesium 254
magnificent number 10,000 178
make love 230
male sex 106, 109
Maltese cross 46, 297, 323
man 109
man dies 109
manji 178
map of the world 253
marcasite 256
marital love 302
married 266
Mars 35, 38, 41, 440
masculine 146
materia secunda 56
materia tertia 56
material wealth 141
matter 138
may it be useful 143
Maya 115
meaning of a sign 8-9
measurement 169
mechanic is needed 105
meekness 303
meeting place 151, 158
melt 184
melting furnace 257
melting pot 258
mem 38
men 109
mercury 119, 124, 258
mercury chloride 127
merged 86
merging with God 57
metal 99
metallum 245
meteorite iron 329
mezzo-staccato 124
Michaelmas 249
microphone 436
migration 179
migrations 171
military expression 97
military power 97, 191
mine tunnel 109
mineral kingdom 252
mineralia 252
misery 183

misfortune 179, 192
mist 148
mix 156, 206
mixture 206, 240
Mjölner 260
modem 239
moderate turbulence 108
modulator 239
money 261
month 227, 295
monument 143
moon 34, 89, 224, 227, 274, 384
moon as a new moon 224
moon elixir 52
moon god 458
moon god Sin 226, 271
moon god Nannan 228
moon's north node 36, 174, 386
moon's south node 36, 386
moose 109
Morning star 43, 225, 299
mortal danger 143
mother 224
mother and child 163
mother earth 163
mouth 189
Mouvement populaire français 68, 245
moveable property 189
movement 87, 104, 107, 168
mutable 89, 182
mystical planet 115
mystical star 303
mythology 193

naudh 183
need fuel and oil 104
negation 126
negative pole 147
Neptune 35, 114–115, 117, 447
new life 241
new or waning moon 226
new or waning moon together
      with a planet 227
next highest suit 262
night 258
night's shelter here 111
nine gifts of the spirit 303
nine-pointed star 303

Nineveh 163
ninth house 37
Nirvana 115
nkyin nyin 194
no bottom reached with sounding 124
no parking 146
non-iconic 7
Nordiska Rikspartiet 68
normal distribution curve 20
north 138, 192
north of the Equator 139
North pole 139
northern 192
not both 146
not identical with 143
not similar to 206
note 233
nothing 103
nuclear charge 192
nuclear physics 270
nuclear power 192
nuclear power plant 270
nuclear reactor 269-270
nuclear research 270

obsolete word 233
ocean current 107
ocean currents 190
ocean travels 195
octagram of creation 303
Odin's staff 261
off 125
offline data storage 239
offline memory storage 345
oil 205
old world 97
oleum empyreumaticum 266
Olympic Games 220
omega 126
on 125
on and off control 125
on/off switch for the radio function 241
once cultivated but now wild growing
      plant 233
one 146
oneness 146
onion 188
online storage of data 260

only one 149
open vessel 111
opening up 102
openings 102
opposite of P is true 166
opposition 35
or 146
orb 249
orbit of the sun 104
order in which the sons were born 242
Order of the Knights of the Teutonic
    Crusade 68
Order of the Temple Knights 303, 323
organization of the universe 255
óss 189
outgoing migrations 168
output to screen 260
outstanding 146
owner is in 126
owner not home 126

paddle 114
pain 169
parallel with 147
parentheses 87
parties 300
partly overcast 252
partner 224
pärz 110
passive 147
passive intellect 148
path 191
paths 174
patience 303
patriarchal cross 95, 259
pause 227
pawnshops 434
peace 303
peace symbol 253
pebbles 232, 304
pentacle 298
pentagram 298
perennial plants 199
perfection 138
personality 224
phases of the moon 225
philosopher's stone 52
phosphorus 86

Pisces 38, 155
place is not safe 149
planet earth 269, 328
platinum 228
play 239
plug and socket 124
plus 139
Pluto 35, 227
point of intersection 138
pointed cross 233, 244
poisonous 233
police station 220
policeman lives here 143
policeman's badge 302
Polish Resistance Movement 69
pope's cross 144
Portuguese cross 245
positive 146
positive aspect 146
positive charge 139
positive ions 330
potash 98, 111
potassium carbonate 111
potential movement 168
potential power 168
power 146, 168, 178, 179, 328, 436
power off 146
power on 146
power or right to inflict capital
    punishment 256
power stations 45
power supply 110
powerful 146
precious metal 245
precipitate 128
precipitation 128
prepared for destruction 329
present yourselves as former army
    soldiers 192
press together 159
printing error 140
proceed in this direction 108
process of rotting 185
processes of rotting 206
progress 194
projection of self toward new horizons 182
protection against trolls and evil 299
proton 330

Psi 114
purification 56, 450
pushbutton 242
pustule 102
putrefaction 185
putreficatio 53, 56, 185, 206
putty 193

quadruplicities 33
quadruplicity 89, 125, 182, 217
quality 89, 182
quantity 148
quicklime 116, 125, 156
quincunx 36, 240
quinta essentia 57, 138
quintessence 301
quintile 36

radar station 143
radiation 87, 152
radiation of light 152
radio beacon 133
rage 169
rain 132
rainbow 86
raise 107
ram, the sign of Aries 271
rapids 189
ready 188
realgar 134
receptive 147
receptive aspect of man 86
recipient that is not transparent 243
Red Crescent 226
relation or correspondence 133, 147
relation of direction and ordering 103
release of energy 152
religious fanaticism 270
repeat 162
resistance 105
resistor 105
respect 328
result of 106
result of crossbreeding 135
return 169, 194
reverberating furnace 195, 216
reverse 102
reversed grupetto 166

reversible reaction 150
rheostat 105
ring around the moon 257
ring cross 259, 282
rising pressure 330
river 167
road obstruction 140
robbers' cross 244
Roman Catholic Church 259
Roman Catholic cross 328
Roman holy cross 207
Rossback Free Corps 64
rotation 169, 171
ruin 132
ruler of time 202
rune of death 107, 109, 253
rune of victory 191
Russian cross 181
Russian Orthodox Church's cross 144

sacrificial animal 188
safe against splash 233
Sagittarius 38, 182
saintliness 167
sal alcalinus 343
sal ammoniacus 99, 156, 426
sal sedativum 513
sal sedativus 513
salt alkali 242
salt water 248
sand 119, 133
sandstorm 215
Saturn 140, 200, 202, 212
sauvastika 48, 179
Schutzstaffeln 67
Scorpio 38, 216
sea 168, 188
seal of the world 268
second house 37
second son 226
secret tribunals 181
self 194
self-denial 115
semi-square 36
separate from 150
separateness 134
separatist movement 171

seriousness 123, 146
seskiquadrature 36
seventh house 37
severe turbulence 108
sextile 35
sextile aspect 141
sexual love 90, 230
shards of ice 123
shield of David 300
shoal 132, 138
short duration 132
short-range weapon against tanks 123
shut up 123
sidereal zodiac 40
sight worth seeing 268
sign of Sagittarius 124
signal company 191
signalling 329
signals 189
Sigrune 191
silver 132, 225, 236, 269, 284, 384, 460, 500
similarity in one dimension 148
sin 94
single-phase current 146
sixth house 37
skruppel 122
skull 56
sky 86
sleep 192
sleeping place 86
small 132
smile 255
smile sign 230
snow 106, 141, 295
snowstorm 185
sociability 173
soda 254
sodium 254
solar halo 329
soldering alloy used with gold 248
Solomon's seal 298, 300
Solomon's shield 298
solutio 166
solution 149, 166, 498
solvere 166
something incredible or unusual 123
something that is left out 133
somewhat overcast 252

Son 267
soot 138
soprano clef 122
sorrow 248
soul 452
south 147, 167, 192
space between should be lessened 86
specific direction 106
sphere 328
spin drying 168
spiral 12
spirit 126, 167, 452
spirit of life 256, 266
spirit of togetherness 300
spirit of Venus 236
spiritual power or energy that holy
        persons emanate 329
spiritus 126, 301
split 39, 134, 149, 155
splitting 134
spring 228, 252
square 10
squeeze section 150
SS 67
St. Andrew's cross 47
St. George's cross 321-322
St. Hans' cross 268
St. Peter's cross 94
St. Peter's game 163
staff of Adad 130
staff of Apollo 94
staff of a god 126
staff of Jupiter 429
staff of Neptune 98, 429
staff of Poseidon 98, 114
staff of the Devil 98
staff of Zeus 429
staircase 29
stamen 230
standing still 295
star 296
star of Ischtar 271
star of Venus 271
state of transcendental consciousness 227,
        256
stay here 203
steady snowfall 141
steam 167, 174

steel 202, 415, 420, 431, 444
stereo sound 229
stone 133
Stone Age 41
stone bottom at the water's edge 154
stone of wisdom 57
stones 304
storage in the internal memory 236
straight line 12
stream 167, 188
streaming or flowing water 167
street 191
strength 188, 367
strong fire 236, 240, 258
stupa 255
Sturmabteilungen 67
subconscious 224
sublimate 127
sublimation 56, 127
submerged wreck 132
success 296
suitable reading distance 196
sulphur 204, 243, 380, 390, 392,
        416, 450, 516
sulphuric acid 512, 518
sum 86
summer 88, 206
sun 34, 42, 132, 178, 256, 271, 274,
        295-296, 328, 342, 360, 367, 409, 485
sun cross 41, 49, 68, 328
sun god 228
sun god Shamash 315, 328
sun rune 105, 191
sun symbol 330
sun's center 476
sun's mass 338
sun's son 442
Sunday 141, 233
sunlight 409, 485
sunrise 436
sunshine 485
supplement is enclosed 158
support group 232
swastika 48, 64, 178, 207
Swedish hobo signs 62
switched off 242
switched on 242

symbol 5
symbol for eternity 304
symbol for the Ottoman-Turkish Empire
        264
symbol has been found 255
symbol of Constantinople 264
symbol of orientation 97
symbol of power 249
symbolon 5
system 254

T-cross 244
taboo words 263
Tac 107
take this road, it's better 122
take-off will be attempted 108
takes and checks 205
talc 140
tartar 135
tartaric acid salt 124
tartrate 124, 135
Tau cross 112, 244
Taurus, 38, 384
television station 193
Tellus 408
temperance 303
ten 139
tenth house 37
test 118
tetraskele 48, 162
tetraskelion 179
there are friends here 150
there are more tramps on this road 111
therefore 132
they demand hard work here 105
third house 37
third son 300
thread 169
threat 270
threatening skies 238
three units 148
three-foil cross 259
three-leg 28
three-phased alternating current 167
throw down a signalling lantern 147
thunder 193, 328
thunder and lightning 130

thunderstorm of moderate intensity 193
Thursday 189
tick 188
tidal stream at high tide 190
tighten 159
tin 184, 199
tin foil 202
tin oxide 203
tinkal 242
Titans 202
Todesrune 109, 253
togetherness 230, 266
toilet 230
Tor's hammer 48, 260
tourist information 257
tower 143
trails 174
transform into liquid 174
transform into liquid form 105
transformation of self 194
transformer winding 194
transmission of radiation 133
treble clef 122
tree-like plants 201–202
triangle 10, 238
tribal migrations 179
triceps 297
triplicity 33, 217
triskele 28
triskelion 195
tropical zodiac 40
Troy fortresses 163
trustworthiness 303
twelfth house 37
twelve apostles 259
type is damaged or faulty 329
Tyr 107

uncertainty 170
underworld 254
undulations 87
unity 146
universal brotherhood 175
unknown 140
unknown person 140, 192
unreliability 173

unscrew 159
ur 188
uranium 270
Uranus 35, 42, 440, 444
urine 132
uruz 188

vagina 107
varies as 166
varying degrees of cloudiness 254
Vehmgerichte 181
Venus 35, 141
Venus as the Morning or Evening star 227
Venus god 228
very poisonous 143
vessel 88
Vesta's altar 243–244
victory 103, 367
victory rune 67, 191
vigorous heating 236
village 126, 267
vinegar 138, 154
violence 191
virgin dances 163
Virgo 38, 492
visibility 329
visibility is worsened by fog or dust 329
vitriol 206, 252
volume control 239
vulva 107

wan 48, 178
waning moon 225, 252
war 191
warm 146
warm or hot water 296
warmth 409
warning 270
watch out for a dog! 190
water 88, 105, 132, 134, 167, 168, 188, 214,
       228, 229, 248, 255, 294, 301, 308, 342,
       404
water catchment area 258
water clan tribe 29
water mill 485
water of consciousness 172
water of intuition 173
water reservoir 228
water vapor 215

water-bearer 105
waterfall 189
waterproof 233
waves 166
wax 184
way 191
ways 174
weak aspects 35
weak wind 190
wealth 261
weather 296
weather gods 138
weeds 204
well 228, 252
Western triple cross 96
wheel cross 328
whirlpool 169
white frost 103
white lead 96
whole universe 103
whole wave 166
wife 224
wild growing plants 141
wind furnace 257
winds of varying strengths 190
winter 124
woman 109, 238
women 224
wood 262

work 105, 261
work and you'll be given food 114
world evangelization 119, 142
Wuotan's (Odin's) cross 328
wrath 191
writer's lawful right to his or her
      own writings 229
wrong 140, 188

xomsa 232

year 175, 295
yew tree 192
yew-tree rune 191
yin 147
yin-yang 20
yleaster 329
yoke and arrows 68
ypsilon cross 108

zero class 103
Zeus 98, 192, 198, 199, 202, 212,
      520, 535
zinc 200, 387, 447, 520
zinc oxide 388
Zionist movement 301
zodiac of fixed stars 40
zoom 240

Part IV: Graphic Index

Group 1

84, 92

Group 2

86, 12, 13, 275, 531

86, 62, 115, 224

86, 125, 229

87

87

87

87

87

87, 70, 230, 258, 388, 446, 454, 486

87

87, 88

88, 529

88, 124, 385

88, 56

88, 450

88

89, 33, 63, 125, 155, 182, 227, 471, 493

89

89, 73, 172, 214, 229

89

90

90

90, 12, 13, 56, 135, 210, 230, 249, 298, 306

90

91, 38, 42, 52, 109, 182, 201, 230, 289, 306, 349, 385, 410, 443, 472, 499, 521

92, 231, 519

92, 84

92, 84

92, 124

Group 3

94, 10, 60, 73, 138, 244, 287, 318

94, 115

95, 119, 466

95

95

95

95, 46, 142, 181, 245, 324

96, 46

96

97

97, 141

97

97, 245, 444

98, 111

98

98, 54, 484

98, 397

99, 250

99

99, 63, 242

99, 204, 397

99

99, 156, 461

100, 245

Group 4

102, 108, 241

102, 211, 241

102, 71, 108, 241

102

102

103, 106

103, 12, 59, 71, 211, 241

103, 239, 311

103

104

104, 311

104, 36, 505

104

104, 243, 449

104

105, 99

105, 18, 191

105, 174

105, 12, 29, 62, 194, 229, 242, 448

105

106, 152

106, 347

106, 190, 214, 298, 306, 444

106, 68, 191, 253, 304

↓ **107**, 92, 123, 238

⫯→ **107**, 106, 190, 214, 230

--→ **107**

⊤ **107**, 108

→] **108**

△ **108**

⋏ **108**, 36, 240

⟀ **108**

⋀ **108**

Y **108**

Y **109**, 106

Y **109**, 114, 253, 395, 402, 434

⋏ **109**, 253

⍦ **110**, 249, 433

⍦ **110**, 230, 249, 433

ⵊ **110**

⊣⊢ **110**

⊓ **110**, 454

⊔ **111**

π **111**

⊔ **111**, 60, 75

⊥ **111**, 196, 437

--- **111**

⊤ **112**

⊥ **112**, 242

Group 5

Ψ **114**, 98, 155, 480

Ψ **114**

ⵖ **114**, 156, 193, 199, 331, 429

Ψ **115**, 37, 114, 198, 216, 395, 446, 497

ⵖ **115**, 155

Ψ **115**, 116, 156, 210, 427

Ψ **116**

⍦ **116**, 204, 408, 449, 527

⍦ **117**

⍒ **117**, 491

⍍ **117**, 110, 139, 189, 211, 249, 402, 433, 452, 477, 509

⊦ **118**

⊥ **118**, 204, 449

⋀ **118**, 396

⋏ **118**

⟊ **118**, 289

Ѱ **119**, 311, 446

Ⴚ **119**, 88, 124, 311, 385

† **119**

⁙ **119**, 53, 133

Ⱦ **119**, 52, 472

Ψ **119**, 415

Group 6

122, 62

122

122

122, 117, 404

122, 454, 480

123

123

123, 150, 438

123, 132, 146, 257

124

124, 53, 415

124

124, 88, 385

124

124, 135, 395

125

125, 33, 91, 127, 347, 499, 521

125, 242, 252, 343, 424, 451

125, 204

126

126, 75, 347, 476

126

126, 5, 14, 33, 38, 52, 56, 91, 148, 172, 201, 249, 349, 387, 410, 442, 452, 470, 476, 492, 499, 523

128, 53, 56, 387, 416, 523

Group 7

130

130

130

130, 114, 156, 429

Group 8

- **132**, 123, 170, 275
- **132**
- **132**, 229, 269, 284, 455
- **132**, 229
- **133**
- **133**
- **133**
- **133**, 461
- **133**, 152, 460
- **134**, 89
- **134**
- **134**, 14, 39, 89, 155
- **134**, 39, 86, 149, 155, 175
- **134**, 432
- **135**
- **135**, 395, 404
- **135**
- **135**, 171

Group 9

- **138**, 9, 12, 13, 28, 50, 94, 118, 132, 192, 200, 274, 298, 321, 328, 467
- **139**, 47
- **139**, 50, 140, 154, 329, 479
- **141**, 97, 304, 318, 368
- **141**, 8, 35, 150, 185, 272, 295, 347, 397, 464, 528
- **141**, 528
- **141**
- **142**, 63
- **142**, 53, 178, 258, 433, 481, 509
- **142**, 143
- **142**, 325
- **143**, 184
- **143**, 142, 151, 282, 323, 467
- **143**, 150, 190, 233, 466
- **143**, 19, 24, 60
- **144**, 132
- **144**
- **144**

Group 10

146, 138, 470	**148**, 88, 394	**150**, 159, 476
146, 477	**149**, 254, 444	**151**
146, 108, 138, 275, 357	**149**	**151**
147, 357	**149**	**151**, 158
147	**149**, 167	**151**, 286
147, 61	**149**	**151**, 171
148, 33, 61, 127, 172, 214, 311, 390, 471, 521	**150**, 190	**152**
148, 75, 88, 106, 125, 150, 215	**150**	**152**
	150, 139	**152**, 460
	150, 106, 125	

Group 11

✝ **154**

✝ **154**, 433

✝ **154**, 140, 480, 485

✣ **154**, 49, 132, 433, 481

)(**155**, 33, 38, 42, 53, 89, 115, 134, 152, 182, 199, 349, 413, 442, 494, 498

Ж **156**, 98, 114, 199, 260, 429

Ж **156**, 141

Ж **156**

)€ **156**, 206, 240

)(**156**, 99, 461

Group 12

·⊦ **158**, 162

⦂⊦ **158**, 162, 215

⦂⎮⦂ **158**, 215

÷ **158**

⋇ **158**, 248

⋎ **159**

⋎ **159**

Group 13

⚬ **162**, 179

⚭ **162**

⚮ **162**, 48

✕ **162**, 232

⊚ **163**, 29

Group 14

∼ **166**, 111, 170, 214, 372, 377, 397, 498, 519

⌣ **166**, 168

∿ **166**

∾ **166**

≈ **167**, 75, 214, 519

≋ **167**, 148, 214, 394, 519

))) **167**, 174, 215, 229

S **167**, 192, 213, 357, 491

∞ **168**, 359

☺ **168**, 13, 84, 92, 195, 198, 276, 298, 356, 454

☺ **169**, 13, 29, 194, 276, 378, 454

☺ **170**, 400, 429

? **170**, 14, 132

⌒ **170**

☼ **171**, 15, 152, 378, 490

☸ **171**, 14, 179, 359, 378, 501

☸ **171**, 194

☽ **171**, 14, 491

∿ **171**, 33, 38, 42, 53, 73, 90, 105, 127, 135, 148, 196, 201, 349, 384, 418, 470, 493

≹ **173**

♏ **173**, 343, 451

☌ **173**, 170

♌ **174**, 452

♒ **174**, 215

⌒ **174**, 133

☀ **174**, 227, 256, 312

♍ **174**, 216

♌ **175**, 28, 86, 134, 188

♌ **175**

Group 15

卐 **178**, 9, 14, 45, 48, 66, 162, 169, 207, 282, 299, 315, 354, 368, 400

卍 **178**, 48, 68, 162, 169, 268, 283, 297, 360, 373

180

180, 48

180

180

180, 421

181

181, 14, 144

182, 33, 39, 53, 89, 100, 124, 155, 183, 198, 231, 245, 306, 349, 394, 401, 413, 442, 496, 527

183

183

183, 189

183

184

184, 199, 426

184

184, 484

184, 143

184, 388

185

185

185

185

Group 16

⊨	**188**	⋛	**190**, 150	⦓	**193**	
∨	**188**	⌐	**190**, 62	ϟ	**193**, 18	
⅄	**188**, 63	ϟ	**191**, 11, 12, 18, 19, 67, 70, 73, 236, 369, 400	⌐ʒ	**193**	
∩	**188**			⤳	**194**, 14, 360	
⟨⟩	**188**	ϟ	**191**, 318	⊔	**194**	
⊩	**189**, 183, 400	И	**191**, 141, 368	⊓	**194**, 169	
⥮	**189**	⌡	**192**, 18, 368	▣	**195**, 29	
⥾	**189**, 397, 532	N	**192**	⟋	**195**, 444	
⍓	**189**	Z	**192**, 270	⌶	**195**, 216	
⟋	**190**, 508	⟿	**192**	⊥	**196**, 534	
⟋	**190**, 185, 508	N	**192**	⩘	**196**, 171	
⟋	**190**, 214	⌐ʹ	**193**	⊔⊔	**196**	
		⌐	**193**			

Group 17

4   **198**, 37, 52, 91, 127, 184, 203, 332, 384, 410, 426, 443, 471, 500, 522

2ʃ   **198**, 210

ʒʃ   **198**, 155, 182

ᵞ   **199**, 520, 535

Ⱬ   **199**

ᵗⱨ   **199**, 443

Ⱬ   **199**, 53, 98, 212, 387

Ƶ   **199**, 377, 426

Ⱬ   **200**, 199, 387, 443

ʒ   **200**, 37, 52, 91, 117, 127, 143, 175, 201, 204, 258, 302, 307, 464, 502, 522, 535

ℏ   **200**, 38

ʒ   **200**, 14, 201, 212, 332, 392, 417, 441, 471, 491, 500

ℏ   **200**

Ꝁ   **202**, 199, 212

2ⱨ   **202**, 411, 431, 444

2Ƒ   **203**, 184

Ꝅ   **203**, 200, 534

ᵔ   **203**, 60

ʔ   **203**, 99, 115, 397, 411, 445, 454, 534

Ꝅ   **203**, 244

ℏʒ   **204**

Ⱬ   **204**, 125, 248, 254

Ƶ   **204**, 248, 395

+ᶜ   **204**, 449, 527

Ꝥ   **205**

Ꝫ   **205**, 484

ᶇ   **205**

Ꝥ   **205**

≈   **205**

≈   **205**

⟊   **206**

Ƶ   **206**, 184

ᵞ   **206**, 185

Ⱬ   **206**, 156

⚹   **206**

♏   **207**, 119, 174

⧘   **207**

Group 18

~⌐   **210**, 437

Γ   **210**, 415

2   **210**

⌿   **210**

∽   **210**, 116, 125, 380, 411

P   **211**

∬   **211**

Γ   **211**

r   **211**, 63

ℏ   **211**

♭   **212**, 202

⇁   **212**, 206, 252, 425, 466

⌐⌐   **212**, 199, 429

Ʒ   **213**, 408

Ʒ   **213**

V³   **213**, 54, 167, 241, 450

V^c   **213**, 427

↗   **213**, 190, 508

⤳   **214**, 190

♺   **214**, 73

↻   **214**, 376

≃   **214**, 111, 158, 166, 206, 519

♨   **215**, 174

≡S≡   **215**

⁒   **215**, 528

⁒   **215**, 158, 528

♈   **215**

↗   **216**, 444

ℏ   **216**, 195

m,   **216**, 33, 38, 53, 174, 207, 349, 384, 410, 443, 498, 533

m,   **216**, 174

Group 19

⊜   **220**, 63

⚬⚬⚬   **220**, 45, 267

⊗⊗⊗   **220**

⊕   **221**

Group 20

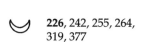 **224**, 7, 13, 34, 37, 53, 217, 228, 236, 252, 269, 275, 332, 377, 384, 392, 418, 458, 487, 499, 512

 **225**, 44, 252, 264, 336, 409, 458, 500

226

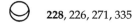 **226**, 242, 255, 264, 319, 377

227, 226

227, 89, 134, 174

227, 412, 532

227

228, 226, 271, 335

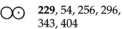 **228**, 252

 228, 53, 377

 229, 54, 256, 296, 343, 404

 229, 243, 267

 **229**, 388

230, 255

230

230, 11, 73, 92, 276, 519

230

231

 232

 232, 13

 232

 232, 162, 376, 403

 233

 233, 263

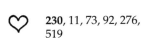 **233**, 255

 233, 205, 285

233, 143

Group 21

 236, 240, 258

 236, 53, 225, 269, 284, 500

236

 236, 297

236, 241, 260

Group 22

238, 306

238, 243, 263, 454

238, 107

238, 240, 294, 307, 390

 239, 236, 243, 260, 294, 308, 367, 392

 239, 367, 400

▷	**239**	⊟	**241**	▽	**243**, 367
⚊	**239**	⊞	**241**	◇	**243**, 289
◪	**239**	〰	**242**, 60, 313, 366, 377	⬙	**243**, 204, 454
△	**240**, 206	⊥	**242**, 380	†	**244**
◈	**240**	⌂	**242**	T	**244**, 68, 112, 245, 324
⋀⋀	**240**, 236	⊐	**242**, 226, 300	⁜	**244**, 47
△̷	**240**	⊔	**242**	†	**245**, 324
▽	**240**	▬	**242**	T	**245**
◁	**240**	▬	**242**	†	**245**, 96
ß	**241**	⊡	**243**, 390	↕	**245**, 68, 100
»	**241**, 282	◁	**243**, 15, 104, 424, 449	♔	**245**
◇◇	**241**	⋈	**243**, 400		

Group 23

♡	**248**, 73, 288	⋓	**248**	⊕	**249**, 253, 408
▽	**248**	⌢	**249**, 433	⊕	**249**, 254
ℭ	**248**, 204, 236, 395	⊛	**249**, 331, 373	ⓦ	**250**
Ⅺ	**248**, 361			⬟	**250**, 303

Group 24

252, 86, 228, 258

252, 125, 225

252, 225, 343, 357, 376, 451

252

252

252

252, 425

253, 249, 277

253, 109

254

254, 249, 401, 431, 513

254

254, 204, 395

254, 424

255, 230

255, 73, 254, 344, 502

255, 228, 249, 294, 344

255, 54, 228

256

256, 229, 404

256, 53, 248, 360, 377, 424, 461, 501, 530

256, 248

257, 60, 348

257

257

257

257, 86

258, 236

258

258

258, 86, 252

258, 142, 509

258, 491

258

259, 426

259

259, 245

259

259

260, 429

260, 236, 366

260, 366

260, 256, 486

260, 347, 432

260, 347, 432

260, 156, 429

261, 242

261

261, 284, 434, 454, 460

262, 53, 427, 454

262, 454

262, 400, 478

262, 233

263, 233

263, 238

263, 44, 46, 226, 264, 288, 336

Group 25

266, 276

266, 61, 220, 230, 248, 302, 432, 487, 513

267

267

267, 70, 220, 248, 266, 287, 350, 420

267

268

268, 297, 360, 369

268, 289, 339

269, 369, 462

269

269, 284, 500

269

269

270, 276, 354

270, 354

270

271

271, 299, 337, 409, 439

271, 42, 49, 178, 228, 277, 315, 328

272

Group 26

274, 8, 10, 12, 62, 86, 103, 125, 229, 242, 342, 404, 447, 477

275

275

275, 425

276

276, 135, 270

276

276

277, 8, 11, 18, 22, 25, 34, 37, 53, 57, 60, 70, 211, 229, 271, 314, 333, 360, 377, 388, 393, 416, 445, 470

278, 18, 387

278, 13, 60, 62, 189, 204, 277, 501

279

279

280

280, 266

280

280

280, 56

281, 132, 370, 460

281, 211, 257, 428, 455

281, 280

281, 415

282, 241, 286

282, 68, 426

283

283

283, 14, 22, 30

283, 14, 95, 339

284, 261, 420, 434, 450, 484

284, 60, 62

284

284

284, 225, 236, 269

285

285

285

285

286

286, 282, 321, 336

286

287, 14, 259, 267, 347, 350, 360, 420

⬠ **287**

⬭ **287**, 269, 349, 360,
380, 462

✷ **288**

✧ **288**

☆ **288**, 299, 317

⚙ **288**, 536

❁ **289**, 339

✠ **289**, 118, 143, 154,
439

♡ **289**

✴ **290**, 228

✴ **290**, 49, 335, 351

Group 27

⊞ **294**

⊞ **294**, 54, 229, 404

⊞ **294**

⬦ **294**

⊠ **295**, 36, 453

▨ **295**, 453, 488

▣ **295**

✳ **295**, 185, 241, 309

▽ **296**

✚ **296**, 48

⋈ **296**, 364, 465

⧖ **296**, 453, 488

⊟ **297**, 236, 268, 304

⊡ **297**

✢ **297**, 14, 46

△ **297**

⟁ **297**, 70, 345

☆ **298**, 12, 14, 43, 44,
142, 178, 226, 318,
345, 370, 409, 490

✡ **300**, 11, 14, 31, 43, 54,
213, 279, 331, 369,
372, 481

✧ **302**

✳ **302**

⬡ **303**, 300

✧ **303**

✳ **303**

✧ **303**, 250

⧖ **304**

⬡ **304**

✚ **304**

✳ **304**

Group 28

306, 10, 12, 13, 33, 37, 54, 91, 155, 236, 238, 256, 301, 314, 339, 347, 384, 393, 442, 486, 497, 515

308

308, 54, 60, 133, 217, 229, 260, 301, 339, 347, 471, 498, 509, 521

308

309, 10, 12, 13, 37, 54, 104, 185, 243, 255, 274, 298, 348, 377, 396, 408, 428, 447, 466, 505

310

310, 487

310, 232, 446

311, 54, 296, 349, 404, 453

311

311, 119

311, 241

311

312

312, 239, 294

312, 372

313, 141

313, 242, 369, 377, 396

313

314, 316, 334, 473

315

315

318

316, 10, 44, 226, 264, 288, 300, 336, 473

318

318

319, 317

319

319, 345

320, 138, 321, 322

320

322, 140

322, 449

323, 15, 143, 467

323, 297

324

324, 42, 68, 142, 154, 245, 319

324, 96, 245, 259

325

325

Group 29

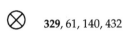 **328**, 14, 24, 33, 36, 41, 49, 53, 70, 199, 271, 282, 312, 342, 388, 392, 408, 425, 478, 493, 512

 329, 61, 140, 432

 330, 61, 356

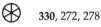 **330**

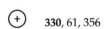 **330**, 272, 278

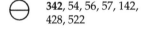 **331**

 331, 249, 357, 372

 332, 302, 358, 414, 443

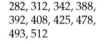 **332**

 333, 32, 43, 141, 220, 227, 264, 271, 288, 298, 316, 345, 351, 356, 384, 409, 462

 333

 338, 254, 424

 338, 425

 339

 339

 339, 283

 339, 268, 289

Group 30

 342, 54, 56, 57, 142, 428, 522

 342, 54, 57, 505

 342, 147

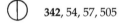 **343**, 125, 451

 343, 18

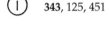 **343**, 14, 54, 281, 342, 381, 396, 428

 343, 451

 344, 46, 289, 510

 344

 344, 55, 86, 308, 391

 345, 347

 345, 297, 331

 345, 288, 333

 346, 347, 460

346

346, 260, 417

347, 344

347, 393, 448

347, 346, 461

348, 53, 110, 132, 241, 295

348, 270

348, 33, 89, 125, 172, 217, 275, 384, 471, 493, 499

349

350, 322

350, 296, 344

350

350

351, 296

351

351, 433

351

351, 14

Group 31

354

354

Group 32

356

356, 330

356

357, 20, 58, 146, 331, 467

357

357

358

358

358, 12, 15, 72, 298, 370

358, 359, 370

359

359, 168

359

360, 194, 278

360, 420

360

360, 14, 17, 467, 490, 496

360, 53, 256, 271, 461, 501, 530

361, 256

361

Group 33

364

364, 30

364, 297, 366

Group 34

366, 104, 376, 405, 484

367

368

366

367, 239

368, 68, 179, 289, 369

366, 396

367

369, 191, 313

366, 62, 242, 313

367, 191, 364

369, 220, 297

366, 57

368, 192

370

368, 19, 67, 191

370, 359

Group 35

372, 32, 182, 312, 333, 386, 431, 487

372

372

372, 60, 166, 214, 519

Group 36

376, 104, 239, 366, 405, 484

376

377, 199

376, 367

376

378

376, 214

377, 14, 166, 347

378

376, 232

377, 60

378, 194

377

Group 37

380

380

381, 490

380, 42, 269, 360, 462, 490

380

381, 432

380, 411, 428

380, 63, 185, 190, 215, 220, 298, 498, 508

381

381, 54, 427, 446

Group 38

⌒ **384**, 14, 269, 284, 500

Ⴆ **384**, 33, 38, 52, 172, 349, 415, 442, 472, 493, 521

Ⴒ **384**

⟡ **384**

Ⴆ **384**

Ⴒ **385**

∝ **385**, 266, 276

Ⴆ **385**, 88, 124, 432

♊ **386**, 36, 174, 333, 450, 487, 532

ᎣᎠ **386**

♋ **386**, 14, 52, 384, 450

℧ **386**, 36, 487

ᴗ **386**, 14, 387

❧ **387**, 421

ᎣᎠ **387**, 449

ᴔᴔ **387**

Ⴆ **387**

○ **388**

℧ **388**, 126

⊶ **388**, 184

☽ **388**

ᴧ **388**

ↆ **388**, 416, 432

Group 39

△ **390**, 240, 307

▽ **390**, 394

⇧ **390**, 53, 348, 392, 415

⇧ **390**, 53, 54, 56, 205, 243, 348, 380, 392, 403, 416, 445, 450, 518

⇧ **391**

⊥ **391**, 54, 55, 344

⇧ **391**

⊠ **391**

▽ **392**, 54, 239, 308, 391

⚥ **392**, 387, 432

♀ **392**, 204, 310, 397, 404, 445

♀ **392**, 243, 390

⇩ **392**, 36, 328

⇩ **393**, 57, 414, 517

⚇ **393**

⚒ **393**

⚇ **393**

⋏ **394**, 401

⋇ **394**, 148, 401

ᴦ **394**, 214

⤳ **394**, 182

⊓ **394**, 53, 390

ᛘ **395**

⚍	**395**	⚎	**396**, 242, 380	⬦	**397**, 189
⚏	**395**, 248	⚌	**396**, 413, 433, 465	⬳	**397**
⚐	**395**, 204, 248	⚑	**396**	⚒	**397**, 204
⚓	**395**, 135, 404, 419	⚔	**396**, 366	Ψ	**397**, 98
		⊓	**396**, 395, 424	⊡	**397**, 1, 295

Group 40

⊢	**400**, 13, 452	⟁	**401**, 63	↓	**404**
⊤	**400**, 243, 262	⩗	**402**, 5, 453	⦶	**404**
△	**400**	⋏	**402**, 394	⦵	**404**
⟂	**400**, 109, 434, 448	⩘	**403**, 390	◇	**404**, 62
⊩	**401**	Σ	**403**	◇	**404**, 62
↗	**401**, 182	⊞	**403**, 232	◇−	**404**
⇝	**401**	⊓	**403**	⊔	**404**
↕	**401**, 480	⊓	**403**	⊐→	**405**
⋀	**401**	⊤	**403**, 516	▪▪▪▪	**405**, 15
		↡	**404**, 395		

Group 41:a

408, 57, 269, 328, 416, 446, 512

408, 414

408, 428, 445

409, 272

409, 37, 41, 43, 52, 53, 70, 91, 115, 127, 172, 183, 198, 210, 220, 319, 334, 345, 384, 393, 411, 425, 442, 473, 513

411

411

411, 53

411

411, 99, 204, 397

411

411

412, 227, 388, 532

412

414, 415, 429, 480

414, 241, 450

415

415, 414, 480, 517

415, 119, 124, 210, 258, 414, 480

415

416

416

416, 55, 467

416, 390, 431

416, 53, 433

417, 346

417

417

417, 37, 42, 172, 201, 216, 384, 444

419

419, 393

419, 393

420, 393

420, 393

420, 448

420

420

421, 181

421

421

421

421

Group 41:b

♀	**424**, 409	⊖	**427**, 213	⚚	**432**, 347, 392, 430
☿	**424**, 125, 437	☿	**428**	♉	**432**, 260
⚶	**424**, 116	⊖	**428**, 257, 453	∞	**432**, 134, 381, 388
⊖⊢	**424**	☿	**428**, 380, 396	♀♀	**432**, 266, 513
♀	**425**, 513	⊕∈	**428**, 380, 445, 480	⋇	**432**, 62, 110
⊕⊢	**425**, 212	☿	**428**, 414	o⋇o	**433**
⊕⊢	**425**, 212	⚕	**429**	⚚	**433**, 110, 127, 249
⊕	**426**, 425, 439	⚕	**429**, 430	⚲	**433**
⚶	**426**, 428	⚕	**430**, 114, 436, 451	⚕	**433**, 388, 481
⊶∈	**426**, 428	⚕	**430**, 412	⚶	**433**, 480
⊖⋋	**426**, 156, 461	∅	**430**, 195, 444, 476	⚶	**434**, 261, 284, 446, 450, 460
⚱	**426**, 116	⊖	**430**, 61, 63	⚕⚕	**434**
♆	**427**	⚚	**430**	⋇	**434**, 109, 395, 401, 448, 478, 530
♆	**427**	◁	**431**	⚕	**434**
♆	**427**	Ⓐ	**431**, 202, 254, 415, 444	⚕	**434**
⚶	**427**, 98	⚘	**431**, 438	⚕	**434**
⚓	**427**, 257	⚶	**431**, 53, 416	⋇	**434**

Group 42

⚘ **436**, 126, 369, 429

Ⴉ **436**

☉ **436**, 437

♀ **437**, 111, 230, 274

♁ **437**

♀ **437**, 210, 424, 438

╱ **438**

❙ **438**

♂ **438**, 35, 224, 252, 275, 314, 347, 453, 529

ϙ **438**

⌀ **438**, 529

⊶ **438**, 260, 431

♀ **438**, 122, 210, 409, 437

☥ **438**, 14, 17, 46, 372, 426, 479

♀ **439**, 46, 112, 118, 425, 479

⚓ **439**, 289

☥ **440**, 439

♀ **440**

♂ **440**, 200, 387, 419

♂ **440**, 9, 38, 41, 52, 70, 91, 97, 106, 127, 149, 195, 202, 211, 281, 332, 384, 392, 415, 424, 446, 491, 500, 513, 533

♂ **443**

♂ **444**, 123

♂ **444**

♀ **444**

⊶ **444**

♂ **444**, 202, 431

♂ **445**, 204

⚲ **445**

⚲ **445**

⚲ **445**

♉ **445**

⚷ **446**, 54, 381, 388, 424, 480, 509, 512

♉ **446**

♅ **446**, 116, 426

♋ **446**

♄ **446**, 311

♆ **447**, 204, 454

⌂ **447**

♄ **447**

□○ **447**, 401

♀ **447**, 116, 446

♃○ **448**, 510

⚥ **448**, 486, 519

⚥ **448**, 434

⟁ **448**

▽ **448**, 5, 393

◇◇◇○ **449**

♋ **449**, 104, 243, 387

♀ **449**, 486

449, 116, 486, 505, 527

450, 390

450, 88

450, 54, 213

450

451, 285, 484

451

451

451, 125, 252, 343, 528

451, 343

451, 429

452

452

452, 13, 400

452

453

453

453, 428

453

453

454

454, 514

454, 262

454, 204, 244, 447

454, 110, 257, 348, 397

455

455, 348

Group 43

458, 384

458, 266, 296

458

Group 44

⁙ **460**, 486   ◉ **461**   ☣ **461**

◯ **460**, 388   ✷ **461**   ⊃⊂ **461**

◎ **460**   ❈ **462**

☢ **460**, 87, 461   ◍ **462**, 287, 338

Group 45

╫ **464**, 143, 154, 450, 481, 491, 515, 526   ╬ **465**, 60, 294, 396, 424, 446, 504, 509   ╪ **466**, 98

                                        ▦ **465**, 60, 387, 504   ⋈ **466**, 296

╫ **464**   ⊕ **465**, 477   ✕ **467**, 351

⊣ **464**   ⊕ **466**, 212, 252, 473   ⋙ **467**, 55, 360, 416, 438, 496

✕ **465**   ⊞ **466**, 95, 142, 323, 479   ✛ **467**, 472

Group 46

Ⅰ **470**   ⋏ **472**   ⊕ **473**, 466

Ⅱ **470**, 89, 119, 127, 148, 172, 182, 201, 349, 413, 472, 488   ⊓ **473**, 484, 518   ⬠ **473**

                                        ⬦ **473**

Group 47

⊖ **476**, 126, 144, 150

⊖ **476**

⌀ **476**, 210, 477

⌀ **476**, 75

☿ **477**

⚔ **477**, 478

⊕ **477**, 323, 477, 484

⊕ **478**, 162, 262, 284, 484

⊗ **478**, 477

⊗ **478**, 458

☀ **479**

⊗ **479**

⊠ **479**, 349

┬ **480**, 415, 528

⚔ **480**

❋ **480**, 114

♀ **480**, 486

♀ **480**

⊶ **481**

╫ **481**, 433

Ⅱ **481**

Group 48

⊥ **484**

� **484**

⊕ **484**, 49, 54, 205

⊛ **484**

)O(**484**, 485

→O← **485**

⅄ **485**

■ **485**, 272, 409

☼ **485**, 486

⊕ **485**, 480

⚙ **486**, 448, 461

⊙ **486**, 62

⊕ **486**

o─o **486**, 53, 55, 147, 266, 416, 433, 447, 449, 481, 527

♀ **486**, 380, 428, 449

o° **487**, 37, 438

●● **487**

o-o **487**

φ **487**, 266, 310, 529

8 **488**

% **488**

8 **488**, 289, 296

Ⅱ **488**, 470

Group 49

ᚻ　**490**, 12

ℐ　**490**, 170

ℐ　**490**

ℓℓℓℓℓ　**490**

🙰　**490**, 15, 171

&　**490**

𝄞　**491**, 5, 73, 171

♌　**491**

∅　**491**, 440, 477, 508, 512

∅　**491**, 175, 258, 502, 535

♍　**492**, 33, 38, 52, 56, 89, 155, 182, 349, 413, 490, 496, 505, 521

♋　**494**

♋　**494**

Group 50

ℴ　**496**, 52, 173, 360, 467, 490

Ω　**496**, 498

ℚ　**498**

ℯ　**498**, 185, 190, 215, 380, 508

§　**498**

♋　**498**, 33, 34, 38, 52, 91, 201, 224, 349, 500, 521, 533

♭　**500**

☪　**500**, 269

℥　**501**, 55

⊙ᵐ　**501**

∞℥　**501**

⊙ℛ　**501**

🜨　**501**, 171

♄　**502**

⚚　**502**, 15

𓂀　**502**

☿　**502**, 92, 415, 504, 531

Group 51

504, 464, 526

504, 60, 63, 465

504

504, 531

504, 517

505, 112, 242

505

505

505, 35

505

505, 199, 384

506

506

506

506

Group 52

508

508

508

508, 185, 190

508

508, 491

509, 54, 424, 446

509, 142, 258

509, 268

509

510, 62, 455

510

510, 448

510

510

Group 53

512, 62

512

512, 446

512, 212, 252, 518

512

513

513, 254

513

513, 266, 432

513

514, 454

514, 536

514, 46

514

514

514

515

515

515, 36

515, 464

516, 476

516, 53, 390

516, 403, 530

516, 69

516

517, 504

517

517

517

517, 393

518, 123, 512

518

518

518, 9, 14

518

519

519, 7

519

519, 420, 448

519, 73, 92, 106, 230, 288

520

520

520

520, 199

520, 33, 34, 38, 53, 91, 172, 349, 418, 442, 493, 499, 534

520

522, 57, 393, 414

523

523, 127, 415, 451

523, 56, 127, 451

523, 128

523

523, 128

Group 54

♭	**526**, 504	⚏	**529**	ℙ	**532**
♩	**526**, 404	φ	**529**, 310, 487	Ɒ	**532**, 35, 216, 227, 412
♩	**526**	♂♂	**529**	⚮	**534**, 196, 411
♪	**526**	⊜→	**529**, 88, 405	√°	**534**, 39, 203
♪	**526**	▲→	**529**	√ᵉ	**534**, 203
O⤳	**526**	▷•	**530**	ℏ	**535**
♂ᵈ	**526**, 254, 424	⊥	**530**	∿	**535**
♂♪	**527**, 322, 449	△ᵉ	**530**, 54	⊿	**535**
♂	**527**, 449	△ᵛ	**530**, 501	⚔	**535**, 193
Ɛ	**527**, 301, 416, 516	⟡	**530**, 63	⊆	**535**
♋	**527**	≈	**531**, 63	Z⁶	**535**, 199
⚥	**528**, 415	⌒	**531**, 63	⬭	**536**, 87, 401
‰	**528**, 488	2/10	**531**, 60	— ⬭	**536**
⌒♪	**528**	▐	**531**	☀	**536**, 288, 461
⌁•○	**528**	¶	**531**	⚟	**536**
⊓	**528**	¶	**531**, 498		
⊕ᴧ	**528**	ℙ	**531**, 504		

Part V: Graphic search index

Definitions

single symmetric

If the sign is drawn on a piece of paper
which is then folded all the lines on the
one half of the sign will coincide with the
lines on the other half.

Symmetry

multi symmetric

One can fold the paper in many ways and the lines on the one
half will still coincide with the lines on the other half.

asymmetric

It is impossible for the lines to coincide if the paper is folded.

open signs

Open-Closed   **closed** signs

both **open and closed** signs

straight-lined signs

**Straight-lined-
soft elements**   **soft** signs

både **straight-lined and soft** signs

signs with **crossing** lines

Crossing lines

signs without **crossing** lines

Search Table

			open signs	closed signs	open and closed
Single symmetric	**soft**	crossing	1	19	37
		not crossing	2	20	38
	straight-lined	crossing	3	21	39
		not crossing	4	22	40
	soft and straight-lined	crossing	5	23	41:a, 41:b
		not crossing	6	24	42
multi symmetric	**soft**	crossing	7	25	43
		not crossing	8	26	44
	straight-lined	crossing	9	27	45
		not crossing	10	28	46
	soft and straight-lined	crossing	11	29	47
		not crossing	12	30	48
asymmetric	**soft**	crossing	13	31	49
		not crossing	14	32	50
	straight-lined	crossing	15	33	51
		not crossing	16	34	52
	soft and straight-lined	crossing	17	35	53
		ej crossing	18	36	54

Helpful hints

If one cannot find the desired sign:

Perhaps the sign is enclosed in a circle or a square. In that case, look in the graphic index for closed signs.

Perhaps the desired sign is a closed one. If you are looking for † and cannot find it, try ✝

Notice that very small filled circles (dots) are regarded as open and soft structures: ⊙

Notice that signs with a combination of straight and soft lines are considered as soft elements : ⇐, ⬦

Notice that many signs initially seeming to be single symmetric are actually multi symmetric.

Notice that groups of closed structures are included as closed signs: ⧉